POLITICS IN NIGERIA

Oladimeji Aborisade
Obafemi Awolowo University, Ile-Ife

Robert J. Mundt
University of North Carolina at Charlottte

Associate Editor: Jessica Bayne
Supplements Editor: Jen McCaffery
Marketing Manager: Megan Galvin
Text Designer: Tom Kulesa
Cover Designer: Kay Petronio

Please visit our Web site at http://longman.awl.com

ISBN 0 321 02539 3

2345678910-- 02010099

The Longman Series in Comparative Politics

Dedication

To Felicia Olayonu Aborisade and Carol Girard Mundt

About the Authors

Oladimeji Aborisade is Professor of Local Government at Obafemi Awolowo University, Ile-Ife, Nigeria, and was Dean of the Faculty of Administration there from 1989 to 1996. He received his Ph.D. in Government in 1977 from the Claremont Graduate Center and has since been on the faculty staff at OAU. On January 13, 1996, the Olubadan of Ibadan Land honored him with the Chieftaincy Title of Balogun Onigegewura of Ibadan Land. During the 1996-1997 academic year he taught African politics and comparative public administration at the University of North Carolina at Charlotte and North Carolina State University (Raleigh) as Fulbright Scholar-in-Residence. Among his other publications is *Local Government and Traditional Rulers in Nigeria.*

Robert Mundt is Professor of Political Science and Interim Associate Vice Chancellor for Graduate Studies and Dean of the Graduate School at the University of North Carolina at Charlotte. His work in West African Politics began with dissertation research in Cote d'Ivoire in 1970-71, where he also taught at the University of Abidjan. Since completing his Ph.D. at Stanford University he has taught at the University of North Carolina at Charlotte. From 1992 to 1995 he and Aborisade directed a project on democratization at the local level in Nigeria, sponsored by the United States Information Agency.

Acknowledgments

The authors would like to acknowledge the assistance of Bob LaGamma, Curtis Huff, Arlene Jacquette, and Charlotte Peterson (representatives of the United States Information Agency) for getting us together, and to our colleagues John A. A. Ayoade, Cecil Brown, Roger Brown, Charles Coe, Chukwuemeka Ebo, Alex Gboyega, Tim Mead, Oladosu Oyelakin, Gary Rassel, Jim Svara, and Deil Wright for helping us compare our two countries. We greatly benefitted from the advice of Gabriel Almond and several anonymous reviewers. All faults in our interpretation are, of course, entirely our own.

Table of Contents

Preface

     In the African context Nigeria is a megastate. Even on a world scale, Nigeria is a major nation. Larger than France or Britain, it claims over one-fifth of the people in Africa south of the Sahara, and has the world's largest black population. Its petroleum and its substantial standing military force guarantee its prominence in international relations; and with thirty-six universities, Nigeria contains a large proportion of Africa's centers of learning and research.

     For these reasons alone, one should know about Nigeria. But learning about Nigeria is also an efficient approach to learning about Africa, because Nigeria embodies much of the variety of African political experience within its borders. Its traditions include the large-scale emirates of the North, and the village-level republics of the Southeast. Although both were administered by Britain, the North and South of Nigeria experienced different versions of colonial rule. Its culture is divided by ethnicity, but also by religion, especially between Christians and Muslims. Its history since independence includes coups, counter-coups, and civil war; recently, as with much of the rest of Africa, Nigeria has been groping toward a renewal of democracy. The problems and prospects of many African mini-states are found in Nigeria, but at a more daunting scale and level of complexity.

     There are, on the other hand, a number of ways in which Nigeria is not "typical" of Africa. We have already noted that Nigeria is the African megastate. With over 100 million people, it is twice the size of the next-largest African country (Egypt), and thus looms over the rest of the continent (see Figure A). On this basis, Nigeria has campaigned actively for a permanent seat on the United Nations Security Council. While size alone does not determine the complexity of a nation's problems, the magnitude of the difference between Nigeria and other African states ensures that its challenges will be especially difficult.

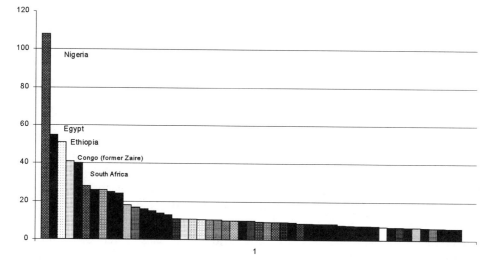

Figure A. African Countries by Population, 1993

Secondly, since the 1970s Nigeria has been economically advantaged in the richness of its petroleum deposits. Nigeria is the only African country among the top ten oil producers, and only a few other sub-Saharan countries (Gabon, Cameroon) produce petroleum for export. Clearly, the availability of this single most valuable commodity gives Nigeria options for development that few African countries possess.

Neither Nigeria nor any other country can stand as a "typical" African country, for Africa is marked by great diversity. Still, if to know Nigeria is not necessarily to know Africa, it is a good place to begin, for there will be little that is surprising in politics elsewhere on the continent to one who is well acquainted with the Nigerian experience.

However, Nigeria's prominent place in the world is more potential than real, because recently Nigeria has been a *sick* giant. Her economy is in tatters, the provision of public services has broken down, and often-promised democracies consistently have been stillborn. A central purpose in this volume is to examine the causes of this illness, and the likelihood of recovery. Our purpose in exploring these issues is not morbid curiosity; as we inventory the resources, both natural and human, with which Nigeria is blessed, we are convinced that in the long run Nigeria will play a major role on the African continent and in the world. Even though no end to this dark period in her history is in sight, we believe that, once the solution to her political dilemmas is found and unlocked, Nigeria will solve the human welfare problems that oppress her people today.

There are already many works on politics in Nigeria.[i] If there is reason for another (besides the obvious need to update some descriptions), it is that, although previous studies have detailed the values and institutions, the military in politics, elections, the economy, external relations and so forth, none so far has put the study of Nigerian politics in a truly general comparative framework. As Nigeria struggles to escape arbitrary military rule and eventually embark on a third republic, a new overview is necessary. The authors of this effort, a team consisting of observers with both an "inside" and an "outside" perspective on Nigerian politics, hope that we can present the reader with an accurate portrayal of this complex country in a format that allows for ready comparison with other countries in Africa and the world.

Central to all political issues in Nigeria is the question of when, and under what conditions, it will be classified among the world's democracies. This description is set in an era that Samuel Huntington has labeled the "Third Wave" of democratization, beginning in 1974 and washing over eastern Europe, the successor states to the Soviet Union, Latin America, and parts of Africa in 1989-1991.[ii] Huntington's wave may already have begun receding, judging from the enumeration done annually by Freedom House, the New-York based human rights organization. Freedom House divides the world's nations into the categories of free, unfree, and partly free. In their 1993 count, the number of unfree countries had grown to fifty-five, from thirty-eight in the previous year; the number stabilized at about fifty-four from 1994 to 1997, about the same number as in 1986. Nigeria appeared to be moving toward democracy with the Third Wave in 1991, but was part of the later receding tide; it is now listed among the eighteen most repressive states in the world.[iii] Nigeria's move toward authoritarianism in the mid-1990s, coming at a time of liberalization on the continent generally, seemed to make it an exceptional case. However, because there was a reduction in the number of elections and in civil liberties ratings across Africa after 1993, Nigeria may simply be a dramatic and highly prominent example of the difficulty in consolidating democracy that the whole continent now experiences.[iv] The Nigerian case presented here will help illuminate the factors conditioning moves toward and away from democracy.

There is a vast literature on the preconditions and correlates of democracy. That literature has burgeoned especially since the end of the Cold War and the appearance of the Third Wave. Among the major questions that have been raised and addressed in other contexts, and that we will consider in the Nigerian case are the following:

♦   What are the <u>political conditions</u> that must be in place for a democracy to be created and consolidated? Synthesizing a venerable literature on this topic,[v] Barry Weingast has recently presented a model of achieving democratic stability based on a "self-enforcing equilibrium," a situation where political elites—those with political authority—would find it in their best interest to respect democratic limits on their behavior, to the point of resignation as their least costly alternative in the case of an electoral defeat. Such a situation provides "self-enforcing limits on state power."[vi] Weingast's model incorporates three elements:

1) *Mass Behavior* - Political elites must expect coordinated resistance should they violate the democratic constraints on their action.

2) *Elite Agreement on the Rules* - Competing elites must arrive at an equilibrium point where each of them (or each elite group) finds their advantage in agreeing to a limiting set of rules of engagement to be greater than unconstrained conflict and violence.

3) *Political Institutions* that "limit the ability of those in power to subvert the system to prevent their opponents from winning the next election."

Although all these factors have been discussed in the democratization literature, Weingast's model combines them in the assertion that democratic stability does not follow the appearance of appropriate democratic values; rather, both stable democracy and citizens' consensus on democratic values come from agreement among elites and the public to compete and to make policy according to a set of rules. Thus, both stability and citizen behavior "reflect the equilibrium" that has been bargained.[vii]

This universal model identifies some problems reaching this stable equilibrium that are directly relevant to the Nigerian case. First, democratic stability is difficult to achieve in divided societies because of the added problems of achieving either elite consensus or the mass coordination of resistance to authority among the various groups or divisions. In this case, an "asymmetric, nondemocratic equilibrium" may be more stable than the preferred symmetric model. In plain terms, the leadership may be able to form an alliance with one group (or some groups) to subjugate another (or other groups).

The elements necessary to apply this model to Nigeria are presented in Chapters Three (political culture), Four (the formation of elites), Five (structure, i.e., an assessment of the stability of the equilibria that have occurred among political elites since independence in Nigeria), and Six (the process, or the conditions of elite interaction and bargaining).

In Chapter Nine, the Conclusion, Weingast's model will be applied to the task of assessing the prospects of democracy in Nigeria, and the Nigerian case will be examined for its usefulness in explicating the model.

♦ Does a successful transition to democracy require that a country experience some prior period of political and economic consolidation and stabilization? Since Seymour Martin Lipset identified, over thirty years ago, a correlation between the level of a country's socio-economic development and the degree to which its political system is democratic, this relationship has been examined, refined, and generally supported by evidence.[viii] Whether economic development and democratization must proceed in a determined sequence, and whether there are necessary intervening variables, is still debated. However, comparative survey data from forty-three countries in 1990 are used by Inglehart to demonstrate that economic development precedes democracy in that "it tends to bring social and cultural changes that help democracy emerge and flourish."[ix] In other words, economic changes do not themselves predispose a society to democratic governance, but rather induce changes in social organization and cultural values that will eventually produce the kind of elite-limiting mass behavior included in Weingast's model. Does this mean that, given its low levels of income and education, Nigeria simply lacks the socio-economic requisites for democracy?

♦ What is the relationship between the Third Wave and the simultaneous spread of a world economy based on free markets? Many have seen a necessary correlation between political democracy and a free market system—in terms of process, between economic liberalization and democratization—with the right to make one's own economic choices a necessary part of the individual freedom that is essential to democracy. On the other hand, the privatization of economies has everywhere resulted in greater economic inequalities. A recent study of democratization in Latin America asks "Could representative democracy coexist with poverty of one sort or another affecting between half and two-thirds of the population? Could democratic rule survive in conditions of growing and acute inequality?. . .Would not demagogues or those nostalgic for bygone times take advantage of the short-term discontent provided by unpopular economic policies and of the democratic openings guaranteed by the liberalization dynamic to jeopardize the entire process by pressuring for redistributive policies or running on populist programs?"[x] In the Nigerian case, one must identify changes in the role of the state in the economy, and specify trends in how private income is distributed.

The organization of this book is meant to facilitate comparison with other countries and to organize answers to the above questions by examining Nigerian politics according to an outline of concepts widely used in comparative political studies. The "mapping" model is that of Gabriel A. Almond and G. Bingham Powell, presented in their *Comparative Politics: A Theoretical Framework* (New York, HarperCollins, 1996). Although their theoretical perspective is developed in much greater detail in that work, the application of their model is presented in sufficient detail in this study so that the Nigerian case can be understood on its own.

The political science literature of recent years is filled with a mild polemic about the relative merits of a "systems" approach as compared to a more state-centered analysis of political life. This is a theoretical discussion of interest only to those readers who intend to master the arcane language of the political science discipline, and is not necessary to an understanding of political life. However, for those who are interested, we take the middle road: This is basically a systems approach—one that views politics as a repetitive process involving individual relationships with institutions (or institutionalized political roles), but it is an approach in which the state is identified as a major actor and a major set of

> ### The Concepts of Liberalization and Democratization.
>
> Liberalization and democratization are two related, but different concepts. Liberalization can be either an economic or a political process. **Economic liberalization** means a move toward greater private ownership of economic goods, and away from state direction of the economy toward reliance on a free market to allocate economic goods. **Political liberalization** refers to increased individual rights, such as freedom of speech and press, the right to organize, the implementation of legal safeguards against arbitrary government actions, and so forth. **Democratization** refers to the acquisition by greater numbers of people of the right to participate in the decision-making process, generally through open, competitive elections. See Linz and Stepan, 1996: 3-4.

institutions, which has its own needs and makes its own demands on the system, even as it usually plays a central political system role in "allocating scarce resources."[xi] The state is some significant part of what is discussed as the political structure in Chapter Five.

Each of the chapters begins with a series of bulleted questions; the reader should find answers to these questions in each particular chapter. Chapter One is an historical introduction that looks at those factors in Nigeria's past important to an understanding of politics today. Chapter Two looks at the political effects of geography and the distribution of natural resources. What are the opportunities for, and limitations on, public policy in Nigeria that result from its physical environment? These include, most importantly, the conditions affecting agricultural production and the sale of primary commodities, the presence of one of the world's richest oil deposits, but also the special challenges to public health in a tropical climate.

Chapter Three builds on the concept of political culture to describe the political beliefs and attitudes of Nigerians today. Important aspects of that culture are ethnic identity, social and economic status, and contact with urban life. The discussion of culture continues with an analysis of the process by which political beliefs and attitudes develop, through the role of such "agents" of socialization as family, primary and secondary groups, formal education, the media, and government-sponsored activities.

Chapter Four looks at recruitment into the political roles that make up the country's decision-making structure. Central to the analysis of any political system is the identification of holders of political power and influence, and of the roles through which power is exercised. An important question to answer in a comparative analysis is how individuals come to occupy formal and informal roles with political influence.

In Chapter Five, we examine the overall structure of decision making in Nigeria—including the place of such state institutions as courts, legislatures, bureaucracies, etc. Of particular interest is the role of federalism in Nigerian politics, because in such a vast and complex country, many of the political decisions that impact Nigerians' lives are not made at the federal level.

Chapter Six describes the political process. There are two aspects of organized influence in most modern political systems. First are the formally organized interest groups such as unions and trade associations, and religious bodies. Additionally, there are the more informal channels of involvement through individual relationships that are often described by the term "clientelism." In this chapter we also consider an institution that in Nigeria has become far more than an interest group: the military. Nigeria differs from many contemporary countries in the absence (probably temporary) of independent, self-generated political parties. Nevertheless, we consider the role parties have played historically in Nigeria, because party politics has shaped much of Nigeria's political history, and will undoubtedly reassume its former importance along with civilian rule.

Policy formation and implementation in the areas of taxation, budgeting, and public expenditures are the concerns of Chapter Seven. Here we look at the important *decisions* governments have made, particularly in raising revenues and in dispersing funds. Consideration of public policy continues in Chapter Eight, with focus on those aspects of governance that do not directly involve raising and spending money. Considered here are the nature of the criminal justice and legal systems, and important and controversial aspects of regulatory policy such as the planning and implementing of the federal census, the role of law in determining property ownership, and the role of Islamic law. This chapter also describes Nigeria's place in the international system. Serious constraints are imposed on Nigerian decision making by the outside world, particularly in the World-Bank-supported Structural Adjustment Program. Dealing with "SAP," as the Structural Adjustment Program is commonly called, leads us into a consideration of the international environment with which Nigerian governments interact. That environment consists of other African countries, world powers, international organizations, and such powerful economic entities as international corporations. Here we consider the critical constraints that the world economy puts on the choices available to a Third World country, even one as large and resource-rich as Nigeria.

The concluding chapter reflects again on the gap between the aspirations of Nigerians and the system's performance to date. It identifies conditions that might narrow that gap, and considers once again the effects of that performance on Nigeria's prospects for democracy, and the additional complication introduced into the model by a heightened level of north–south conflict. We return at the end to consider the large questions posed above concerning the requisites for Nigerian democratization, and to articulate the Nigerian case with the theoretical perspectives embedded in these questions and models.

Our challenge has been to write a book that will be meaningful both in Nigeria and elsewhere. We have tried to build on social science theory, but to write in a vocabulary that is familiar to any well-read person. We ask the reader's indulgence if we have occasionally fallen short of reconciling these goals.

END NOTES

i. See, most importantly, Guy Arnold, *Modern Nigeria* (London: Longman, 1977); Eme O. Awa, *Federal Government in Nigeria* (Berkeley: University of California Press, 1964); Paul A. Beckett and Crawford Young, eds. *Dilemmas of Democray in Nigeria* (Rochester: University of Rochester Press, 1997); James S. Coleman, *Nigeria: Background to Nationalism* (Berkeley: University of California Press, 1958); Larry Diamond, *Class, Ethnicity and Democracy in Nigeria: The Failure of the First Republic* (Syracuse: Syracuse University Press, 1988); Larry Diamond, Anthony Kirk-Greene, and Oyeleye Oyediran, *Transition Without End: Nigerian Politics and Civil Society Under Babangida* (Boulder, CO: Lynne Rienner, 1997); *An Introduction to Nigerian Government and Politics* (Bloomington: Indiana University Press, 1982); Tom Forrest, *Politics and Economic Development in Nigeria* (Boulder: Westview, 1995); Richard A. Joseph, *Democracy and Prebendal Politics in Nigeria: The Rise and Fall of the Second Republic* (Cambridge: Cambridge University Pres, 1987); Tunji Olagunju, Adele Jinadu and Sam Oyovbaire, *Transition to Democracy in Nigeria (1985-1993)*, (Ibadan: Safari Books, 1993); Richard Sklar, *Nigerian Political Parties: Power in an Emergent African Nation* (New York: NOK Publishers, 1983); C.S. Whitaker Jr., *The Politics of Tradition: Continuity and Change in Northern Nigeria, 1946-66* (Princeton: Princeton University Press, 1970).

ii. Samuel Huntington, *The Third Wave: Democratization in the Late Twentieth Century* (Norman, OK: University of Oklahoma Press, 1991).

iii. Adrian Karatnycky, *The Comparative Survey of Freedom 1995-1996* (http://www.freedomhouse.org// Political/summary.htm).

iv. Michael Bratton and Nicolas van de Walle, *Democratic Experiments in Africa* (New York: Cambridge University Press, 1997), pp. 3-6.

v. See, for example, Joseph A. Schumpeter, "The Crisis of the Tax State," in *Joseph A. Schumpeter*, ed. Richard Swedberg (Princeton, Princeton University Press, 1991 [1918]); Dankwart A. Rustow, "Transitions to Democracy," *Comparative Politics* (2, April), pp. 337-363; Robert A. Dahl, *Polyarchy: Participation and Opposition* (New Haven, Yale University Press, 1971); Terry Lynn Karl, "Dilemmas of Democratization in Latin America," *Comparative Politics* (23, October), pp. 1-21; Juan J. Linz, *The Breakdown of Democratic Regimes* (Baltimore, Johns Hopkins University Press, 1978); and Gabriel A. Almond and Sidney Verba, *The Civic Culture* (Princeton, Princeton University Press, 1963).

vi. Barry R. Weingast, "The Political Foundations of Democracy and the Rule of Law," *American Political Science Review* 91 (2, June, 1997), pp. 245-263.

vii. Weingast, "The Political Foundations of Democracy and the Rule of Law," p. 254.

viii. Seymour Martin Lipset, *Political Man (Garden City, NY: Doubleday, 1960);* Larry Diamond, "Economic Development and Democracy Reconsidered," in Gary Marks and larry Diamond, eds. *Reexamining Democracy (Newbury Park: Sage, 1992)*; Adam Przeworski and Fernando Limongi, "Modernization Theories and Facts," *World Politics* 49 (January, 1997), pp. 155-183.

ix. Ronald Inglehart, *Modernization and Postmodernization: Cultural, Economic, and Political Change in 43 Countries* (Princeton: Princeton University Press, 1997), p. 180.

x. Jorge G. Castañeda, "Democracy and Inequality in Latin America: A Tension of the Times, in Jorge I. Domínguez and Abraham F. Lowenthal eds. *Constructing Democratic Governance: Latin America and the Caribbean in the 1990s* (Baltimore: Johns Hopkins University Press, 1996),pp. 43-45.

xi. From the classic discussion by David Easton; see his *A Systems Analysis of Political Life* (New York: John Wiley, 1965), p. 451. Tom Forrest argues that "the state has been given too much centrality in recent writing" on Nigeria (*Politics and Economic Development in Nigeria*, p. 4).

Administrative Map of Nigeria

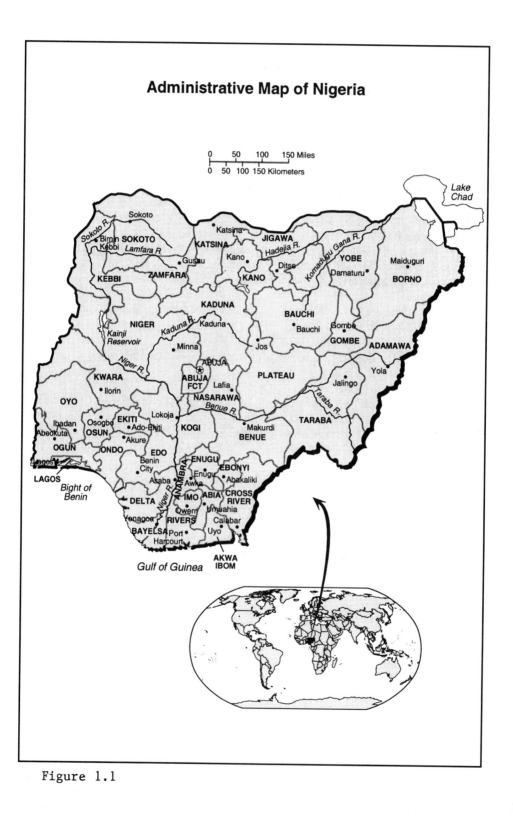

Figure 1.1

Chapter 1

THE EFFECTS OF HISTORY

♦ What kinds of political systems existed in Nigeria before the colonial experience?
♦ How did this region come to be the British colony of Nigeria?
♦ How did the colonial system structure the nature of independent Nigeria's politics?
♦ Why and how did the military come to occupy the center of Nigeria's political stage?

Over thirty years ago, sociologist Clifford Geertz titled a volume on the developing nations *Old Societies and New States.*[1] This is an apt characterization of Nigeria, for although the concept of Nigeria dates only to 1914, and the independent state only to 1960, the cultures that compose it have ancient roots.

In one sense, then, there are "many" Nigerias. That is, there are distinct political cultures with precolonial origins, and there are the varied colonial experiences of North, East, and West. We will consider these causes of variety separately.

The Enduring Effects of Precolonial Events

Our images of precolonial Africa have been plagued by misunderstandings, sometimes in the form of simple ignorance, but often the result of prejudice. Many in the industrial world still view traditional Africa as "primitive," composed of a series of "tribes." Because Africans have frequently referred to their ethnic groups as "tribes," and to the conflicts among those groups as "tribalism," these terms may seem appropriate to our discussion of ethnicity in Nigeria. The problem from an outside perspective is that the term "tribe" has been applied indiscriminantly to small groups of villages or whole empires, and often in conjunction with the adjective "primitive." Thus "tribe" has lost any specific meaning, and imparts prejudicial notions. One may ask whether, if the Yorubas or Igbos of Nigeria are tribes (of thirty or forty million), are not the less numerous peoples known as Norwegians or Irish also tribes? What is the distinction? And if ethnic conflict in Africa is "tribalism," the same phenomenon in Yugoslavia, Britain, Germany, or the United States deserves the same label.

A common response to condescending attitudes toward Africa is that "Africa had its empires also." As we shall see, this is quite true. However, to insist on the presence of empires as proof of advanced culture is to accept that the successful implementation of authoritarian rule over large numbers of people is "civilized." It can be argued that those peoples who developed complex systems of limitations on their rulers at the village level were at least as sophisticated in their political thinking as those who built empires. And all these peoples interacted in trade, cultural diffusion, and war for many centuries before the creation of today's nation states, and their belief systems were as complex and nuanced as any in the world.

To reiterate, there was no single Nigeria a century ago. Some of the peoples inhabiting the land that now constitutes Nigeria were organized only at the village or extended family level (e.g., the Igbo in the Southeast), while in other areas there were kingdoms and states. Where one group had subjugated the peoples around them, we can identify empires, such as that of Kanem-Bornu around Lake Chad between the eleventh and fourteenth centuries, the Oyo Empire in the Western region of present-day Nigeria (thirteenth–eighteenth centuries) or the Fulani Empire of the nineteenth century (see Figure 1.2).[2]

There has probably been settled agriculture in Nigeria for several thousand years, spreading from its origins in southwest Asia to the Nile valley and across the Sahara. An advanced culture flourished at Nok, in northern Nigeria between about 500 b.c. and 200 a.d., as evidenced by the famous masks and sculptures found there along with evidence of the smelting and use of metals. Trade between peoples of present-day Nigeria and the Mediterranean region flourished with the introduction of the camel to North Africa (about 100 a.d.). It was through those routes that Islam was introduced into Nigeria no later than the late eleventh century (in the Kanem Empire), thus just a few centuries after its birth in Arabia.

The Hausa people began forming city-states in northern Nigeria between 1000 and 1200 a.d., and came under the influence of Islam no later than the fifteenth century. By the next century, mosques and Koranic schools were flourishing and Hausa princes were involved in the international rivalries of Morocco and the Ottoman Empire. The fortunes of these systems waxed and waned through the centuries, but they were decisively changed when non-Hausa court officials rose against them early in the nineteenth century. These

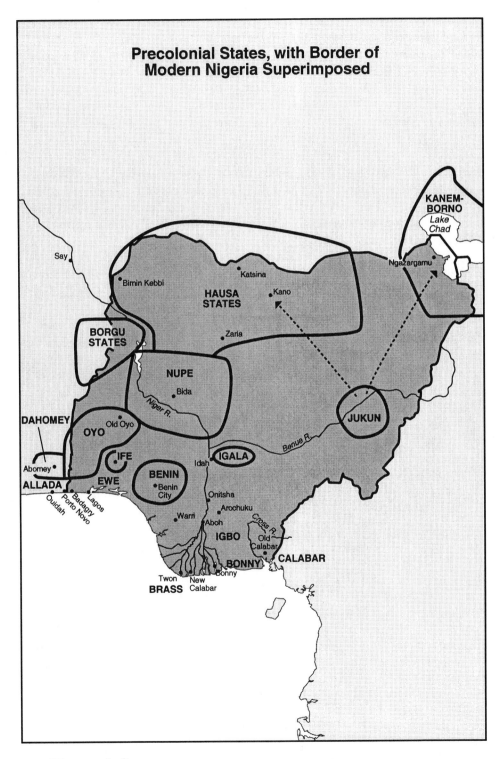

Figure 1.2

officials were Fulani, a people with their origins in western Sudan, but who had entered into the Hausa lands as herders, and more importantly, as teachers, traders, and eventually court advisers. They were generally ardent Muslims, who found the Hausa leaders lax in their faith and decadent. A Fulani scholar and preacher, Usman dan Fodio, inspired a revolt against the Hausa kings that was both religious and political (he found audiences responsive to his denunciation of taxes, even among Hausa commoners). A Fulani-dominated caliphate was established, with Usman dan Fodio's son as sultan, in Sokoto, now northern Nigeria. This Fulani Empire controlled most of the North until the British defeated the Fulanis in 1903. Sokoto retains its role as the Muslim religious capital of Nigeria to this day. The Hausa and Fulani cultures have become so intertwined, with extensive intermarriage and with Hausa the primary language of both, that the dominant culture of the North is usually referred to as "Hausa-Fulani."

In the forest region, sophisticated bronze and clay sculptures are early evidence of the existence of advanced societies among the Yoruba and Bini peoples of the Southwest, with kingdoms emerging between the twelfth and fifteenth centuries at Oyo, Ife, and Benin. In the seventeenth and eighteenth Centuries the kingdom of Oyo subdued its rivals and extended its control over the entire area of southwest Nigeria. These political systems developed intricate methods of limiting the powers of their rulers. For example, the ruler of Oyo, the *Alafin*, was chosen by a council of chiefs, the *Oyo Mesi*. Crowder recounts that

> if they felt the Alafin had exceeded his powers, [the Oyo Mesi] could divine that all was not well between the Alafin and his spiritual double and force him to commit suicide
> . . .However, the Oyo Mesi were restrained from abuse of this power by the fact that one of their number had to die with the Alafin. [3]

In Yoruba tradition generally, *Obas* or chiefs were held in check by Oro societies, who could express the people's displeasure with their rulers in ritually sanctioned ceremonies.

Highly decentralized societies, often on that basis labeled "primitive," also had effective systems of political checks and balances. Anthropologist Paul Bohannon has described the historical socio-political organization of the Tiv people of Nigeria's "Middle Belt" as one of "segmental opposition." He explains that the Tiv family structure was based on a lineage extending back through male ancestors about seventeen generations to a common ancestor. At the lowest level, brothers might be in competition, but they are seen as absolutely equal to one another, and join with one another in opposition to their paternal cousins. At the next level, however, cousins form a unit in opposition to more distant cousins. As one follows this system to ever more inclusive levels, "two lineages opposed in one context may join forces in another as a single lineage against an external lineage or against foreigners." This simple form of organization, based on the equality of opposing segments, would not allow any individual to assume generalized authority over others: "If one person is given more authority than another, the lineage system ultimately breaks down and will not work: Its segments are no longer equivalent. If authority is vested in a man from Lineage *A*, all others can dissociate themselves by invoking the fissions in the system." Also, the lineage system "acts as a system of built-in checks and balances that generally allows warfare to take place without getting out of hand. In theory—and usually in fact—fighting is stopped short when it embroils two equal and opposed lineage segments."[4]

Clearly, limited government has sources other than the *Magna Carta* and comes in a variety of forms. This is a very important point, because imported political structures of the British or American model have not worked well in Nigeria, and constitution makers are often exhorted to develop structures that derive from Nigerian tradition and experience. There is a problem with this advice, in that Nigeria has many traditions and a wide variety of experience, and it is not obvious which institutions and practices from Nigerian tradition would be widely applicable. We cannot conclude that the question should not be addressed; it seems self-evident that political structures deriving from a people's own experience will be more legitimate to them than imported models will be. However, the difficulties in drawing from either imported or indigenous practice ensure that the constitution writer's task will not be simple.

Because Nigeria was defined through the colonial experience, we must ask how and why the eventual domination of Nigeria's peoples by Great Britain occurred. The immediate cause for British interest in West Africa was trade, and the first such international trade of any importance was in slaves. Late in the fifteenth century, Portuguese explorers visited Benin, and stimulated a redirection of trade from the North to the Atlantic coast. Although Benin–Portuguese relations initially involved a variety of products, the development of plantation economies in the Americas created a demand for labor that was not filled by volunteers, and high demand led to great profits; thus did African trade come to be dominated by the export of slaves. Coastal groups began exchanging captives for goods with European trading ships as early as the sixteenth century (see Figure 1.3). Wars among the various kingdoms assured a plentiful supply of captives, particularly in southwestern Nigeria. For the next three hundred years this trade was sustained: Benin, Lagos, Bonny, and Calabar thrived as slave trade centers exporting upwards of twenty thousand persons per year to the Americas.

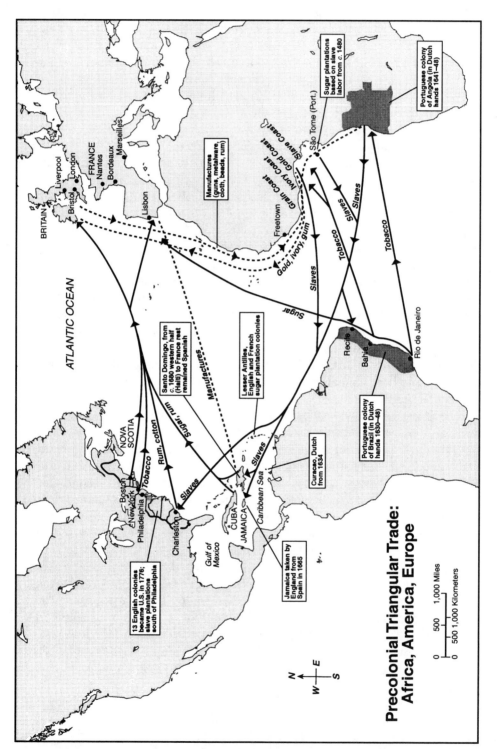

**Precolonial Triangular Trade:
Africa, America, Europe**

Figure 1.3

Nigeria lost some of its most able-bodied inhabitants in that time,[5] and, to quote Crowder:

> The three centuries of contact between Europe and Africa which were focused on the slave trade brought to the latter none of the benefits of the technological innovations of the former except in the form of cast-off firearms with which slave wars could be the better prosecuted. As far as this relationship was concerned, then, these were a barren three centuries.[6]

In 1807 the British Parliament outlawed the slave trade. In a remarkable turnabout, the British navy replaced British slave ships and began patrolling the West African coast to cut off the trade, which was not, however, completely eliminated until about 1850. The trading patterns that had been established were gradually converted to other goods, in the Nigerian case to palm oil and other agricultural products as well as ivory and timber. In the earliest phase, the European traders relied on coastal peoples to serve as intermediaries, but their economic self-interest led them to try to establish direct contact with inland societies and to influence and ultimately control the coastal authorities. British consuls established themselves on the coast and began to intervene in the politics of local communities, favoring for ruling positions those candidates who would give them commercial advantages. In the mid-nineteenth century, French and British representatives competed among themselves for these relationships, but the British succeeded in forcing the French out by forming alliances against them and in signing treaties of British protection and trade along the coast. These treaties between unequals became increasingly favorable to the British as they first established commercial, and then political control.

The Colonial Interlude (1900–1960)

With tongue in cheek, a Nigerian journalist once described his nationality in this fashion: "Today, the conglomeration of tribes assembled compulsorily at the 1884 Berlin conference are assigned as Nigerians—for want of a substitute collective noun."[7] Indeed, it says something about Nigerians' problems with self-definition that the name "Nigeria" was itself coined by Flora Shaw, an Englishwoman who later married Sir Frederick Lugard, the architect of colonial Nigeria. (Reference to the Niger River as a defining feature for the country is, however, certainly appropriate. The Niger flows from the Futa Djalon highlands in Guinea, through the Sahelian countries of Mali and Niger, and divides Nigeria first north and south, then east and west as it curves toward its delta on the Gulf of Guinea; see map,

Figure 1.1). Enahoro's characterization refers to the origins of Nigeria's boundaries, and those of most countries of contemporary Africa. In order to avoid the danger of war resulting from the competition for colonies, the great European powers met as the Conference of Berlin in 1884–1885 and divided Africa into spheres of influence. In effect, the European powers decided to seize control of the continent rather than merely trade with its rulers and merchants, and to divide it into spheres of influence. In a wave of negotiations, imperialist wars and conquests, their efforts were successful, and by the beginning of World War I (1914) maps of Africa showed clearly drawn lines with areas color coded according to the European power claiming control. Crowder cites Hilaire Belloc for a pithy explanation of British military success in the colonial expansion:

> *Whatever happens we have got*
> *The maxim gun and they have not.*[8]

Thus, the Royal Niger Company was granted a royal charter in 1886 to control Nigerian trade. That charter was revoked and replaced in 1900 by the creation of the Colony of Lagos and the Protectorates of Northern and Southern Nigeria.

Nigeria was itself created in 1914, when the Northern and Southern Protectorates (including Lagos) were brought under a single colonial administration. This unifying action proved to be largely symbolic, as its two parts continued to be governed separately. The Northern and Southern Provinces replaced the protectorates, each under a lieutenant governor. Northern Nigeria remained apart as such political structures as a legislative council evolved in the South. Northerners did not sit on the Nigerian Legislative Council until 1947. Indeed, the North proved to be the perfect setting for the concept of "indirect rule" elaborated by Governor Lord Lugard: The British administration would not intervene directly in everyday life in its colonies, but would instead support the rule of traditional leaders such as the Fulani emirs. This, Lugard argued, was the most efficient means of controlling the colonies. In Southern Nigeria, however, educated elites arose to challenge the authority of the traditional rulers where they existed (as among the Yoruba). Indirect rule among the Yoruba not only became less tenable as modernization progressed; it also distorted the traditional powers of the *obas*, who as we saw in the discussion of the *Alafin* of Oyo above, were subject to various checks and balances on their authority. Under the British, the *obas* evolved into much more powerful political figures than had been the case in precolonial times.[9] In southeastern Nigeria, among the Igbo and other peoples, there really were no traditional kings or chiefs. Attempts to create village chiefs where the concept was unknown produced results that were sometimes comical and often tragic. Novelist Chinua Achebe has an English colonial officer describe such a situation:

. . .Chief Ikedi was still corrupt and high-handed but he had become even more clever than before. The latest thing he did was to get his people to make him an *obi* or king, so that he was now called his Highness Ikedi the First, Obi of Okperi. This among a people who never had kings before! This was what British administration was doing among the Ibos, making a dozen mushroom kings grow where there was none before.[10]

Poor understanding of complex socio-political systems also caused the British administrators headaches among the Tiv of the Middle Belt in the Northern region. As we have seen, Tiv society was organized according to lineages in "segmental opposition." Bohannon noted further that

there is no role above the level of compound head that can be called by a title to which authority in any sense may adhere. Political leaders can be described, and the functions of leadership discussed—but any man who performs the tasks of leadership can be described with the words. The words describe acts, not roles. [British administrative officials]. . .kept assuming that these descriptive words were in fact names for official positions. The British then tried to tie down each of these "positions" to a given individual, thereby creating a static system of the sort to which they were accustomed. Tiv refused to have power concentrated in the hands of any given individuals, with or without offices.[11]

Thus the different applicability of indirect rule served to further distinguish the political experiences of the regions, and of different peoples within the regions.

In addition to the impossibility of applying indirect rule to some societies, the British colonial administration faced the problem of incompatible objectives. The right of a European colonizing nation to claim a territory was tied up, in the words of the Conference of Berlin, in "effective occupation," thus the need to create a visible administrative infrastructure. "Competing predators were swift to advance their own claims to ungarrisoned territory."[12] But providing security for one's possessions abroad was inherently expensive, and governments insisted that the colonies must be financially self-sufficient, and it was not immediately obvious how to go about taxing nonmonetized economies. The first and most obvious approach was a simple head tax on the population, but southern Nigerians were especially hostile to this approach. Instead, colonial authorities there relied heavily on the introduction of export-oriented agriculture, with taxes levied on the profits thus obtained.[13] In order to make the colony self-sustaining, Britain needed to encourage an export economy, and therein lay the long-term colonial dilemma: The conversion of peasant societies from a subsistence to a market orientation decayed the foundations of traditional rule. Except in the North, chiefs and kings had no traditional right to collect taxes, yet this became an essential part of their role in the colonial system. Also, the development of a modern system of transportation and communication, necessary to stimulate commerce, encouraged the movement of people to cities from the countryside, and from one part of the country to another, all under the protection of the colonial authorities. Urbanized populations and immigrants from other cultures could scarcely be expected to show deference to traditional rulers, nor did they see any good reason for paying taxes.

Along with commerce and administration, the British brought missionaries and education. Missionaries of many denominations—Anglicans, Presbyterians, Catholics, Baptists, Adventists, and others—brought the gospel to Nigeria, although only to the South; the northern emirates had an understanding with the colonial administration that Christian proselytizing would not be permitted in their domains. Christianity spread especially rapidly in the Southeast, and somewhat less so in the Southwest; with it went formal schooling. As Nigerian children learned the English language and customs, they acquired the tools with which to challenge colonial rule on the rulers' own terms. However, the Western-educated elite that emerged from this process came largely from the South. Thus, the culture is divided north and south along religious lines, but the difference has to do with much more than religion.

Modern constitutional development began within a few years of the creation of Nigeria as a single colony, with elective office first provided in 1922. An early nationalist leader, Herbert Macaulay, established a political party soon thereafter. As a Nigerian-centered political life grew up among the formally educated, other organizations arose, and the British colonial administration was pressed with demands for participation. The spirit of the times was captured by Nigerian author Wole Soyinka in this recollection:

> . . . suddenly there was Oge-e-e-ed* and there was Ze-e-e-ek.** His oratory, we learnt, could move mountains. Some young, radical nationalists were being jailed for sedition, and sedition had become equivalent to demanding that the white man leave us to rule ourselves.[14]
>   *Ogendengbe (Herbert) Macaulay
>   **Nnamdi Azikiwe, nationalist leader

From then until independence, constitutions promulgated by various governors (and named after them) were always somewhat behind the expectations of Nigerian political activists. What southern politicians judged conservative, however, was usually seen as radical by the conservative elites in the North, which ultimately could imagine its interests protected only through a federal constitution that left primary powers with the regions, including even the right to determine when and under what rules to become self-governing. These differences of opinion among Nigerians concerning the political evolution of the country were largely a product of the colonial administration's regional approach to governing, which cemented the country's self image as a conglomerate of three regions. They resulted in 1954 in the creation of a federal system composed of three regions: Northern, Eastern, and Western, each dominated by a single ethnic group: The Hausa-Fulani controlled the North, the Yoruba the West, and the Igbo the East. Under pressure from their leaders, the Eastern and Western regions were granted self-government in 1957; the North became self-governing in 1959.

Box 1.1 The Story of Wole Soyinka

Wole Soyinka was born in 1934 in Abeokuta, Western Nigeria, the child of teachers. He finished secondary school at Government College in Ibadan, then attended University College (now the University of Ibadan), and the University of Leeds (England), receiving a B.A. honors degree in English in 1957. He returned to Nigeria in 1960, the year of independence. Soyinka's political activities resulted in his arrest (and release) in 1965 on charges of pirate radio broadcasting. He became involved in efforts to mediate the Biafran War in 1967, and was arrested and held for over two years (during which time he wrote *Poems from Prison*). Much of his work satirizes and criticizes political corruption and injustice. He joined the faculty at the University of Ife in 1976, but in the 1970s and 1980s he held a variety of visiting professorships in Britain, the United States, and Ghana. Soyinka has written novels, drama, poetry, autobiography, and literary criticism, and his renown resulted in the award of the Nobel Prize for Literature in 1986; he was the first African to be so honored. He has become increasingly politically active in recent years, and so vociferously attacked the continuation of military rulers in power that his passport was taken and his life was in danger. He slipped out of the country and has continued to attack from abroad.

Nigeria was one of the few colonial entities in Africa that had to solve a serious boundary question before independence—in most cases, the arbitrary lines drawn by Europeans at the Conference of Berlin were unquestioningly adopted as frontiers of the new African states. In the Nigerian case, the territory in question was the British Cameroon. Cameroon, bordering Nigeria on the east, had been a German colony from 1884 through World War I. The Treaty of Versailles that reorganized the world following Germany's defeat in that war had assigned her colonial possessions to the League of Nations, which farmed them out as mandates to the victorious powers. Technically they were not colonies, and the mandate status suggested that those countries receiving them had a responsibility for their social and economic development. Cameroon, which lay between British and French colonies in West Africa, was divided between Britain and France in 1922, and the two mandates became United Nations trusteeships in 1947. The British in effect governed their mandate as part of Nigeria. As Nigeria moved to independence, varying demands came from British Cameroon: The northern region shared a common Kanuri culture with that part of Nigeria across the border; on the other hand, inhabitants of the southern portion of the trusteeship felt more in common with French Cameroon. Southern Cameroon was granted autonomy from Eastern Nigeria in 1954, and a 1961 referendum in the whole British trusteeship determined that the north should become part of Nigeria and the south become a part of the new Republic of Cameroon. Independent Nigeria, born on October 1, 1960, was definitively configured once the Cameroonian question was resolved. However, the southern part of the border between Nigeria and Cameroon was not clearly determined, and has remained a point of sometimes violent contention between the two countries to this day.

Undoubtedly, many British colonial administrators truly believed they were "preparing" Nigeria for the introduction of a pluralist democratic constitution. Yet the experience of colonial rule was an experience in authoritarianism: Colonial administrators were first and foremost held responsible for achieving acquiescence to their policies. In order to maximize their effectiveness, they systematically attacked whatever checks, balances, and responsibility of rulers to their citizenry had existed previously. The deliberate and gradual introduction of representative institutions must be seen against a backdrop of long-term arbitrary rule. Modern discourse on democracy usually stresses the necessity that it emerge from internal inconsistencies and contradictions in a once-authoritarian society. From that perspective, It is obvious that colonial rulers could not shape a democratic constitution and insert it into an alien society. In Nigeria, as over most of Africa, the attempt to impose foreign institutions of democracy was doomed to failure.

We have titled this discussion "the colonial interlude," to emphasize the brevity of a sixty-year period in historical time. Yet the thrust of the discussion is to emphasize the severely destructive effects of that experience. Often the historian focused on a particular country or region fails to put explanations for the evolution of that political system in comparative perspective. It has been left to the skeptic to ask why, if colonialism played such a large part in Africa's current desperate situation, are other formerly colonial areas in Latin America, the Pacific Rim, and the Middle East so much better off today? In a recent comparative history of colonialism, Crawford Young argues for the uniquely destructive effects of the particular forms of colonialism experienced in Africa.

A first dimension of the differences noted by Young was the later time period of African colonization. Africa was the last world region to be colonized by Europe, which had (1) accumulated experience and knowledge on techniques of domination (in the British case, especially in India); and (2) set itself apart socially through an unfolding ideology of racial and cultural superiority that more completely marginalized the colonized populations in their own lands. The colonial system that emerged in Africa, Young explains, was actually quite autonomous from the European governments that created it, and very removed from influence from the subject African cultures. The style and structure of operation it developed became the model to which, or from which, independent states had to adapt. Specific differences in the application of colonial rule in Africa included the speed with which it was established; the ruthlessness with which the European powers pushed to extract the continent's resources; the use of head taxes, and of forced labor for public works and even private enterprise (even though slavery had long since been prohibited); the relatively advanced technology (as in communications) available to the colonialists; and the contemporaneous apogee of racism in European thought. On the other hand, because colonial rule in Africa ended later than in other regions, in its later phases it was imbued with a heavy dose of paternalistic development ideology; the first independent governments were compelled to "outbid" the claimed accomplishments of latter-day colonialism, and to avoid asking for commensurate sacrifices. Finally, Young observes, indigenous African religions were not structured to provide the "insulation" or competing vision to European culture that Islam and the major religions of Asia could offer (and which probably accounts for the rapid expansion of Islam in twentieth-century Africa).[15] The various dimensions of colonial impact on contemporary Nigeria are considered in several succeeding chapters, notably in our discussion of culture in Chapter Three and of the political process in Chapter Six.

This recounting of pre-independence history is not presented simply "because it's there," as though it were a mountain to climb. Rather, an awareness of these experiences is critical to an understanding of political conflict in independent Nigeria. Although the colonial experience was brief in the context of human history, the Europeans left more than their technology; they left their political ideas, which were difficult to reconcile with precolonial values and structures. For example, even though many modern Nigerians remain profoundly Yoruba or Hausa, is there a role for *obas* and emirs in modern Nigeria? This is not just a clash between the "traditional" and the "modern," because there are many, perhaps hundreds of "traditions." The blending of these various influences was all the less likely given the short amount of time allowed for political evolution prior to independence. Nigerians and other Africans are today grappling with the resultant confusion, which has produced political instability, economic woes, and constant military interventions. And the difficulties on Nigeria's road to national unity are obviously related to the absence of any start in that direction prior to independence. One scholar suggests two possible views of Nigeria's situation at independence in 1960: "Either there was no workable basis for the concept of one Nigeria. . .or else the emergence of a national identity called Nigeria was genuinely believed to be possible and practicable."[16] Posing the question in this way demonstrates how problematic was the country's existence from the very beginning.

Adjusting to Independence And The Biafran War

The short period from 1957 to 1965 brought the formal independence of a majority of African states. Those who had been mobilized into independence movements in the 1950s were euphoric, imbued with the spirit epitomized in the biblical paraphrase of the Ghanaian leader Kwame Nkrumah: "Seek ye first the political kingdom, and all else will be given unto you." The 1950s had seen more economic and educational progress than any other colonial period, and it was widely assumed that this line of development would proceed at an even faster pace once governments were in African hands.

The "honeymoon" thus celebrated proved to be very short for Nigeria's independent governments at the federal and state levels. Within two years, conflict had torn apart the ruling coalition in the Western region. The next year suspicions about the national census (discussed as a long-term policy issue in Chapter Eight) destroyed what little trust there was among the regions. Finally, in 1965, law and order broke down in the Western region over election-related fraud and violence, and the military ended the First Republic in a January 1966 coup.

THE MILITARIZATION OF NIGERIAN POLITICS

Given the central importance of military rule in Nigeria's independent history, and the prevalence of military coups generally in Africa and other less-developed regions, it is instructive to preface our discussions of the country's road to military rule by first exploring a logically prior question: How did Nigeria's military become interested in a dominant political role? As late as 1961, over half of Nigeria's officer cadre were still British. The military training of the Nigerian officers had been infused with "the subordination of the military to their political masters and a purely instrumental role for the military." Nonetheless, the younger grades of officers, and especially the more highly educated among them, were also affected by nationalism. As one of the leaders of the first coup explained,

> My first impressions which really distressed me was that [the army] was *not* a nationalistic organization and it was far from being revolutionary. A nationalistic army would first of all be ideological. Secondly, it would be political. Thirdly, it would be patriotic. . .Ideologically, the core of the revolutionary officers had agreed on a programme of action to be implemented if we had successfully taken the reins of power into our own hands.[17]

By 1966, many Nigerians, especially among the elites who had enthusiastically greeted independence, had become disillusioned with the independent regime. Their sentiments were articulated in Chinua Achebe's novel *A Man of the People*; Achebe depicted a corrupt and violent state, in which an idealistic challenger for power is beaten down by an old, self-serving politician. At the novel's end, Achebe accurately foretold the first coup.

Thus, the officer corps' first intrusion into politics was, as far as we can tell, based on their nationalistic ideology, and on the corresponding rapid decline in legitimacy of the civilian regime. They, and other Nigerians, were dismayed by the politicians' inability to stay within legal and constitutional limits in the struggle over the Western region's elections in 1964.

The First Coup (January 1966) - Those who planned and carried out the first coup were mostly majors, i.e., at the middle ranks of the officer corps. Although some senior officers had received reports of a possible coup attempt, it does not appear that any of them were informed of the actual plans. The plotters, who had been discussing the need for such an operation for about two years, planned for simultaneous strikes in the capitals of each of the four states, Ibadan in the West, Enugu in the East, Benin in the Midwest, and Kaduna in the North, as well as in the federal capital, Lagos. They intended to eliminate senior federal officials and military officers, and, at least ostensibly, the premier of each region. In the words of one of them, this was "a short list of people who were undesirable for the future progress of the country or who by their positions at the time had to be sacrificed for peace and stability."[18] Early in the morning of January 15, 1966, the coordinated attacks began. The majors succeeded in capturing and killing the federal prime minister, Sir Abubakar Tafawa Balewa, and the minister of finance, Festus Okotieboh; the premier of the Western region, Chief Akintola; the premier in the North, Sir Ahmadu Bello (traditionally titled the Sardauna of Sokoto). Accidentally (or in the belief of many Northerners, intentionally), the premiers of the East and Midwest, both Igbos, escaped death.

Box 1.2 What Happens During a Coup? How the "Majors' Coup" of 1966 was Thwarted.

"The conspirators in Lagos reassembled at the rendezvous at the Federal Guard officers mess at the Dodan Barracks, only to find that the rest of the army was by now being mobilised against them. For Major General Ironsi and a few of his senior officers had managed by one means or another to evade capture or assassination. Ironsi appeared at the Police HQ, pistol in hand, at 3.20 a.m., and ordered the troops on guard there to return to barracks because they were engaged on an 'unlawful operation'. He found his way up to Ikeja, where he was able to rally the 2nd Battalion to him with the help of Lt. Colonel Njoku; and by the time one of the conspirators, Captain Oji, arrived there at 4:00 a.m. to reconnoitre, it was too late." (Luckham 1971, pp.21-22)

The narration in Box 1.2 describes the immediate activities of Major General Aguiyi Ironsi. The conspirators numbered only about 30 officers and 100-150 enlisted men, in an army with 500 officers and 10,000 troops. They were thus, in Luckham's words, "clearly overextended from the start."[19] When Ironsi had regained control of the army he met with senior civilian officials and asked that the military be given power. A demoralized cabinet acquiesced.

It will never be known what Ironsi knew of the conspiracy beforehand, although presumably enough to save his own life. Whether intentionally or accidentally, the plot to eliminate the highest civilian and military leadership in the country had been carried out by Igbo officers, and had spared the senior Igbo officials. General Ironsi was in a delicate position.

In one of the most detailed analyses of the situation of the Nigerian military in 1966-1967, Robin Luckham argues that the violence within the Nigerian armed forces was largely the product of "the pace at which military institutions were transferred [from British command to Nigerian] and the structure of the situation in which this took place."[20] Luckham notes that the hand-over of command from British to Nigerian officers was hurried because of the political demands of independence. As a result, promotions were first very rapid (with a small difference in age and experience between senior officers and junior officers and enlisted personnel); then, once positions were "Nigerianized," advancement would be very slow. Igbos had been promoted earlier because of their generally higher educational backgrounds. However, political considerations were catching up with this merit-based ethnic imbalance in other areas of government service, and Igbo officers had reason to believe their careers were in jeopardy. The coup leaders had more than their ethnicity in common; they were also mostly graduates of Britain's military academy at Sandhurst, and from the same few cohorts. For example, among the conspirators were all four of the Igbo officers who entered Sandhurst in 1959.[21]

Two very different perspectives have been handed down concerning the motivation for the January 1966 coup. The first, provided by the public statements of the conspirators themselves, is that it was conducted by fervent young nationalists who were disillusioned with the corruption and inefficiency in government. The second, widely accepted in the North, is that it was a thinly disguised Igbo conspiracy. Ultimately, the difference may not be important, because whether the plotters were nationalists attempting to create a merit-based state, or Igbos attempting to dominate Nigerian politics, the effect in other regions, and especially in the North, would be equally threatening.

In summary, it is important to remember that Nigeria's first military coup was not a simple seizure of power. The captains and majors who planned it failed to carry it out successfully, and left the army in disarray. General Ironsi, as the general officer commanding, probably had no knowledge of the plan, and certainly took no part in it, but he warned the civilian government that a civil war would ensue unless they turned power over to him, and they acquiesced.[22] In this roundabout way, Nigeria entered its first period of military rule.

The Second Coup (July 1966) - Soldiers from the North were so outraged by the outcome in January that their officers dared not go near them. The situation was most serious in the regiment stationed in Ibadan, which had lost both its current and a past commander in the coup violence. Order was not restored until the unit was put under the command of a Northern lieutenant colonel. It was widely believed that General Ironsi had played an active role in the plot.[23] The rapid promotion of the "best qualified" replacements for those killed and arrested shifted the balance among commanders and high-level staff further in favor of Igbo officers, thus confirming suspicions of an Igbo plot. "During the first month after the January 15 coup, Igbo officers held every post of any importance in the army except Chief of Staff (Army). . . and commander of the 1st Brigade." Even after Ironsi compensated soon thereafter by appointing Northerners to two battalion command positions, Igbos were overwhelmingly dominant in the command structure.[24]

Ironsi was certainly sensitive to his delicate situation, but seemed driven by the belief that, if he were absolutely fair and impartial (not systematically favoring his own region), and if he acted as a patriotic Nigerian, his decisions would be accepted. In that spirit, he struck what he thought was a blow against "tribalism" and regionalism in his Decree no. 34 of May 1966, abolishing the federation and replacing it with a unitary state.

Order had never completely been restored in the army after January, and by July, according to Luckham, "Northern soldiers were already in a semi-mutinous state."[25]   However, their officers were reluctant to lead them in revolt, and it was only after they became convinced that Ironsi was directing a plan of Igbo domination that they put together their plan for overthrow and carried it out a few weeks later (see Box 1.3). The Northern coup was planned to disarm Igbo officers and men across the country, but it failed in the Eastern region, even though a majority of the personnel in the major unit there were

---

Box 1.3 The Second Coup July 1966

"The revolt began late at night on 28 July in the Abeokuta Garrison, where Northern officers and men broke into a meeting in the officers mess, shot their commander [and other Igbo officers]. . .It was (it seems) two or three more hours before they got themselves organised and were able to take over the armouries and disarm the Eastern Troops. In the event it gave time for the supreme command to receive a warning in the early hours of the morning of the 29th and for the Chief of Staff (Army), Lt Colonel Gowon, to put all units on the alert. . . By the time, however, that Army Headquarters were able to contact Major General Ironsi and his host at Government House, Ibadan. . .it was too late. At about 5:00 a.m. they were surrounded and their guard disarmed . . .Ironsi himself was not confronted until 9:00 a.m. when Major Danjuma of the 4th Battalion went upstairs in Government House with an escort, saluted him, questioned him and ordered his arrest." (Luckham, 1971, pp. 64-65)

Northerners.[26] This outcome was to be particularly significant because the military governor in the East, Lt. Colonel Chukwuemeka Odumegwu Ojukwu, then emerged as the leading figure in the Eastern region's secession.

IGBO MASSACRE AND CIVIL WAR

In the confusion following the July coup, many Northern officers, including Lt. Colonel Murtala Muhammed (later a military head of state) argued for the secession of the North from Nigeria. However, many prominent civilian figures argued strongly against the breakup of the country, and the Northern officers acquiesced to keeping their units in Lagos only on the condition that Lt. Colonel Yakubu Gowon, the army chief of staff and the most senior Northern officer, assume control of the government. On August 1,

1996 Gowon announced by radio that he had taken the title of Supreme Commander and Head of the Military Government. One major figure was not a party to this agreement, and immediately denounced it: the military governor of the Eastern region, Col. Ojukwu.

Gowon immediately rescinded Ironsi's Decree No. 34, and proposed creating a federal system of eight to fourteen states (see further in the discussion on federalism, Chapter Five). However, discussions of Nigeria's future were cut short by the outbreak of what has more recently been termed "ethnic cleansing," in this case of Igbos living in the North. Rioting had broken out across Northern Nigeria six weeks previously, following Ironsi's announcement of the unitary republic, with gangs invading Igbo sections of towns, looting their shops and killing the owners. An exodus toward the East had begun at that time, which swelled significantly with the July coup. By mid-August, the *New York Times* reported that 300,000 easterners had left the North; the *Times* of London put the figure at 500,000. Simultaneously, a much smaller number of Northerners began to move in the opposite direction.[27] As the "brain drain" of educated easterners began to take a toll on public services, military officials urged the civil servants among them to stay at their posts. During the first weekend of October 1966, violence again broke out in the North against Igbos and other Easterners, and in the East against Northerners; reports of each in the other region rapidly inflamed passions, and before the weekend was over, somewhere between 5,000 and 50,000 people had been killed and a panicked exodus of the estimated two million Igbos living in the North had begun.[28]

"Thus the lines were drawn for the East's *de facto* withdrawal from the political control of the center, and the secession and civil war that followed in 1967."[29] However, that outcome was not preordained, for all the major actors each originally had a range of options that overlapped with others, and the breakdown of bargaining was not inevitable.[30] The combination of factors that led to secession included the massacres, the position of Ojukwu at the head of a battalion and in control of the regional government and the Eastern media, and the failure of Western and Midwestern leaders to follow the Eastern lead in secession. Several months of negotiation began between the Gowon government and Colonel Ojukwu's command in Enugu, the Eastern regional capital. Ojukwu's objective was to maintain control of military and security forces in the East, whether as part of a confederation or through secession if necessary. Ojukwu thus refused to accept any arrangement that put him under the command of central authorities. As negotiations continued, Ojukwu developed a self-standing military command headquarters in Enugu, and began negotiating for arms shipments. Negotiations were conducted at a distance because of Ojukwu's doubts concerning his safety outside his own region, but a last series of face-to-face talks were held in January 1967 in Ghana at the invitation of that country's military government. An apparent agreement reached there was variously interpreted by the different sides upon their return to Nigeria, and was never implemented.

Late in May 1967, Gowon issued a decree abolishing the four regions and creating twelve states. Northern solidarity was broken, but more important to the Igbos was the fact that the Eastern region would now consist of three states, with non-Igbo majorities in two of them; the ports and oil facilities would be outside Ojukwu's control. Gowon hoped to forestall secession, but instead precipitated it: "On 30 May. . .Lt.-Col. Ojukwu broadcast a dawn message declaring Eastern Nigeria a sovereign independent state and proclaiming the birth of a new Republic of Biafra."[31]

Colonel Ojukwu (soon promoted to general in the Biafran army, as was Gowon in Nigeria) had overwhelming and immediate support among the Igbo, and a propaganda effort in support of Eastern independence built on the popularity of this position already expressed by immigrants from the other regions. However, the minority peoples of the Eastern region were ill-at-ease at the prospect of living under Igbo domination, and without them Ojukwu's command was threatened with loss of the oil fields, access to ports, and a multiethnic, territorial rationale for independence. People such as the Ogoni, who lived in the Niger delta oil fields, felt particularly torn, and ultimately experienced great suffering in the conflict.

The month of June 1967 passed with no military activity, but the issue was brought to a head by the competition for control of oil royalties. When Ojukwu's government used its control of the oil fields to get agreement from the international oil companies to pay at least part of the royalties to Biafra, the federal government launched its attack.[32] The next month (August 1967) a Biafran force invaded the Midwest, briefly occupied Benin City, and threatened to march on Lagos. The federal forces reorganized, however, and soon drove the Biafran army back over the Niger River. Although the war dragged on for two more years, it was thenceforth a matter of slow attrition of the Biafran position. Biafra's cause had dimmed once other regions decided against breaking from Nigeria. Led by Obafemi Awolowo, leaders in the West had immediately fallen in behind the federal cause, ending Ojukwu's hope of a general disintegration of Nigeria into its regions. Following the Biafran invasion of their region in August, leaders in the Midwest (except for Igbo officers stationed there) also declared their support of the federal government, as did most of the Eastern minorities. The Ojukwu regime shift from persuasion to coercion against the minorities exacerbated the situation.[33]

The Biafran War was truly a civil war in the most grim connotation of that term. The civilian population, especially in the Midwest Region battleground, suffered enormously. The violence is vividly described in Nigerian literature of the 1970s, notably in Buchi Emecheta's novel *Destination Biafra.*[34] At the same time, Biafra's predictions to its own people and the world of genocide at the hands of federal forces were unfulfilled. The federal army generally remained disciplined as it advanced into Biafra, and Igbos were quickly reintegrated into Nigerian life after the war.

Through the last two years of the war (1968-1970), Biafra's hope lay in convincing international organizations and foreign governments to pressure Nigeria into a negotiated settlement. The Biafrans proved to be excellent propagandists, and aroused considerable sympathy for their plight in the United States and Britain. Various religious groups, Oxfam, and the International Red Cross provided emergency relief by airlift. Some African governments offered clear support to Biafra, a support Nigerians suspected grew from a desire to see their country divided up and thus reduced in influence. This was thought especially to be the case with Côte d'Ivoire (the Ivory Coast) under President Houphouet-Boigny, who favored Biafra with

---

Box 1.4 The War's End.

"The formal reconciliation ceremony took place at Dodan Barracks, Lagos, on 15 January. An emotion-filled Gowon welcomed his five former brother officers. . .by their Christian names. Later he embraced the armistice delegates outside on the lawn and congratulated them on their 'return to the fold.' 'Biafra now ceases to exist,' declared Effiong. 'We have been reunited with our brothers,' replied General Gowon in a champagne toast, confirming the idiom he had purposely adopted throughout the war in his refusal to refer to the Biafrans as 'enemies. . .but as fellow countrymen who had been led astray by an evil clique.' 'But for Ojukwu's madness,' he added, 'such a thing would not have happened to this country.'"

A. H. M. Kirk-Greene, *Crisis and Conflict in Nigeria*, vol. 2, pp. 143-144.

French support. When the war ended, relations among these countries were accordingly strained.

Finally, in January 1970 Ojukwu fled Nigeria for asylum in Côte d'Ivoire, and the Biafran field commander, Lt. Colonel Effiong, surrendered unconditionally. General Gowon announced a general amnesty (see Box 1.4).

NIGERIA AFTER THE CIVIL WAR

On October 1, 1970, General Gowon announced a "nine-point" program for a return to civilian rule by 1976. Four years later, he issued an amendment: Achieving civilian rule in 1976 would be "unrealistic." In the meantime, Nigeria's petroleum revenues had grown astronomically, and had been the basis for unprecedented corruption in the Gowon administration. He was overthrown in a bloodless coup in 1976 by Murtala Muhammed, who actually began the return to a civilian system.

Conclusion

Obviously, Nigerian history did not end in the 1970s. In the following chapters we treat the twenty years since then as a single "contemporary" period in Nigerian political history. It is a period marked by the alternation of civilian and military governments, and by an economy based on oil. The country's experience with various constitutions in the past twenty years is described in Chapter Four, while the country's experience as a major petroleum producer is considered in Chapters Two and Seven.

Many important aspects of Nigeria's political and economic development were given brief attention in this chapter, because they are better discussed in the topical chapters that follow. For example, the independence movements of the late colonial period, the precursors of later political organizations, are described in the sections on parties and interest groups.

Awareness of the events covered in this historical review is necessary to an understanding of contemporary Nigerian politics, and especially to our later consideration of this essential question: Was the difficult situation in which Nigeria finds itself today essentially preordained by the interplay of precolonial and colonial conditions, or should blame be laid on the country's political leadership since independence?

ENDNOTES

[1]1. Clifford Geertz, Old Societies and New States: The Quest for Modernity in Asia and Africa (New York: Free Press of Glencoe, 1963).

2.This discussion relies principally on Anthony Oyewole, *Historical Dictionary of Nigeria* (Metuchen, NJ: Scarecrow Press, 1987), Michael Crowder, *The Story of Nigeria*,(London: Faber and Faber, 1978), and James S. Coleman, *Nigeria: Background to Nationalism* (Berkeley: University of California Press, 1971).

3. Crowder, *The Story of Nigeria*, p. 41.

4. Paul Bohannon, "The Tiv of Nigeria," in James L. Gibbs Jr., ed. *Peoples of Africa* (New York: Holt, Rinehart and Winston, 1965), pp. 523-525, 532-533.

5. While this tragic process deprived most of its victims of their cultural roots, aspects of Nigerian culture survived in parts of the West Indies and especially Brazil. The Nigerian author of this book visited Rio de Janeiro and observed the play of *ayo*, a

traditional game, and the worship of *Yemaja,* a traditional Yoruba god. He discovered that *esusu,* a local banking system, was transplanted to the West Indies.

6. Crowder, *The Story of Nigeria,* p. 68.

7. Peter Enahoro, *How to be a Nigerian* (Ibadan: Caxton Press, 1966).

8. Crowder, *The Story of Nigeria,* p. 183.

9. Crowder, *The Story of Nigeria,* pp. 201-203.

10. Chinua Achebe, *Arrow of God* (New York: Doubleday-Anchor, 1969), p. 65.

11. Bohannon, "The Tiv of Nigeria," p. 533.

12. Crawford Young, *The African Colonial State in Comparative Perspective* (New Haven: Yale University Press, 1994), pp. 96-97.

13. Young, *The African Colonial State in Comparative Perspective,* pp. 124-133.

14. Wole Soyinka, *Aké: The Years of Childhood* (Ibadan: Spectrum Books, 1981), p. 200.

15. Young, *The African Colonial State in Comparative Perspective,* pp. 45, 76, 280-281.

16. A. H. M. Kirk-Greene, *Crisis and Conflict in Nigeria,* vol. 1, *January 1966-July 1967* (London: Oxford University Press, 1971), p. 3.

17. A. Ademoyega, *Why We Struck: The Story of the First Nigerian Coup* (Ibadan: Exams Publishers, 1981), pp. 27, 33. Quoted in Dele Olowu, "Centralization, Self-Governance and Development in Nigeria, in James S. Wunsch and Dele Olowu, eds. *The Failure of the Centralized State* (Boulder, CO: Westview, 1990), p. 206.

18. Major Nzeogwu, quoted in Robin Luckham, *The Nigerian Military: A Sociological Analysis of Authority and Revolt 1960-67* (Cambridge: Cambridge University Press, 1971), p. 31.

19. Luckham, *The Nigerian Military,* p. 33.

20. Luckham, *The Nigerian Military,* p. 4.

21. Luckham, *The Nigerian Military,* p. 48.

22. Dudley, *An Introduction to Nigerian Government and Politics,* p. 79.

23. Luckham, *The Nigerian Military,* p. 51.

24. Luckham, *The Nigerian Military*, pp. 56-57.

25. Luckham, *The Nigerian Military*, p. 64.

26. Luckham, *The Nigerian Military*, p. 66.

xxvii. Kirk-Greene, *Crisis and Conflict in Nigeria*, vol. 1, pp. 48, 57.

28. Kirk-Greene, *Crisis and Conflict in Nigeria*, vol. 1, pp. 62-67.

29. Luckham, *The Nigerian Military*, pp. 67-68.
xxx. Luckham, *The Nigerian Military*, pp. 336-337.

31. Kirk-Greene, *Crisis and Conflict in Nigeria*, vol. 1, p. 97.

32. Kirk-Greene, *Crisis and Conflict in Nigeria*, vol. 1, pp. 103-104.

33. Kirk-Greene, *Crisis and Conflict in Nigeria*, vol. 1, pp. 328-332.

34. Buchi Emecheta, *Destination Biafra* (New York: Allison andn Busby, 1982).

Chapter 2

ENVIRONMENTAL POTENTIAL AND LIMITATIONS

- ♦ What non-political conditions affect a political system's ability to respond to the needs of its population?
- ♦ What is the level of poverty in Nigeria compared with other countries? What are the most reliable indicators of wealth and income?
- ♦ Why has Nigeria's record of economic development been so dismal?
- ♦ Why are most of Nigeria's people so poor?

In a systems approach to politics, the term "environment" takes on a wide definition, almost "that which is not political but which conditions or affects the political process." It allows us to preface our discussion of politics by describing the physical, cultural, and economic conditions, as well as the relationships with other political and economic systems, that limit the choices that political actors may make or enhance those options. These elements of the environment are, of course, themselves the result of historical trends, some of which were described in the preceding chapter.

The environment of Nigerian politics consists of the physical resources within the country's borders, the limitations which its physical environment imposes on productivity, the nature and health of its economy, its social and cultural patterns (introduced in Chapter One, and developed further in Chapter Three), and its interactions with other countries and international economic and political systems. Beyond simple description, we can use this analysis to address the debates concerning the sources of Nigeria's problems.

We need to know whether these problems are the result of physical environment, history, and socio-economic context and the constraints which these environmental conditions impose on Nigeria's policy options, or whether they result from the Nigerian political process and the policy that Nigerian governments have made. The first approach—the environmental explanation—was first addressed in the previous chapter, where the historical legacy, especially of colonialism, was addressed. It is further considered in this chapter, in terms of contemporary environmental constraints. The second approach to explanation, in the nature of the Nigerian political process and its policy decisions, is considered in Chapter Seven.

The Socio-Economic Situation

Nigeria is counted among the world's less-developed, or Third World countries. The term "Third World" was coined to distinguish the poorer, non-industrial regions of the world—Latin America, Africa, and south Asia—from the industrial and capitalist "First World" and the industrial and communist "Second World." With the demise of the Soviet Union and her sphere of influence, the "Third World" distinction no longer seems appropriate, but it has become part of the vocabulary of international affairs. Here, we use the terms "Third World" and "less-developed" interchangeably.

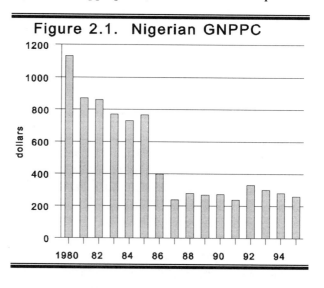

Nigeria's gross national product (GNP) in 1995 was $29 billion, or $260 per capita. This put it well below the World Bank criterion for "low-income countries," which for 1995 was a per capita GNP of less than $765. Furthermore, during the period of 1980 to 1991 GNP per capita actually *declined* by 1.7 percent annually, and in 1987, was only one-fourth the 1980 level (Figure 2.1). The gross national product per capita (GNPPC) is the most commonly used quantitative indicator of development. Among countries at comparable development levels, it is a useful and valid indicator for comparing the size and growth of economies. However, it has serious deficiencies as a measure of well-being. This is obvious if the reader in an industrial country considers the prospect of surviving for a year on a Nigerian's average share of the total value of goods and services produced in that year—$260 in 1995. Among the deficiencies of GNP as a standard for comparing economic conditions are:

1) *Its failure to include productive activities that do not pass through the marketplace.* Rural populations often raise much of their own food, produce their own building materials, process their own fertilizers, etc.

2) *Its failure to fully account for the informal sector of the economy.* Especially among urban populations in less-developed countries, many people are self-employed as petty traders, or are hired for wages that go unreported. This informal sector may include as much as 75 percent of the urban work force in West Africa.[1]

3) *Its failure to account for different price levels.* How well one can live on a given income will depend on the prices of the things one must buy. It is frequently the case in less-developed countries that "high-tech" and imported goods are more expensive than in advanced industrial countries, while locally produced goods, especially food, are relatively less expensive. To compensate for this problem the International Monetary Fund introduced a measure, the Purchasing Power Parity (PPP), which

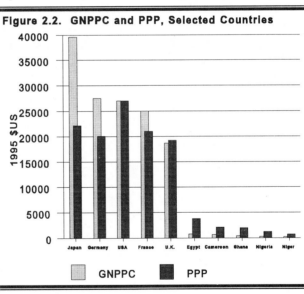

Figure 2.2. GNPPC and PPP, Selected Countries

adjusts GNPPC by taking into account the cost in each country of a given "basket" of goods. The GNPPC and PPP measures for Nigeria, some advanced industrial countries, and other African countries, are shown in Figure 2.2.

The figure shows that wealthier countries tend to have PPP ratings that are lower than their GNPPC, while the opposite is true for developing nations. Clearly, however, the gap is still wide between the purchasing power ratings in the two categories of countries.

4) *Its failure to take into account inequalities in the distribution of income and benefits.* Because Nigeria's GNPPC of $260 is obtained by dividing total GNP by population, it is a mean share of GNP. Because some Nigerians are

very wealthy, there are obviously many whose share of GNP is well below the mean. Less-developed countries tend to have income distributions that are less equal than in developed countries, and to have relatively few people at middle-income levels. Thus, while the PPP may adjust the GNPPC of Third World countries upward, the number does not reflect the disposable income of most people. It is important, of course, to note that GNPPC is *not* a measure of personal income, but rather represents the average share of goods and services produced. Thus, it includes one's share of highway pavement, parking lots, jet fighters, and other such goods that are not part of an individual's disposable income.

Given all these difficulties with arriving at precisely comparable statistics on differences in wealth among nations, it is often more instructive to abandon reliance on income or wealth comparisons, and to focus instead on indicators that more directly measure quality of life. One such measure used by many national and international agencies is the *infant mortality rate (IMR)*, defined as the number of deaths per one thousand live births after the first year of life. This measure might seem too specific to be an indicator of overall quality of life, but it is defensible when one considers the many factors that contribute to the IMR: The availability of health and sanitation services, food supply, the health of parents, especially the mother, and so forth. Nigeria's IMR for 1995 was 80. Most industrial nations have IMRs of less than 12, and international health organizations have set 50 as the maximum IMR that can be said to characterize a society "meeting basic human needs." IMRs for various countries are shown in Figure 2.3.

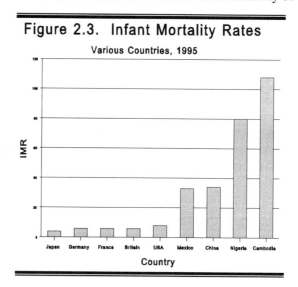

Figure 2.3. Infant Mortality Rates

Various Countries, 1995

Environmental Conditions That Contribute to Nigeria's Problems with Agricultural Production and Marketing

Having measured the severity of Nigeria's economic problems, we move again to an explanation for these conditions, always with an ultimate purpose of determining whether they are beyond correction by human agents, or whether they represent a failure on the part of political leaders and other political and economic forces to take appropriate remedial actions. Among the environmental conditions that must be considered are, first of all, those limiting the country's ability to produce food and other necessities, and to profit from the marketing of agricultural products.

In comparison with more developed countries, poor countries generally have low agricultural productivity, both per unit of land and per worker. Furthermore, agricultural producers must deal with wide fluctuations in prices for their products, and they are left to their own devices should a natural disaster such as drought or flood wipe out their source of income. To what degree could these problems be addressed by political and economic decision-makers?

Low agricultural productivity in Africa has been ascribed to a wide variety of factors, in various complex mixes. Those factors include *ecological constraints* (poor soils, erosion, drought, diseases and pests), *labor shortages* caused by migration to urban areas; *primitive technology* due to a lack of capital; *resistance to change*, aggravated by an aging farm population and low status of farming in the education of youth; *inefficient marketing*, because of inadequate transportation infrastructure and trade restrictions; *underinvestment,* from unavailability of credit, low prices, unstable pricing policies, and *unfavorable terms of trade* between agricultural and other sectors.

CLIMATE AND RAINFALL

A particular ecological constraint that has been much studied and much discussed is long-term *desertification*. In the 1970s, world attention was focused on a drought that devastated the Sahel region of Africa—the semi-arid band to the south of the Sahara Desert. It affected both West and East (especially Ethiopia) Africa, and brought a wide variety of international agencies into the region to provide famine relief, to drill new and deeper wells, to introduce new farming techniques, and to try to prevent "overgrazing" of a "fragile ecosystem." It was widely believed, and reported in highly credible sources, that the Sahara was advancing south.

It has since been determined that the drought of 1969-1974 did not represent a permanent shift in climatic conditions, but that it was an episodic event, like others reported in 1913, 1926, and 1949. However, if the worst of the drought ended in 1974, the dry spell continued at least until 1985, and "no dry spell of similar length can be shown from the rainfall records except, possibly, that of the 1860s and 1905-15—when records were scarce."[2] In northern Nigeria, the lack of rainfall in 1972 and 1973 destroyed part of subsistence farm output in both years, and the second was worse than the first. The resulting food shortage was widespread. Commercial output was also destroyed. In the absence of income, savings (especially livestock) were liquidated. A dearth of grazing and fodder caused widespread animal mortality. The market, on which people now depended for food imported from outside the region, was subject to inflation.[3]

Northern Nigerian peasants used an entire arsenal of strategies to counter drought-induced famine; one of those strategies was to sell land, thus increasing the overall inequality of land ownership.[4] This is an example of a ripple effect, as conditions in the physical environment have economic and social effects that work against certain public policy objectives.

Nigeria's government can hardly be blamed for the drought, but the severe weather conditions may have had direct political effects: Although the collapse of Nigeria's last civilian regime in 1983 may be "overdetermined" in the sense that it has more than enough sufficient explanations, the drought in the years just preceding the 1983 coup at least exacerbated the seriousness of other constraints on the Second Republic's options.

THE INHERITED ECONOMIC SYSTEM

In Chapter One we considered the retarding effect of colonialism on Nigerian political development; here we want to consider how colonial policies shaped the Nigerian economy, especially in marketing, labor supply, and investment. We will then explore the interaction of those policies with the country's natural environment.

Since early in the colonial period southern Nigerians have been producing cocoa, palm oil, timber, and rubber. The timber, sold mostly as tropical hardwood for use in furniture and construction, has come from the now dwindling rainforests in the South. In the North, the principal market products were cattle, hides and skins, cotton, and peanuts.

The growth of trade in these commodities was not entirely spontaneous. The British interest in Nigeria was primarily commercial, with its origins in the United Africa Company (UAC). When the UAC was granted a charter as the Royal Niger Company in 1886, it was given police and judicial power, and authorized to collect taxes and to oversee commerce. Not surprisingly, its policies were directed toward developing the Nigerian economy to be compatible with British needs. Also, public sentiment in Britain was never solidly in favor of creating a colonial empire, and powerful voices were raised in Parliament in favor of keeping the costs of empire to a minimum. Colonial administrations were under heavy pressure to be self-sufficient, i.e., to develop local sources of revenue to cover their costs of administration. As a result, colonial administrators took such measures as necessary to lure or force peasant farmers away from subsistence and into commercial farming, particularly of export crops. Furthermore, cost-efficient marketing meant emphasis on just a few of the most needed products; in Nigeria (and elsewhere in West Africa), these turned out to be palm oil, cocoa, peanuts, and cotton. Thus British raw material priorities and the need to provide a self-sufficient colonial administration distorted African economies toward dependence on the sale of a small number of primarily agricultural commodities. In Nigeria, these policies were hugely successful, as the rail line completed to Kano in 1911 stimulated cash-crop exports. Cocoa exports grew from 5,000 tons in 1914 to 30,000 tons in 1922 to over 100,000 by the late 1930s.[5] Farmers in western Nigeria became so wholly dependent on income from cocoa sales that by the 1950s they were purchasing one-half to three-fourths of the calories they consumed.[6]

Beyond its need for fiscal self-sufficiency, the colonial administration did not greatly interfere with the social, political, and market forces defining Nigerian agriculture. Its agricultural policy was largely guided by the political imperative to maintain the stability of the countryside, and it did not encourage the replacement of peasant agriculture by large-scale plantations.

The combination of population growth and the commercialization of agriculture began to strain relationships between agricultural techniques and the ecology that had been in place for centuries. A visitor to the tropics from North America or Europe, surrounded with the lush vegetation of a tropical country, may be excused for concluding that agricultural products might almost grow themselves in such an environment. However, tropical agriculture is vastly different, and in some ways more difficult than that of temperate zones. For example, the deep, fertile river loam that characterizes the best temperate-zone farming areas is nonexistent in tropical Africa; its humus content depends on the slowing of bacterial activity that winter brings. Humus does not build up in tropical soils, which remain fragile and easily leached of their nutrients.

After World War II, colonial officials sometimes assumed that productivity could be greatly increased in tropical regions with the introduction of "modern" methods; not often recognized were the different ecological conditions of production in a tropical setting. Lush tropical rainforest could not simply be replaced by plantations. Rainfall patterns (dry and rainy seasons), constant high temperatures, and soil conditions meant that farming techniques effective in England or North America would be unsuccessful or even disastrous. Only gradually, and much later, were the efforts of agronomists applied to maximizing agricultural production in the tropics, especially to food production for local consumption. There is still a large "research deficit" between the level of resources expended for agricultural research in temperate zones, as opposed to tropical zones.

In conclusion, Nigeria came to independence with an economy typical of Africa and other Third World areas. It was based on the production and export of agricultural commodities, principally palm oil (of which Nigeria was the world's leading exporter) and cocoa. It was also an agricultural economy based predominantly on small farmers whose labor force consisted mainly of family members. Because Nigeria was larger and more ecologically diverse than most African colonies, its agricultural production showed greater diversity than in the typical case; still, production for export in each of its regions was focused on one or a few commodities, and the country as a whole depended on commodity markets in the industrial capitals of the world for its foreign exchange.

POLICY CHOICES OF INDEPENDENT GOVERNMENTS

Until the oil boom years of the mid 1970s, Nigeria led Africa in production of peanuts and palm oil, and was second only to Ghana in production of cocoa. Like other newly independent countries, Nigeria broke with some colonial economic development policies, especially as concerned the need to diversify production. But the need for foreign exchange meant that the emphasis in agriculture would remain on exportable commodities, even as a large proportion of investment capital was directed toward industrialization. Economists in both the industrial and Third World countries associated industry with prosperity, and agriculture was seen as the "cash cow" from which to extract savings for investment in other areas. Also, Nigerian government officials, trained in the need to balance budgets, balanced appropriations bills with overly optimistic estimations of "expected revenue." When these fell short, the difference was made up from cash reserves accumulated by the Central Produce Marketing Board.

> Since those reserves were derived from the price differential between what was paid to the farmer and what the Board earned in export earnings. . .for close on a decade, Nigeria existed only through the exploitation of her farmers.[7]

Thus, governments were motivated to keep the prices they paid for exportable commodities low, in order to fund other programs. Many scholars have found that independent governments also tried to satisfy urban demands for cheap basic food products by holding down the price paid to farmers on food for the domestic market. This was said to contribute to the unattractiveness of agricultural work, and to enhance the lure of the cities.[8]

Tom Forrest challenges the applicability of such views to Nigeria, where he finds that "there is no history of widespread and persistent intervention by the government in domestic food production and markets in Nigeria," and he sees the problem as an extension of arguments in a "voluminous literature" on marketing boards and export crops.[9] We will further examine the impact of Nigerian agricultural policy in Chapter Seven; here it is important to observe that food production for domestic markets has a different set of dynamics than agricultural production for export.

Forrest goes on to question the presumed relationship between the oil boom and a drop in agricultural production due to an exodus of labor and in fact questions the large literature suggesting that Nigeria has had, or is projected to have, a food shortage. According to his logic, the oil boom led to an increase in urban incomes and an in-migration to Nigeria that actually boosted prices of food compared to other commodities. The rapidly increasing revenues from petroleum exports reduced the government's desire to tax agriculture, and so prevented a rise in farmers' costs. At the same time, as the naira (the national currency) increased in value and tariffs were reduced on imported food, imports boomed and the volume of agricultural exports dropped. He finds a mixed and complicated picture of food production in Nigeria, but cites several studies demonstrating an increase in food production in some localities. Forrest himself questions whether there is a sufficiently reliable data base to make any categorical statement on these relationships, but his contribution is significant because it raises fundamental questions concerning widely accepted theories on problems of African agriculture.[10] He does agree with other researchers that the distortion of Nigeria's labor market by oil had serious effects on such major export crops as cocoa, palm oil, palm kernels, rubber, peanuts, and cotton,[11] however, this oil-boom disruption seems to have merely enhanced a process already underway. As early as the 1950s, Western region cocoa farmers saw their investment of labor and capital as a stepping stone to other occupations—trading for women, service jobs for men, and education and nonagricultural careers for their children. (Berry documents that most of the children of farmers in two villages she studied had left those villages to work or attend school, and had become teachers, drivers, mechanics, and traders.) This meant that cocoa production had been in competition with other demands on the labor market for a long time before oil appeared.[12]

These trends continued even though the price paid for cocoa increased during the 1970s; it did not keep up with inflation, and better options were available. Thus during the oil boom, agriculture in general, especially at certain peak periods of need, suffered from a shortage of labor in competition with jobs related to the urban construction boom and with the growth of the informal economy.[13]

Cocoa exports were briefly stimulated in 1986, when the Cocoa Marketing Board was eliminated and private purchasers entered the market. Demand was sufficiently stimulated that these buyers were offering farmers as much as 6,000 naira per ton, compared to a price of 1,600 naira the preceding season. However, the purchasing system proved to be poorly organized, which was reflected in the poor quality of the Nigerian cocoa entering the market. The government responded by reinstituting a system of purchasing licenses.[14]

It is clear that agricultural exports dropped off rapidly in the 1970s, and although food production grew somewhat, production per capita was declining. By 1982, over 90 percent of consumed wheat, 50 percent of rice, and 20 percent of corn was imported. Imports were stimulated by the effect of rising petroleum prices and government spending that funded relatively cheap food imports, while a shortage of labor in the countryside prevented the growth of domestic food production. However, a 1985 survey of rural households showed that 90 percent of returning migrants went to their home villages, and only 20 percent of those reported that they did no agricultural labor. The rationalization that Nigeria's growing dependence on imported food was explained by a shortage of labor in the countryside seemed to hold no longer.[15]

Conditions That Create Quality-of Life Challenges Unique to Poor Tropical Countries like Nigeria

HEALTH AND DISEASE

Health problems pose one of the most serious challenges to the country's political system. Beyond their direct effect on the quality of life, they greatly (if unmeasurably) reduce Nigeria's economic productivity, and drain resources from other needs. Efforts to improve health are described in Chapter Seven.

Physical illness is a part of the human condition everywhere, and the higher disease rates of poorer nations are largely explainable by the lack of resources necessary to acquire medicines, medical facilities, and personnel. But environment contributes as well: There are virtually no diseases present in temperate areas that are not also endemic in the tropics (although some arrived recently: gonorrhea, syphilis, and influenza were introduced to Nigeria by soldiers returning from European service during World War I).[16] However, the reverse is not true, as carriers of some of the most common human diseases can only survive in tropical climates. The most prominent example is malaria, discussed below.

Table 2.1. Prevalence of Diseases in Nigeria, 1986: The Top Ten

Disease	Number of Cases	Cases per 10,000 Population
Malaria	1,020,071	1,028.9
Dysentery (all types)	185,904	187.5
Measles	115,743	116.7
Pneumonia	82,312	83
Gonorrhoea	42,306	42.7
Whooping Cough	42,193	42.6
Schistosomiasias	26,975	27.2
Meningitis (both types)	17,168	17.3
Leprosy	14,659	14.8

(From Toyin Falola, "The Crisis of African Health Care Services," in T. Falola and Dennis Ityavyar, eds. *The Political Economy of Health in Africa* (Athens, OH: Ohio University Center for International Studies, 1992), p.

10.

Various river-borne diseases also account for long-term illness and fatalities (see schistosomiasis in Table 2.1), contributing especially to the high mortality rate among children. As with agricultural problems, these diseases can be attacked with research and its application; yet a vastly disproportionate share of the resources applied to health problems world-wide is focused on ailments more common to the industrialized world.

In Nigeria specifically, the most difficult health problems include:

Malaria - This is one of the most prevalent infectious diseases in the world, but is limited to warm climates. It is endemic to most of the African continent and to all regions of Nigeria. Occuring only where its vector, the anopheles mosquito, can survive, it is a leading cause of illness and death in the developing world. Of an estimated 300 to 500 million clinical cases of malaria per year in the world, tropical Africa accounts for more than 90 percent, and it is the most common disease in Nigeria (Table 2.1). Data for 1970-1975 in a locality in Nigeria showed that malaria was responsible for 20 to 30 percent of infant mortality.[17] In tropical Africa, virtually every long-term resident carries the malaria virus, and although large proportions of the population are affected by it, it is usually not fatal after childhood.

Malaria is, however, almost always extremely debilitating and has a documented effect on labor productivity.

Guinea Worm - This infection is transmitted through contaminated water supplies. It is a parasital infection that is not fatal, but it causes repeated illness and occasionally permanently cripples its victims. In areas of highest incidence, it is thought to be the most significant health-related cause of absence from work or school. In 1987, the World Health Organization (WHO) estimated that there were three million cases in Nigeria—the highest number in any country in the world.

Schistosomiasis - This infection is caused by blood flukes, which enter through the skin when the human body is in an infested fresh water pond or stream. Like guinea worm infection, schistosomiasis is debilitating rather than fatal. Such infections are certainly less serious in one sense than the fatal diseases, yet they are even more serious in their economic effect, in that they incapacitate people, who can no longer work but must be cared for, often for long periods. Incidence of schistosomiasis has increased where reservoirs are created behind large dams, as at the Kainji Dam in Nigeria.[18]

AIDS - the presence of AIDS in Nigeria was only confirmed in 1987. In comparison to some countries in Central and East Africa or the United States, and in comparison to Nigeria's problems with other diseases, AIDS was not considered a major health problem in Nigeria until quite recently: In 1990, the infection rate for either HIV type 1 or 2 was estimated at less than 1 percent of the population, which would have put it in fourth place in Table 2.1. However, the number of cases has been increasing, with 5,500 active AIDS cases by July, 1996, and the number of HIV positive cases is now estimated at 2.2 percent of Nigeria's population. Because of the stigma attached to the disease it is likely that many cases are unreported.[19] The death from AIDS of a popular Nigerian music star, Fela Ransome-Kuti, in August 1997 focused unprecedented attention on this new health problem.

In addition to long-term, endemic diseases, *epidemics* can seriously disrupt health planning for years, as in the case of cerebrospinal meningitis. There is a belt across the Sahel region with a long dry season and low humidity for about five months, with wind-borne dust storms. Because it is relatively cool, people in the North spend long periods indoors in this period, which promotes contagion, and respiratory diseases are common. There were serious outbreaks in 1986, 1989, 1996 and 1998. Meningitis can be treated at an early stage with antibiotics, and there is a preventive vaccination available, but lack of funds and health infrastructure ensure that such epidemics will have more serious effects in a less-developed country. (There were also political and cultural factors at work in Nigeria: The 1996 outbreak occurred at the time of the annual Muslim pilgrimage to Mecca, and Saudi Arabia temporarily prevented entry to their country from the affected countries. Thus, Nigerian officials were reluctant to reveal the true magnitude of the epidemic.) In three months in 1996, 100,000 West Africans (including 50,000 in northern Nigeria) were infected, and more than 10,000 died (including 5000 Nigerians). Dr. Marc Etchegorry of Doctors Without Borders called it "by far the worst [epidemic] that sub-Saharan Africa has ever seen."[20]

Other epidemics in Nigeria in recent years were an outbreak of yellow fever in 1986 and of Lassa fever (a contagious viral disease first identified in 1969 in the northern Nigerian town of Lassa).

POPULATION GROWTH

Nothing is more striking to a visitor to Nigeria than the youth of the population; everywhere there are multitudes of children. It has been estimated that about one-half the Nigerian population is less than fifteen years of age. Children are considered a valuable resource in labor-intensive agricultural societies, and in a country with high infant mortality rates and no social security system in place,

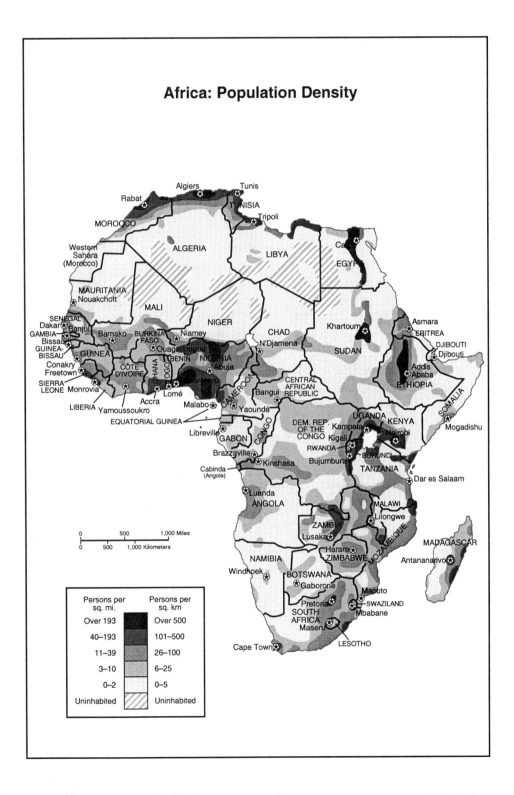

Africa: Population Density

parents would be imprudent not to have enough children so that some would grow up to provide for them in their old age. This utility at the individual level becomes dysfunctional at the societal level, of course, as increasing populations struggle to survive on a limited physical environment. Nigeria already claims one of the highest population densities in Africa, as is obvious from a population density map (Figure 2.4). Yet, during the 1980s the population of Nigeria grew 3.1 percent annually, while GNP grew only 1.7 percent per year. The urban population is estimated to have grown 8 to 10 percent per year, and in the urban environment children become economic liabilities. Thus, the dependency ratio (the proportion of the nonworking population to the working population) has steadily risen since the early 1960s, placing a great strain on the country's underdeveloped facilities for the provision of social welfare and education."[21]

Because there has not been a widely accepted census since 1963 (see the discussion of the census issue in Chapter Eight), population totals for Nigeria vary widely: The much-cited *World Military and Social Expenditures (1993)* reported a total of 115.5 million Nigerians in 1990, while the United Nations found 108.5 million that same year; however, the World Bank estimated the 1991 population to be 99 million, and the government's official population count for 1991 was 88.5 million. Although the 1991 census figures are hotly disputed because of their implications for the distribution of resources, it is likely that the earlier long-term projections were considerably inflated. But if we use the most conservative count (the official census) and if we accept the World Bank's growth rate of 3.1 percent per year as accurate, Nigeria's population pressures will soon be staggering (Figure 2.5):

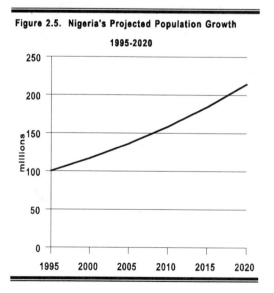

Figure 2.5. Nigeria's Projected Population Growth

1995-2020

From 88.5 million in 1991, the total reached 100 million in 1995, and it will double this 1995 population in 2018. The most important factors in this trend cannot be controlled: As in most developing countries, the rapid population increase in Nigeria may largely be traced to advances in health care, especially for children. Mortality rates among infants and young children have been dropping while the birthrate remains relatively constant. We can expect counter pressures from urbanization (children are economic liabilities in the urban environment, whereas they are assets in the village), the expansion of education (the education of women in particular has been found to be closely related to a declining birthrate), and the availability of birth control information.

URBANIZATION

Nigeria shares a pattern of urbanization common in Africa: Although the country is still primarily rural (60.7 percent), it is urbanizing rapidly: Nigeria's population is projected to be over 50 percent urban by the year 2010. In the process, the development of urban infrastructure is added to the long list of demands on government. The problems associated with urbanization are seen primarily in the largest city, Lagos. While the country's total population has been growing at an annual rate of between 2.5 and 3.1 percent, Lagos has grown 11.4 percent per year, and some parts of Lagos grew at double that rate. The density of its population is 151,500 per square mile, compared to New York City's "mere" 11,500 per square mile. Of all the world's seventy-five largest cities, only Hong Kong is more densely settled. In 1950, Lagos had a population of 290,000; in 1975, 3.5 million, and in 1995, 9.8 million. By the year 2000, the Lagos urban area is projected to have a population of 12.5 million, and by 2010, 21 million—1.5 times more than in present-day metropolitan New York.[22]

What draws people to Lagos? Few Nigerians will ever admit to liking the lifestyle of this huge, crowded city, but clearly there are economic opportunities there for many people. In 1975 over 55 percent of the country's industrial firms were located in the Lagos metropolitan area, producing 70 percent of gross industrial output. If petroleum is excluded, 75 percent of both imports and exports pass through the port of Lagos. It is clearly the country's commercial and financial capital. Lagos offers the highest income levels in the country for professionals and skilled workers, although it also burdens them with the highest cost of living. For unskilled migrants, on the other hand, the opportunities in Lagos are limited: With an official unemployment rate of over 20 percent, Lagos has over 50 percent of its labor force in the "informal economy," meaning street vending or day labor. Most people do not have the opportunities, available in more rural areas, to use farming as a back-up source of income, or to pool resources with an extensive kinship network.[23] Inequalities in income and quality of life are extreme in Lagos.

A permanent departure from the village to the city would imply an uprooting with cultural, social, and political, as well as economic, effects. Sociologists have written of the "alienation" resulting from such a change, and this view leads to the assumption that alienated masses thronging city streets are susceptible to radical political mobilization. However, recent studies of the urbanization process in many locations have shown that the process of becoming a city dweller is often very gradual; complete displacement is such a longterm process that the socio-cultural effect is not nearly as dramatic as might have been imagined. Rather, "Third World societies may be increasingly characterized as bi-local populations, relatively stable in their demographic composition, but composed of individuals in constant motion between village and nonvillage places."[24] An observer of the movement of Hausa villagers from northern Nigeria to the cities and commercial farming areas of the South does not find support for the notion that they are being progressively absorbed into urban life, and reports that even during the drought of the early 1970s there was very little permanent out-migration from the North.[25] On the other hand, the Lagos urban area has also experienced a growth in its permanent population, especially from the Yoruba-speaking areas that most immediately surround it.

The implications of this rapid but impermanent urbanization are several: First of all, in Nigeria and in most Third World contexts, urbanization does not lead to the rapid conversion of peasants to an urban proletariat. However, the migrant lives at the margins of urban society, working usually in the informal economy, for part of the year. "He finances his own considerable travel, yet provides urban services at rock bottom prices. . .Only continuing rural poverty can make such an unequal participation appear attractive."[26] Migrants are also likely to be at the margins of political life, although in times when survival is especially precarious they may respond to mobilization efforts that target their ethnic and religious identities and values.

Box 2.1 A Note on Data

In this and subsequent chapters, we present a great amount of quantitative data that demonstrate change over time and compare Nigeria with other countries. There is always a danger that statistical analysis in political economy and other areas will start from an assumption of accurate data. This should never be assumed, and especially in Nigeria. Watts quotes a study of Nigeria in the *Economist*, which announced:

"This is the first survey published in the *Economist* in which every single number is probably wrong. There is no accurate information about Nigeria. Nobody knows within a margin of error of about one-third, how many people the country contains, where they live or how much they produce."

The data problem may even explain vastly different interpretations of the effect of the Nigerian oil boom on agriculture, and thus, some of the differences of opinion described above. We assume that the data, even though suspect, are reasonably useful in demonstrating broad trends.

As farmers work increasingly in the urban environment, the result may be that a smaller labor force is available for agricultural work. The picture is complicated, in that urbanization will be strongest when employment opportunities in the countryside are at their lowest; but if the urban opportunity becomes attractive enough, the pool of agricultural workers will shrink. Unless the productivity of the remaining workers increases, this could mean a drop in food production per capita.

In the Nigerian case, it is commonly understood that the oil boom of the 1970s created urban employment opportunities that drained labor from the countryside, and that they did not all return when the economy soured; this helps to explain why Nigeria, self-sufficient in food at independence, became heavily dependent on food imports, paid for from oil revenues.

If the economic downturn in the 1980s did not stop the population flow to the cities, it did slow it considerably. The cities had benefited disproportionately from the boom, and urban residents were hardest hit by the "bust." Exact numbers are unavailable, but it appears that many migrants returned to the village (or shifted toward longer stays there), and young people were discouraged from leaving the countryside.[27]

The Role of Commercial and Industrial Activity in the Economy

THE IMPACT OF COLONIALISM

In order to profit from Nigeria's agricultural production, a European-dominated commercial sector was created, both to buy and export Nigerian commodities, and to import and sell foreign goods in the large Nigerian market. Because commerce and finance were controlled by foreigners, there was at first little possibility for participation in this network by Nigerians, except in commodity production and petty trade.

In the late colonial period, however, the foreign monopolies began to give way; between 1949 and 1963 Nigerian traders' share of the export trade grew from 5 to 20 percent of the total. The agricultural marketing boards described above provided capital for a foreign-investment shift from commerce to industry in the late colonial period. This new emphasis was maintained by the first independent regime, although the nature of the foreign enterprises was changed by the "Nigerianization" of their personnel. Still, by the 1950s, most ambitious young Nigerians were entering politics or the civil service, and the indigenous capitalists were weak and disorganized in comparison with the expanding state.[28]

THE ROLE OF THE PRIVATE SECTOR AFTER INDEPENDENCE

African entrepreneurs are sometimes depicted as mere rentiers, that is, those who use political power and influence, especially in controlling access to international trade, rather than market-based activities to accumulate private wealth.[29] Forrest believes that this argument has some validity in the Nigerian case, but has been exaggerated; he finds "substantial private productive accumulation" in the country, and that "long-run, private trajectories of accumulation take place to a large extent independent of the state and those who control it." This is especially the case in the East, where some communities have "a long tradition of trade and community autonomy," and where the Biafran conflict reduced access to political influence for some time.[30] A visitor to Nigeria cannot help but be impressed with the multiple evidence of entrepreneurship operating in the shadow of the oil economy and the state and patronage system that oil supports. Our assessment of the economic environment of Nigerian politics must take into account this vital private sector and its potential for growth. At the same time, industrial and commercial growth have not been what the country's development planners had hoped for at an earlier time. Nigerian industrial development policy is examined in Chapter Seven.

Natural Resources: Boon or Curse for Nigeria's Economic and Political Development?

The proposition that natural resources could be a country's curse might seem ridiculous, yet the interaction between the exploitation of Nigeria's mineral wealth and its political and economic development has been at best a mixed blessing.

PETROLEUM

The magnitude of Nigeria's petroleum reserves did not become apparent until the 1950s, with the first shipload of crude exported in 1958. Nigeria's oil was found to be especially high quality because it is "sweet," that is, containing a very low sulphur content. Its location also was a strategic advantage to importing industrial nations, for its position on the Atlantic Ocean guarantees access to a source of high-grade oil in times of crisis in the Middle East (as during the Gulf War in 1990). Following the end of the Biafran War, Nigerian petroleum production began to boom (Figure 2.6). The quantity and value of crude oil produced grew at a dramatic rate through the 1970s, and in some years Nigeria ranked as high as fifth in the world in oil production, then fell to about tenth place (it was in twelfth position in 1993). Although one must assume the presence of such a valuable mineral resource to be an asset to any country, its effects on Nigeria were not all beneficial.

Nigeria is characterized in the literature on development in oil-producing states as having, at least theoretically, a "high absorptive capacity:" This means that it has the ability to absorb capital in productive investment, not for consumption of imports. Besides Nigeria, this category includes Mexico, Indonesia, and Venezuela. In language compatible with our concept of the *environment* in which political processes occur, Michael Watts has identified a list of "common features and structurally similar choices and constraints" that are common to "high absorber states"; To the degree that conditions in these countries are common, we have evidence that Nigeria's situation is not the result of its own record of decision-making, but derives from the nature of petroleum production in such a country. The "nature" of petroleum production does not refer to anything inherent in the product,

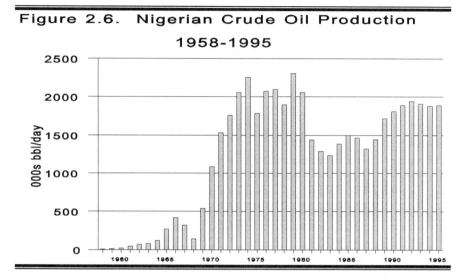

Figure 2.6. Nigerian Crude Oil Production 1958-1995

but rather to the fact that the oil industry is "inherently global and internationalized and inseparable from the complex circuits of production and exchange dominated by multinational firms." Third World oil-producing countries do not have the option of extracting and refining oil for their own use or export on their own terms, because they lack the technology and infrastructure to do so. Furthermore, the oil industry in such countries characteristically has few economic links to other sectors of the domestic economy. Finally, the profits from oil exploitation all go into governmental accounts, which tends to strengthen the country's center as opposed to regional or local governments, and which expands the role of government in the society and economy.[31]

In the Nigerian case, absorptive capacity is only high in theory, based on a high demand for capital. In fact, when the impact of the oil boom began to be felt, there were no investment institutions in place that could handle the sudden inflow of wealth, and large amounts of money were still given over to immediate consumption. Also, the country's economy became distorted by the great disparity of value between petroleum and the agricultural products traditionally grown: Soon, young workers were abandoning their farms and villages and flocking to the cities and the oil fields. The once-basic exports of peanuts, cotton, and palm oil almost disappeared from this list of exports; however, the export of cocoa and rubber began to increase again by the late 1980s.[32]

Production and export of oil has always been primarily managed by international oil companies, which have negotiated prospecting and mining leases, or concessions for the exclusive right to prospecting and production in a given geographical zone. Shell-BP had the original concession, but the development of offshore activities opened the way in 1961 for Mobil, Texaco, and Gulf to enter the scene. These leases are for limited time periods, and have often been renegotiated.

However, Shell remains the single largest producer, having produced over half of Nigeria's crude oil in 1990.[33]

A world oil glut beginning in 1981 brought the glory days of seemingly limitless oil revenues to an abrupt end. Demand for petroleum fell because of the combined effects of a worldwide economic recession, a decline in industries that were particularly heavy users of petroleum products, and the substitution of nuclear and electrical energy and coal in industrial, commercial, and residential use in the industrial world. Also, oil from the North Sea brought Britain and Norway into the list of exporters, in direct competition with Nigeria and other members of the Organization of Petroleum Exporting Countries (OPEC). The demand for OPEC oil dropped from 31 million barrels per day in 1979 to 18 million in 1983 and 14 million by the third quarter of 1985.[34] In April 1982, production of crude oil in Nigeria dropped from 2.1 million to .9 million barrels per day (Figure 2.6), and oil export revenues fell correspondingly, from $1.35 billion to $.7 billion per month.[35] In the preceding decade, Nigeria had become dependent on oil revenues to cover the rising cost of exports and to finance large-scale development projects. As was commonly the case in the Third World, Nigeria fell behind in its debt payments, the economy was disrupted, and the government was forced to impose unpleasant austerity measures. There was a further fall in oil prices in 1986, pushing the country into a severe recession from which it has never recovered. Moreover, Nigerian fortunes became even more closely tied to oil revenues as the only dependable source of foreign exchange; Figure 2.7 shows that the source of Nigeria's hard currency shifted dramatically from agricultural products to petroleum in the

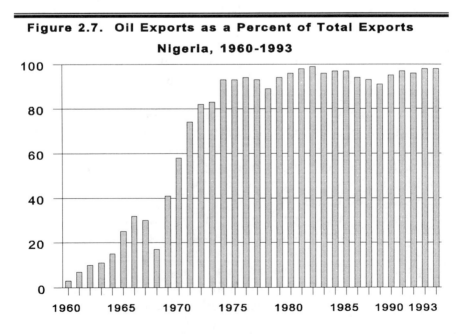

Figure 2.7. Oil Exports as a Percent of Total Exports Nigeria, 1960-1993

early 1970s, and that since that time petroleum has accounted for over 90 percent of export earnings. Oil production has been remarkably unaffected by most regime changes and other political events in Nigeria. As described in Chapter One, only the Biafran War had a seriously disruptive effect on the industry. Although government policies toward the oil companies has changed over time, this has been in response to changes in the world oil market, rather than a result of philosophic differences among regimes. However, the unstable nature of the political system itself has affected the development and productive efficiency of the oil industry.[36]

Nigeria has proven oil reserves (as of late 1995) of 20.8 billion barrels, ranking it twelfth in the world (two-thirds of proven reserves are in the Middle East, with Saudi Arabia holding one-fourth of the world total itself). Nigeria's share of the world total is 2.1 percent. At present rates of production, and if no further reserves are discovered, Nigeria's supply will be exhausted in thirty years. As most new reserves have been found in the Middle East, the projection is plausible. However, the reserve/ production ratio is not fixed by geology; it depends also on the rate of investment in exploration. This in turn depends on world prices for oil, refining capacities, etc., but also on Nigeria's willingness and ability to offer the necessary incentives.[37] And in the long term, should the reserves be exhausted, planning in Nigeria must prepare for the transition to a more conventional diversified economic base.

Nigeria has significant deposits of other minerals as well. One that has been tapped only marginally is natural gas, of which there are 3.1 trillion cubic meters of proven reserves, or 2.2 percent of the world's total (over 70 percent of natural gas reserves in the world are in the former Soviet Union and the Middle East). Natural gas is released as a by-product of oil drilling, but most of it in Nigeria has simply been "flared off," i.e., burned as it is released into the air. Flaring consumed 99 percent of gas production in the early 1970s; this figure was reduced to 76 percent by the 1990s, but it was still the highest of all OPEC countries. The Nigerian National Petroleum Company (NNPC) has been negotiating a project to market liquified natural gas (liquification allows for export) since 1976, but political conflict delayed its implementation. Under a deal between NNPC and the Chevron corporation, the first tanker of liquified natural gas left Nigeria for the United States in September 1997.[38] Marketing of natural gas for domestic use has been slowly increasing, from 1.1 million tons in 1986 to 4.6 million in 1993, but this still represents just .2 percent of world production for the latter year, or one-twelfth the proportion the country's share represents of world reserves.[39] Environmental considerations support the construction of a natural gas pipeline to the far north of the country, to reduce the consumption of wood for fuel, and thus slow the process of deforestation. In the mid-1980s, fuelwood accounted for 44 percent of domestic fuel use in Nigeria's urban areas. Environmentalists debate the merits of flaring vs. simply releasing the natural gas into the atmosphere, each of which poses its own hazards to the environment. Nigerian flaring released 30 million tons of carbon dioxide into the atmosphere in 1989. The marginal damage caused by this release has been estimated at $7.5 million per ton. Still, the economics of the choice for Nigeria to date are in favor of continued flaring.[40]

Among other mineral resources, coal has been mined in the Southeast (near Enugu) since 1906; however, it is apparently not of sufficient quality to be used at Nigeria's steel complex at Ajaokuta, which relies on imported coal and iron ore.[41] There has been production for export of Columbite, tin, gold, zinc, and lead. Until 1968 Nigeria was Africa's leading exporter of tin, but production has declined since then. In fact, the value of petroleum production continues to dominate production and to distort the Nigerian economy, as well as its political system.

THE DISTRIBUTION OF NATURAL RESOURCES: POLITICAL EFFECTS

Nigeria's oil fields are found especially in Rivers and Bayelsa states (near the city of Port Harcourt), as well as in Akwa Ibom, Abia, Cross River, Delta, and Imo states. The Niger delta basin covers 70,000 square kilometers, or about 8 percent of the country. As a resource that is both geographically concentrated and far more valuable than any other natural resource, Nigerian petroleum presents a classic problem for distributive justice. To Nigerian federal governments, they are a "national patrimony." Awareness of their potential value was an important motivation behind the Eastern region's declaration of independence as Biafra in 1966, and oil certainly helps explain why the rest of the country was so obstinately determined to keep the region within Nigeria. But had Biafra maintained its independence, the question of oil field ownership would not have gone away, for the people who traditionally inhabited that area were minorities in the Igbo-dominated Biafra. And although the federal government won the civil war, local peoples express their grievances about the spread of oil wealth over the whole country while their land pays the price of environmental degradation from the oil operations and southern Nigerians in general wonder why the riches should be shared with the distant North. There is some prospect that oil may be found in the North, in the Chad basin in Borno State and the Sokoto basin in the Northwest, because there is a sedimentary geological structure in those places like that in the Niger delta.[42] This gives technical support to the claims of some northerners that the oil is below *all* of Nigeria, but just rises to the surface in the delta! In any case, discoveries of oil in the North would help with this major distributional problem.

The International Environment

The world is increasingly interdependent. Even a superpower like the United States has found its ability to plan for its own economic future constrained by the ability of capital to flow across international borders. However, the poorer a country is, and the less competitive and less diversified its economy, the more likely it is to suffer limitations on its control of its own destiny. Nigeria, like most African countries, has been profoundly affected by its birth at the height of the Cold War, and by the sudden change from a bipolar to a unipolar world with the dissolution of the Soviet Union thirty years later. During the Cold War, strong pressures were put on new nations to choose sides. The Great Powers were highly concerned that movement to the other side could pose a strategic threat, especially in the loss of access to natural resources. Foreign aid to developing nations was granted as a reward for loyalty to the West or the East, and was withheld by the other side for the same reason. Nigeria at independence was considered to be conservative and "pro-Western," especially in contrast to such radical regimes as that of Kwame Nkrumah in Ghana. The prime minister at independence, Tafawa Balewa, announced the country's gratitude "to the British whom we have known first as masters, then as leaders, and finally as partners, but always as friends."[43]

The close economic relationship between Britain and Nigeria began to weaken as independence neared and other countries were attracted to the potentially large Nigerian market. Britain's share of Nigerian trade declined steadily from 45 percent of imports and 72 percent of exports in 1954-1956 to 16 percent of imports and just 5.2 percent of exports in 1986. Large Western corporations were joined by Indian, Greek, Syrian-Lebanese, and Nigerian entrepreneurs in import and wholesale activities. In 1967 Britain still accounted for over half the stock of foreign investment, and dominated manufacturing, trade, banking and the oil industry,[44] but its role continued to decline. In contrast to the continued strong French presence in Nigeria's francophone neighbors, there are few obvious reminders of the British colonial presence in Nigeria.

Whether the western presence was British or international, many Nigerian intellectuals equated the West's capitalism with colonialism, which they contended was continued after independence through economic ties they regarded as *neocolonial*. Political discourse through the first thirty years of Nigerian independence was often based on the ideological poles of capitalism and socialism, and relationships with the major powers involved staking a position between the two camps. The outcome of the debate was largely on the pro-Western side, and "even though Nigeria's overall dependence on foreign countries gradually declined in 1960-1966, her economic dependence on capitalist countries in the 1960s was still substantial enough to severely limit the ability of her political system to cope with domestic political crises."[45]

In the civil war that resulted from the Eastern region's declaration of independence as Biafra in 1967, Britain, joined by the Soviet Union, sided with the Nigerian federal government, while the United States generally tried to maintain an independent stance in the face of widespread popular sympathy in the United States for Biafra. The West was best equipped to prospect for Nigeria's oil fields, and only the West had the technology to extract and market this natural resource. As described above and in Chapter Seven, a close relationship developed between the federal government and some of the world's major oil companies.

In the 1970s, the West began to be represented in developing countries more and more through its major financial agencies, the International Monetary Fund (IMF) and the World Bank. The latter sponsored a series of Agricultural Development Programs in Nigeria, first to promote the growth of traditional export crops, but later defended as means to increase the production of food as well. The World Bank had earlier subsidized the first and largest multipurpose dam and reservoir project in the country, the Kainji Dam, and in this and other ways promoted the large-intrusive-project approach to development.

The end of the Cold War brought a new era to the relations of Nigeria and other poorer nations with the industrial world. The West's fear of the spread of communism had caused them to pay some attention to even the smallest and least-endowed countries. In the colonial period, Britain had provided virtually all foreign aid from the developed world to Nigeria. In the Cold War environment at independence, Nigeria adopted a deliberate policy of diversification in its relationships that diluted British influence and brought aid from the United States, Canada, the European Common Market (now the European Union), Japan, and Sweden.[46] In the 1990s, however, those Third World countries without significant resources or with serious developmental problems are simply less interesting to the developed world; it is commonly perceived that Africa particularly has been "marginalized." In the Nigerian case, official loans and grants have not loomed large in recent years in any event, given access to oil revenues; foreign aid represented only about two dollars per person in 1990. On the other hand, Nigeria's importance as a source of oil means that it will never be completely off the agenda for the West.

Another problem in Nigeria's relationship (and that of Africa as a whole) with the industrial world has been much more serious: A massive and increasing international debt. Nigeria shared in a common Third World experience following the oil crisis of 1973. A sudden boom in oil prices resulted in huge new deposits in the world's banks. At the same time there was a parallel boom in the prices of major commodities, including the cocoa, cotton, and peanuts that Nigeria had traditionally produced. The surge in bank deposits without an increase in the demand for credit posed a serious problem to the lending agencies: They had to find borrowers. Looking at the increasing value of Nigeria's commodities, they found the country to be extremely credit-worthy. Although Nigeria's military government at the time was already busy spending the booming oil profits, the demand for new infrastructure and for an expansion of public services was great. The lending agencies had little difficulty convincing the Nigerian government to borrow additional sums. This borrowing seemed to make sense for all sides, given high inflation, rising prices for commodities, and the "excess liquidity" of bank deposits. Between 1973 and 1977, Africa's total debt increased from $9 billion to $27 billion. Nigeria's debt burden was increasing even in the height of the boom in prices for its products. Late in the 1970s, commodity prices fell, while oil prices remained high; African governments borrowed at an even faster pace, and the continent's total indebtedness increased between 1978 and 1982 from $27 billion to $72 billion. Commercial lenders lost interest in loans to Africa, and the slack was taken up by the international financial institutions, principally the IMF and the World Bank.[47]

Indebtedness continued to increase in the 1980s, from $8.9 billion in 1980 to $34.5 billion in 1991; by 1991 it represented 257 percent of the annual value of the country's exports, and 109 percent of GNP. The annual cost of servicing the debt consumed 25 percent of the value of exports, and this heavy burden almost ensured that the debt would continue to grow. The question of how to deal with the external debt has been a principal focus of political discussion in Nigeria over the past decade.

The central political problem for Nigeria involves the severe conditions the IMF has attached to its help: Devaluation, and eventually a floating exchange rate for the national currency, the naira; the termination of trade restrictions, including protection for domestic producers; and the elimination of subsidies for domestic gasoline consumption. These and similar measures to reduce the cost of government and to reduce its direct role in economic activities have been the contents of "structural adjustment programs" (SAPs) demanded by the international agencies as conditions for debt relief. Nigerian governments are in a "no win" situation on this issue: Austerity measures that cut allocations for public services or subsidies are extremely unpopular. However, just the servicing costs on the foreign debt of $25 billion equal over 70 percent of Nigeria's annual export earnings, and no new funds can come into the country, and creditors will not talk about the situation unless the Nigerian government is in agreement with the IMF on how to manage the debt. Nigeria is typical of many African and Latin American countries in the constraints placed on its freedom to form independent economic policies by the need to make burdensome and unpopular debt payments and to satisfy the international lending agencies on measures taken to restructure its economy.

The end of the Cold War also changed the way that western governments viewed the nature of political regimes in Africa. Even the most authoritarian and corrupt governments could maintain friendly relationships with the United States and Europe if they were staunchly anticommunist. By 1990, however, even as Africa became more marginal to the West's concerns, such interest as was shown gave new support to the emerging movement toward democratic rule on the continent. It is generally believed by Africanists that neither the collapse of the one-party Soviet model or the new pressures from the West were nearly as important in this wave of democratization as were unfolding events in Africa itself. Yet, the pressure became constant for military regimes to sponsor constitutional conventions and elections. Partly this is based on a belief that parliamentary democracies on the Western model offer the most stable support for the market-based and foreign-investment-friendly economies that the West prefers. But there is also an idealistic component in Western support of democracy that became relatively more salient when overriding Cold War concerns disappeared.

In the Nigerian case, this meant that the West constantly encouraged the Babangida regime to move toward an elected civilian government. Foreign aid funds from Britain and the United States were directed toward democratization projects, and World Bank and IMF representatives included political criteria in their discussions of conditions for loan restructuring and new loans. When President Babangida abruptly annulled the outcome of the 1993 presidential elections, and his successor General Sani Abacha abolished the local and state elected positions (see Chapter Six), reactions from the West were very hostile. The United States suspended its aid programs, suspended direct air routes between Nigeria and the United States (the latter ostensibly because of security conditions at Lagos' Murtala Muhammed Airport), and, by naming Nigeria a major drug-trafficking country, called into effect provisions of the Foreign Assistance Act that prohibited Export-Import Bank financing and required U.S. opposition to multilateral bank loans to Nigeria. Eventually, the American government recalled its ambassador. The British denied visas to Nigerian military officers and ended its military training programs (although it continued to sell tanks to the Nigerian military and maintained a small aid program). Japan suspended its aid program.[48] The most effective pressure from these countries, of course, would have been the suspension of oil purchases, but this would have had negative effects at home too costly to be considered.

At least as concerns trade policy, Nigeria's membership in the Organization of Petroleum Exporting Countries (OPEC) has provided some balance to its relationship with the industrial West. Since Nigeria became a member in 1971, OPEC has provided models and specific binding agreements that have resulted in more favorable conditions in negotiations with petroleum companies than it is likely to have been able to negotiate alone. Since the 1980s, however, the increased production of oil from the North Sea has come in direct competition for Nigeria's markets, and has put the country at the margin between the Atlantic Basic producers and the Middle-East-dominated OPEC. This has caused OPEC to see Nigeria as a weak link in its defense of prices, as Nigeria has often led the way in OPEC in cutting prices to match British and Norwegian prices. OPEC was also concerned when Nigeria helped form the African Petroleum Producers' Association (APPA) with Algeria, Angola, Benin, Cameroon, Gabon, Libya, Cote d'Ivoire, and Egypt. Half of these do not belong to OPEC; the Middle East members of that organization have raised concerns about the threat a competing organization like APPA might represent to producer solidarity.[49]

A final aspect of Nigeria's international environment is its regional context, West Africa. As an accident of colonial rule, Nigeria came to independence entirely surrounded by former French colonies—Benin (formerly Dahomey), Niger, and Cameroon. (Although Cameroon is officially bilingual, and the region adjoining Nigeria is predominantly English-speaking, the country has maintained strong ties with France.) France and the French-speaking West African countries have been suspicious of Nigeria's intentions, and have developed close economic ties among themselves. As a result, Nigeria has had difficulty in developing the leadership role in the region that its size and strength would suggest.

Chapters Seven and Eight discuss the efforts of Nigeria's leaders to overcome its regional handicaps, to deal with the country's debt problems, and to counter Western hostility to prolonged military rule.

END NOTES

1. World Bank, *World Development Report 1995* (New York: Oxford University Press, 1995), pp. 34-35.

2. Michael Mortimore, *Adapting to Drought* (Cambridge: Cambridge University Press, 1989), p. 137.

3. Mortimore, *Adapting to Drought*, p. 189.

4. Mortimore, *Adapting to Drought,* p. 196.

5. Sara Berry, *Cocoa, Custom, and Socio-economic Change in Rural Western Nigeria* (Oxford: Clarendon Press, 1975), p. 221.

6. Sara Berry, *No Condition is Permanent* (Madison: University of Wisconsin Press, 1993), p. 72.

7. Billy Dudley, *An Introduction to Nigerian Government and Politics*, p. 230.

8. See, e.g., Robert H. Bates, *Markets and States in Tropical Africa: The Political Basis of Agricultural Policies* (Berkeley: University of California Press, 1981) and Bates, *Essays on the Political Economy of Rural Africa* (Cambridge: Cambridge University Press, 1983).

9. Forrest, *Politics and Economic Development in Nigeria*, p. 181.

10. Forrest, *Politics and Economic Development in Nigeria*, pp. 184-85.

11. Forrest, *Politics and Economic Development in Nigeria*, p. 186.

12. Robert Shenton, "Nigerian Agriculture in Historical Perspective: Development and Crisis 1900-1960," p. 44, and Sara Berry, "Oil and the Disappearing Peasantry: Accumulation, Differentiation, and Underdevelopment in Western Nigeria, in Michael Watts, ed. *State, Oil, and Agriculture in Nigeria* (Berkeley: Institute of International Studies, University of California at Berkeley, 1987), pp. 204-5.

13. Michael J. Watts, "Agriculture and Oil-Based Accumulation: Stagnation or

Transformation?" in Watts, ed. *State, Oil, and Agriculture in Nigeria* (Berkeley: Institute of International Studies, University of California at Berkeley, 1987), p. 74.

14. Johny Egg, "La nouvelle insertion de l'agriculture nigériane dans le marché mondial," in Daniel C. Bach, Johny Egg and Jean Philippe, eds. *Le Nigeria: Un Pouvoir en Puissance* (Paris: Karthala, 1988), p. 190.

15. Johny Egg, "La nouvelle insertion de l'agriculture nigériane dans le marché mondial," p. 191.

16. Dennis A. Ityavyar, "The Colonial Origins of Health Care Services: The Nigerian Example," in Toyin Falola and D. Ityavyar, eds. *The Political Economy of Health in Africa* (Athens, OH: Ohio University Center for International Studies, 1992), p. 73.

17. World Health Organization Web Site, Malaria Control Programme, July, 1995. [Current version is found at http://www.who.ch/ctd/diseases.]

18. World Health Organization, "Disease sheet: Schistosomiasis (or Bilharziasis), http://www.who.ch/ctd/ diseases/shis/shissit.htm.

19. Helen Chapin Metz, ed. *Nigeria: A Country Study* (Washington: Federal Research Division, Library of Congress, 1992), pp. 150-152.

20. New York Times, May 8, 1996, p. 1; Helen Chapin Metz, Nigeria: A Country Study, p. 150.

21. Patrick Smith, "Economy," *Africa South of the Sahara* (London: Europa Publications, 1994), p. 660.

22. Data from the United Nations Population Division, 1994, and the *Statistical Abstract of the United States*, 1995.

23. Sandra Barnes, *Patrons and Power* (Bloomington: Indiana University Press, 1986), pp. 11, 13.

24. Sidney Goldstein, *Circulation in the context of total mobility in Southeast Asia* (Papers of the East-West Population Institute 53, 1978), cited in Mortimore, *Adapting to Drought*, p. 198.

25. Mortimore, *Adapting to Drought*, pp. 198-99.

26. Mortimore, *Adapting to Drought*, p. 199.

27. Johny Egg, "La nouvelle insertion de l'agriculture nigériane dans le marché mondial," p. 191.

28. Forrest, *Politics and Economic Development in Nigeria*, pp. 8, 23-26.

29. See especially, Jean-François Bayart, *The State in Africa* (London: Longman, 1993).

30. Forrest, *The Advance of African Capital*, (Charlottesville: University Press of Virginia, 1994), pp. 246-251.

31. Watts, *State, Oil, and Agriculture in Nigeria*, "Introduction," pp. 9-10.

32. Forrest, *Politics and Economic Development in Nigeria*, p. 220.

33. Sarah Ahmad Khan, *Nigeria: The Political Economy of Oil*, (Oxford: Oxford University Press, 1994), pp. 20-22.

34. Akin Iwayemi, "Le Nigeria dans le système pétrolier international," in Daniel C. Bach, Johny Egg and Jean Philippe, eds. *Le Nigéria: Un Pouvoir en Puissance*, p. 32.

35. Peter O. Olayiwola, *Petroleum and Structural Change in a Developing Country* (New York: Praeger, 1987), p. 62.

36. Ahmad Khan, *Nigeria: The Political Economy of Oil*, pp. 5, 11-14.

37. *BP Statistical Review of World Energy, June 1996* (London: BP Statistical Review, 1996); Ahmad Khan, *Nigeria: The Political Economy of Oil*, pp. 40-43.

38. Ahmad Khan, *Nigeria: The Political Economy of Oil*, p. 14; Agence France Presse, 3 October 1997.

39. *BP Statistical Review of World Energy, June 1994*, pp. 18, 20.

40. Ahmad Khan, *Nigeria: The Political Economy of Oil*, pp. 163-64, 180 (fn. 16).

41. Forrest, *Politics and Economic Development in Nigeria*, p. 151.

42. Ahmad Khan, *Nigeria: The Political Economy of Oil*, pp. 39-40.

43. Quoted in E. Wayne Nafziger, *The Economics of Political Instability* (Boulder, CO: Westview Press, 1983).

44. Tom Forrest, *Politics and Economic Development in Nigeria*, pp. 36-37.

45. Nafziger, *The Economics of Political Instability*, p. 51

46. Nafziger, *The Economics of Political Instability*, p. 60.

47. David Gordon, "Debt, Conditionality, and Reform: The International Relations of Economic Restructuring in Sub-Saharan Africa," in Thomas M. Callaghy and John Ravenhill, eds. *Hemmed In: Responses to Africa's Economic Decline* (New York: Columbia Press 1993), pp. 92-96.

48. Forrest, *Politics and Economic Development in Nigeria*, p. 238.

49. Ahmad Khan, *Nigeria: The Political Economy of Oil*, pp. 28-31.

Chapter 3

POLITICAL CULTURE AND SOCIALIZATION

♦ What are the patterns of political beliefs and values?
♦ What do we mean by the term *civil society* as applied to Nigeria?
♦ What was the effect of colonialism on political beliefs and values?
♦ How important is ethnic (tribal) identity in Nigerian political culture?
♦ What part does religion play in Nigerian political values?
♦ How strong is Nigerian nationalism?
♦ How strongly do Nigerians believe in and support democracy?
♦ How strong are political ideologies in Nigeria?
♦ What role do women play in Nigerian politics?
♦ What is the meaning of clientelism, prebendalism, and patrimonialism?
♦ How do Nigerians react to political corruption?
♦ How and from what sources do Nigerians acquire their political attitudes and values?

Political Culture

The term "political culture" refers to the "collective political attitudes, values, feelings, information, and skills" in a society or in a nation.[1] A first point of comparison of national political cultures is the degree to which they are homogeneous, that is, the degree to which citizens of a country share common attitudes, values, and so forth. The political culture of Nigeria is extremely heterogeneous and complex. Analysis of it must take into account the presence of a Western value system overlaid on those of its various precolonial traditions; it must assess the impact of a variety of religious beliefs and of the continuing effects of Christian and Muslim proselytizing efforts. With the colonial experience and since then have come new divisions based on social class, and on the different experiences of urban and rural dwellers. The whole range of modern political ideologies can be found among the belief systems of the politically active population. Here we will give greatest attention to attitudes among various categories of Nigerians toward the state of Nigeria, and to the various regimes that have governed it. We will also look at the vitality of civil society, and to the political implications of religious beliefs, ethnic identity, social and economic status, and contact with urban life.

CIVIL SOCIETY

The concept of civil society has played a significant part in liberal democratic thought, beginning at least with John Locke and other philosophers who saw government as a social contract. For them, it was necessary to have a concept for the collective or institution which entered into contract with rulers in the name of the people. It has more recently been defined as "public political activity that occurs in the realm between the state and the family."[2] It is a theoretical concept, not an empirical entity, and its value rests in the need to have a countervailing power to the state if one is to have limited government, or liberal democracy, since individuals cannot defend themselves alone against a powerful state. Empirically, we will use this concept first in our discussion of political culture, and in Chapter Six, in our discussion of interest groups and political parties, which collectively form the most frequently cited institutional manifestations of a modern civic culture.

Crawford Young's analysis of the uniquely destructive impact of colonialism in Africa starts from its effect on African political traditions:

> For most of the continent, what did exist by way of a shared political tradition commonly understood by rulers and ruled was swept away by the nature of the colonial partition . . . extant, perhaps partially "civil" societies . . . experienced a deconstruction in the cognitive realm. An "invented" Africa took form, the product of an external imagination, reconceived as the subordinated other . . . the colonial state . . . transformed non-European areas into fundamentally European constructs.[3]

As the colonial culture denigrated traditional African institutions (and in this respect the missionaries played a powerful role alongside the administration), Africans could gain an audience in the colonial system only if they learned European forms of discourse. Resistance to colonialism came in several forms, either based on traditional values, or by turning European values against the new rulers. While both forms of resistance occurred, it was only the latter that "fit" the artificial boundaries of the new states, and ultimately it was the latter form of resistance and protest—using European metaphors—that brought political independence. In the process, then, precolonial understandings between rulers and ruled on the limitations of authority were destroyed or made irrelevant, and no such understandings were permitted under colonial rule. At independence the political culture of Nigeria and other states had only the most fragile of civic cultures.

ETHNIC IDENTITY

Ethnologists have identified over 250 ethnic groups in Nigeria, based on language and cultural traits. A project to survey the world's languages has documented 6170 human languages, of which 420, or almost 7 percent, are spoken in Nigeria, and most of that number are spoken in no other country.[4] One must use such numbers with great caution, for the point at which a separate dialect becomes a separate language is arbitrary, and language and other cultural features are not static. As we have seen, ethnic identities are not primordial; Young's analysis of the colonial impact highlights the role of colonial authorities, the British in particular, in *promoting* ethnic identity and consciousness:

> Europeans applied to Africans their own system of ethnic classification and accepted without question that Africans should use the same distinctions and concepts. Thus, ethnic boundaries were territorialized . . . Small entities, deemed unnaturally or unhealthily fragmented, were amalgamated under a common label. Large states were dismantled to form units of convenient scale, in the name of freeing "tribes" held in thrall to tyrannical rulers.[5]

It is critical to our understanding of ethnicity to know that such identities are not permanent, and certainly not genetic, that they are shaped in interaction with the environment, and that in the particular case of Nigeria, identities such as Igbo and Yoruba are largely a product, intended or not, of the colonial experience.

In urban areas especially, there are complex interminglings of peoples. As people adopt each other's cultural traits, as they intermarry or modify their religious beliefs, ethnic identities become ever more difficult to pin down and quantify. Nevertheless, almost all Nigerians can give a ready answer to a question about their ethnic identity, and the most straightforward counts of ethnic groups are based on the number of individuals who *claim* a given identity.

Nigerian ethnic groups vary tremendously in size, and three of them are particularly numerous and influential in the country's politics. A central point to remember about Nigerian political culture is that the influence of the three major groups is a great cause of concern to the remaining fragmented minorities. Because there has been a high degree of geographical separation of ethnic groups in Nigeria (a result of the country's policies during and since the colonial period), Nigerians can easily identify the origins of their fellow citizens by observing their dialect (or accent in English), their manner of dress (if it is traditional), and in some cases by "tribal marks," patterned facial scars that formerly were created as part of rites of passage to indicate ethnic identity. There are also differences in wealth and political awareness among ethnic groups, as a result of the historical factors identified above. The three major groups are the Hausa, the Yoruba, and the Igbo, and we should discuss each in turn.

Hausa-Fulani people mostly live in the northern half of the country. As noted earlier, this hyphenated identity came from the imposition of Fulani rule over the Hausa population in the nineteenth century. The two cultures became intricately intertwined, although they have never become completely homogenized. Thus, the term "Hausa" is often used as a short form of "Hausa-Fulani," but may also refer to that which is distinctively Hausa in the hyphenated culture, including the language.

Hausa is spoken as a common language by peoples who describe themselves with such various ethnic identities as Fulani, Gwari, Nupe, Tiv, and Kanuri, and some scholars have asserted that there is no single Hausa ethnic group, and that "Hausa" is only a linguistic term. "Hausaland" actually straddles the border between Nigeria and Niger to the north, a former French colony, and the people in these two countries maintain many cultural and commercial ties.[6] A greater proportion of Hausas have continued to engage in subsistence agriculture and to live in rural villages than is true of southern Nigerians. There are sizeable Hausa communities in cities all over Nigeria, where they carry on trade and commercial activities while maintaining kin and client relationships with their home region. Among Nigerians, the Hausa have a "reputation of having a special 'genius' for trade. On a closer analysis, much of this 'genius' turns out to be associated, not with a basic personality trait, but with a highly developed economic and political organization which has been evolved over a long period of time."[7] The vast majority of Hausas (but not all) are Muslim. In their various sub-ethnic, religious, rural/urban, homeland/diaspora contexts, the Hausa share an identity that is, in William Miles' terms, "fluid, multilayered and evolutionary."

Hausa ethnicity became an important political identity as a form of northern solidarity against perceived threats of cultural and political domination from the South. As described in Chapter One, under colonial rule northerners were spared from "cultural imperialism":

> The incumbent [Hausa-Fulani] political hierarchy was defeated but not humiliated; peace with not only honor but advantage within the British framework was provided to the Fulani elite. Mesmerized by the mobilizing force of Islam and conscious of the thinness of the red line of British forces, the colonizer gave careful deference to hierarchy, language, and religion. The Fulani

rulers were confirmed in their functions; Hausa was used as a language of administration; and Christian missions were excluded from Islamic areas.[8]

The rulers' complacency disappeared after World War II, when it became likely that Nigeria would come to independence as some kind of unit in which mass political mobilization would be important. They shrewdly adopted "northern" solidarity as their public frame of reference, which could include Kanuri and other non-Hausa Muslims in the North,[9] and they have been largely successful in using this larger concept for political mobilization. The contemporary political significance of "Hausaness" and its overlapping identity with "northernness" is clear: When Brigadier Sani Abacha (later head of state) announced the 1983 coup, Miles joked to a Hausa village chief that as Abacha was an ethnic Kanuri from the northeast of the country, the historic Kanuri kingdom of Bornu would once again rule the area. The chief replied, "Well, as long as he's Hausa, it's all right."[10] The Hausa heartland is itself still organized as a series of emirates: Each of the major cities in northern Nigeria is the seat of an emir, one of the kings through whom the British applied their system of indirect rule. There is no official role for the emirs in modern Nigeria, and their unofficial role is hotly disputed, even in the North. Yet they retain great influence in their localities and, through Hausa prominence in national politics, in the rest of the country as well.

Crawford Young summarizes the evolution of Hausaness as a political framework in this way:

> In the nurturant security of colonial indirect rule, identity was related to locality, town and emirate rather than to a still-vague Hausa community; self-awareness as Hausa was most visible amongst the migrant Hausa trading clusters in southern towns. the invocation of Northern rather than specifically Hausa-Fulani patriotism was at once optimizing electoral tactic and testimonial to the diffuseness of the Hausa-Fulani cultural self-consciousness.[11]

Beyond ethnic identity, can we describe a set of political attitudes and beliefs that distinguish the Hausa from other Nigerians? It is difficult to find balanced treatments of this delicate issue. For many southern Nigerians, the traditions of rule in the Fulani emirates was "absolute, despotic, and extortionary."[12]

In accepting such a system, northern Nigerians, epitomized by the Hausa, are viewed in the South as obsequiously deferential to authority, easily accepting of a centralized, authoritarian state, and thus ill-prepared to participate in democratic institutions. To the degree that the North has been behind in educational achievement, and since education is commonly held to be a necessary corequisite for high participation levels,[13] to that degree the northern peasant is unlikely to be as politically aware at the national level as his southern counterpart. Furthermore, since Islam is widely interpreted in northern Nigeria to discourage the participation of women in politics, we can expect an even greater difference in propensity to political activity among women in the North and South. This does not mean, however, that the North is a political monolith. Elections have been vigorously contested in the North: In the 1979 presidential election, the "official" northern candidate, Shehu Shagari, was beaten by opposition candidates in two northern states (Borno and Kano), and even southern candidates did well in some areas. This voting is often based on clientelism; that is, individual voters are not simply determining which individual candidates and programs they prefer, but are "guided" in their choices by influential politicians at various levels. Still, it is necessary to conclude that the preferences of voters in the North are frequently guided by rational considerations of group advantage; ethnic preference plays a role, but it is only one factor among others in the northern voter's calculations. Writer Wole Soyinka calls northern solidarity a "carefully propagated myth" developed by a "desperate minority." This may be literary exaggeration, but in an insightful account of election politics in a northern Nigerian town, William F. S. Miles showed the many facets of Hausa society that produced, although within a rather narrow range of values, real interparty competition at the local level.[14]

The *Igbo* (also, especially formerly, spelled Ibo) occupy the southeastern part of the country, from the banks of the Niger River east. This was historically a region of thick rainforest. However, most of the region is now developed for market agriculture, with Igbo farmers growing palm products, rice, and yams. The Igbo people lived in politically independent villages, usually no larger than eight thousand people, and did not have a sense of common Igbo identity until the colonial period.

Ethnologists noted very early on that the Igbo were an exception to generalizations about the absence of achieved status in traditional societies. Describing the Afikpo subgroup of the Igbo, an anthropologist wrote:

> In their admiration for the self-made man the Afikpo seemed to field workers to be 200 percent American. Great effort is exerted in the amassing of wealth toward conspicuous consumption, traditionally in the form of title-taking, that is, joining a title society by paying a high initiation fee and giving a series of feasts to members . . . Afikpo impress outsiders as self-assertive, verbal people, clear in their aspirations and explicit as to the role of others in helping them or hindering them in achieving their goals. The Ibo people as a group are often described by non-Ibo as 'pushing' or 'aggressive,' and it seems very possible that it is their concern for strength and achievement that lies behind these observations.[15]

It is perhaps a related trait that the Igbo are known for the enthusiasm with which they adopted those aspects of Western culture that seemed to aid such achievement. Although the encounter with British colonialism was a wrenching shock forcefully described by Chinua Achebe in *Things Fall Apart*, the Igbo responded enthusiastically to Western education and the missionaries who brought it, and aggressively sought advancement in modern commerce and civil service. Also, in spite of their historic isolation and fragmentation, Igbo people emigrated widely throughout the country and seem to have been less concerned than other groups with maintaining separate communities where they are "strangers." (In Nigeria, the term "stranger" refers specifically to a person living outside his or her "home" community.) They were employed on the basis of their education and modern skills in all parts of the country, including the North, and were preponderant in the first promotions of Nigerian military officers.

As described in Chapter One, Igbo officers led the first military coup in 1966, and thousands of Igbos living in northern cities were attacked and killed in the reaction to that coup. The Igbos retreated to their home region, and the next year

---

Box 3.1 The Story of Chinua Achebe.

Chinua Achebe and Wole Soyinka are the two most prominent writers in Nigeria. Both frequently have used political themes, and their works are important sources for understanding Nigerian political culture. Achebe, the son of a mission teacher, was born in 1930 in the Eastern region. Beginning in 1954 he worked for the Nigerian Broadcasting Corporation, then served in the Biafran Ministry of Information during Nigeria's civil war. He has been a visiting professor at several U.S. universities. Among his works are a sequential trilogy of novels, *Things Fall Apart, Arrow of God*, and *No Longer at Ease*, that follow several generations of an Igbo family through the colonial period. The last of these chronicles the attempt of a young civil servant to avoid falling into political corruption. In *A Man of the People*, he describes the struggle of an idealistic young man against a corrupt politician (and predicts Nigeria's first military coup). *Anthills of the Savanna* describes an African country under personalistic military rule. Achebe has received many literary honors and awards.

---

followed the call of one of their own, Lt. Colonel Ojukwu, in the secession from Nigeria of Igbo-dominated Biafra. The three-year civil war that ended in the defeat of Biafra in 1970 caused them great hardship, but within a few years Igbos were again active in commerce (they were by then generally barred from government work in other localities) across the land. Nevertheless, the Biafran experience and the civil war left long-term mistrust between the Igbos and other Nigerians.

The *Yoruba* mostly live in the southwestern part of Nigeria, including the metropolitan area of Lagos, the former capital and major urban center. Smaller numbers of them may be found in neighboring Benin and Togo. Traditionally subsistence farmers, rural Yoruba people began growing cocoa and palm products for export in the colonial period. The Yoruba have a long tradition of commerce, and both men and women are prominent in trade networks and markets throughout West Africa. Although they share a common language, traditional religion, and myths of origin (all the Yoruba groups claim to be descendants of Oduduwa, the first man, who came directly from God to the world at Ile-Ife), the pre-colonial Yoruba were divided into over fifty independent and warring kingdoms that give them separate identities today as Ijebu, Egba, Awori, Oyo, Ekiti, Igbomina, and others.

Thus, as with the Hausa-Fulani, the Yoruba identity is of recent vintage. The most prominent Yoruba political leader in the movement to independence, Obafemi Awolowo, wrote in his autobiography that throughout history the Yorubas had warred amongst themselves:

> When the Portuguese and the British had visited their coasts in the course of their slave trade, the Yoruba had shown no qualm of conscience in conducting violent and merciless slave raids on one another . . . the mutual hatred and acerbity which were attendant on them lingered . . . I thought that it was in the best interests of Nigeria that the Yorubas should not be reduced to a state of impotence, into which they were fast degenerating.[16]

There had never been a single political entity termed "Yoruba," although there had been the Oyo and other kingdoms composed of Yorubas, and it was returned slaves who first identified the Yorubas as a single culture.[17] As with the "Hausa-Fulani" designation, the Yoruba identity emerged largely in response to the manipulations of political leaders who felt threats from outside their region.

The Yoruba kingdoms were marked by complicated institutions that balanced power between an *oba* (king) and lineage chiefs, as in the relationship between the Alafin of Oyo and the Oyo Mesi described earlier. In their effort to impose indirect rule, the British upset these structures by supporting the *obas* against all challengers. In the process, the *obas* frequently became autocratic and lost much of their legitimacy with their own people; their influence in contemporary politics varies greatly, but is generally much less than that of the Northern emirs.

Because the Yoruba had, on the one hand, a highly stratified society complete with kings and, on the other hand, were quite receptive to missionaries and their schools, they are often seen as in an intermediate position between the stratified and change-resistant Hausa and the egalitarian and innovative Igbo. In their sometimes strident assertion of their identity and interests, they seem also to have provoked their share of mistrust among other Nigerians, as their candidates have generally been shut out of national leadership positions.

The Middle Belt refers to the area in the southern part of the original Northern Region (now in the states of Niger, Kaduna, Kwara, Benue, Plateau, Bauchi, and Gongola), primarily inhabited by non-Hausa, largely non-Muslim peoples. These peoples have occupied an ambivalent position in the country's North-South conflict. Largest in number and influence in the Middle Belt are the Tiv, whose traditional socio-political system of "segmental opposition" was described in Chapter One. They strongly resisted the imposition of a hierarchical administration by the British, to which they responded with various cults and movements. In their efforts to understand and control the Tiv, the British isolated them from other groups. Not surprisingly, they were violently opposed to efforts to extend Muslim emirate control over their area at independence and thereafter, and their resistance led to army interventions in 1960 and 1964.[18]

GROUP	Percent of Population
Hausa and Fulani	29.5
Kanuri	4.1
Tiv	2.5
Nupe	1.2
Yoruba	20.3
Edo	1.7
Igbo	16.6
Ibibio-Efik	3.6
Ijaw	2.0
Others	18.5

Table 3.1 The Distribution of Ethnic Identities in Nigeria. (Based on the 1963 Census; Census efforts of 1973 and 1991 did not include questions on ethnicity.)

The distribution of Nigerian ethnic groups is presented in Table 3.1. It is helpful to remember that approximately one-half of the country's population is in the North, and about one-fourth each in the Southeast and Southwest. The Hausa represent about two-thirds of the North's total population, the Igbo about two-thirds in the East, and the Yoruba about two-thirds in the West. Thus, other groups represent about one-third in each region, and one-third overall.

Given the ethnic-based strife so common in the world today, it should not come as a surprise that group identities are deeply rooted and emotionally charged in Nigeria as well. As we have seen, ethnic rivalries often have their roots in precolonial warfare, and are frequently refreshed by economic rivalries. While nationalism may serve as a cement where the feeling is shared by a country's entire population, the same feeling at a subnational level can destroy a political system. In Nigeria as elsewhere, outsiders often fail to perceive the complexity of these attachments. They are multilayered, and different levels of association can become charged at different times, as demonstrated in the Ibadan/Ijebu rivalry (see Box 3.2). Strong ethnic ties often are felt and expressed in kinship terms, and thus are often central to the definition of self.

There are, however, two common misperceptions about ethnicity that can be illustrated in the Nigerian case. The first is, as we have noted previously, an erroneous understanding of ethnicity as *primordial*. While ethnic identity often has ancient roots, this does not mean that one's ethnic identity is identical with that of one's distant ancestors. In Africa, and in Nigeria in particular, we see extraordinary change, as in the bonding of two separate groups to form the Hausa-Fulani culture, in the emergence of a "Yoruba" identity over what were previously separate

> **Box 3.2. The Ijebu/Ibadan Controversy.**
>
> Ibadan is one of the two largest cities in Nigeria. An old Yoruba city, it is plagued by an historic rivalry between its two major groups, the Ibadan and the Ijebu—both claiming descent from Oduduwa. (Oduduwa's descendants seem as quarrelsome as Abraham's!) The Ijebu lived closest to the coast, and thus were the first to enter into commerce with European traders. Their attempt to control trade with the interior, i.e., with Ibadan, is said to have produced their longstanding animosity. At the same time, the animosity is not always felt at the individual level, for intermarriage between the two groups is common.

societies in conflict, and in the formation of an Igbo identity among villagers who previously were largely unaware of one another. Both in the colonial period and since, ethnic identities have been manipulated for political purposes. Commenting on his country's political experience, Nigerian political scientist Claude Ake concluded:

> There is nothing inherently conflictual about ethnic differences. They lead to strife only when they are politicized, and it is the elites who politicize ethnicity in their quest for power and political support. [19]

Ake's statement could as easily be applied to Rwanda, Bosnia, and many other locations.

The second common error concerning ethnicity is to think that it is inevitably eroded by exposure to such "modern" institutions as the mass media, secular education, and urbanization. Any truth in this proposition is surely only evident over the very long term, and again we can use as examples several years of recent history in the former Yugoslavia and Rwanda. Political scientists have looked at this central issue as one of "nation building," that is, the development of affective attachment to the modern state. However, for ethnic identities the same process appears as "nation destroying," as nation-builders 'teach' subordinate peoples to embrace the new national identity that the state would ostensibly represent.[20] In the late twentieth century we have learned how little we know about manipulating such identities, as demands for autonomy of groups that were supposed to disappear remain as loud as ever. In Nigeria, and in Africa generally, the potential for states to come apart at the seams led the Organization of African

---

Box 3.3. The Conflict Between Modakeke and Ile-Ife.

Early in the nineteenth century, Yorubas from Old Oyo were driven south by a Fulani invasion, and some settled in and around Ile-Ife. They were at first well-received by Ile-Ife's traditional ruler, the Ooni, but soon got into a violent quarrel with the local population. The Oyo refugees were then reduced to servitude, and some were sold into slavery. Later, however, in an internal dispute, they sided with the ruler, who rewarded them with a settlement of their own, Modakeke. Strife continued between the two groups, and in an 1882 battle the Modakeke burned down the sacred city of Ife. Throughout the colonial period, the Ooni often used their conflict to play one group against the other. As independence neared, the Modakeke sought a local government independent of Ife. Also, the Ife leaders supported the Action Group (party), while Modakeke supported the National Congress of Nigeria and the Cameroons (NCNC). After independence, Ife and Modakeke were in the same local government (Oranmiyan), but fought constantly until Oranmiyan was split in 1989. There was peace until August, 1997, when the military government moved one local government from an Ife to a Modakeke location and then to supposedly neutral ground. Violent conflict broke out among young men of each side. Whole villages were burned and nearly 200 lives have been lost, or perhaps, according to the *Abuja Mirror* (February 18-24, 1998) over 1000 lives. Two Seventh-Day Adventist schools with no obvious relevance to the struggle were burned to the ground with no one claiming responsibility. The conflict continued into 1998.

Unity to state as a given that the boundaries between states established at independence are permanent, however artificially they were created at the Conference of Berlin. The question is not definitively resolved for Nigerians, who continue to ponder whether the various subnational identities in the country can ever be consolidated into a national identity that all can embrace.[21]

In Nigeria some of the first associational groups were based on the perception of common ethnic bonds in "nontraditional" settings. As a student in London, the early nationalist leader Obafemi Awolowo formed the *Egbe Omo Oduduwa* as a cultural organization grouping expatriate Yorubas. This group was to become the basis for the Action Group, the political party Awolowo later formed.

Because the major ethnic groups are regionally based, political issues affecting such groups are often defined geographically, and Nigeria has preserved a sense of permanent attachment between a people and its "traditional" homeland to the degree that it is undoubtedly more difficult to become a "citizen" of another state in Nigeria than it would be for a Nigerian to acquire citizenship in many foreign countries. The ethnic exclusiveness found in each state and local authority is euphemistically referred to as Nigeria's "federal character." This term first appeared in the Nigerian Constitution of 1979, in a section providing that federal government appointments in each agency must reflect the ethnic and regional distribution in the country; similar requirements have been imposed at the state level. This explicit reference to ethnic origins has had strong effects on the nature of national policy.

Thus, as Nigerians respond to educational or economic opportunities in other parts of the country, they find it necessary to organize into ethnic associations for protection and promotion of their interests. Hausas in the South usually live in a ghetto called the *Sabo*, where they speak their language and practice their Muslim faith. Nigerians at the lowest socio-economic level often belong to a single association—that of their ethnic group. As P. C. Lloyd pointed out years ago, the more educated members of these "stranger" communities will often overlay the purely ethnic associations with others in which they interact across ethnic lines.[22]

Multiple ethnic identities even at the local level have had a fragmenting effect on political structure. Particularly since 1976, there have been numerous disputes over the siting of local government headquarters, with the "loser" often petitioning to the state and federal governments for a division of the local government area. Examples include the conflict between Ifon and Erin in Osun State, the Ife and Modakeke in Oranmiyan local government (see Box 3.3), the Igbogbo and Ikorodu in Ikorodu local government, in Delta State between the Ijaw and Itsekiri peoples (resulting in intergroup violence in March, 1997), and in Efon Alaye, a town that preferred to be administered directly through the governor's office in Akure rather than to cooperate with the nearest local government. (They finally were given their own local government as one of 183 new local governments created in 1996.) Local ethnic conflict affects policy outputs as well, where local governments build health centers or markets that are not used by some ethnic groups, thus throwing off planners' projections. (Group leaders often protest that they were not consulted in planning the facilities, that they are sited too far from them, etc.)

Ethnic group identities are often reinforced by language exclusiveness. Although colonialism left the country with English as a common official language, it is not the first language of the vast majority of the population, and certainly does not have the emotional attachments inherent in the indigenous languages. Access to modern politics is strictly limited by the access to English language that only formal education can provide (see below). However, in the midwest and eastern regions (the Niger delta and the Calabar and Cross River areas), individuals without much formal education may speak "broken" English, also known as "pidgin" English, using a simplified syntax, grammar, and vocabulary that render it a distinct dialect. Pidgin developed as a means of commercial exchange with Europeans, and is often used by market women and other traders. In modern Nigeria it is a valuable means of interethnic communication (oral), but because it is normally acquired on the street and in the market, its use connotes low socio-economic status.

RELIGION

All the peoples of Nigeria had their own religious institutions and beliefs in place long before the arrival of Christianity and Islam. In some cases these earlier beliefs have maintained their vigor, especially among many Yoruba.

However, the missionaries brought their religion with formal education in the southern regions; most major Christian churches are well established in the South, and indigenous Christian sects have split off from them in a myriad of denominations. Not surprisingly, the Christian denominations in the South tend to

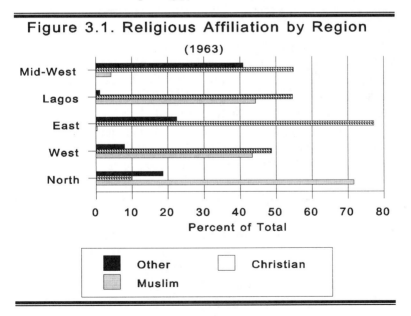

Figure 3.1. Religious Affiliation by Region

From J. N. Paden, *Religion and Political Culture in Kano* (Berkeley: University of California Press, 1973, p. 44

be geographically concentrated, with a higher proportion of Roman Catholics among the Igbo, a Baptist concentration among the Yoruba of Ogbomoso, the Evangelical Church of West Africa predominant in Igbomina and Kwara State, etc. A significant proportion of Yoruba—perhaps half—are Muslim.

In the Middle Belt, the non-Hausa and primarily non-Muslim region in the south of the old Northern region, North American Christian missionaries were particularly active. Prominent among these was the Sudan Interior Mission (SIM) with headquarters in Toronto and a Nigerian center at Jos. By the 1970s retiring foreign missionaries were being replaced by indigenous Nigerians, who reorganized the SIM and other missionary groups as the Evangelical Community of West Africa (ECWA).[23] This "Nigerianization" of the clergy has been occurring in all the previously missionary-based Christian denominations.

Under the agreement between the colonial administration and the northern emirates, Christian proselytizing was barred from the North, and, except for the "strangers" living there, almost the entire population is at least nominally Muslim, and the Hausa bring their religion with them when they move south. This movement is offset by the establishment of churches in northern cities by immigrants (mostly Igbos) from the South.

Figure 3.1 shows the breakdown of religious affiliation in the country's four regions (as of 1963) and Lagos. That census reported the population to be 49 percent Muslim, and 34 percent Christian, with 17 percent following traditional African religions. However, the census figures are widely suspect (and religious affiliation was not requested in later census attempts). Furthermore, the distinction between a Christian or Muslim and a traditional believer is sometimes quite arbitrary. Nevertheless, Figure 3.1 shows, if only roughly, the overlay of religion on region that, along with ethnicity, intensifies the North-South cultural split.

In a survey conducted in 43 countries in 1990-91, respondents were asked the importance of religion, and of God, in their lives. In Nigeria, fully 85 percent replied that religion was very important, and nearly 100 percent of Nigerians said that God is important in their lives. These were by far the highest proportions of any of the countries sampled. The identities we examine here, then, are not superficial.[24]

The religious divide in Nigeria is put in dramatic perspective by Samuel Huntington, who has recently divided the world into nine "civilizations." He foresees that "fault lines" among these civilizations will be the major loci of conflict in years to come, and notes specifically that "the overwhelming majority of fault line conflicts. . .have taken place along the boundary looping across Eurasia and Africa that separates Muslims from non-Muslims." The greatest potential for strife, he suggests, is where these lines divide countries. [25]

Before the 1970s there were very few attempts to manipulate religion for political purposes in Nigeria. In the period since then, there has been a decided rise in expressions of religious fundamentalism among both Christians and Muslims, often expressed outside the traditional Christian denominations and the "established" Islamic hierarchy (see Box 3.3). The fundamentalist wave in Nigeria coincides with a world-wide rise in fundamentalist movements,[26] but seems related in Nigeria to the rapid influx of wealth as part of the oil boom of the 1970s, and the collapse of the oil economy at the end of that decade. The case can be made that the most sensitive political issues now involve religion rather than ethnicity. This is more dangerous, because as we have seen, religious identity is a central defining characteristic to most Nigerians, because the sharp north-south divide is blurred by multiple ethnic identities, but is focused by the Christian-Muslim dichotomy. Finally, Nigeria has a special problem in that the country is almost evenly divided between Christians and Muslims, whereas in almost all other African states Muslims are either the large majority of the population or compose a clear minority.[27]

The brother of Usman dan Fodio, the leader of the nineteenth-century *jihad* in northern Nigeria, wrote a four-volume work on the nature of legitimate Islamic

---

Box 3.4 The Story of Mohammed Marwa Maitatsine.

"Maitatsine originated from Marwa, a town in northern Cameroon . . . After studying locally, he spent most of his life in Nigeria, first visiting Kano in 1945, where he became known as a controversial preacher and commentator on the Koran. His illegal preaching and abusive critique of authority led to his imprisonment and exile to Cameroon in 1962 or 1963. [Later] he took residence [in Kano], and by 1972 he had attracted a number of followers and Koranic students . . . In 1975 he was arrested by the Nigerian police for slander and public abuse of the political authorities. Nonetheless, Mohammed Marwa made the *hajj* during this period so that he was accepted as orthodox by the religious authorities. He attracted a large following . . . By 1980 he was recognized as a mystical religious leader with a substantial income, a large following and the protection of armed guards . . . From the late 1970s Marwa's preaching and the militant activities of his followers led to arrests and violent confrontations with nonbelievers and the police. His community, composed largely of youths . . . and unemployed migrants, self-consciously divorced itself from the mainstream Muslim community both socially and spatially . . . .[During the Kano insurrection of 1980] Maitatsine was killed by Nigerian security forces."

Source: Paul M. Lubock, Islamic <u>Protest and Oil-Based Capitalism</u>, p. 269

---

government. It specifies that a state must be judged in terms of its "provision for social welfare, popular participation, justice, and human rights," and that *Sharia* (Muslim religious law) must be fully implemented. It does not allow for the possibility of a conflict between secular concepts of justice and welfare and those in the *Sharia*. These values are well-rooted in the region: A survey of 686 students at Bayero University in Kano in 1983 found that 92 percent of them "believed an Islamic state was inherently superior to a secular state."[28] In the 1980s the Maitatsine Islamic movement, composed largely of young men marginalized in the socio-economic changes of the period, rioted against the Christian presence in northern Nigeria (as well as against police repression)[29] with loss of life estimated in the thousands (see Box 3.4). The Grand Kadi of Northern Nigeria stated in 1987 that "a Muslim could not accept a non-Muslim to lead the nation and that if a Muslim leader was not acceptable to Christians, the country would have to be divided into two parts."[30] On the other hand, a failed coup against the Babangida regime in 1990 is widely thought to have been a "Christian coup against the northern Muslim leadership."[31] Because fundamentalist elements in both Christianity and Islam are more frequently finding it unacceptable to live in a pluralist society, those seeking a basis for political stability in Nigeria must be sensitive to finding a balance between the two major faith groups. For that reason there was great distress in the South when, in 1986, President Babangida proposed that Nigeria join the Organization of the Islamic Conference (OIC). The OIC had been formed at a meeting of foreign ministers of Muslim countries in 1970. Its stated aims were to (1) protect Islamic holy sites; (2) encourage Islamic solidarity among Muslim states; (3) end colonialism and imperialism; and (4) assist in the liberation of Palestine.[32]

The print media were flooded with statements of support of the move and strident denunciations, and threats of violence were voiced in those parts of the country already experiencing religious-based tensions. The Catholic archbishop of Lagos declared that Christian soldiers could not serve a formally Islamic state.[33] In 1991, Babangida asserted that Nigeria's OIC membership was "in abeyance," which is perhaps the only status for the issue that will not exacerbate religious tensions. The issue was raised again in June, 1997 when Industries Minister Haladu represented Nigeria at a meeting of the "Developing Eight" Third World governments that was ostensibly organized around economic issues but at least coincidentially consisted of major majority-Muslim nations (Bangladesh, Egypt, Indonesia, Iran, Malaysia, Pakistan, Turkey, and Nigeria).

At the elite level, attitudes on the role of religion in politics are much more moderate, and perhaps not so different from what would be found in the United States. A survey of political views of elites—both Muslim and non-Muslim, and including professionals, executives, civil servants, teachers, politicians, and trade unionists in Lagos—was reported in a study of public opinion in the Muslim world.[34]

These urban elites showed strong agreement with the statement that "Religious values should play a larger role in our society," that "(o)ur schools should provide more religious instruction for our children," and that "Western mass culture runs counter to our traditional values (see Table 3.2). On the other hand, most of them oppose religious extremism, and support freedom of religion and a separation of religion and politics. It seems clear that there is a class dimension in attitudes to the role of religion in politics in Nigeria, with elites more aligned to views prevailing in the West.

Statement	% Agreeing	% Disagreeing	Don't know
Religious values should play a larger role in our society.	79	18	3
Our schools should provide more religious instruction for our children.	89	8	3
Western mass culture runs counter to our traditional values.	66	29	5
Religious extremists are a threat to our way of life.	89	10	1
Religious groups should be separated from the political life of our country.	64	34	2
Freedom of religion is an important function of government.	98	2	0

Table 3.2. Views of Religion and Politics, Lagos Elites (from Pollock and El Assal, eds., *In the Eye of the Beholder*, pp. 45-51.

The opposing camps of Christianity and Islam are not monolithic in Nigeria. This is obvious among Christians, who are splintered into many denominations, with new ones forming almost constantly. The principal focus for unity among Nigerian Christians is clearly the "Islamic menace." On the other hand, struggles between orthodox and reformist Muslims continue to threaten northern solidarity, and northern (Hausa-Fulani) Muslims are said to be highly critical of the purity of Islamic practice among Muslim Yorubas, where women are rarely subjected to the conditions of seclusion prevalent in the North.[35] This helps explain why Yoruba Moshood Abiola's Muslim identity did not result in support among northern leaders for his claim to have won the presidency in 1993.

The politicization of religion has not only involved inter-denominational conflict. Fundamentalist and millenarian movements often result from anxieties about rapid socio-economic change. Mohammed Marwa Maitatsine, whose *'yan Tatsine* movement grew up during the oil-boom 1970s (Box 3.4), condemned the corruption and materialist values of Kano's established secular and religious elites. The term Maitatsine came from the Hausa for "the one who damns," and Marwa "damned all who enjoyed modern, Western consumer goods: automobiles, radios, watches, televisions, and even buttons." Brutal police agent reactions to their dissent provided them with a focus for their discontent.[36] Although the evils decried by fundamentalist leaders are not necessarily political in nature, security agents will often be at the focal point of conflict, especially where dissenting opinions are not well protected. Although all recent military leader have been Muslims, this has not prevented concerns about the role of Islam in Nigeria from causing political tension within the Islamic community. The arrest of Shiite Muslim leader, Ibrahim El Zak Zaky, by the Abacha regime in 1996 has resulted in large-scale demonstrations supporting his release in Katsina and Kaduna in the North and later in Lagos. El-Zak Zaky was accused of inciting the public against the government.

THE EVOLUTION OF NIGERIAN NATIONALISM

All of our preoccupation with conflicting Nigerian subcultures should not obscure the fact that the British colonial administration was responding to Nigerian nationalist forces when they granted independence in 1960. There were three major sources of nationalist sentiment. The first was a small number of freed slaves from North America and others of African descent from the Caribbean who settled on the West African coast and developed a culture unrelated to any of those indigenous to the country. Nationalist fervor also grew out of the experience of Nigerians who fought for the British in World War II and felt frustration at the lack of recognition of their service on the part of the administration.[37] A third category of nationalists consisted of those Nigerians who studied in England and especially in the United States, including one of the most prominent among them, Nnamdi Azikiwe (see Box 3.5). Although they came from a variety of ethnic backgrounds, these activists developed a sense of Nigerian nationalism in their quest for independence, and succeeded in forming cross-ethnic alliances. Here again, Crawford Young focuses our attention on the paradox of "nationalism" in Nigeria: These leaders were forced to identify with a "nation" that rose from their own collective experience *as defined by an alien power*. The object of patriotic allegiance was indeed a foreign creation in which they had been involuntarily included. "Formerly acknowledged as determining the boundaries of anticolonial engagement, the units of colonial partition became sanctified, even sacralized—a process symbolized in the 1963 charter of the Organization of African Unity (OAU), which declared colonial boundaries definitive and immutable."[38]

We have seen the expressions of nationalism that ostensibly fueled the first Nigerian coup; some would suggest that the military is more prone to nationalistic loyalties than most other segments of society.[39] A sense of Nigerian national identity seems to have been stimulated by the Nigerian civil war: Although ethnic rivalry played an important role in the two military coups before the Biafran War, that conflict brought together a military force that was cross-ethnic (excluding, of course, most Igbos, who were at the heart of the Biafran succession). Although the officer corps has come to be dominated increasingly by Muslims, it has continued to recruit nationally, and the desire to forge a nation has been among the motives and rationales for the behavior of many a young officer since then.

Still, opposed to the factors favoring the development of nationalistic sentiments is the paradox that British colonialism created the entity on which national identity is to be focused. Secondly, to the degree that any community identity is forged in distinction to outsiders, Nigerian nationalism lacks a common

---

Box 3.5 The Story of Nnamdi Azikiwe.

Although an Igbo, Nnamdi Azikiwe was born in Zungeru in Northern Nigeria in 1904. He received his basic education in Nigeria, then went to the United States where he studied at Lincoln University (Pennsylvania), Stores College (West Virginia), and the University of Pennsylvania. He also worked in the United States as a coal miner, laborer, and dishwasher. Upon his return home he joined the Nigerian Youth Movement. His interest in self-rule led to his presence at the founding of the National Council of Nigeria and the Cameroons, and to his founding of a pro-self-rule newspaper, the *African Pilot*. He then moved to the Gold Coast (now Ghana), where he published an article, "Has the African a God," that resulted in a sedition charge. He won his case on appeal, and went on to serve as the premier of the Eastern region, and from 1963 to 1966 as president of Nigeria. Later in life he was given a traditional title. He died in 1996 at the age of ninety-two.

---

enemy or "other." Colonial rule, and later the Biafran secession, provided such a point of focus, but there have been none in recent years. It is for these reasons that the Nigerian state is by and large seen by Nigerians not as the focus of their sense of collective identity, but as "a purveyor of services and employment that belong[s] to no one."[40] Looking at Africa as a whole, Peter Ekeh finds two separate publics in political life: (a) an *amoral civic public* from which one expects benefits but which is not important in one's definition of one's duties; and (b) a *moral primordial public*, defined in terms of one's ethnic groups, to which one's relationships were predominantly phrased in terms of duties.

Ekeh elaborates on the particular case of Nigeria:

> . . . most Nigerians have deep sacred feelings about their ethnic groups. In fact many do sacrifice their lives and their life savings in the service of perpetuating these primordial groupings. They gain little in return from them. In other words, their relations to the more primordial public is one-sided: In terms of their *duties* to preserving and servicing it but not in terms of benefits or rights from it. Contrariwise, the relationships of Nigerians to the amoral civic public are predominantly in terms of one's expectations of *rights* from the government, with little conception of concomitant duties to it.[41]

We would take issue with Ekeh's use of the term "primordial," which, as noted above, wrongly suggests that ethnic identities are ancient and unchanging when many of them are more recent than colonialism. It is not their *antecedence* that makes them more powerful forms of identity than is Nigerian nationalism; rather, they are simply more satisfying in distinguishing self from other in contemporary Nigeria. Ethnic identities set the bounds of trust. We must also emphasize that the more powerful ethnic identities may not always be on the level of "Igbo," "Yoruba," or "Hausa." Often they are more local, reflecting conflict *within* one of the larger groupings. But Ekeh's formulation is useful precisely because it emphasizes the *comparative* strengths of different identities.

Similarly, particular regimes have not achieved a high degree of *legitimacy* among the population, except as the ethnic composition of that regime's institutions creates a sense of trust in it in corresponding sectors of the population. In Nigeria, trust in government is more readily achieved on the basis of ethnic ties than in any other way.

Although sentiments of loyalty to the Nigerian state may be weak, the above discussion does not preclude a high degree of awareness of that state, if only as "a purveyor of services and employment." The degree to which a national political culture has evolved in Nigeria can be assessed by an examination of orientations toward national (federal) political institutions. A general approach to political orientations is to categorize them as *parochial, subject,* and *participant. Parochials* are those who are only vaguely aware of government, a rare situation if strictly defined. However, some people are usually connected to national-level political institutions only through indirect relationships, especially in remote rural areas. *Subjects* are those whose only orientation to national institutions is in passive obedience to rules emanating from them. *Participants* are informed about politics, have expectations of political institutions, and give support to different political leaders.[42] What factors affect the relationship between individuals and the state in Nigeria? Nigerians with a participant orientation toward public political activities can be identified by (1) exposure to formal education and (2) involvement in the modern economy. There are many Nigerians, particularly in rural areas, and especially in the North, who are parochials. However, this does not mean that such people are unaware of Nigerian political institutions or the effect of policy on them personally. Thus, one may be unaware of, and uninterested in, issues of general concern, but still have to deal with local government officials on issues affecting oneself and one's family. In Nigeria, as elsewhere in Africa and the Third World, such concerns are likely to be handled through *parochial contacting*, meaning that they approach people with influence to enlist their aid in obtaining favorable rulings on matters affecting them personally. In the cross-national study conducted in the late 1960s, Nigerians were more likely than those in other countries to feel that the "government could help solve personal and family problems": Of those who had such problems (a higher proportion than in other countries), almost half mentioned the government as a source of help, especially on questions of jobs, income, and education.[43] In most cases, contacting government for services in Nigeria is part of a *clientelist* arrangement: Citizens go to an individual who is politically influential for help, and are expected to "pay" for help through a long-term arrangement that may include payment in kind (as in bribes, or in Yoruba, *egunje*), or by turning out to vote when asked to do so, even while remaining parochial in terms of interest in politics. In other words, political activity is widespread and virtually all-embracing; interest in public affairs is strongly conditioned by education and employment.

Is anything left of the sense of Nigerian nationhood that was felt by at least some of the urban and educated class at independence? Very little, apparently, if we can believe Wole Soyinka's recent assessment:

> And so, if you pose the question . . . "Do you believe in Nigeria as a nation?" the answer from many sections [is at best] an ambiguous, qualified "Yes," hedged about with conditions, but those who wish to be truthful to the evidence of their hearing must admit that the mood of the nation . . . amounts at best to a vote for the reconsideration of the nation status as it now exists.[44]

Soyinka's dire forecast is that, if the election of June 12, 1993 is never revalidated, "Nigeria as a nation has no future history."[45]

DEMOCRATIC NORMS AND VALUES

In order to assess Nigeria's chances for achieving political democracy, consideration must first be given to the distribution of norms that might support the existence of democratic institutions. Robert Dahl has identified one such norm as most important in this respect: the legitimacy of opposition. Manifested as tolerance by a regime for criticism, opposition, and competition for control, this is an obvious prerequisite for stable democracy, and a rare and fragile characteristic.[46] The performance of political activists in Nigeria from 1960 on suggests that it has not been a predominant trait there, even among the educated elite, and even under democratic civilian regimes. As single parties gained control in each region, opponents were treated very roughly, often in the physical sense, with armed thugs hired to disrupt their meetings and attack their leaders.[47]

Most students of democracy would specify that a sense of community, although not part of the definition of democracy, is a necessary precondition to achieve democracy. "The people cannot decide until somebody decides who are the people."[48] Although most regimes and political movements in Africa at least accept existing state boundaries as inevitable,[49] it is clear that in Nigeria some political activists have begun to question that inevitability, and to imagine different state boundaries, or at least a much weaker center. The belief that individuals have equal political rights as Nigerians may not be unanimously shared, and it may be difficult to make democracy work in such a cultural context.

Nevertheless, while an interest in the welfare of the nation over that of more particular groups may not characterize large numbers of Nigerians, even among the politically active, it can still be said that truly Nigerian characteristics of political culture have emerged across a large proportion of the politically aware population. Larry Diamond identifies two widely held values: freedom and public accountability.[50] A survey of university students by Beckett and O'Connell (1977) found a more nuanced view of democracy: Democracy was defined in terms of results such as good government and responsiveness, rather than by process; politicians were denigrated, and there seemed to be little confidence in the wisdom of the electorate. Yet, as a "bottom line," a large majority of the students still favored a full, election-based democracy, and in a national survey conducted in March/April 1997, 94 percent of respondents felt that honest elections constitute a key democratic right. Yet, after long periods of military rule, ideas about democracy may have become more confused. In the 1997 national survey, only half the respondents believed it is an important right to be able to "openly criticize the government."[51]

THE ROLE OF IDEOLOGY

As we have seen, Nigeria's leaders have generally displayed an approach to problem solving that has been described as "pragmatic," and that has rarely been presented in an overtly ideological fashion, particularly as concerns questions of political economy. We know that even in advanced industrial countries, only a minority of the general population thinks in ideological terms,[52] and in less-developed countries with lower levels of education, we would expect the proportions to be even lower. But the thinking of political elites, including academics, some public officials, and younger military officers has been quite influenced by modern ideological conflicts. In academe, sympathy with socialism

---

Box 3.6 The Igbo Women's War of 1929.

"In November of 1929, thousands of Igbo women. . .converged on the native Administration centers. . .The women chanted, danced, sang songs of ridicule, and demanded the caps of office (the official insignia) of the Warrant Chiefs. . .At a few locations the women broke into prisons and released prisoners. Sixteen Native Courts were attacked, and most of these were broken up or burned. . On two occasions, British District Officers called in police and troops, who fired on the women and left a total of more than 50 dead and 50 wounded. No one on the other side was seriously injured. [The women's actions were] an extension of their traditional method for settling grievances with men who had acted badly toward them."

Source: Judith Van Allen, 1976, pp. 60-62

among political scientists and economists has been quite common, especially before the breakup of the Soviet Union. As in many Third World countries, Nigerians often resent the preponderant role played by foreign interests in the modern sector of their economy, and, as we will see in Chapter Seven, that resentment has been greatly fueled by the country's subjection to the Structural Adjustment Program of that epitome of foreign influence, the World Bank. Nigeria is, on the one hand, a country many of whose citizens are

quick to take advantage of market conditions. On the other hand, its economists and political (especially military) leaders favor a centrally planned economy as a developmental model, and in the Inglehart of 43 nations in 1980, only the Chinese respondents expresses a higher level of support for government ownership of productive enterprises.[53].

THE POLITICAL ROLE OF WOMEN

In Nigeria's ethnic diversity, the position of women has varied considerably. In Igbo, Yoruba, and other southern Nigerian traditions, women had considerable control over their own affairs in what anthropologists label "dual-sex" systems. That is, there were parallel systems of political and social organization for men and women.[54] P. C. Lloyd concluded that "the Yoruba wife's status is characterized by great overt submission to her husband together with considerable economic independence."[55] In southern Nigeria, women were especially prominent in the markets, which they organized by commodity sections, with leaders in charge of market activities and with associations that set prices and settled disputes. Market women provided some of the most effective organizations in Nigeria in asserting themselves before colonial officials, and gave crucial support to the emerging political parties and independence movements.[56] This is not surprising: Scholars of colonial history contend that women *lost* most of their autonomy under colonialism, because British custom at the time gave women less control of their own affairs than did the African societies they controlled. A famous case in point is the Igbo Women's War (referred to by the colonial government as the "Aba riots"), in which Igbo women used traditionally sanctioned means of protest against taxation and were harshly repressed by the colonial government (see Box 3.6).

In the North, Islamic custom has greatly restricted the role of women in society. Although Hausa women have considerably more freedom than their counterparts in the Middle East, including significant roles in local production and trade, they have generally not been allowed an active political role, and were not given the right to vote or to hold office at independence (northern women voted for the first time at the national level in 1979).

The contemporary pattern of involvement of women in political leadership is similar to that of many countries: Nigerian women vote in equal numbers with men in most parts of the country, but in the 1992 National Assembly elections, only twelve of 584 members of the House of Representatives were women, and only one of 170 senators. It is revealing that there are no women mentioned as individuals in most accounts of Nigerian politics. We will return to the role of women in Nigerian politics in the next chapter.

Box 3.7 Definitions and Explanations of terms commonly used in describing Nigerian Society and Politics

Patrimonial - characterizes a political system organized along kinship lines, of which one essential characteristic is "the presence and ultimate authority of a ruler and the general legitimating role of a traditional ideology." [Joseph, p. 66]

Clientelism (patron-client relations) may be defined as "a special case of dyadic (two-person) ties involving a largely instrumental friendship in which an individual of higher socio-economic status (patron) uses his own influence and resources to provide protection or benefits or both, for a person of lower status (client) who, for his part, reciprocates by offering general support and assistance, including personal services to the patron." [Joseph, pp. 55-56] Usually, "clientelism is a many-tiered phenomenon. The coming together of a series of patron—or middleman—client exchanges forms a network, an extensive network of people bound together by reciprocal obligations may stretch across large segments, or the whole, of a society so that it forms a system." [Barnes 1986, p. 9] Clientelism differs from patrimonialism in that the relationships that compose it are based on *contractual* rather than kinship ties.

Prebendalism. "A prebend is an office of state which an individual procures either through examinations or as a reward for loyal service to a lord or ruler." Weber stresses that such an office normally has lifelong income, compensations for "actual or fictitious office duties; they are goods permanently set aside for the economic assurance of office." This is true in Nigeria in the case of ministerial appointments, or positions on government boards. It also applies, however, to "individuals within the nominally private sector." Prebendalism is a component of patron-client relations in Nigeria, for in order "to obtain and keep clients, one must gain a prebendal office; and to be sure that in the distribution of prebendal offices an individual or his kin have a reasonable chance of procuring one, clients must be gathered together to make their collective claims . . . " [Joseph, pp. 56-57]

Sources: Garth and Mills, From Max Weber; Richard Joseph, Democracy and Prebendal Politics in Nigeria; Sandra T. Barnes, Patrons and Power.

CLIENTELISM

Clientelism was a feature of almost all Nigeria's precolonial traditions, especially the most hierarchical of them like the Hausa emirates and the kingdoms of the Southwest. It is based on a series of patron-client relations, defined by James C. Scott as a relationship "in which an individual of higher socio-economic status (patron) uses his own influence and resources to provide protection or benefits or both, for a person of lower status (client) who, for his part, reciprocates by offering general support and assistance, including personal services to the patron." The related terms "patrimonialism," "clientelism," and "prebendalism" are defined in Box 3.7. The place of clientelism in present-day Nigeria is discussed in greater detail in Chapter Five. Here we can note its cultural aspect, namely that there is a common approach to political action or administrative decision-making in Nigeria which is to create or enter into reciprocal relationships with others at higher or lower levels of influence, and to build a career through advancement in such a network of patron-client relationships. To those who value such relationships, political actions or administrative decisions are not seen as blind applications of statutes or procedures, or as widely applied public policies, but as benefits to individuals that result from reciprocal exchanges. What is less universally accepted (and often roundly condemned) is the conversion of this system into a market, such that political and administrative decisions are sold to the highest bidder, or sold according to some price list. When a public position is seen primarily as a source of revenue to the "gatekeeper" occupying that position, we are beyond a traditional understanding of reciprocity or clientelism and into pure corruption of the kind exemplified by the police officer or customs agent accepting a bribe for not applying the law. We have no empirical evidence on the degree to which market corruption has become accepted in Nigerian culture, but it is widely condemned in public and in the mass media, and the rationale for overthrowing regimes in Nigeria has generally included the need to eliminate and to punish corruption.

POLITICAL CORRUPTION

As one travels on Nigerian roads there are frequent police checkpoints and barricades. Ostensibly in place to check for arms and smuggled goods, their actual function is to extort payments from travelers by uncovering various minor violations. Many Nigerians do not take offense at this behavior, noting that police officers' pay is low, and often comes late. Travelers leaving the country through the Murtala Muhammed International Airport in Lagos are routinely asked for "gifts" or subjected to harassment designed to elicit bribes by police and customs officials. This, of course, is petty activity compared to the huge sums which high government officials have extracted from investors and contractors, sometimes as much as 25 percent of a contract. Pervasive corruption has been a problem ever since the late colonial era; it was the central theme of Chinua Achebe's novel *No Longer at Ease*, in which an idealistic young administrator is gradually pressured by personal problems and the "everybody's doing it" argument into accepting bribes for help in getting scholarships for students. Achebe is only one of many Nigerians who have condemned corruption; each political regime has come to power promising to eliminate the practice and punish offenders, only to fall into the same pattern. The problem seems to have gotten worse: In the first period of civilian rule (1960-1966), there were hardly any corruption scandals in the army. Once the military came to power, however, they were caught up in the already powerful patronage networks, and their socialization as neutral authorities was sorely and successfully tested by tempting business deals.[57] Corruption was greatly aggravated by the huge sums of money that passed through officials' hands as a result of the oil boom: Unprecedented forms of flagrant corruption appeared when huge revenues began to fill the federal treasury of General Yakubu Gowon in the early 1970s. His military governors spent large sums on openly lavish lifestyles, thus tarnishing the image of the military, which had supposedly come to power in reaction to the corruption of the First Republic. The coup against Gowon in 1975 was a direct result, as was the assassination of his successor General Murtala in 1976. Succeeding regimes have all found it impossible to control the demands of those in public office that they share in a "national cake" made almost entirely of petroleum, and Achebe asserts that corruption has grown more "bold and ravenous" under each new regime.[58] In a 1994 survey of international experts attending conferences on corruption, respondents were asked to rate a select group of countries as to the seriousness of their problem with corruption; Nigeria was ranked the highest.[59] Similarly, a German-based non-profit organization formed to fight corruption, Transparency International, reported that a 1996 survey of persons in international business rated Nigeria the most corrupt country in the world.[60]

It is fair to conclude that the Nigerian public is highly ambivalent about the corruption problem, frequently complaining about it and condemning it, but generally resigned to its pervasive presence. (A national survey found that 85 percent of respondents agreed or strongly agreed with the statement, "The majority of public officials are corrupt." Those with higher levels of education were more likely than those with little or no formal education to agree with the statement.)[61]

The activities described above fit the definition of corruption anywhere in the world. It is not simple to determine, however, at what point "politics as usual" becomes corruption. Corruption is most simply defined as the use of public office for private gain.[62] In almost every culture the informal norms allow that individuals will exchange political favors to at least a limited degree on the basis of friendship, kinship, and reciprocity. Early treatments of corruption in Africa often pointed to these as traditional social and political values: The "good" person would use political influence to help relatives or friends, or to repay past favors; only the "selfish" person would refuse to do so. Achebe's novels *Man of the People* and *No Longer at Ease* treat the conflict between these normative expectations and the bureaucratic imperative that the administrator will use general decision rules and criteria in making decisions . . . that they will be made "by the book." Some have argued that, to some degree, the use of such connections is even useful, or at least that the expense of eliminating all corruption exceeds the benefit to be obtained from such an accomplishment. Political scientist Samuel Huntington once observed that "the only thing worse than a society with a rigid, overcentralized dishonest bureaucracy is one with a rigid, overcentralized, honest bureaucracy," and Robert Klitgaard bases a singular approach to controlling corruption on the maxim "the optimal level of corruption is not zero."[63]

Varda Eker hypothesized that "extreme devotion to one's family precludes very strong morality in other spheres," creating in Edward Banfield's term a society of "amoral familists." According to Eker, "Strong allegiances to one's kin impose powerful restraints on one's self-interestedness in that context. Simultaneously, it weakens to the point of obliteration all other moral restraints, such as the integrity of office, the devotion to one's country, the good of the public, and the dues to one's class or profession."[64] Absolute incompatibility between loyalty to the family and to other social units is difficult to sustain, at least in Nigeria with its strong ties to enduring local traditional authorities and to religious congregations. Yet, it is worth recalling that loyalty to the nation is an extremely battered concept in Nigeria, and that even the relatively stronger constructs of ethnic identity are largely the product of colonialism and the reaction to it. In that context, the belief can grow that "the 'correct order of things' is that actions taken on behalf of 'strangers' should be rewarded . . . From Old Testament times, gifts have always been an honourable and conventional way of showing respect . . . In developing countries, Biblical norms still prevail . . . Corruption enjoys the status of a condemned but understood prodigality." This does not completely explain the rapacious greed with which powerful figures have enriched themselves at public expense. Eker finds that Nigerians share with other modern societies an equation of "success and its public demonstration, especially through great material extravagances." Negative reaction is muted because "the roots of the vast majority are not in the urban centers but in the villages, where the structures of authority are still undisputed."[65]

Political Socialization

We continue the discussion of culture by examining the process through which Nigerians have developed the political beliefs and attitudes just described. This process of acquisition of beliefs and attitudes about politics is known as political socialization. It is commonly studied by looking at the separate and then combined effects of those social institutions that commonly play the greatest role in this process, institutions identified therefore as "agents" of socialization. Universally important agents of socialization include the family, primary and secondary groups, formal education, the media, and government-sponsored activities.[66] A word of caution is in order, however, before we compare the political socialization process in Nigeria with that in well-established liberal democracies.

Analyses of political socialization in the "First World" assume a certain stability of the institutions that are the objects of that process. We treat the fluidity of party alignments in France or the effects of major events such as the Vietnam War in

America as exceptional, whereas in Nigeria people have grown up under political arrangements that shift constantly, even to their very core. Add to this the upheaval of major population shifts toward the city, and of the sudden and dramatic impact of petroleum on the culture as well as on the economy, and the need for a different perspective on socialization is apparent. Nevertheless, there is a universal quality to the importance of the agents of socialization identified above, even as the nature of those agents and the objects of political attitudes and values they shape may differ greatly from those in Europe or North America.

THE FAMILY

Our previous discussion of ethnic identities should not obscure the fact that within these groupings, and of greater significance historically and even today, is family identity. The family, whether nuclear or extended, remains the core unit of political activity in Nigeria. In many Nigerian traditions, families were identified with a particular trade or role in society. Thus, among the Yoruba a family of warriors is called *Jagunjagun*, farmers are *Agbe*, and traders are *Onisowo*. To traditionally minded Nigerians such identification remains important to the determination of one's appropriate role in modern politics. However, parents' level of education is also a critical variable in determining awareness of and interest in the political process.

Many Nigerians have grown up in polygamous families. In Nigeria there is

> **Box 3.8 Terms Describing Marriage to More Than One Spouse**
>
> In anthropological usage, polygamy is a general term for marriage to more than one spouse. *Polygyny* is preferred to describe the marriage of one man to more than one woman (and *polyandry* for the reverse). However, polygamy is the term in general use in Nigeria and elsewhere in English-speaking Africa.

no law preventing a man from taking more than one wife, although Muslims are theoretically limited to a maximum of four and Christians of mainstream denominations to one. All indigenous traditions in Nigeria sanctioned polygamy, and little stigma is attached to the practice. Some Christian denominations in Nigeria enforce monogamy only on those men who hold office in the church. However, in the economic difficulties of the 1980s and 1990s few have the resources to support more than one household and formal polygamy, especially in urban households, is rare.

The fact that "family" is defined broadly in most African societies should be kept in mind when the family unit is considered as a political unit. A politician may be able to count on the support of literally hundreds of individuals based on actual kinship ties, and even larger numbers if one considers as "family" clan affiliations based on a sense of kinship affiliation even where exact genealogical ties cannot be demonstrated, but where there is still a belief in a common ancestor. Kinship provides the most powerful sense of identity and loyalty to many in Nigeria and elsewhere in Africa and is the model (and often the real-world basis) for clientelist relationships.

SCHOOLS

In most contemporary nations, the schools play a central role in developing a sense of community among citizens. This is clearly an important mission in Nigerian schools, and balancing various loyalties is a delicate task for Nigerian educators. Also, formal education is one of the principal benefits Nigerians expect from government. The school certificate is highly regarded throughout the developing world as a means to economic and social advancement, and this is especially true in Nigeria: "It seems safe to say that by the 1930s and 1940s no people in the world placed a higher value on education or regarded its consequences more optimistically than did the inhabitants of this area."[67]

Western education, first brought by missionaries in 1842, was a hundred years old when the colonial administration first directly invested in it. As Nigeria approached independence in the 1950s, policies to achieve free, universal, and compulsory education were quickly elaborated in the southern regions of the country by the first elected legislatures in the early 1950s, and both regions were soon investing massively in expansion of their educational systems, especially at the primary level. Universal Primary Education, or "U.P.E." as it came to be known, was a highly popular campaign slogan, but it also responded to Nigerian idealists who saw mass education as a necessary base for modern nationhood. Education was a regional responsibility at independence, and the education gap between the North and the South appeared to be widening. In 1976, the federal government announced a national policy of U.P.E., the planners of which "thought that education could promote children's views of themselves as Nigerian citizens first and then as a member of an ethnic group. It could also equalize opportunities as citizens all received a basic level of education."[68] The U.P.E. policy led to a common national curriculum of mathematics, science, social studies, religious knowledge (Christian or Islamic), language arts, arts and crafts, and physical education. For each content area a common syllabus was developed.[69]

Beyond that basic agreement, however, Nigeria has struggled with how to shape the curriculum and how to make it available. Into the 1970s, the traditional British curriculum was followed: six years' primary education, five at the secondary level, two years leading to the higher school certificate, and three years to a university degree. Based on a 1973 report, the system was changed to a 6-3-3-4 system, essentially the American model. At the same time, there was an introduction of vocational subjects into the secondary schools, so that secondary graduates would have skills directly relevant to employment. The oil boom of the 1970s stimulated a massive wave of secondary school expansion, and the university system grew from five in 1962 to twenty-seven in 1985; by 1996 there were thirty-six universities, thirteen of them created and supported at the state level. In addition to the universities, the higher education system includes sixty-nine poytechniques and

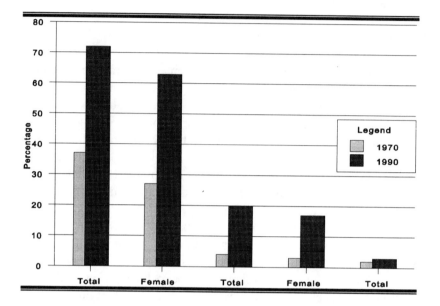

Figure 3.2 Percent of Age Groups Enrolled in School. Source: Federal Ministriy of Education, *Statistics of Education in Nigeria* (Lagos, 1990), p. 7

colleges of technology and of education.

Given the high level of religiosity in Nigeria, it is not surprising that religious groups are asking for permission to establish their own universities. Seventh-Day Adventists, Baptists, and Catholics already run parallel degree programs affiliated with established universities, the Adventists with Andrews University in the United States, the Baptists with the University of Ibadan, and the Catholics with the Catholic University of Kinshasa (Congo Republic). However, the federal government has yet to approve the creation of any private universities.

Even in the prosperous 1970s, the educational boom was challenged by a lack of resources, for there were insufficient properly trained instructors at all levels. With the economic collapse of the 1980s, funds for education dried up, and education suffered at all levels. More than ever, equal access became illusory, a problem that is more acute as one moves from the primary to the secondary and to the post-secondary level. The bias is on the one hand socio-economic—children of the elite occupy a disproportionate share of the seats—and also reflects gender: In

1990, there were seventy-six female pupils in primary school to every one hundred males, and seventy-four to every one hundred males at the secondary level. Figure 3.2 shows that 72 percent of the primary-school-age population was in school in 1990 (compared to 68 percent for sub-Saharan Africa as a whole). Sixty-two percent of males and forty percent of females are literate, which is about at the continent-wide mean. As a result, there has been a substantial reduction in the proportion of political parochials, although there is a widened gap in this respect between North and South. Data by region are not available, but it is clear that the national-level data mask persistent regional disparities: Total attendance figures would be higher, and the gender difference in access to education lower, if the data were for the southern half of the country only. Also, differences in the preparation of teachers and the availability of materials from north to south suggest that the quality of education is also lower in the North. For example, only 37 percent of northern teachers reported that their students had textbooks, compared with 59 percent in the South.[70] There have been indirect political effects of this gap, going back to independence: At that time, as the number of secondary graduates increased in the South, many of them sought jobs in the North, and were embittered at northern rejection. At the same time, northerners grew alarmed at the prospect of being inundated by educated southerners. Differences in educational achievement thus contributed to the resentments that exploded in violence in 1966. More recently, the fact that Christians of the Middle Belt region of the North had greater educational opportunities than others in the Northern region (because of the mission schools there) meant that a large proportion of the officer cadre from the region were from these non-Muslim minority groups, which has been a source of conflict in the military. Northern political dominance in the face of higher educational achievement in the South continues to aggravate interregional political conflict.

Language is an aspect of community building that is almost taken for granted, but decisions on language usage in school can have a major impact on political attitudes. As noted previously, English is the official language of Nigeria, an historical accident resulting from British colonization, and from the use of English in Christian mission schools. English is the vehicle of instruction in Nigeria in secondary and post-secondary school. Furthermore, English is the language of government and, for the most part, of the mass media. Because English is a second language in most Nigerian homes, school plays an especially critical role enabling access to the political system; it is significant, then, that primary-level instruction is generally given in the major indigenous language in a locality, since (Figure 3.2) no more than 20 percent of the population of appropriate age is enrolled in post-primary education. The teaching of English (essentially, as a foreign language) is emphasized at the primary level, but teachers themselves often have limited competence in English. Results of a survey of primary teachers showed that their "facility at comprehending more complex, abstract and/or technical material in English was limited. Therefore, even when such material was available, they chose not to read it because it was usually in English and therefore too difficult for them to comprehend."[71]

As a nation-building effort, the three major indigenous languages— Hausa, Igbo, and Yoruba—are (in principle) also taught through secondary school, and are topics in the Senior School Certificate examinations. (There is frequently a problem in finding qualified teachers who are willing to live in other regions of the country.) Proficiency in English is required for admission to university, where the local languages are used only in programs where they might specifically be required. The

connection between English usage and government activities gives added weight to the usual relationship between education and political efficacy.

Language has never loomed large among the major issues in Nigerian politics, perhaps because the official language is "foreign." However, Nigerians have also been tolerant of linguistic pluralism. When minority leaders expressed concern about the provision for three indigenous languages, the Babangida government approved *twenty-seven* languages for "mother tongue" education, meaning that they could be used in the first three years of elementary school. That this was a symbolic act is seen in the fact that only nine of these languages are written; furthermore, the students in any given locality speak a variety of languages at home, and those speaking minority languages will be disadvantaged. Still, even *symbolic* language tolerance is important in a plural culture.

The reader should not conclude that the language issue has never been raised. In the first year after independence a bill was introduced in parliament that would have made Hausa the country's lingua franca. Chief Anthony Enahoro, from a southern minority group, denounced the proposal:

> . . . I deplore the continuing evidence in this country that people wish to impose their customs, their languages, and even more their ways of life upon the smaller tribes. My people have a language, and that language was handed down through a thousand years of tradition and custom. When the Benin Empire exchanged ambassadors with Portugal many of the new Nigerian languages of today did not exist. How can they now, because the British brought us together, wish to impose their language on us?

The bill did not pass, and the issue was laid to rest. However, in 1990 the executive secretary of the Nigerian Educational Research and Development Council under the Babangida government announced a survey of languages to prepare the country for the adoption of a national or official language; it was said that Hausa, Igbo, and Yoruba would qualify as candidates. That initiative also did not result in action, and the three major languages continue to be taught.[72] Nigeria is among a large number of Third World countries who are fated to live with the colonial tongue as an official language, simply because in this way no particular group is advantaged over the rest.

Whatever the effect of intentional socialization in the schools, the very fact of being there is centrally important in shaping one's political self. Studies of political culture since the seminal *Civic Culture* have affirmed the effect of education as a predictor of political participation. This is especially true in less-developed countries, where the cultural gap between those with and without formal education is especially great. A late-1960s survey of Nigerians from the three southern regions (at that time) found the relationship between the most basic levels of education and interest in politics (Table 3.3) to be extremely strong. However, in a 1997 survey, respondents with no formal education claimed a *greater* interest in politics than those with an education. Although the 1997 study differs from the earlier survey in that it includes the north, Nigerians would point out that the educated population has grown both fearful to discuss politics openly, and apathetic about the political process because of frequent disappointments.

THE MASS MEDIA

The presence of a lively and politically independent press goes back at least to Azikiwe's *West African Pilot*. By the time of independence there were a considerable number of competing newspapers in Nigeria (virtually all published in Lagos, then distributed nationwide). The country is rather unique in the less-

Table 3.3 Nigeria: "High" Interest in Politics by Education

Educational level	Percent "High" on Interest in Politics late '60s	1997
None (illiterate):	7%	37%
Some Primary:	31	18
Primary plus:	81	28-31

Source: Verba, 1978:27; Opinion Analysis, USIA, 1997.

developed world in the variety of privately owned newspapers and magazines, reflecting a diversity of viewpoints. At present the newspaper with the largest circulation is the *Daily Times*, which claims a readership of 100,000. It is likely that the combined circulation of daily newspapers is less than one million, or about one per one hundred people.

The political effect of the press is limited in a country with 58 percent adult illiteracy. However, among those with a secondary education or greater—those most likely to be politically active—reading a paper has been almost a daily ritual. In a 1964 survey of southern Nigerian schoolchildren, between 73 and 100 percent of respondents (the percentage varying according to level in school), reported that newspapers were their principal source of information about politics.[73] Today, newspaper readership includes all politically active Nigerians, and the perspectives in the press undoubtedly have a wide word-of-mouth circulation. (As of 1993, word-of-mouth was cited as a news source by 86 percent of Nigerians.) Also in 1993, 45 percent of adult Nigerians reported that newspapers were a usual source of national information, but the proportion was 91 percent of college graduates and 63 percent of urban dwellers.[74] Conversations among educated Nigerians would be difficult to imagine without newspapers. In recent years, access has been limited by cost, and papers must be shared: Although a newspaper at 50 naira (60 cents U.S.) or a magazine at 100 naira ($1.25) is inexpensive by Western standards, these prices put the purchase of print media out of reach of many students and urban workers. Also, since 1995 the government has decreed that state funds cannot be used to buy newspapers, thus ending the practice where a government office or university department would buy a copy to which the staff had access. Governments have made sure they had a voice in what has, at least until recently, been an independent press: The government controlled the *Daily Times* during the Babangida years, which, according to Wole Soyinka, was full of whatever fabrications the regime found useful.[75]

The 1964 survey found that the second most important source of political information was radio. Twenty-nine years later, the order was different: Virtually all adult Nigerians (99 percent) get news of their country from domestic radio, and 64 percent of them list domestic television as a source of news. This reflects the fact that radio ownership is almost universal (90 percent of households own at least one radio, compared with 70 percent in 1989). Television sets are found in 50 percent of households, up from 38 percent in 1989.[76] Until 1992, radio and television were state-controlled, and thus faithful purveyors of the government's "spin" on political events. Although there are now a few private television and radio stations which compete financially with the state-owned channels, they do not show great political independence. However, the shortwave broadcasts from BBC, the Voice of America, and other outside sources have been available as independent sources for decades; today, indigenous television must compete with satellite news services. Although only a tiny proportion of the country's population had direct access to shortwave broadcasts, or now have access to satellite telecasts (estimated at 4 percent of college graduates), such advanced communications technology does permit outside views of Nigerian events to be introduced into the country, then spread by word-of-mouth or reflected in the print media. A 1997 survey finds that

61 percent of Nigerians rely on foreign media "for information about internationally accepted principles of democracy and citizenship," with the BBC the most trusted sources (39 percent) followed by CNN (16 percent).[77]

Under the more authoritarian regimes there has been a high level of tension between government and the press, and the life of a journalist has not been easy. Many have been arrested, especially since passage of the Public Officers (Protection Against False Accusation) Decree of 1984, which "made it an offence to make any false report in the press or to bring the federal government or public officers into ridicule or disrepute through the media. As in other countries, the government began using the supply of newsprint as a way to control the press.[78] In one case in 1986 a prominent critic of the government was killed by a letter bomb. Since 1994, particularly under Abacha, many newspapers have been shut down (three media companies, controlling fifteen publications, were banned between June and August of that year), and the rest frightened into silence. The regime points to the existence of independent newspapers as evidence of press freedom in Nigeria, but journalists for these publications report that they are routinely surveilled; editors are regularly arrested, and photographers and reporters have been beaten by police while on the job. Eighteen journalists were arrested or detained in 1995 alone.[79] Journalists allege that government security agents are responsible for two arson attacks on news organizations, and the near death by gunfire of a newspaper publisher between December 1995 and February 1996.[80] In Wole Soyinka's judgment:

> Apart from the valiant remnant of that press, functioning with an erratic sword grazing its neck, the nation's voice is contracted to two newspapers run by the government. . .as well as the electronic media, across which that dictatorship has placed a stranglehold . . .But the existence of a vigorous risk-taking underground press speaks volumes, and this remains one of those signs that inform us that the combative spirit of a nation is not yet extinguished.[81]

A newcomer to the media scene is the underground "Radio Democrat," which now calls itself "Radio Kudirat" in honor of the murdered wife of Moshood Abiola. Radio Kudirat harshly criticized the Abacha regime and claims to represent the National Democratic Coalition (NADECO), a human rights organization. Its broadcasts from a secret location (or locations) is an indication of the sense of oppression now felt in the country. The government has so far been unable to find and permanently suppress it. It is rumored that the government has serious reservations about the spread of electronic mail across Nigeria's borders, but has so far been unable or unwilling to eliminate it.

THE STATE

The Nigerian government has at its disposal the modern means of mass communication that oil revenues have allowed it to develop to a high degree. Periodically it launches propaganda campaigns on one issue or another, as in Operation Feed the Nation and Free Primary Education (1970s), the War Against Indiscipline (WAI) (1980s), or the Road Safety Operation (1990), for which the government recruited author Wole Soyinka as director.

It is not always easy to determine whether the motive for a regime-sponsored propaganda campaign is sincere or cynical. However, the WAI campaign was launched within a few months of the military takeover of 1983—since which time Nigeria has been constantly under military rule. It coincided with military tribunals bringing corruption charges against officials of the Second Republic and firing civil servants, and with efforts to intimidate the press. The WAI went through a series of themes. The first was "queuing"—instilling the habit of waiting in line for public services and accommodations rather than crowding to the desk. The next theme was "work ethic." The third was "patriotism and nationalism," the fourth "anticorruption," and the fifth "environmental sanitation." Perhaps because it was essentially unfunded, and thus not open to corruption, WAI was popular. It was sometimes promoted harshly, as by "WAI brigades" acting on their own or increased harassment by police. There was visual evidence of effectiveness in implementing the last theme, in the increased cleanliness of state capital streets and the removal of hawkers and persons in the street trades.[82]

In a more general sense, the government also makes decisions on language policy and applies them. Language interacts with ethnic and national identity, as in the decision to offer Yoruba, Igbo, and Hausa in schools nationwide, while promoting national identity through its use of English as the official language of government. The latter policy, without a practical alternative, has the effect of distancing government from the uneducated rural populations.

As part of its "transition program" to democracy (1986-1993), the Babangida regime inaugurated a "Directorate for Social Mobilization," also known as MAMSER (Mass Mobilization for Self-Reliance, Economic Recovery, and Social Justice.) MAMSER's ostensible purpose was to shape a political culture at the mass level that would be congenial to a democratic system. It planned the distribution of its messages through rallies, lectures, advertising, drama, school curricula, and music. Considerable resources were devoted to this effort: Offices were established in each state and a full-time "social mobilization officer" was named to each of the (then) 453 local governments. However, many questioned MAMSER's effectiveness, and some critics questioned its sincerity, and that of the government that sponsored it, as well. The purpose of MAMSER in the Abacha regime was unclear, and in 1995 it was abolished and replaced by the National Orientation Agency (NOA). The NOA has a much smaller cadre of personnel than did MAMSER, and their financial support is assigned to the local governments. In 1990 the Babangida regime had also established a Centre for Democratic Studies (CDS) in Abuja, to conduct research on democratization and present seminars on that topic for government officials. From an extensive central compound in a rural corner of the Federal Capital Territory, the CDS ran training seminars for thousands of local government councilors and chairmen on democratic governance as well as on administrative and fiscal procedures. Similar training was provided to the officers at all levels of the two political parties created by the Babangida administration (see Chapter Six). Later, state and federal officials received the same training. As it did with MAMSER, the Abacha regime allowed the CDS to remain in existence for two more years, perhaps as a form of "lip service" to democratization. Finally, the CDS was closed in 1996 and its facilities in the Federal Capital Territory were made available to the Law School formerly in Lagos (which provides the final year of

training required of any person who seeks to be admitted to the Nigerian bar). Staff members of the CDS either returned to their prior positions or were assigned to various ministries.

Efforts to promote a "cult of personality" around General Abacha are unprecedented in Nigerian experience. Abacha lapel pins were necessary apparel for army officers; television sets, wrist watches, and sacks of rice appeared under the Abacha brand, and "new publications began weaving tales of the miraculous birth and heroic deeds of the President, while billboards bearing the slogan 'Abacha is the Answer' were cropping up. . ."[83]

Cooperation with this campaign of personal glorification was overwhelmingly based on opportunism or fear, not belief. Indeed, Nigerian political attitudes are far more likely to be affected by everyday contact with the state than by direct, intentional efforts of the state to shape attitudes. In Nigeria's federal system, that effect will come largely through contact with local officials. Rural residents without English-language proficiency will find that, even, at the local level, officials are much more educated than they, and generally expect and get deference as rural citizens seek services or deal with regulations. Government is remote, and must be approached through some form of informal mediation. For those with formal education, contact with local government is relatively simple; furthermore, because Nigerian policy is to hire civil servants from their home areas, there is neither a social nor a cultural difference between educated citizen and public servant. Nigerians have come to expect to pay for expeditious service, and while they are aware of norms of honesty and ethics that are higher than the behavior they perceive, they are not unduly scandalized by the difference. Perceptions of policy makers at all levels are not usually the result of direct contact. Nigerians generally express great cynicism about the motivations of policy makers, civilian or military, but for the most part this results from media accounts of venality and corruption. Whether through direct contact or media portrayal, they most often get what they expect from governmental officials, which of course becomes a self-fulfilling prophecy:

The Complete Nigerian civil servant unlike his predecessor is not self-effacing behind an array of coded titles. You meet him here, you see him there, and you talk to him yonder. He is eager to make your acquaintance. He takes you into little corners to confide in you.

For instance, he tells you how much it would cost you to have your file speeded up, which I think is very nice.[84]

CONTACT WITH URBAN LIFE

Massive population movements from the countryside to the cities is a nearly universal characteristic of less-developed countries. In the Nigerian case, this movement was accelerated by the oil boom of the 1980s, as employment opportunities opened in construction and in other economic activities stimulated by the massive infusion of wealth into the economy. From 1970 to 1991, Nigeria's urban population increased from 20 percent to 36 percent. The subsequent economic downturn left many of the new urban residents in an economically marginal position that was all the more precarious because they were removed from the possibility of subsistence production that is the option of peasants when the demand for marketed goods is low or prices are artificially held down. In such an environment, the urban residents are said to be "available" for political mobilization; they are physically close to political institutions that might be held responsible for their problems, and communication about political events can spread quickly. In Nigeria, political unrest is directly felt in Lagos, where most national political institutions are located. This political consideration is seen to have contributed to the regime's decision to move the federal government to a new capital in Abuja, much farther to the north.

POPULAR THEATER, TRADITIONAL MUSIC

As of the early 1980s, there were more than one hundred commercial theater troupes touring the Yoruba-speaking region of Nigeria, playing generally to packed houses, and leading to television and radio spin-offs and photoplay magazines. The content of the scripts performed by these groups is rarely directly political. However, one theme that is very prominent is wealth. Some plays make a distinction between riches that result from honest work and the ill-gotten gains of robbers and schemers. They suggest that "there are no poor people, only lazy people," and "if you stay honest and put your trust in God, he *will* make you rich; you *will* become wealthy." Thus, popular theater did not contribute to the emergence of class consciousness or class antagonisms, but rather reinforced a conservative interpretation of the massive inequalities in private wealth.[85]

Some political messages are put to music: During the Biafran War, musicians pleaded with Biafran leader Ojukwu to negotiate an end to the suffering:

Yoruba:	Emeka lo bebe boya Gowon yio gba--Zce.
	Ori Okere O koko la wo O
	Bawi fomo eni agbo O, Ojukwu O.
English:	Emeka, go and plead with Gowon, perhaps he will concede,
	A squirrel's head is always good on a plate,
	If a child is warned he must listen: Ojukwu, please listen.

The music was all the more traditional in that the words were conveyed by talking drum. Since Yoruba is a tonal language, it can be "spoken" by drums. In southwestern Nigeria, drums have long been used to call people's attention to an urgent problem.

RELIGION

Training in the predominant religious denominations of Nigeria is not necessarily oriented toward the state or political activity, but because of the important role of religion in many Nigerians' lives, it is not surprising that religious institutions and religious leaders may affect political orientations. A dramatic example addressed earlier has been the activity against political authorities in northern Nigeria inspired by religious leaders Alhaji Mohammed Marwa Maitatsine (Box 3.4) and Ibrahim El-Zak Zaky. In the 1970s, the rapid urbanization of the country produced a marginalized stratum of youth in the towns and cities of northern Nigeria. Fundamentalist Muslim reformers were active at the time, with financial support from Saudi Arabia and other Arab countries. The fundamentalist message, especially as preached in the Izala (short for the Society for the Removal of Heresy and Reinstatement of Tradition) movement proved appealing to the young urban migrants, and directed them religiously and politically against the dominant leadership in the North. They were thus mobilized into the region's political factionalism:

> Religion is a powerful instrument of mobilization in Northern Nigeria. . . ambitious politicians and local notables supported the creation of the Izala movement. . .support for a religious movement by a politician offers political rewards. This is all the more so given the fact that religious leaders mediate between the politicians and the civil society. Moreover, with the pledge by the military to hand over power in 1979, and with the

heightened inter- and intra-party competition, one observed an intensification of contacts between politicians, local notables and religious leaders.[86]

CONCLUSION

This exploration of the many facets of Nigerian political culture and the socialization process that has produced it is based on the assumption that the culture must be understood if one is to predict what the nature of future Nigerian regimes will be, or whether there will even continue to be a single Nigerian state. But just how critical is the depth and breadth of belief in such democratic value as the legitimacy of opposition to the likelihood that Nigeria will achieve a stable democracy? How important are the beliefs of ordinary citizens, as compared to the beliefs of educated and wealthy elites? How critical to stability and to the continued existence of Nigeria are the divisions we have identified along ethnic and religious lines to stable democracy, or even the continuance of the state? We will return to these questions in the concluding chapter, after we have described the nature of the political process and those who participate in it.

END NOTES

1. Gabriel A. Almond and G. Bingham Powell, *Comparative Politics: A Theoretical Framework* (New York: HarperCollins, 1996), p. 43.

2. Michael Bratton, "Civil Societies and Political Transitions in Africa," in John W. Harbeson, Donald Rothchild, and Naomi Chazan, eds. *Civil Society and the State in Africa* (Boulder, CO: Lynne Rienner, 1994), p. 56.

3. Crawford Young, *The African Colonial State in Comparative Perspective*, p. 223. The internal quote is from V. Y. Mudimbe, *The Invention of Africa: Gnosis, Philosophy, and the Orders of Knowledge* (Bloomington: Indiana University Press, 1988), p. 1.

4. Barbara F. Grimes, ed. *Ethnologue: Languages of the World,* 11th edition (Dallas, TX: Summer Institute of Liguistics, 1988).

5. Young, *The African Colonial State in Comparative Perspective*, pp. 232-233.

6. The results of this arbitrary division of a civilization by French and English colonizers is described in *Hausaland Divided* by William Miles (Ithaca: Cornell University Press, 1994)..

7. Abner Cohen, *Custom and Politics in Urban Africa: A Study of Hausa Migrants in Yoruba Towns* (Berkeley: University of California Press, 1969), p. 9.

8. Crawford Young, *The Politics of Cultural Pluralism* (Madison: The University of Wisconsin Press, 1976), p. 277.

9. Young, *The Politics of Cultural Pluralism*, pp. 277-278.

10. Miles, *Hausaland Divided* , p. 46.

11. Young, *The Politics of Cultural Pluralism*, p. 278.

12. Olowu, "Centralization, Self-Governance, and Development in Nigeria," p. 201.

13. See S. M. Lipset, "The Social Requisites of Democracy Revisited," *American Sociological Review* 59 (February), pp. 93-139.

14. Soyinka, *The Open Sore of a Continent* (New York: Oxford University Press, 1996), pp. 6-7; Miles, *Elections in Nigeria: A Grassroots Perspective* (Boulder, CO: Lynne Rienner, 1988)..

15. Phoebe Ottenberg, 'The Afikpo Ibo of Eastern Nigeria," in James L. Gibbs Jr., ed. *Peoples of Africa* (New York: Holt, Rinehart and Winston, 1965), p. 6.

16. Young, *The Politics of Cultural Pluralism*, pp. 278-279.

17. P.C. Lloyd, "The Yoruba of Nigeria," in Gibbs, ed. *Peoples of Africa,* p. 551; Young, *The Politics of Cultural Pluralism*, p. 279.

18. Bohannon, "The Tiv of Nigeria," pp. 543-544; Okwudiba Nnoli, *Ethnic Politics in Nigeria* (Enugu: Fourth Dimension Publishers, 1980), pp. 237-239.

19. Claude Ake, "Rethinking African Democracy," *Journal of Democracy* 2 (1, Winter), p. 34.

20. Claude E. Welch Jr. and Marc Sills, "The Martyrdom of Ken Saro-Wiwa and the Future of Ogoni Self-Determination," *Fourth World Bulletin* 5 (Nos. 1–2, Spring/Summer), pp. 5-6.

21. See the conclusion of Veronica Nmoma in "Ethnic Conflict, Constitutional Engineering and Democracy in Nigeria," in Harvey Glickman, ed. *Ethnic Conflict and Democratization in Africa* (Atlanta: African Studies Association Press, 1995) p. 345.

22. P.C. Lloyd, *Africa in Social Change* (London: Penguin, 1972), p. 210.

23. John N. Paden, "Nigerian Muslim Perspectives on Religion, Society, and Communication with the Western World," (Washington, D.C.: Office of Research, U.S. Information Agency, 1990), p. 8.

24. Ronald Inglehart, *Modernization and Postmodernization* (Princeton, NJ: Princeton University Press, 1997), pp. 84, 86.

25. Samuel P. Huntington, *The Clash of Civilizations and the Remaking of World Order* (New York: Simon and Schuster, 1996), p. 255-56.

26. Almond and Powell, *Comparative Politics: A Theoretical Framework*, pp. 53-54.

27. Naomi Chazan and Victor T. LeVine, "Africa and the Middle East: Patterns of Convergence and Divergence," in John W. Harbeson and Donald Rothchild, eds. *Africa in World Politics* (Boulder: Westview Press, 1991), p. 208.

28. Barbara J. Callaway, *Muslim Hausa Women in Nigeria* (Syracuse: Syracuse University Press, 1987), p. 93.

29. Paul M. Lubeck, "Islamic Protest and Oil-Based Capitalism: Agriculture, Rural Linkages, and Urban Popular Movements in Northern Nigeria," in Watts, ed. *State, Oil, and Agriculture in Nigeria.*

30. Forrest, *Politics and Economic Development in Nigeria*, p. 117.

31. Chazan and Levine, "Africa and the Middle East," p. 207.

32. See Mir Zohair Husain, *Global Islamic Politics* (New York: HarperCollins, 1995), p. 211.

33. Murray Last, "Tradition musulmane et diplomatie," in Bach, Egg and Philippe, eds. *Le Nigéria: Un Pouvoir en puissance*, pp. 272-73.

34. David Pollock and Elaine El Assal, eds., *In the Eye of the Beholder: Muslim and Non-Muslim Views of Islam, Islamic Politics, and Each Other* (Washington, D.C.: Office of Research and Media Reactions, U.S. Information Service, 1995), pp. 45-51. The Nigerian respondents (n=100), randomly drawn from a list of "opinion leaders" in Lagos, were surveyed in September-October 1994.

35. Murray Last, "Tradition musulmane et diplomatie," p. 271.

36. Lubeck, "Islamic Protest and Oil-Based Capitalism," pp. 270, 285-89.

37. P.C. Lloyd, *Africa in Social Change*, p. 81.

38. Young, *The African Colonial State in Comparative Perspective*, p. 241.

39. See Eric A. Nordlinger, *Soldiers in Politics* (Englewood Cliffs, NJ: Prentice-Hall, 1977), pp. 37-39, and sources cited therein.

40. Forrest, *Politics and Economic Development in Nigeria*, updated edition, p. 3.

41. Peter Ekeh, "Colonialism and Development of Citizenship," in Onigu Otite, ed., *Themes in African Social and Political Thought* (Enugu, Fourth Dimension Publishers, 1978), pp. 318-319, quoted in Tunji Olagunju, Adele Jinadu and Sam Oyovbaire, *Transition to Democracy in Nigeria (1985-1993)*, p. 39.

42. See the discussion of *process propensities* in Gabriel A. Almond and G. Bingham Powell, *Comparative Politics Today: A World View* (New York: HarperCollins, 1996), pp.37-39.

43. Sidney Verba, "The Parochial and the Polity," in Verba and Lucien W. Pye, eds. *The Citizen and Politics* (Stamford, CT: Greylock Publishers, 1978), pp. 3–28.

44. Soyinka, *The Open Sore of a Continent*, pp. 130-131.

45. Soyinka, *The Open Sore of a Continent*, p. 131-132.

46. Robert A. Dahl, *After the Revolution* (New Haven, CT: Yale University Press, 1971).

47. Larry Diamond, "Nigeria: Pluralism, Statism and the Struggle for Democracy," in Diamond *et al*, eds. *Democracy: A*frica (Boulder, CO: Lynne Rienner, 1988), p. 40-43.

48. W. Ivor Jennings, *The Approach to Self-Government*, (Cambridge: Cambridge University Press, 1956), p. 56.

49. Bratton and van de Walle, *Democratic Experiments in Africa*, p. 11.

50. Diamond, "Nigeria: Pluralism, Statism and the Struggle for Democracy."

51. Paul Beckett and James O'Connell, *Education and Power in Nigeria* (London: Hodder and Stoughton, 1977); "Nigerians Lack Wide Understanding of Democracy," *Opinion Analysis* (Washington, D.C.: Office of Research and Media Reactions, U.S. Information Agency, April 30, 1997). This report is based on a national survey of 2130 adults, conducted by the marketing research firm Research International.

52. Russell J. Dalton, *Citizen Politics* (Chatham, NJ: Chatham House, 1996), pp. 15-39, especially 35-37.

54. See Kamene Okonjo, "The Dual-Sex Political System in Operation," in Nancy J. Hafkin and Edna Bay, eds. *Women in Africa* (Stanford: Stanford University Press, 1976), p. 45.

55. Lloyd, "The Yoruba of Nigeria," p. 565.

56. Kole Ahmed Shettima, "Engendering Nigeria's Third Republic," *African Studies Review* 38 (3, December), p. 85.

57. Luckham, *The Nigerian Military*, pp. 113-114.

58. Chinua Achebe, *The Trouble with Nigeria* (Enugu: Fourth Dimension Press, 1983), p. 42.

59. L. W. J. C. Huberts, "Expert Views on Public Corruption Around the Globe," (Amsterdam: PSPA Publications, Department of Political Science and Public Administration, Vrije Universiteit Amsterdam, 1996), pp. 9-10.
60. Antony Goldman, "Same Salary, Three Lifestyles: Corruption's Toll on Nigeria," *Christian Science Monitor*, February 5, 1997, p. 8.

61. "Nigerians Lack Wide Understanding of Democracy," *Opinion Analysis*, April 30, 1997.

62. For a simple definition of corruption, see Stanislav Andreski, "Kleptocracy as a System of Government in Africa, p. 346; also, M. M. McMullan, "Corruption in the Public Services of British Colonies and Ex-Colonies in West Africa," in Arnold J. Heidenheimer, ed. *Political Corruption: Readings in Comparative Analysis* (New York: Holt, Rinehart and Winston, 1970), p. 319.

63. Samuel Huntington, *Political Order in Changing Societies*, (New Haven: Yale University Press, 1968), p. 69; Robert Klitgaard, *Controlling Corruption* (Bloomington: Indiana University Press, 1988).

64. Varda Eker, "On the Origins of Corruption: Irregular Incentives in Nigeria," *Journal of Modern African Studies* 19 (1), pp. 175-76.

65. Eker, "On the Origins of Corruption," pp. 177-178.

66. The following discussion draws on Crawford Young's treatment of socialization in his chapter on "Politics in Africa" in the Fifth Edition of Almond and Powell, *Comparative Politics Today*.

67. Abernethy, *The Political Dilemma of Popular Education* (Stanford: Stanford University Press, 1969), p. 18. The following description of educational development draws on this same source.

68. Cynthia S. Sunal, Dennis W. Sunal, and Osayimense Ose, "Nigerian Primary School Teachers' Perceptions of Schooling During the Second Decade of Universal Primary Education," *African Studies Review* 37 (3, December), p. 52.

69. Sunal, Sunal, and Ose, "Nigerian Primary School Teachers' Perceptions of Schooling," p. 59.

70. Sunal, Sunal, and Ose, pp. 59, 61.

71. Sunal, Sunal, and Ose, pp. 62-64.

72. F. Niyi Akinnaso, "The National Language Question and Minority Language Rights in Africa: A Nigerian Case Study," in Ronald Cohen, Goran Hyden and Winston P. Nagar, eds. *Human Rights and Governance in Africa* (Gainesville: University Press of Florida, 1993), pp. 191-92.

73. Abernethy, *The Political Dilemma of Popular Education,* p. 194.

74. Matthew Claeson and Elaine El Assal, eds. *Global Information Sources: Where Audiences Around the World Turn for News and Information,* (Washington: Office of Research and Media Reaction , U.S. Information Agency, 1996), p. 4, citing a BBC-commissioned survey among 3000 adults in sixteen cities and rural areas in four regions: North, Central, Southeast, and Southwest.

75. Soyinka, *The Open Sore of a Continent*, pp. 43-44. Soyinka describes *Daily Times* galley proofs found in Babangida's home after his fall from power featuring the headline WOLE SOYINKA IN SEX AND FRAUD SCANDAL.

76. Claeson and El Assal, eds. *Global Information Sources: Where Audiences Around the World Turn for News and Information*, p. 4

77. "Nigerians Lack Wide Understanding of Democracy," *Opinion Analysis*, April 30, 1997, p. 18.

78. Forrest, *Politics and Economic Development in Nigeria*, p. 97.

79. Leonard R. Sussman, "Press Freedom: Media Controls," *Freedom House* (http://www.freedomhouse.org/Political/sussman.htm).

80. Josh Arinze, "Nigerian Press Under Fire From Military Leaders," Christian Science Monitor (May 22, 1996), p. 19.

81. Soyinka, *The Open Sore of a Continent*, pp. 122-23.

82. Forrest, *Politics and Economic Development in Nigeria*, p. 94.

83. *New York Times*, April 4, 1998.

84. Peter Enahoro, *The Complete Nigerian* (Lagos: Malthouse Press, 1992), p. 121.

85. Karin Barber, "Popular Reactions to the Petro-Naira," *Journal of Modern African Studies* 20 (3), pp. 433, 445-450.

86. Ousmane Kane, "The Rise of Muslim Reformism in Northern Nigeria," in Martin Marty and Scott Appleby, eds. *Accounting for Fundamentalism* (Chicago: University of Chicago Press, 1994).

Chapter 4

POLITICAL RECRUITMENT

- ♦ How are important political decision-makers chosen?
- ♦ Why is the process through which African political leaders emerge so personalistic?
- ♦ Is there a regional bias in Nigeria's national leadership?
- ♦ What have been the roles of elections and civil-service recruitment in the recruitment of Nigerian political elites?
- ♦ What part does clientelism play in the recruitment of these elites?
- ♦ How have military careers translated into political careers?
- ♦ Do civil servants (bureaucrats) still play an important role in political decision-making and administration?
- ♦ Under what conditions can women be politically active?
- ♦ Under what conditions can elections play an important rule in elite recruitment in the future?

Every society, even the most democratic, has a relatively small number of individuals with major roles in the making of political decisions. According to one study of African politics, the leaders of African states rise through a system of "personal rule." Political elites are not chosen in such a system through impersonal rules, but through relatively unstructured processes that often deteriorate into fights. Most of the regimes Nigeria has known, especially under military rule, would fall under a particular category of personal rule known as "princely rule." In this system the ruler is:

> a political strongman who at least temporarily succeeds in dominating everyone else and in effect transforming politics into administration—"autocratic rule."[1]

Some might be tempted to see the Abacha regime, with its more authoritarian style, as having approached the category of "tyrannical rule," in which rulers and their supporters "conduct themselves in a wholly abusive and unrestrained manner." But the very scale and complexity of the country may prevent the most rapacious leaders in Nigeria from matching the excesses of an Idi Amin (Uganda, 1971-1979) or Jean Bedel Bokassa (Central African Republic, 1966-1979).

Personal rule comes about from the very newness of a state, its lack of an institutional tradition, or a shared political tradition or political culture. The origins of Nigeria and other African states as colonial constructs—that is, without a precolonial identity—virtually guaranteed that they would pass through some period of personal rule.

We will now identify the individuals who have headed the political elites of the Nigerian polity, and the factors and procedures that determine why they rose to power.

All the chief executives of Nigeria since independence are identified in Table 4.1. Several conclusions are apparent: First, northerners have dominated the leadership of the country under both civilian and military rule, in the first case because census and voter enrollment figures show that the population of the North is about the same as in the East and West combined, and in the case of the military regimes, because of increasing dominance of the officer corps by northerners. This imbalance in the military was clearly observed in the Buhari regime of 1983-1984, and was temporarily redressed in Babangida's broadened Armed Forces Ruling Council. However, reshuffling in 1989 led to new public perceptions of northern dominance. (Some northerners use ethnic stereotypes to defend their dominance, saying that the Igbos are entrepreneurs, the Yorubas administrators. . .and the northerners born leaders!)[2]

In our consideration of elite recruitment, we must go beyond national executives, cabinet members, and ruling councils to consider the recruitment of state or regional and local elites as well. At independence in 1960, the departing colonial power—while they could still impose procedures that had evolved in the British context—required a transfer of authority through elections. How was it determined who would stand for election? Political parties had formed around the independence movements (and around those, as in the North, that sought to prepare for a perhaps unwelcome independence). The leaders of those parties were the nationalist elites who had learned the vocabulary and metaphors of British colonial figures, missionaries, and teachers, and who now based their claim to power on their familiarity with "external models of rule and development." "Confrontation of the colonial state with a catalogue of its iniquities had earned the right to succession; the elite's rule was justified by a schooled vision denied to the unlettered masses. The schoolroom, however, was the colonial state."[3] In fact, younger idealists in Nigeria criticized the first generation of leaders for their uneducated, rural, old-fashioned behavior; they did not sufficiently resemble the British model! And in Achebe's novel *A Man of the People*, an idealistic educated young man fights the power of a

Dates	Name	Title	Ethnicity	Cause of Departure
1960-Jan. 1966	Tafawa Balewa	Prime Minister	Hausa-Fulani (North)	Coup (killed)
1963-Jan. 1966	Nnamdi Azikiwe	President [appointed]	Igbo (East)	Coup (Removed)
Jan.-July 1966	Aguiyi Ironsi	Military Head of State	Igbo (East)	Coup (killed)
July 1966-1975	Yakubu Gowon	Military Head of State	Middle Belt of Northern region	Coup (removed)
1975-1976	Murtala Muhammed	Military Head of State	Hausa-Fulani (North)	Coup (killed)
1976-1979	Olusegun Obasanjo	Military Head of State	Yoruba (Southwest)	Handed power to civilian government
1979-1983	Shehu Shagari	President	Hausa-Fulani (North)	Coup (removed)
1983-1985	Muhammed Buhari	Military Head of State	Hausa-Fulani (North)	Coup (removed)
1985-1993	Ibrahim Babangida	Military Head of State	Gwari (North)	Forced out of office
Aug.-Nov. 1993	Ernest Shonekan	interim Head of State [appointed]	Yoruba (Southwest)	Forced out of office
Nov. 1993 - May 1998	Sani Abacha	Head, Provisional Ruling Council	Kanuri (North)	died in office
May 1998	Abdulsalam Abubakar	Head, Provisional Ruling Council	Gwari (North)	

Table 4.1 Nigerian Chief Executives, 1960-1998

corrupt politician of the older generation, whose party newspaper launches this attack upon the young intellectuals:

> Let us now and for all time extract from our body-politic as a dentist extracts a stinking tooth all those decadent stooges versed in text-book economics and aping the white man's mannerisms and way of speaking. We are proud to be Africans. Our true leaders are not those intoxicated with their Oxford, Cambridge or Harvard degrees but those who speak the language of the people. Away with the damnable and expensive university

education which only alienates an African from his rich and ancient culture and puts him above his people. . .[4]

Long before they championed the election of executives and legislative bodies, colonial authorities introduced the concept of merit-based appointment into the civil service, and appropriate values and practices have certainly affected recruitment into government service. Nevertheless, most Nigerian traditions of public service require that more personal, particularistic values also play a role. The process was described thirty years ago to anthropologist Ronald Cohen by a young civil servant in Maiduguri in the far northeast of Nigeria:

> If you want a job in the. . .department, one of your relatives should find the name of a person in the department who is known to help people. Your relative then goes to greet him in the evening and gives him some money and perhaps other gifts. The man who can help then tells your relative to come back at such and such a time and he will let him know the result. Then he will try to find a job in the department, probably by using some of the money your relative gave him. Then the job is yours. . .sometimes it takes a long time.[5]

Recruitment into political positions at the local level generally has excluded "strangers," even though they may be long-time residents of a community and, of course, Nigerian citizens. There have been some exceptions: Ever since the 1950s, the Ibadan city council has allowed any resident of the municipality to stand for a council seat; in some cases, Hausas, Ijebus (a non-Ibadan Yoruba group), and immigrants from Edo and Delta states in the Southeast competed successfully. In Jos, in Nigeria's Middle Belt, two Igbo residents of the city were elected to the Jos Local Government Council in the early 1990s. What this means is that where "stranger" elements in the population are sufficiently numerous and the council is elected by districts, they can run and win. In most places, however, regulations have expressly limited candidacy to indigenous candidates. In addition to simple democratic fairness, the advantage of creating a multiethnic council is that it stimulates a sense of identity and participation in the community on the part of populations that are otherwise forever excluded. The overriding characteristic of recruitment into political or administrative office, however, has been, in the words of the 1978 constitution, the effort faithfully to "reflect the federal character of Nigeria"—that is, to fill positions so as to have a government at every level that is an ethnic microcosm of the locality or state it controls, and to have equal representation at the federal level. The 1978 constitution took concrete steps in this direction in requiring that there be at least one minister from each state in the federal cabinet, and more generally provided that there "be no predominance of persons from a few states or from a few ethnic or other sectional groups in [the federal government] or in any of its agencies."[6] It was hoped that through this quota system interethnic peace could at last be realized. As we shall see in our discussion of structure, the latest constitutional proposals include the requirement that the top elected offices at the federal, state and local levels be rotated through a number of geographic zones, to ensure that every group will eventually take a turn at leadership. Unfortunately, because Nigerians have no official "ethnic" identity— they are legally simply Nigerians residing in given states and local government areas—federal character is not based on personal ethnicity, but on origin by state.

With well over two hundred ethnic identities in the country, allocations of positions based on federal character do not necessarily represent minorities within states. In a complex political structure, "fair" allocation is also not obvious: The Ogoni and others claim to be underrepresented in Rivers State, with two of seven cabinet commissioners, two directors-general of twenty-nine, and two of three federal commissioners from the state. Other people looking at the same numbers believe they are overrepresented.[7]

Competence for administration (as measured by education, experience, and other "objective" criteria) mixes with influence based on clientelist networks and ethnic balance in a variety of patterns to produce the political elites of Nigeria.

The Military as a Political Elite

In the early years of independence, Nigeria's political elite was not well established, and was relatively open to entry and advancement by ambitious young men. Among the paths to power, a military career ranked relatively low in prestige, especially among educated southerners. On an impressionistic basis, Luckham found that the earliest generation of military officers were from relatively lowly backgrounds: "Farmer, clerk, catechist, trader, primary school teacher, lower paid employee of the government or one of the large public corporations. . .or non-commissioned officers in the army, are all fairly typical of the occupations of their fathers."[8] In an effort to speed the replacement of remaining British officers, the Balewa government actively recruited university graduates into the officer ranks. One result was the introduction of large numbers of educated Igbos into officer ranks; another was the politicization of the army: Three of the first six university graduates to enter the army led the first coup.

Some students of the role of the military in politics and society have identified military officers as "a strong source of anticommunal sentiment. . . The capacities of the military for developing national identifications derive from the unity of its organizational environment. . .men of various regional and ethnic backgrounds are given a common experience and come to think of themselves as Indians, Egyptians, or Nigerians."[9] However, such conclusions exaggerate the effect of military training and experience, which "neither eradicate nor replace communal loyalties. They constitute an additional set of values, the two existing together despite their inherent contradictions."[10]   Because African militaries were developed through the colonial structure, that is, imported from Europe, they, like every other governance structure, were "impregnated by African socio-cultural norms."[11]

Igbo officers in newly independent Nigeria were rapidly promoted based on their educational advantage. Their ideological and nationalistic feelings against a corrupt and ineffective regime coupled by fears that competency-based advancement would give way to quotas for Hausa-Fulanis led to the first coup of 1966 (see Chapter One). In the process, Igbo officers advanced rapidly, but ultimately became the targets of a Hausa reaction.[12]   Still, the Nigerian officer corps has remained multiethnic. A Yoruba general, Olusegun Obasanjo, emerged as the head of state following the assassination of Murtala Muhammed in 1976.   There has been a continued evolution toward the dominance of northern officers, but the process is still incomplete.

Because the military has controlled the country continually since 1983, a commission in one of the armed services has recently come to be seen as the most regular path to political power. It seems that the ethos of the military has changed in this regard. The first coup-makers in 1966 professed great regret at the necessity to intervene, and promised that their stay would be temporary. They were removed

---

Box 4.1 The Story of Ibrahim Babangida.

General Ibrahim Babangida was born in Minna, Niger State. He is identified ethnically as a Gwari, although he is considered by many to be a part of the Hausa-Fulani elite. He joined the army in 1963 and was trained in India, Britain, and the United States.   He was involved in the coups of 1975 and 1984, and personally confronted Lt. Colonel B. S. Dimka, the leader of the 1976 attempted coup that cost the life of General Murtala Muhammed .   Under the Second Republic (1979-1983) he was in charge of operations and military planning, and was a member of the Supreme Military Council under the Muhammed, Obasanjo, and Buhari governments. He led the coup against Buhari, following which he became head of state. Babangida was the only one of Nigeria's military rulers to take the title of President. He narrowly escaped assassination in 1990. In June 1993 he annulled the presidential elections, formed a provisional government, and resigned. He lives in retirement in his hometown, Minna.

---

and killed in the second 1966 coup before their sincerity could be tested. The longevity of General Gowon's regime was made necessary by the need to prosecute the civil war, and then to lay a constitutional framework for civilian rule. When Gowon seemed inclined to settle in for the long term, he was removed, and Generals Murtala Muhammed and Obasanjo set and abided by their 1979 deadline. Thus, through the first period of military rule, although there was serious profit-taking on the part of many military leaders, none of them expected to have long-term political careers.

The second round of military power (1983 to the present), seems to have produced a gradual change in the perspectives of at least some military officers. Many observers have wondered at the military leadership's action in annulling the 1993 presidential election results and in abolishing the state and local elective offices already filled. Most feel that if Abiola had been allowed to assume power, he would have been unable to deal effectively with the country's problems, would quickly have lost an already dubious legitimacy, and would thus have prepared the way for a return of the military with acceptance by the population. As it was, the Abacha regime has faced serious resistance, and has had to rule on the basis of force, at least in much of the southern half of the country. Many assume that his actions, while certainly supported by elements in the North that could not stomach a Yoruba president, also reflect the strong desire of a new generation of military officers to enjoy the fruits of power that come from oil revenues and various forms of "rent-seeking." (Rent-seeking is an economic concept widely applied to the efforts of those occupying public office to obtain income from those who benefit from their decisions on the allocation of resources their positions control. . .essentially through the corruption of public office.) The country has witnessed open jockeying for positions as state governors or chairmen of local governments, which have been allocated according to military rank: National-level offices are usually filled by generals, brigadiers, or colonels; state governors are mostly colonels. After the abolition of elected local councils in 1993, local chairmen were lieutenant colonels and majors, often retired from active service. (This presumably changed with elections held for local chairmen by the Abacha regime in March 1996, although Abacha decreed the next year that he could replace the elected mayors if in his judgment they were "acting contrary to national interests.") While some proportion of the officer cadre prefer a professional military career, it is no longer clear that the politicized officers will willingly give up their offices. Military appointments to government posts also "reflect the federal character of Nigeria," but on the basis of a nationwide allocation: Northern officers are appointed in the northern states, Yorubas and others from the Southwest to states in that region, etc. From one-half to two-thirds of all military personnel still come from the Middle Belt or the South, and given the southern advantage in education, they hold most positions requiring technical knowledge.[13] However, the highest military positions have recently been dominated by northerners, without which Abacha's control of the country could not have been maintained. Even northerners are not always reliable, witness the death sentence that a secret military tribunal meted out to General Shehu Yar'Adua, a native of Katsina, former Vice Chairman of the Supreme Military Council under Obasanjo, a leading candidate for president in 1993, and until early in 1995 reputed to be one of the most influential individuals in the country even after Abacha seized power. (Yar'Adua died in prison December 9, 1997, at the age of 54.) Nor do lower-ranking officers necessarily support those controlling the political system; in the 1993 election, press reports claimed that a majority of junior officers had voted for Abiola.

The views of junior officers are important, because senior officers have begun to follow a pattern of rather early retirement, followed by work with private-sector economic activities. Junior officers now expect to advance rather rapidly to fill the positions created by retirement.[14] This leads to a pattern of elite circulation

---

Box 4.2 The Story of Sani Abacha.

General Sani Abacha was born in 1943 in Kano in northern Nigeria. He joined the army in 1962 and went to Britain for officer training. He held a number of senior military posts, including director of army training. He played important roles in the coups of 1983 (which he announced on the radio) and 1985. He was an ally of Babangida, appointed by him to chief of Defense Staff and chairman of the Joint Chiefs in 1990. After the annulment of the 1993 presidential election, Abacha was named defense minister, the only military member in the interim government of Ernest Shonekan. In November, 1993, Abacha dismissed Shonekan and created his own Provisional Ruling Council, with himself as chief of state.

Abacha claimed to be preparing the country for a return to civilian rule with the election of a president in October, 1998, but most observers agreed that he was structuring the situation so as to himself become president. He was prevented from achieving this objective by his death on June 8, 1998, reportedly of a heart attack.

Sources: Forrest: Politics and Economic Development in Nigeria, pp. 239, 240; Political Leaders in Black Africa, p. 1

---

which does not, however, necessarily lead to an end of military rule, as new generations of officers appear demanding their turn to take advantage of political power for personal enrichment. Because junior officers often have not waited for a return to civilian rule before they stage their own coup, Abacha reassigned junior officers with greater frequency than previously, in order to reduce their ability to organize a revolt. Abacha was himself probably Nigeria's most experienced coup leader, having taken a leading role in three of them and having put down two coups in 1990 and 1995; with him at the top, military coups became a less likely avenue of advancement to leadership. In December 1997 the government announced the discovery of a coup plot against Abacha, and launched a wave of arrests beginning with the chief of general staff, Lt. General Oladipo Diya and eventually over one hundred more mostly military conspirators. Diya and most of the other detainees were Yorubas, and the Yoruba presence in the armed forces was from that point seriously diminished.

Abacha made some attempts to achieve a wider legitimacy. Like all military leaders before him, Abacha felt compelled to promise an eventual return to elected civilian rule, even as the sale of that promise was pitched to a completely cynical public. In November 1996, the regime announced to both domestic and international audiences the formation of Vision 2010, a program based on the creation of a 170-member committee (headed by the erstwhile interim national executive Ernest Shonekan) to plan how to improve the quality of life and guide the country's economy into the next century.

In Chapter Eight we will discuss Nigeria's recent military interventions in other West African countries. These activities also seem designed to enhance the Abacha regime's prestige at home and abroad.

The regime even tried to capitalize on Nigeria's victories in the 1996 Atlanta Olympic Games. Nigeria won its first gold medal ever in the women's long jump, and this quickly paled in light of a surprise gold medal in the national passion, football (i.e., soccer). This was the first time any African country had won first place, and Abacha, in declaring the next Monday a national holiday, emphasized Nigeria's ability to succeed despite efforts to make it a pariah state. Abacha supporters introduced Abacha-brand consumer goods such as flour and even television sets, and staged pro-Abacha rallies in Abuja and around the country to "demand" that Abacha declare himself a candidate for president in the 1998 elections. Could such obvious manipulations of symbolic politics overcome widespread cynicism? Yet, even though it is more cost-effective for any regime to rule by consent, it is not clear that this regime needs enhanced legitimacy for its survival.

Box 4.3 The Story of Abdulsalam Abubakar.

Born in Minna in 1942, Abubakar shared his father's home as a child with former head of state Ibrahim Babangida, and the two have remained very close. He attended secondary school from 1957 to 1962 in bida, then studied at the Kaduna Technical Institute before joining the air force. He switched to the army, which sent him to the United States for military training in 1975-77 and 1982. In 1981 he commanded a Nigerian battalion as part of a peacekeeping force in Lebanon. He rose to senior military rank in the late 1980s, and to the rank of Major General in 1991. He was named chief of the defense staff by Abacha. Following Abacha's funeral (June 8, 1998), a late-night meeting of the Provisional Military Council named him Abacha's successor.

The Professional Bureaucracy

The military regimes also rely on civilian public administrators, however, and these have been recruited in generally the same ways, whether under military or civilian leadership. Nigerian universities have produced large numbers of trained public administrators, and they have followed long-term careers in federal, state, or local administration that, at least in the early years, were not affected by changes at the top. An analysis of the educational backgrounds of the "administrative class" (assistant secretaries to permanent secretaries) just before the restoration of civilian rule in 1979 showed that only 11 percent of them had no advanced degree. Seventy-two percent had a bachelor's degree, 9 percent held the master's, 3 percent the doctorate, and 6 percent had professional degrees.[15] An appropriate educational level had come to be expected in the civil service.

Civil service assignments at the local level are made by the Local Government Service Commission (LGSC) in each state, which also monitors Local Government Area (LGA) personnel actions and procedures. Discretion in hiring was taken from the LGAs in the 1976 reforms because it was perceived that arbitrary, corrupt, and prejudicial hiring and promotion practices had undermined the morale of local personnel, leading in turn to difficulty in recruiting competent individuals. Of course, local councils complained that since personnel were not responsible to them for their jobs, management and discipline are difficult. In response to these complaints, President Babangida abolished the LGSCs in January 1992, but reinstated them in August of the same year in the face of "immediate and accelerated relapse to the decadence of the mid-1950s."[16]

Most of the military governments have also given ministerial positions to experienced civilian administrators. The quality of Babangida's early ministerial appointments was evaluated by Forrest as "probably higher than under any previous government, military or civilian."[17] Even the transition government named by Babangida upon his departure was mostly civilian. Finally, Abacha was able to co-opt a number of former civilian ministers, governors and prodemocracy activists into his administration, including Abiola's vice-presidential running mate as foreign minister, and other erstwhile supporters of civilian rule as attorney general and finance minister. More recently he has drastically reduced the number of civilians in the top levels of government.

In many cases, administrators were thought to prefer to work for military officers rather than with civilian politicians. In a survey of former members of the Western region House of Assembly during the Gowon regime, most respondents thought that civil servants did not want a return to civilian rule, and that they had more power under the military than the civilian regime; civil servants interviewed at the time generally agreed.[18] There has been some upheaval in the civil service in regime changes: An estimated 11,000 administrators were removed when Murtala Muhammed took over and took vigorous action against corruption. But, to the degree that the administrative system has continued to function through the many regime changes, it has been able to do so because of the permanence of the civil service.

The neutral, apolitical civil service has, however, been greatly affected by political instability, to the extent that top officials must demonstrate their loyalty to the military or civilian leaders in charge. The directors general, comparable to permanent secretaries in Britain, formerly were shielded from changes in political leadership, but a change in this status was made official in 1988, when the appointment of directors general was put under the discretion of the ministers and commissioners. This meant that the directors general were no longer necessarily civil servants, and it reduced the possible scope of advancement for career civil servants and confined their careers within a single ministry.[19] Having seen the flaws in this system, the Abacha regime is considering a return to the permanent secretary model.

The Role of Women in Politics and Administration

In all the various aspects of political leadership described heretofore, we have not discussed any individual woman among nationally influential leaders. In Chapter Three, we noted that women had various levels of power and influence in precolonial societies, but that the structure of influence emerging from British colonial rule effectively denied women a political role at any level in Nigeria. Women have been practically invisible during the military regimes, although some local "chairmen" appointees have in fact been the wives of military officers, and General Babangida's wife Maryam played the role of "first lady" to a degree unprecedented in Nigeria. She was allocated significant sums of federal money for her Better Life Program, which built women's centers across the country to offer job training, literacy programs, health-care information, and the like. But if the role of women in military regimes has been barely visible, it has not been much more in evidence under civilian regimes: There were no women on the 50-person committee that drafted the constitution of the Second Republic. In the Constituent Assembly that debated that draft document, there were 5 women out of approximately 250 members. There were "women's wings" of the Second Republic political parties, but they participated very little in general decision-making. Finally, in the 1979 parliamentary elections, 17 women ran for the 450-seat House of Representatives, of whom 3 were successful; 5 women ran for seats in the 95-member Senate, and one of them won. In a rare exception to the pattern, a woman, Bola Ogumbo, was nominated as the running mate of Aminu Kano by the People's Redemption Party (PRP).

There was no greater participation by women in the political activity leading up to the never-achieved Third Republic: there were 14 women in the 567-member Constituent Assembly. There were 159 female members of the 453 Local Government Councils, of which only 6.9 percent were chairpersons. As a result of elections at the state and national levels, 27 women were among 1172 legislators in State Houses of Assembly, and they were one of 90 senators and ten of 593 representatives.

> [In the campaigns of 1979] women were merely mobilizing agents who campaigned, sang and danced at rallies and were rewarded with token appointments and a few yards of cloth.[20]

In many Third-World contexts, women achieve prominent political positions through family or marriage connections to prominent male politicians. Indira Gandhi (daughter of J. Nehru) and Benazir Bhutto became prime ministers of India and Pakistan respectively on this basis. This has also happened in Nigeria: Kudirat Abiola was one of the seven wives of Moshood Abiola. After her husband's arrest she became involved in a dispute with one of Abiola's sons, concerning who controlled the famous prisoner's legal defense. She also was known to be particularly adamant in the family that they should continue to support Abiola's claim to the presidency, and was thus against any "deal" with the Abacha regime. Her activist role in politics labeled her as controversial, even as "Nigeria's Winnie Mandela," and her murder on the street in full daylight on June 4, 1996 was suspected by opposition groups to have been carried out by government agents. The government, for its part, was investigating other family members. Whether Kudirat's tragic end is related in any way to the fact she is a woman (and presumably a Muslim wife) is difficult to say.

In Yorubaland, the daughter of the *Ooni* (traditional ruler) of Ife, Mrs. Tejumade Alakija, combined this credential with a degree from Cambridge University to rise to head of service of Oyo State, and then became pro-chancellor of the University of Nigeria, Nsukka. On the other hand, the daughter of Obafemi Awolowo wore her father's cap in campaigning for governor of Lagos State in 1983. She was unsuccessful in this campaign and in later efforts in electoral politics, largely because electioneering was not seen as an appropriate women's activity in that culture, even for the daughter of one of its most successful politicians.

In making politics the almost exclusive domain of men, Nigeria follows the typical pattern in Africa and is not very different from most other countries of the world.

Conclusion: A Role for Elections?

It is still too early to know whether the "Third Wave of Democratization" will result in any *consolidated* democracies in Africa, this in the sense that contenders for power accept the outcome of elections whether they win or lose. To this point, there has been only a very small number of cases in Africa where a sitting executive has voluntarily surrendered power as the result of an electoral defeat. Most elections, if they offer any genuine choice, are *plebiscitary*; opponents are not given the means to campaign as effectively as the incumbents, and the vote is carefully structured to result in a vote of confidence for the incumbent.[21]

Even the fairest elections in the history of independent Nigeria have not been contested on a level field. It is widely expected that, should the current regime continue with scheduled elections, the process will be structured to produce a result acceptable to the military rulers.   This is no reason to despair of democracy, however. The literature on democratization, as molded into the Weingast model described in the Preface, suggests the necessity to proceed gradually to the point where incumbents find that their best option is to accept a defeat. Most democracies have experienced piecemeal consolidation, witness the evolution that has been taking place in Mexico over the past few decades. Expectations of absolute fairness are unrealistic even in the most advanced democracies, where the increasing financial burden of campaigning has made fairness elusive.   The challenge to democratic-minded Nigerians is to devise an electoral process that will be legitimate among its various constituencies, and can evolve into a process that eventually wins over the propensity to personal rule.

END NOTES

1. Robert H. Jackson and Carl G. Rosberg, *Personal Rule in Black Africa* (Berkeley: University of California Press, 1982), pp. 19-20.

2. Adams, "Reign of the Generals," p. 29.

3. Crawford Young, The African Colonial State in Comparative Perspective, p. 284; Tom Forrest, Politics and Economic Development in Nigeria, pp. 105-6 .

4. Chinua Achebe, A Man of the People, p. 4.

5.Ronald Cohen, The Kanuri of Bornu (New York, Holt, Rinehart and Winston, 1966), p. 107.

6. The Constitution of the Federal Republic of Nigeria, Article 14(4).

7.Claude E. Welch, Jr., Protecting Human Rights in Africa, p. 134; Welch and Marc Sills, "The Martyrdom of Ken Saro-Wiwa and the Future of Ogoni Self-Determination," p. 8.

8. Luckham, The Nigerian Military, p. 111. Luckham identified Ironsi and Gowon as from humble backgrounds, but noted exceptions to the rule who came from rich or powerful backgrounds, including Murttala Muhammed and Colonel Ojukwu.

9. Morris Janowitz, The Military in the Political Development of New Nations, pp. 63, 81.

10. Eric A. Nordlinger, Soldiers in Politics: Military Coups and Governments, p. 40.

11. Jackson and Rosberg, Personal Rule in Black Africa, pp. 33-34.

12. Nordlinger, Soldiers in Politics: Military Coups and Governments, p. 41.

13.Adams, "Reign of the Generals," p. 28.

14. Tom Forrest, Politics and Economic Development in Nigeria, p. 125.

15.Koehn, Public Policy and Administration in Africa, p. 16.

16. O.O. Oyelakin, "Implementation of the Executive Federal Presidential System of Government at the Local Government Level: Its Logic, Merits and Constraints," Paper presented at the National Workshop for Directors of Local Government at the State Level, Obafemi Awolowo University, Ife, July 21-23, quoted in Timothy D. Mead, "Barriers to Local Government Autonomy in a Federal System: The Case of Nigeria, p. 168.

17. Tom Forrest, Politics and Economic Development in Nigeria, p. 106.

18.Henry Bienen with Martin Fitton, "Soldiers, Politicians, and Civil Servants."

19. Helen Chapin Metz, ed. Nigeria: A Country Study, pp. 239-40.

20. Kole Ahmed Shettima, "Engendering Nigeria's Third Republic," pp. 61-98.

21. Jackson and Rosberg, Personal Rule in Black Africa, pp. 269-270.

Chapter 5

POLITICAL STRUCTURE

♦ What is the constitutional history of Nigeria?
♦ Why has it been so difficult for Nigerians to reach a consensus on an appropriate constitution?
♦ Who has held the decision-making roles in independent Nigeria?
♦ What constitutional institutions would work best in Nigeria?

It is not obvious that we can realistically describe the "structure" of the decision-making process in a country that has experienced seven successful coups, two civilian constitutions, and a particularly amorphous arrangement since General Babangida annulled the elections of 1993. It is, however, useful to be familiar with the range of constitutional arrangements the country has known, the patterns in their evolution, and the traits that a future constitution is likely to exhibit.

Crawford Young cites a personal communication from Mamadou Diouf, of Senegal, on the different context of constitutional development in Africa and the West, in terms highly relevant to Nigeria:

The African constitutions imported from London, Paris, or Washington became inverted versions of those after which they were modeled. The historical logic which led to the appearance of constitutionalism in Europe is a logic of resistance by civil society, the dominated vis-à-vis the dominators. The constitution serves to limit the power of the state and to guarantee the liberty of the citizen. In Africa it served to guarantee the authority of the state and the uncontrollable and uncontrolled exercise of power by the occupants of the state apparatus. And for this reason the constitution undergoes constant modifications.[1]

Constitutions in Nigeria have lacked the articulated support of a civil society necessary to buttress them against clientelist demands on office holders and the blatant grabs for power of the military. Still, Nigeria is simply too large and complex to have experienced the single-party or "president for life" type of rule common in smaller African states, although Sani Abacha may have pushed farther in that direction than any previous ruler. Rather, constitutions have been developed in a context of bargaining among various elites, and have come closer with each attempt at achieving the type of equitable compromise that could result in a more permanent constitutional arrangement.

The first political institution in which Nigerians participated as Nigerians was the legislative council mandated by the Clifford Constitution of 1922, which provided for elected representatives from Lagos. The elective principle was introduced in this way and stimulated political activity. A new constitution was granted following World War II (the Richards Constitution of 1946) that established advisory regional Houses of Assembly. The Macpherson Constitution of 1951 gave those bodies real powers to tax and to appropriate funds, provided that the regional houses would have a majority of elected seats and a majority of Nigerians in the cabinet of each house, and also established a Federal House of Representatives, with most members selected from the regional bodies. There were two additional, incrementally more democratic constitutions before that which granted independence in 1960. Through these successive changes elective office was extended to local and regional governments and the first provisions for a federal structure were introduced.

Nigeria has a rich experience in the *writing* of constitutions, and its politically active population has been absorbed in constitutional discussions almost continually since independence. One author joins Babangida himself in pointing to the anomaly that three years (1975-1978) were spent writing the constitution of the Second Republic, but less than one year was allotted to organizing the political system—especially the parties—for its implementation.[2] It is perhaps not surprising that the regime thus created lasted only four years. Two major issues have been involved: the relationship between the national government and state and local entities, and the fashioning of national-level institutions that will provide a balance of power along with effective authority.

Federalism

Nigeria's experiments with a range of governmental structures allow us to assess the strengths and weaknesses of various constitutional arrangements as they have been applied there. Of particular interest is the role of federalism in Nigerian politics, because in a country as vast and complex as this, many of the political decisions that impact Nigerians' lives are not made at the national level. The term "federalism" often connotes an abstract exercise in constitution writing, but given what is at stake, nothing could be farther from the truth. For ethnic minorities in

Nigeria and elsewhere in the world, federalism has meant freedom from oppression by a majority. Thus, unless the population of a political unit is highly homogeneous, demands for decentralization of authority are common in political life.

From the time that colonial authorities first considered the matter, some form of federal organization seemed necessary in Nigeria, if only because of the colony's size and ethnic complexity. Early nationalist leaders, including Nnamdi Azikiwe and Obafemi Awolowo also advocated a federal arrangement for independent Nigeria; the unitary Richards Constitution of 1946 proved very unpopular in all areas,[3] and, a federal system composed of three regions was established as the basis for Nigeria's move to independence in 1954. In a uniquely Nigerian scenario, two of the regions, the Eastern and the Western, were accorded self-governing status in 1957; the North followed in 1959. Therefore, a very decentralized federal system was already in effect at independence; the Constitution of 1960 was explicitly federal, dividing responsibilities between the federal government and the three regions. Federalism has been a constant in all the constitutions (1963, 1979, and 1989) developed since that time, and was unequivocally the choice of the 1994-1995 Constitutional Conference convened by Abacha.[4] Indeed, it is difficult to imagine a stable political structure that would not allow a considerable devolution of power at least to leaders of the three major ethnic groups.

There have been two attempts to impose a unitary system since independence: In the first coup in 1966, General Ironsi attempted to end the autonomy of the then four regions, and there seemed to be a similar thrust in the aborted coup of 1990. The first effort at a unitary state resulted in large-scale communal rioting and the Nigerian civil war. General Ironsi and his advisors expressed the belief that ethnic tension was exclusively the result of manipulation of public opinion by politicians. As Nordlinger summarizes their approach to power,

> Hostile expressions of tribalism and regionalism would be averted by denuding the politicians of their power, by refusing to consult with them or the country's "natural" political leaders, the chiefs and emirs. National unity was to be achieved, not by consultation, bargaining, and accommodation, but by banning all political activities and organizations; and then within this presumed political vacuum, by issuing a unification decree.[5]

The military technocrats seemed to believe that the validity of their uniformly merit-based system of recruitment to office would be self-evident to the diverse population of Nigerian citizens. In retrospect, it is hard to believe that they did not foresee the explosion in the North at the issuance of Decree 34 (creating a unitary government and abolishing regional quotas in the national civil service). Yet, even if they had been more considerate of public opinion in their move toward the unitary system, it is doubtful that it ever could have been implemented without bloodshed.

After the second coup of 1966, it was accepted on all sides that Nigerians would not accept a unitary state, and one of General Gowon's first acts was the repeal of Decree 34. The question that remained was, would the country break apart completely, would there be only a weak confederation with most power at the regional level, or would there be a real federal system with a powerful federal government?

Some northern leaders had initially supported secession from the federation, but came around to supporting a federal system, even to the point of accepting the demands of minority groups (especially in the Middle Belt of the North) that the four regions be broken up into a larger number of states. Leaders in the Eastern region opposed both a strong central government and the creation of new states, even before violence broke out against Igbo residents of the North (see Chapter One). After that violence they were irreconcilable, and in any case no longer felt safe attending meetings where northern troops were present.[6] The higher military leaders were some of the foremost proponents of a strong center, and were particularly unwilling to see the armed forces regionalized. The federal bureaucracy was of course also a powerful interest in favor of the center. On the other hand, as the East under Lt. Colonel Ojukwu moved closer to secession, leaders such as Chief Awolowo and the military governors of the West and Southwest Regions also began to talk of splitting up the federation, with Awolowo demanding the withdrawal of northern troops from the West. When Ojukwu did announce secession, Lt. Colonel Gowon coopted the leaders of the Midwest and West with positions in a Federal Executive Council, and at the same time decreed the creation of a twelve-state federation, with six states in the North, and three each in the East and West. This system emerged intact from the civil war, and was the basis for future federal arrangements, even as the number of states multiplied and the country passed on to (and away from) civilian rule. [7]

In 1990, a coup was attempted by a group of Middle Belt junior officers, with the financial support of a businessman from the Midwest. The immediate cause for the officers' discontent may have been a shake-up in the top military leadership in which senior midwestern officers seemed to lose out. However, the coup plotters did manage to take over a radio studio and announced that five northern states would be removed from Nigeria, and that a unitary government would be instituted. In spite of a spirited attack on Dodan Barracks (the military headquarters in Lagos), the coup was put down. In part because its program was seen as extreme, it received little public support.[8]

Thus, reactions to two real efforts toward a unitary system for Nigeria, actions spaced twenty-four years apart, were decidedly cool. Rather, the country has seen an evolution toward more and smaller states, responding to the demands of minority ethnic groups, or of subcultures within the three dominant culture groups, to have their own states. The original three regions were decidedly unbalanced, with the Northern region (and its dominant Hausa-Fulani leadership) containing 79 percent of the total territory and over half the population. The decision to create twelve states from four after the Biafran secession was based on the belief that a federal system that broke up the control of states by the three major ethnic groups would contribute to national stability. The creation of new states happened to fit the federal government's military strategy as well: Minorities in the East were wary of Igbo domination, and some of them had long been demanding states of their own. The new division created Rivers State around Port Harcourt that effectively cut the Ojukwu regime from its port , the oil fields, and petroleum facilities. Federalism is a serious game indeed! The number of states increased to nineteen in 1976, to twenty-one in 1987, to thirty in 1991,and to the current thirty-six in 1996. Had the military not intervened in 1983, plans were underway in the National Assembly to bring the total number of states to 48.[9] There is, of course, no "optimal" number of states; every time a new one is created, the minority that becomes a majority in the new state faces fear of domination and demands for autonomy from still smaller minorities. The situation finds its analogue in Canada, where Quebec separatists seek an independent, French-speaking Quebec. . .but a Quebec in which Indian Tribes are now demanding autonomy from Quebec.

The overwhelming preference for a federal state in Nigeria reflects the belief that federalism mitigates regional and ethnic conflict. A monumental study of ethnic conflict determined that the effect of federalism in a multiethnic country depends on how state lines are drawn, i.e., whether or not they produce ethnically homogeneous units.[10] The classic case here is Switzerland, where, according to Horowitz, homogeneous cantons have reduced ethnic conflict because the most important issues are decided locally.[11] The same might hold true for Nigeria, but for the fact that petroleum revenues are distributed from the top, and thus have made control of the center by far the greatest prize. Even given the preeminent importance of the federal government, however, the number of states is critical, for states compete for federation wealth, and the competition might be even more deadly if there were still just three or four regions.

The first, pre-independence, federal constitution in 1954 gave the central government control of foreign relations and defense, the police, large-scale financial and trade policy, and major modes of transportation and communication. The regions controlled primary and secondary education, agriculture, public health, and local government. The regions had their own judicial systems, public services commissions (for the hiring of civil servants), and agricultural marketing boards. Both levels participated in establishing economic development programs, in higher education, and in labor policy.

In the face of formal federalism, powerful forces have dictated that the preponderance of power in Nigeria will be at the national level. First, there is a fiscal condition that calls the federal concept into question: As we will see, all levels of government derive the greater portion of their revenues from the national oil monopoly, distributed through the national government. Figure 5.1 shows how the proportion of state funding provided by the federal government has gradually increased. It is important to note that the absolute value of revenues generated by

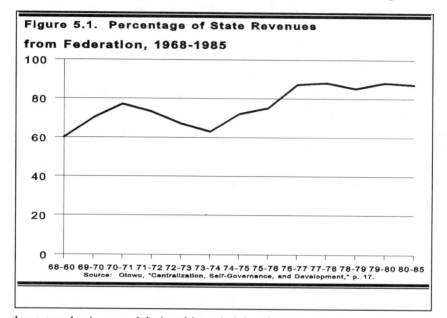

Figure 5.1. Percentage of State Revenues from Federation, 1968-1985

Source: Olowu, "Centralization, Self-Governance, and Development," p. 17.

the states also increased during this period, but that growth rate was far outstripped by the growth in federal revenues. The relative power to generate revenue is likely the best litmus test available for determining the true level of autonomy of various levels of government in a federal system. Secondly, beyond the fiscal facts of life, Nigeria's federalism has been effectively curtailed by military government control for twenty-nine of thirty-eight years of independence. It has been difficult to define federalism in practice when the country has been subject to a military chain of command.

Finally, many in Nigeria's political and social elite, including many academics, federal civil servants, and some junior military officers, have espoused strategic or ideological positions on the country's development that have mandated dominance by the federal government, in order to be able to see plans through at that level. Foreign, including Western, development specialists have in the past shared this predilection for strong government. For many years the ranks of academic and government planners in Nigeria included ideological leftists, although that position is less common in the post-Soviet era; but it also included ultra-nationalists on the right, who have been impatient with the dispersion of political power, including some leaders in the various military coups. In the words of a prominent Nigerian scholar:

> In the second half of the twentieth century, [federalism and limited government] are unrealistic in the case of post-colonial, ethnically

heterogenous and rapidly developing societies (like the Nigerian one) for which an assertive and dominant role by the federal government is both desirable and necessary--desirable for national integration, necessary for the socio-economic transformation of the economy[12]

However, there is another school of thought that finds "decentralization, both as a process and as an end state in terms of organization and operations . . .closely related to the quality of governance in countries at every level of development, but particularly in developing countries."[13] Decentralization as an instrumental value started reasserting itself with the "small is beautiful" movement in the 1970s,[14] and is the preferred choice now, at least among those development specialists representing official agencies. Any permanent civilian constitution for Nigeria will undoubtedly be genuinely federal, and, as always, the definition of state and local government boundaries will be a central issue confronting any regime, whether civilian or military.

Local Government

In Nigeria's colonial experience, there was no autonomous local government. Rather, the purpose of "native authorities" was to implement policies determined in Lagos. In 1951, toward the end of the colonial era and as part of the preparation for independence, limited local authority was given to elected councils in the Eastern and Western regions. The north followed later with a system that allowed more autonomy to traditional rulers. Still, in the first sixteen years of independence both civilian and military regimes let local government stagnate. During the civil war, local governments were totally managed by administrators named by the federal government. After the war, a number of variations in local administration were tried, including a "council manager" system said to resemble that in place in many communities in the United States, but which differed in the very important respect that the managers were posted to their positions by the central government, not by the councils with whom they worked. Since precolonial days Nigerians still had not experienced local governments that they controlled.

In August 1976, as the first phase of a programmed return to civilian government, the Obasanjo regime introduced a comprehensive Local Government Reform, declaring local government to be an independent "third tier" of government.[15] Three hundred and one Local Government Areas (LGAs) were constituted, with populations of 150 to 800 thousand.

Initially, these LGAs were headed by professional civil servants, which, under the 1979 constitution, served with an elected Local Government Council, and an advisory council of traditional chiefs. The functions of these local governments were specified to include primary education, public health services, and the development of agriculture and natural resources (other than minerals). When the military returned to power in 1983, they again abolished the elected councils and appointed administrators. In preparation for the never-achieved Third Republic, the Babangida regime issued a Local Government Decree in 1989 that established an "executive presidential system of government." This reform brought the U. S. presidential model to the local level (where it is rare in the United States); that is, there was an elected executive (chairman) and an independent council with its own leadership, and with the power of impeachment to wield against the executive.

In principle, the three-tiered federal system that has remained in place since 1976 means that the local level is given explicit constitutional recognition. This is in contrast to the United States, Australia, and Canada, whose constitutions recognize only the federal and the state or provincial levels, and where local governments are controlled by the latter. Germany is more like Nigeria, in that the federal Basic Law in place since after World War II (which became the Constitution of the United German People in 1990) explicitly recognizes and protects communes (Gemeinden) and countries (Kreise); however, states (länder) are given the authority to oversee local government operations.[16] In Nigeria likewise, the Local Government Decree of 1989 instructs states to provide for the "structure, composition, revenue, expenditure and other financial matters, staff, meeting and other relevant matters for the local governments in the States." In implementing the provisions for state and local government in the transition to the Third Republic constitution (suspended in 1993), states were explicitly ordered to establish departments of local government, but with the caution that "state/local Government relations should now be defined in terms of guidance, assistance, support and encouragement rather than control."[17] Already in 1988, the military government had ordered states to abolish their Ministries for Local Government in place of Departments of Local Government; with the exhortation that local governments should be liberated from "unwholesome bureaucratic constraints," with their speed of action enhanced, and "in firm control of local affairs."[18] Of course, federal military governments have themselves often interfered in the constitutionally guaranteed functions of local government, and the abolition of the elected positions of chairmen and local councils in the last days of the Babangida regime was a major setback to local autonomy.

A major constraint on LGA autonomy, as described in Chapter Four, is that civil service personnel are hired for LGAs by state Local Government Service Commissions; this system was adopted with some reluctance because of widespread abuses in local government hiring.

The 1976 reconstitution of local governments was incorporated into the constitution of the Second Republic. The Federal Military Government had created the LGA boundary lines in Lagos with minimal consultation locally, and communities were not allowed to change them. This decision was in line with the general approach to establishing local governments since independence, which was to cluster local communities and to ignore traditional relationships among such communities, partly to weaken the influence of chiefs who had been supported by the colonial administration.[19] Nevertheless, military rulers have relied on traditional leaders in many locations to resolve local-level conflicts. . .It was a meeting of *obas* rather than civilian or military administrators that negotiated a cease-fire in the Ife-Modakeke violence in 1997. The military administrations did not, however, specify the role of such leaders in a local government that was presumably under the control of an elected council. However, when the country returned to civilian rule in 1979, elected state officials were much more receptive to demands for subdividing local government areas, especially in return for electoral support.

In our discussion of culture, we noted the effect of ethnic fragmentation on the creation of local government boundaries. A further impetus toward more local governments was the Revenue Allocation Formula, which awarded 10 percent of federal revenues to local governments. The assumption was that more local governments in an area would draw a greater proportion of this allocation. A new local government would, specifically, mean a government headquarters with more localized services and a nucleus for expanded infrastructure. Finally, parties and other political organizations normally had their bases in local government areas; thus, more local governments meant greater density in the party structure.[20] Within a year there were 716 local governments, an increase of 238 percent. Although these smaller units had the virtue of bringing government closer to the people, the many local administrations placed a heavy burden on a country with limited financial and human resources. What resources there were were exhausted in overhead expenses, with very little available for capital projects. Local governments themselves have lost (generally to the states) what little potential they once had for generating revenue; consequently they were unable to provide the services demanded by local populations. Inter-ethnic competition to ensure responsive government produced units that were unable to respond to those who had "won" their own local governments.

The situation was alleviated by the next military government: After seizing power on December 31, 1983, they returned the country to 301 local governments, plus four in the new Federal Capital Territory. Even the military was susceptible to local demands, however: The number again began to grow, and now at the "grass roots" there are 774 LGAs.

The powers of local government also have varied over time, and ironically, seem to have been greatest under military rule. "The federal civilian governments have generally been impotent in their ability to prevent state governments from weakening local government, ostensibly in exercise of their constitutional rights over local government." States often took over functions from local governments, presumably to perform them more efficiently, but also to justify keeping an appropriate share of the federation revenue allotment due the local governments. It was politically not feasible for local government chairmen appointed by state governors to challenge the authority of state government, but once local chairs began to be elected, such challenges occurred. The Nigerian scholar Alex Gboyega believes that, under a competitive civilian regime, local councils would be emboldened to assert their rights, which "ultimately, is the only way the states can be restrained from unwarranted interference."[21]

On the other hand, states are not entirely unjustified in arguing the need for greater control of LGAs. Especially under elected leadership, corruption has debilitated many LGAs; if funds are provided by the federal government, and corruption enters into the discretion with which the funds are spent, local citizens are not likely to demand accountability, because the expenditures are not supported by locally collected taxes. The argument seems persuasive that effective autonomous local government cannot be achieved without giving local governments the means

---

Box 5.1. Impermanence as an Obstacle to Local Government Capacity.

"Enugu Chair Ono.. explained the dual threats of impeachment and political defeat as impediments to long-term perspectives. Many of the villages in the jurisdiction of the Enugu LGA lack electric power. To get a permanent supply of electric power would require the cooperation of the National Electric Power Authority (NEPA). NEPA is a notorious bureaucracy and unlikely to plant the necessary towers and string wires to a village promised electricity by a candidate for chair of an LGA. Small generators, however, can bring electricity quickly to a village, though a generator may break down, be stolen, or vandalized and though fuel may be hard to get in a small village, an LGA chair that supplies a generator can claim credit for bringing electricity, even though it is only a temporary and cost-ineffective solution to the needs of people in small villages. 'If I knew I was going to be chair for two or three years, then I could start planning for electricity for villages.'"

Quoted from Mead, "Barriers to Local Government Capacity in Nigeria," p. 169.

---

to raise their own revenues, and then requiring them to do so.

Nigerian local government has been beset by the problem of impermanence, not only of geographical boundaries, but of form of rule. We have seen that each change at the national level has brought disruption at the local level, compounded by local government reorganizations at other times. Local governments were first created to replace "Native Authorities" in 1952, with three tiers: divisional, district, and local. This system continued until the first period of military rule (1966). In both periods of military rule, local administrators, with or without councils, have been appointed. In 1988, the nonpartisan election of local councils was one phase of the return to civilian rule, but the councils then elected were dissolved the next year when partisan elections were held as a provision of the new constitution. Those councils were then replaced by appointed councils as one of the last acts of the Babangida regime in 1993. Finally, the Abacha regime conducted new elections for local council chairmen and councilors in March 1996, and new party-based elections for these positions (including 183 new local governments) in December of that year. This instability, compounded by the limited fiscal autonomy of local governments, does not promote effective governance. Under conditions of instability, it is impossible for officials to plan "future-oriented policies," because of the necessity to focus on short-term survival (see Box 5.1). This short-term perspective is common among elected officials in any country, who find it difficult to look beyond the next election. It can also be a problem for career officials whose tenure is not protected from the winds of political change. In some Nigerian locations, there was a perception that local officials *should* rotate quickly in and out of office, to give others a chance to "share in the 'business opportunities' that service represents."[22]

The politics of *state governments* has in turn often been dominated by local ethnic rivalries, as states have been called upon to settle local government boundary disputes and to decide on the competence of various traditional institutions. Pressures analogous to those at the local level have led to an expansion of the number of states. The three colonial regions, which became the states of federal Nigeria, quickly became four in 1963 with the creation of the Midwest State. With the outbreak of civil war in 1967, the country was divided into twelve states, which number was increased to nineteen in 1976; the number continued to grow to the present thirty-six in 1997 (plus the Federal Capital Territory; see maps, Figure 5.2).

At the same time, it is clear that the country was most truly federal in character when there were three, then four regions under the First Republic. The multiplication of states since that time has broken the power of the old regions, and the process has been simultaneous with the concentration of power at the national level that military rule and oil wealth have dictated. The best measure of the relative strength of various levels in a federal system is undoubtedly fiscal: In the First Republic, regional expenditures about equaled those at the federal level; by the mid-1970s, federal expenditures were about 70 percent of the total. States also grew more dependent on the federal budget: At independence the regional governments were receiving about 55 percent of their revenue from the federal government; by late in the 1970s the proportion had risen to over 80 percent. At the same time, various regimes have, either operationally or through constitutional mandate, handled the federal budget allocation according to fixed across-the-board percentages of federal revenues. In 1979, the distribution formula was 76 percent to the federal level, 21 percent to states, and 3 percent to local governments. States had great political influence under civilian rule, and won a change to 55 percent for the federal government, 30.5 percent to the states, 10 percent to local government, and 4.5 percent to be split among them for various purposes.

The practice in the period of military rule since 1983 has been for the federal government to provide blanket allocations of funds to states, with little control on how those funds are spent. State-level budget deficits have not been closely controlled. When external lenders began putting constraints on Nigerian budgets in the 1980s, limits were placed on the amount of Nigeria's external borrowing that could be spent by states. The result, however, was that the states received federal loans instead to allow them to maintain constant levels of expenditure. In one sense, then, the system is more federal than one would expect when the states are so completely dependent on the federal government for funds; the control that might have accompanied these transfers was simply never applied.[23]

The political tensions in various localities and regions now finally converge at the national level, the source of most government resources. Federal governments have attempted in recent years to calm the ethnic struggle with a Nigerian version of affirmative action based on the country's "federal character." Various regions (and thus ethnic groups) are guaranteed a proportionate share of positions in federal institutions, thus ensuring balanced representation in the implementation of policy. This is an application of the *consociational* model, a common solution where countries are deeply divided by religion or ethnicity. If appointments were made on competence alone, the educational advantage of the southernmost populations would result in them having a disproportionate share of civil service jobs. The major exception to apportioning positions according to federal character may be an indication of priorities: The Nigerian national football (soccer) team is *not* selected with attention to geographic representation!

Both the 1979 and 1989 constitutions, as well as Abacha's Constitutional Conference of 1995, describe a three-level federalism. In such other large federations as the United States, Canada, and Australia, the constitution focuses on the federal-state relationship, with local government principally in the domain of the state or province. Thus, the fact that Nigerian constitutions have specified a uniform structure and common functions for local government is rather unusual. While there are, no doubt, advantages to this uniformity of structure and function, it does not allow for local governments to reflect the diversity of local cultures present in the country, nor is experimentation possible of the sort that has produced the manager and commission systems at the local level in the United States. However, since colonial times, local government has really been little more than local administration of federal policy, a situation unlikely to change until local governments acquire independent sources of revenue. Clearly, the demand for creation of local governments cannot be explained by the control of decision-making in an oil-centralized system. Rather, ever-more-local government is attractive because of the formula-driven allocation of funds that supports local activities. In 1981, the Second Republic's National Assembly decided on an across-the-board allocation of 10 percent of federal revenues and 10 percent of state revenues to the localities. However, not only were state governments unwilling to abide by this mandate, but they frequently tapped for their own purposes the federal allocation that was transmitted to them for distribution at the local level. To remedy this situation, the 1989 constitution provided direct payment of the federal allocation to local governments, and in 1990 that allocation was increased to 15 percent of federal revenues.

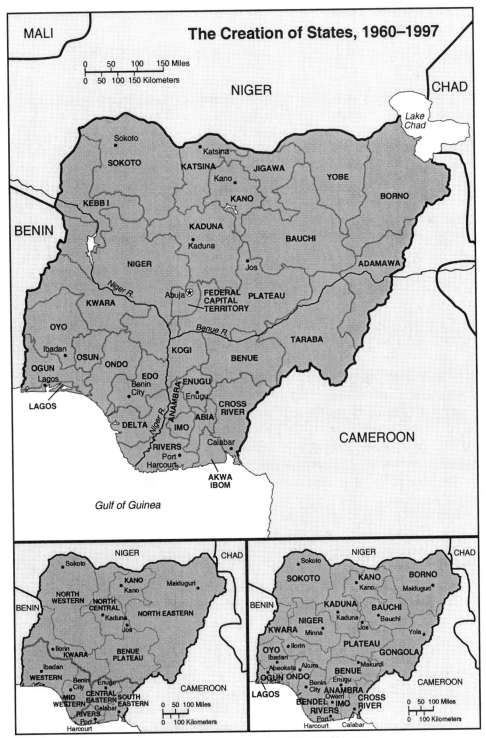

The Creation of States, 1960–1997

Lower left: Dark border shows original three regions, increased to four by the creation of the Midwestern Region, and to twelve in 1967. Lower right: Nineteen states, 1976–1991. Above: 30 states 1991–1997. (Current 36 states are shown in Figure 1.1)

Figure 5.2

The process of subdividing administrative and political units has placed great demands on the supply of human and financial resources, as seen in the growth of the public sector. Employment in the public service may serve as an indicator of the growth of government. At independence, there were 71,693 employees of federal and regional government; by 1974 there were about 630,000, not counting the 250,000 in military service. A study of local governments in 1978-1979 found another 386,600 positions at that level, not counting general laborers or district or village heads. The drop in oil revenues in the mid-1980s brought an end to government growth, however; the Buhari administration imposed a 15 percent across-the-board personnel reduction that started a long period of stability in government employment.[24]

Some have suggested[25] that genuine practice of federalism would help to cure Nigeria's political problems, which almost always involve the tremendously large stakes in the oil-rich nation's federal government. Perhaps a limited national government with limited access to resources would result in a federation that was not viewed as a high-stakes zero-sum game.

Parliamentary vs. Presidential Government

Without exception, British colonies came to independence with a parliamentary system based on the mother country's Westminster model. Initially Nigeria followed the Commonwealth pattern, with a ceremonial governor-general named by the British monarch. In 1963 the formal structure was redesignated a republic, with Nnamdi Azikiwe as president with mostly ceremonial powers. The parliamentary system was maintained, with a prime minister as effective executive. Because Nigeria's first experience with civilian rule ended disastrously in 1966, it is not surprising that the previous system was called into question as a new constitution was being framed in the 1970s.

The 1979 constitution of the Second Republic was unabashedly modeled on the American presidential model: An independently elected president was balanced against a two-house National Assembly at the federal level, with governors and legislatures following the same model at the state level.

Beginning in 1985, the Babangida regime outlined a thoughtful and detailed process for the return to democratic civilian rule. Many Nigerians and foreign observers were skeptical as to his true intentions from the very beginning, and their skepticism was proven fully justified when the whole elaborate structure of the 1989 constitution was scrapped in 1993. The Abacha regime almost immediately called for deliberations on a new constitution, conveniently forgetting that the 1989 system had not been tried and found wanting. In spite of this unfortunate context, it remains the case that the 1989 constitution was the product of careful deliberation on the weaknesses of past structures; Nigeria's previous transition to civilian rule had clearly been unsatisfactory, and most of the measures taken under Babangida seemed to address real problems. Thus, any earnest attempt at writing a new constitution can hardly avoid coming to some of the same conclusions. For this reason, the 1989 constitution merits some attention as Nigeria looks to the future.

The long debate on the relative merits of parliamentary and presidential systems became more vigorous with the plethora of constitution-making that has covered the former socialist countries and many formerly authoritarian systems in the Third World. Nigeria, with experience with both systems, offers a useful case in point.

Juan Linz has argued in favor of parliamentary systems, especially in countries with "deep political cleavages." Linz points out that most of the world's stable democracies are parliamentary regimes, and that the United States is exceptional as a presidential democracy with long stability. A major weakness in the presidential arrangement, according to Linz, is that, should the parliament and presidency fall under the control of different parties, there is no constitutional answer to resolving the stalemate. Secondly, he points out that, although the fixed-length terms of office in presidential systems provides stability, it does so at the expense of flexibility in dealing with midterm crises of confidence, which cannot be resolved until the next scheduled election. Finally, he points to the "zero-sum" characteristic of the presidency; as there is no way to divide it up, one group in a multiethnic society will win it totally and the others will be left out.[26] Another vigorous defender of the parliamentary system, Arend Lijphart, advised that it be combined with proportional representation as a means of electing members of parliament. Nigeria has elected its parliaments from single-member districts under all of its civilian constitutions. According to Lijphart, minorities tend to be underrepresented in such a system, and when it is combined with a presidential regime, "a president almost inevitably belongs to one ethnic group, and hence presidential systems are particularly inimical to ethnic power sharing."[27]

In its short existence, the Nigerian Second Republic did not experience the situation where the National Assembly was controlled by a party other than the president's. However, it is clear that Nigerians have been greatly troubled by the fact that the president will inevitably be from a single ethnic origin.

In response to Linz and Lijphart, Donald Horowitz cites W. Arthur Lewis, who in a lecture on politics in West Africa over twenty-five years ago blamed the legacy of Westminster parliamentarism for the emergence of authoritarian regimes after independence. According to Lewis, the parliamentary system is "winner take all," in that a majority in the parliament cannot be checked by a minority, and thus has no need for compromise and coalition building—in effect, the "zero-sum" situation that Linz attributes to the presidential regime. Horowitz points out that under the Nigerian Second Republic, the president worked with a coalition in the legislative body. Horowitz argues for an electoral system that "ensures broadly distributed support for the president," which has been a provision of both the Second and Third Republic constitutions of Nigeria. In Horowitz's words,

To be elected, a president needed a plurality plus distribution. The successful candidate was required to have at least 25 percent of the vote in no fewer than two-thirds of the then-nineteen states. This double requirement was meant to ensure that the president had support from many ethnic groups. . .the aim was to shut out ethnic extremists and elect a moderate, centrist president. This is precisely the sort of president the Nigerians elected under the new system. The extremists, in fact, were elected to parliament, not the presidency. . .In choosing a presidential electoral system with incentives for widely distributed support, the Nigerians were rejecting winner-take-all politics. They aimed instead for a president bent on conciliation rather than on conflict. They succeeded.[28]

Horowitz suggests further that, had Nigeria adopted a presidential system from the beginning, its conflicts would have been moderated; rather, under the parliamentary system of the First Republic, winner-take-all politics in parliament exacerbated conflict and excluded minorities from participation in government.[29]

In their recent deliberations, Nigerian constitution-makers have followed the same line of reasoning. The disorder in the Second Republic might have brought presidentialism into disrepute as part of an overall unfortunate experience, but the principal aspects of the presidential system were maintained and extended to state and local levels of government in the 1989 constitution. Like the 1979 document, it provided for a directly elected president, with a limit of two terms in office (this time applicable to executives at all levels of government), and a bicameral National Assembly with a lower House of Representatives and an upper Senate.

The belief was widespread that the three levels of government had been too hastily constituted in 1979: Elections of the national Senate, the House of Representatives, the state Houses of Assembly, and the state governors had been held at intervals of a single week; two weeks after the ballot for governors, the president was elected. The 1989 constitution both reversed the order of elections to local, then state, then national, and spaced them much farther apart. The process was to take place over a five-year period, ending in 1990 (later extended to 1992, then to 1993).

The constitutional provision for just two political parties was mandated by Babangida, and many questioned the compatibility of such a provision with true freedom of political activity and expression, and wondered if it would exacerbate the North-South split in the country's political culture; yet, it promised to minimize ethnic-based presidential politics, especially when combined with the proviso carried over from the 1979 document that to win, a presidential candidate must have significant support across the country. In 1979 the rule was that the winner needed to obtain at least one-fourth of the vote in two-thirds of the states (a parallel rule was applied in the election of governors, that they received at least one-fourth of the votes cast in at least two-thirds of the local government areas in a state); unfortunately, the logical uncertainty in how to determine two-thirds of nineteen states caused great confusion. The 1989 constitution provided that the victor win at least one-third of the votes in each of at least two-thirds of the states.

The constitutional dilemma for multiethnic countries is whether to adopt a system like the parliamentary-proportional representation model that gives voice to minorities but does little to force them into consensus, or a presidential-plurality system that pushes toward consensus, but may break apart in the process. It seems likely that any new civilian system in Nigeria will be presidential rather than parliamentary, but the question will continue to be debated. Nigeria's problems with achieving stable constitutional rule have made it an important case study in arguments over the relative advantages of the two systems in conditions of cultural pluralism.[30]

It is clear that Nigeria has had an unsatisfactory experience with constitutional civilian government. The fault, however, does not seem to lie with any inherent defects in the various constitutional frameworks, but in the so-far intractable nature of Nigerian pluralism. A constitutional document cannot succeed at papering over a lack of trust among the country's subcultures. The lack of trust among the major ethnic and religious groups, and between major and minor groups, have led some observers to suggest a "zoning" arrangement as the only constitutional arrangement that will ultimately be able to hold Nigeria together. This plan would essentially extend "federal character" arguments to the single top executive, by providing that the presidency rotate automatically among the various geographical zones in the country, such that every major group could have a turn at the controls. In a 1995 radio broadcast, Sani Abacha proposed a plan whereby

> six key executive and legislative offices will be zoned and rotated between six identifiable geographical groups. . .North-East, North-West, Middle Belt, South-West, East Central, and Southern Minority. The national political offices, which will be filled by candidates on a rotational basis, are: the president, vice-president, prime-minister, deputy prime-minister, Senate president and the speaker of the House of Representatives. This power-sharing arrangement, which shall be entrenched in the constitution, shall be at federal level and applicable for an experimental period of 30 years.[31]

The report of the Constitutional Conference of 1995 gave a general endorsement to zoning at all levels of government, in specifying that "the presidency shall rotate between the North and South. . .the governorship of a state shall rotate amongst the three senatorial districts of the state, while the chairmanship of a local government shall rotate among the three sections into which each LGA shall be divided by the state electoral commission.[32]

The zoning idea was first proposed by the National Party of Nigeria (NPN) in 1979 for its own offices: According to its constitution, the presidential candidate, the vice-presidential candidate and the party chairmanship would be allocated to the three major regions. That year, the NPN nominated and elected a Hausa-Fulani president and an Igbo vice-president, with a Yoruba as party chairman.[33] Unfortunately, no party-based electoral system has been in place long enough in Nigeria to test whether party leaders would follow through on such a promise.

Such a system would have a precedent: After years of political violence in the 1940s and 1950s, the two major parties in Colombia agreed, in 1957, to "sixteen years of parity between the two parties in all branches of government down to the levels of mayor and janitor. The Liberals and Conservatives would alternate the presidency." That system was extended, formally and informally, until 1986.[34] It brought peace in the short run, and may have contributed to a transition to "real" pluralism in the 1980s. Colombia has not achieved stable democracy, although the reasons for instability include factors much more powerful than constitutional structure.

There are, of course, problems: In what order would the zones be designated? Would people have confidence that the zoning plan would stay in place through a complete rotation? How receptive would minorities in each zone be to this plan, knowing they would probably never have a chance for nomination? Since they seem to have been electorally advantaged by conventional arrangements, can northern politicians (and military officers) be persuaded to accept the plan? The answer seems to be that such a new constitutional concept would only get serious consideration if the costs to these groups of existing arrangements were raised through serious movements toward secession, or sustained disruption of the oil-based economy. As Nigerians grow more desperate in their need for relief, such pressures may yet arise, and may in fact already be present. But even if the plan were adopted, would it reduce or aggravate regional and ethnic identities? Would the short rotation inspire corrupt office-holders to even more rapacious rent-seeking, knowing they would only be in a given office for one term?[35]

The Judiciary

Nigeria came to independence with a well-established legal system that included a court system and a thriving legal profession in the British tradition. The federal and state courts have traditionally been integrated into a single system of trial and appeal courts. Thus the 1989 constitution would have provided a Supreme Court, a Court of Appeal, and state and federal High Courts with original and appellate jurisdictions. Traditional authorities have maintained their greatest influence in their judicial powers, for states have explicitly been allowed to constitute customary and *Shari'a* (Muslim Koranic law) courts, both original and appellate. Ten northern states have maintained *Shari'a* courts, an additional point of contention between Muslim authorities and those who see such official recognition as divisive.[36]

It has been one of the greater anomalies of Nigeria's often chaotic politics that the independent judiciary has survived, even through military regimes that rule by decree. The final blow to judicial independence may have come, however, under the Abacha regime, which showed no inclination to respect any semblance of legal system autonomy. It has reacted to court orders by changing the rules—even constitutional provisions—that might be used against it. Thus, in November 1994, when attorneys for the president of the National Union of Petroleum and Natural Gas Workers (NUPNGW) filed a claim of illegal detention, the government announced that it had doubled—from three to six months—the length of time a suspect can be held without being charged, and at the same time barred courts from ordering the government to produce detainees in court. Finally, it established special tribunals for robbery and firearms violations, for the trial of Ken Saro-Wiwa and others in Ogoniland, and for those accused of supporting coups against Abacha in 1995 and 1997.

The Role of Traditional Authorities

We have seen that kings and chiefs whose legitimacy is rooted in precolonial systems have continued to play a role in Nigeria's politics. In Chapter Two, we saw how the colonial administration applied the principle of indirect rule (even in those cases where there were not the traditional rulers through whom it could be applied), which incorporated precolonial rulers and their successors into the governing system. Where this intervention was great, it resulted in removing the legitimacy from those rulers whose people saw them as mere tools of colonial rule. The role assigned to traditional rulers under Lord Lugard's indirect rule model inevitably resulted in at least the appearance that chiefs sided with the colonial rulers against their people. This loss of legitimacy was especially true among those who received a western education, and who, in a sense, had adopted European values. It was also particularly true where colonial administrations assigned to traditional rulers the task of tax collection.[37]

Thus, in most African countries the fate of traditional rulers was in doubt at independence. In most cases, the new leadership was Western-educated, without any standing in the traditional hierarchies. Many of the leaders of newly independent African states blocked kings and chiefs from any formal role, and in some cases even attempted to eliminate chieftaincies completely. It is important, however, to survey the wide variety in the colonial position of traditional leaders, and in their post-independence roles.

In Nigeria, chiefs and kings fared relatively well, especially in the North. Given the education gap between North and South, plus the minimal intrusion of the British presence in the northern emirates, the traditional leaders of northern Nigeria were most secure. The first prime minister, Tafawa Balewa, had close ties to the most powerful northern figure, the Sardauna of Sokoto. The political preeminence

---

Box 5.2 The Career of the Atta of Igala in Modern Nigerian Politics.

The incumbent Atta, Alhaji Aliu Ocheja Obaje, CBE, CON is the twenty-third Atta in the Ayegba Oma Idoko dynasty, which may date from the middle of the fifteenth century. He was born in 1917, and received formal education at Idah, Dekina, Ibadan Teachers' College and the Institute of Administration, Zaria (where he also became a lecturer). He has had a wide range of working experience as a teacher, an accountant, and as a lecturer. . .He officially assumed kingly responsibilities according to Igala tradition in September 1956 when the Achadu sent the Ikabi to him to give him essential insignia of office. In 1957, he was presented with one political staff of office by the British administration, promoted to first class chief in 1959 and has remained the Atta to date. He was a member of the Nigerian delegation to the Constitutional Conference in London in 1957. . .He was a member of the northern House of Chiefs and a minister of state in the Northern Nigerian Government. . .When states were created in 1967, the Igala area was placed in the West Central State, with its capital at Ilorin. . .An administrative reorganization carried out in 1974 divided Igalaland into three smaller units [each with] a Local Government Council under the chairmanship of a traditional ruler. The Atta was made head of one of the three councils. This was a serious miscalculation. . .by appointing chiefs hitherto subject to the authority of the Atta to chairmanship positions, the government seemingly equated the position of the Atta to those of the new chiefs. In July 1977, the Atta vehemently opposed the plan of the Benue State military administration to condone and allow the separate existence of traditional councils in Igalaland. In the end [the military commander] put the Atta in prison, the first time ever that an Atta was thus detained. . .with pressure from all corners, the Atta was released a few days later. As first chairman of the Benue State Council of Chiefs, he led a delegation of chiefs to the Council of State meeting in Lagos in 1980. In 1980, President Shagari named him first chancellor of the Open University of Nigeria.

(Abridged from Tom A. Miachi, "The Role of Atta Igala in Nigerian Politics" in O. Aborisade, ed. Local Government and Traditional Rulers in Nigeria, pp. 83-88).

of the North and the strong conservatism characterizing that region meant that, especially there but elsewhere in the country as well, chiefs would play an important, if informal role. The emir of Zaria once explained to the authors that he played no formal role in government, although he was consulted by local authorities; some of those same local authorities were in the room, and were careful to keep their heads lower than the emir's.

The above discussion must not be interpreted to mean that the traditional rulers are above the federal government. Recalling indirect rule in the colonial era, in 1996 the military government dethroned the sultan of Sokoto, Ibrahim Dasuki, for "unbefitting behavior," which apparently related to his business involvements. The staff of office was turned over to Mohammed Maccido, at whose enthronement official dignitaries "bowed until their heads touched the ground"[38]—acting in this respect quite unlike the colonial authorities.

One of the most extreme examples of the endurance of traditional political institutions is in the far northeast of Nigeria, in Borno State, where the Kanuri are the dominant ethnic group. Royal dynasties of Kanem, then of Bornu, have ruled there for perhaps a thousand years, and avoided conquest during the jihad of Usman dan Fodio. The current dynasty gained control in Bornu in the early nineteenth century, and was later snatched from military defeat by the British, who established them in a new capital at Maiduguri in 1905 and incorporated them into the system of indirect rule. Maiduguri is still the capital of Bornu State.[39]

Under colonial rule Bornu maintained its identity, but was directed by the British in the development of a hierarchical administration that altered the relationship of the traditional leader, the *Shehu*, his court and the Kanuri people. Certainly the independence of Nigeria has had its effects on Kanuri society and politics, but only as a gradual evolution. Ronald Cohen studied Kanuri culture in two phases of field study, one in 1956 and 1957, the other in 1964 and 1965, thus before and after independence. His comments on the transition are revealing:

> . . . detailed questions about various traditional practices indicated that there have been few changes at the cultural and social level. At the political level where there were English District Officers and other officials of the regional government, now these posts are filled by Nigerians, generally from other parts of northern Nigeria. However it is for the most part correct to use the present tense in describing Bornu . . .[40]

It is remarkable that Bornu was described as though it were an independent state exercising "foreign relations" with the rest of Nigeria. Not only the traditional ruler, but the entire politico-administrative structure, remained intact. Eventually there were changes, first with the creation of twelve states in 1967, which removed the emirs' control of the courts and prisons and the right to appoint *Alkalis* (traditional Muslim judges). More profound change came with the Local Government Reform of 1976, with the elected local councils it established throughout the country. At first, emirs were appointed to these councils alongside the elected representatives, but were removed with the return to civilian rule in 1979, since "traditional rulers must be kept out of the Local Government Councils and therefore neutralized from partisan politics [in order] to continue to be the father of everybody in their domains." From this point, the emirs' jurisdiction has been restricted to "traditional and cultural matters," and to advising the Local Government Councils.[41]

Bornu, of course, is the extreme of continuity with the past. In most of Nigeria there is great ambivalence about the role traditional leaders play, and the role they should play. Those with little or no precolonial legitimacy, as among the Igbo, disappeared, although chiefs continue to be named as recognition for their individual accomplishments. Controversy about traditional leaders has probably been greatest among the Yoruba, where precolonial rulers had held significant power, but where many young people had attended mission schools, gone on to higher education, and were unwilling to see the *obas* have real political power. Nevertheless, *obas* with appropriate educational backgrounds have been appointed to high administrative positions: For example, the Ooni of Ife, Sir Adesoji Aderemi, was appointed governor of the Western region after independence. In the competition with modern local bureaucracies, "traditional rulers and chiefs have seized the initiative by providing leadership on a wide range of issues confronting their communities."[42]

In sum, highly educated Nigerians often see traditional authorities as representatives of a premodern system, out of place in a "rational" political framework, especially one with democratic values and institutions. But many others, especially in rural areas, maintain great respect for their chiefs, and still others are personally ambivalent. So-called "modern" figures sometimes seek the honorary title of chief, "bestowed on them by the traditional rulers. . .in appreciation of the recipient's service to the community."[43] It has been estimated that each traditional ruler in Nigeria bestows at least fifty chieftaincy titles per year, for a significant fee plus annual payments thereafter.[44] Individually, chiefs and kings remain influential, and in some cases wealthy and successful in the business world. Chieftaincy titles are not merely honorific; they quite probably contribute to success in the private sector, which helps to explain the demand for them.

Nigeria's first constitution provided for a House of Chiefs modeled roughly on Britain's House of Lords in each of the four regions. There was no formal role for them under military rule from 1966 to 1976, but the Obasanjo military regime's Local Government Edict in 1976 provided for bicameral local governments with an elected council and a traditional or emirate council. Under the Second Republic (1979-1983) chiefs could be named to the national Council of States or to state Councils of Chiefs. However, their powers in either case were purely advisory.[45] Under military rule since 1983, chiefs have had no formal *collective* position in Nigerian politics; however, higher-level chiefs are still considered civil servants and receive a state salary. The issue of an appropriate political role for chiefs in a future constitution remains contentious. Given the varied traditions of rulership in the country, it is unlikely that a uniform role for chiefs can be found that will be satisfactory to all. Bringing chiefly legitimacy into a new constitution would probably entail some discretion for states and local governments in defining their role. For this reason, traditional rulership and federalism are intricately entwined.

Under those periods of military rule when elected governments have been abolished at the local level, chiefs, kings, and emirs constitute the only representatives of local areas with any official standing, and could be influential should they choose to adopt a spokesman role. Along this line, Victor Ayeni has proposed an "ombudsman" role for traditional rulers—essentially their former judicial functions without legal or political standing. They would be ready to hear complaints with a minimum of formality (especially orally) and expense, represent to political authorities those whose complaints were found justified, and provide binding arbitration. Ayeni argues that this role would be appropriate precisely because, in contrast to the colonial period, the

> **Box 5.3: The Conferral of a Chieftaincy Title on This Volume's Co-Author.**
>
> The title Balogun Onigege Wura of Ibadan Land was conferred on Professor (Chief) Oladimeji Aborisade on January 16, 1996 by the Olubadan of Ibadan Land in Council. The title was in recognition of his support for and belief in education at all levels and his achievements as a teacher and writer and for his community service. The title is a traditional Yoruba approximation of "Academic Administrator and Intellectual," and helps the less-educated public appreciate the titleholder's contributions. Although the Oba did not take payment for this title, celebration of the conferral involved a high cost of entertainment of well-wishers, relatives, friends and professional colleagues—perhaps one thousand guests in all.

traditional leaders would have no formal powers or connections to state authorities, and thus would be in a position to act independently. He is not entirely successful in specifying such a role for chiefs in Nigeria's various traditions, and it might prove impossible to do so in some cultures, and in areas where traditional rulers have largely been discredited. But the ombudsman role might enhance the rulers' prestige with those who now hold them in low regard, and would not compromise (and might promote) democratic institutions in a new constitution.[46]

The Structure of Military Rule, Buhari Through Abubakar (1983 – Present)

Beginning with the first coup of 1966, military regimes have abolished and prohibited political parties and movements, as well as a broad range of independent interest groups. Only in the military-directed return to civilian rule leading to the Second Republic (1979-1983), in the aborted transition to the Third Republic under

Babangida, and in the elections sponsored by the Abacha regime in 1996-1998 have such institutions been allowed, but carefully restricted, controlled, and manipulated. As we have seen in our discussion of federalism, political power has been centralized as well. The formerly elected local authorities and state governors are replaced by military officers of appropriate ranks in the hierarchy. Following the first coup of 1966, General Ironsi created simple institutions of rule: A Supreme Military Council (SMC) consisting of Ironsi and the then four regional military governors, and a Federal Executive Council (FEC), essentially a cabinet composed of federal permanent secretaries. Parallel organizations were constituted in each region. Upon taking power after the second coup in 1966, General Gowon left this structure in place, but added several positions as "civilian commissioners" for former politicians such as Chief Obafemi Awolowo. This system was made more complex under General Obasanjo by the insertion of a Council of States—composed of the military governors of all twelve, then nineteen, states—between the SMC and the FEC, simultaneously removing governors from the SMC, leaving it as both the top of the military command structure and the top executive body. Also, new rules forbade the presence of civil servants at the meetings of any of these groups unless they were specifically invited. This reflected a feeling that "bureaucrats" had been too influential in the policy process.[47]

In the period after the return of military rule in 1983, Muhammed Buhari, and then Ibrahim Babangida headed a collective military regime known as the Armed Forces Ruling Council (AFRC). Shortly after coming to power, Babangida further elaborated his administration through the appointment of a Political Bureau of seventeen members. This institution had something of a public relations role: Composed largely of university academics and formally charged to develop an outline for the transition to civilian rule, the Political Bureau traveled the country seeking expressions of opinion on how to structure the future. In 1987 Babangida created a Constitution Review Committee (CRC) of forty-six members, which reviewed and revised the 1979 constitution. The government then (in 1988) created a Constituent Assembly which was to review the work of the CRC and recommend a constitution to the AFRC.[48] This structure was much more elaborate than that of most military regimes, in Nigeria or elsewhere, a fact which, along with the careful elaboration of an electoral process, led many to believe that the Babangida administration was managing a sincere and careful transition to civilian rule. Larry Diamond, observing that the five-year transition program cost about 14.6 billion naira, almost half the amount of the whole 1990 federal budget, concluded that "It is hard to imagine that a military government would expend so much intellectual and material effort if it were not serious in its intention to exit."[49] With a series of delays in the transition in 1989-1992, skepticism grew again.

As President Babangida's actions in 1992-1994 further modified and postponed the return to civilian rule, his standing with the population, and even within the military, moved ever lower. When he delayed announcing the outcome of the June 12, 1993 presidential election, apprehensions grew, for it was popularly believed that Moshood Abiola had won. Two days after the election, initial results released by the National Election Commission showed that Abiola had won in eleven of fourteen states. Later, the private human rights coalition Campaign for Democracy published election results indicating that Abiola had won in nineteen of the thirty states. A few days later, the military government declared the election invalid. At the same time, Babangida promised new elections, and promised a return to civilian rule. In January 1994, he appointed a transition committee chaired by a Yoruba, Ernest Shonekan, to carry out the "disengagement program." Shonekan was named head of state on August 26, 1993, and Babangida vacated the capital without fanfare—in a technical sense meeting his deadline for the restoration of civilian rule. However, Shonekan had virtually no support—the fact that he is from the same state (Ogun) as Abiola did little to legitimize him even there. The uproar in the southwest at his abrupt removal and replacement by Sani Abacha was not over his departure, but stemmed from the disappointment felt there that civilian rule had been postponed indefinitely.

The ruling military group under Sani Abacha and Abdulsalam Abubakar is known as the Provisional Ruling Council (PRC), with approximately twenty-five members. The membership of the PRC has shifted, as when Abacha dismissed the heads of both the army and the navy for challenging his leadership during the 1994 strikes, and especially following the charges of a 1997 coup presumably led by the vice-chairman of the PRC, Lt. General Oladipo Diya. In any case, the PRC has not functioned as a rule-making body; rather, policy decisions are made by Abacha and small groups of his advisors, without any institutionalized process.[50]

General Abacha maintained the myth of a return to civilian government. Without explaining how a new effort would be different from that which evolved from 1985 to 1993, he appointed a constitutional commission and an electoral board to plan the selection of delegates to a new constitutional conference. Abacha at first set no deadlines, although in April 1994, the government announced that a first phase of its transition program would be completed on January 17, 1995. At that time, constitutional measures would be announced and political parties allowed to resume activities. In the meantime, there are two contending scenarios playing out: In the first of these, the regime-sponsored Constitutional Conference was inaugurated on June 27, 1994, and heard Abacha tell them that "we in the present government in Nigeria are committed to ensuring that there is speedy and unimpeded transition to a civil democratic rule in which we shall not be participants. We are, in short, arranging to surrender power through a peaceful and orderly process."[51]

However, two weeks prior to the opening of the Constitutional Conference, on the anniversary of the annulled election, Moshood Abiola had declared himself president. A warrant for his arrest for treason was immediately issued; Abiola was arrested on June 23 and charged with three counts of treason. One count stated that he "solicited, incited, addressed, and endeavored to persuade people to take part in unconstitutionally overthrowing the head of state," an ironic indictment from a government whose leader seized control by force. A lengthy judicial struggle then began, with the Lagos High Court and the Federal High Court in Lagos ordering that he be produced. The Abacha-appointed attorney general simply ignored the request. Abiola, reportedly in poor health, remained in custody until his death of a reported heart attack on July 7, 1998. Had he lived, it is unlikely that he would have been allowed to assume the office he claimed. His wife Kudirat had vigorously campaigned for his release, but was gunned down in an ambush in June 1996 by unnamed assassins. His son Kola Abiola has since negotiated for his father's release, but the government's conditions are stiff:

> Abiola must give a guarantee not to make political utterances or grant interviews to the media, accept to be banned from participating in politics for three years; apologize to the Nigerian state for the crisis engendered by the June 12 debacle; agree to a confinement to house arrest or a trip abroad to a country to be decided upon by the Abacha regime.[52]

Powerful leaders like Shehu Yar'Adua, a delegate to the constitutional conference, a retired general, and a nearly successful presidential candidate in 1992, could have caused difficulty for the PRC in the absence of progress toward restoring civilian institutions, and such activity was presumably the cause for the arrest of Yar'Adua and others in April, 1995, and their subsequent secret trials and harsh sentences. (Yar'Adua died in prison on December 9, 1997.) On June 27, 1995 the Constitutional Conference submitted a draft constitution to the PRC which was never formally adopted. However, on October 1, 1995 Abacha announced a new three-year transition schedule ending with a return to elected government at all levels by October 1, 1998. The specifics of this program generally followed the recommendations of the Constitutional Conference, specifying a multiparty system in which any party with at least ten seats in the National Assembly would be proportionately represented on the Federal Executive Council (cabinet), with the rotation by zone of principal executive and legislative officials for a period of 30 years. A new constitution is to be formally adopted at the end of the transitional period (in 1998).

Civilian-Military Diarchy

Politics at the macro level in Nigeria has in the past decade taken on the form of a succession of military regimes that are constantly planning a return to democracy—with no progress toward that goal. The use of the term "transition" has been so stretched that current descriptions of the Nigerian regime refer to "transition without end,"[53] or "permanent transition."[54] In the details of this tableau, administrative and judicial proceedings have continued as though a constitutional structure were in place. Given the long involvement of the military in Nigeria, it is difficult to foresee a time when Nigerian military officers will be completely depoliticized. Accordingly, there have been various efforts to institutionalize a power-sharing role for the military. Richard Joseph has termed the sharing of power between the military and the bureaucracy in earlier military regimes a "civil-military diarchy."[55] A broader application of the concept of a civilian-military diarchy form of government was proposed by the famed nationalist Nnamdi Azikiwe in 1972:

> . . . there should not be an immediate transfer of power to complete civilian rule; rather a *modus operandi* should be devised for a combined civil and military government that should rule this country. . .for five years, after which period the continuation of such a regime should be reviewed in the light of experience and reason.[56]

The idea stayed alive through the constitutional debates of 1979, during which it was proposed that power would be shared during a fifteen-year transition period between the military and a civilian regime. In the 1992 constitutional debates, the diarchy concept took the form of a proposed coexistence of elected governments at the state and local levels, with a federal military administration "assisted by" an elected National Assembly.[57] This was, in shortened form, the situation between the local elections of 1990 and the annulment of the 1993 presidential election.

If the military controls the choice of a "civilian" president, that individual will have to maintain the support of the military he leaves behind. Thus, there will clearly be some kind of diarchy in place, although it remains to be seen if it will be codified in any form of constitution.

Conclusion

J. Isawa Elaigwu argued prophetically that plans for the Third Republic had not dealt with an appropriate post-1992 role for the military. Steps he suggested to incorporate a still-not-depoliticized military in a civilian regime included:

> (1) appointing a military officer as minister of defense, as is frequently done in Latin America;
> (2) electing representatives of military personnel to legislative bodies; and
> (3) application of military skills (e.g., in engineering and health) to developmental tasks.[58]

It is doubtful that these measures would, in themselves, have prevented the suspension of the transition in 1993. But Elaigwu makes a strong argument that, even a transition planned and managed by the military itself must strive to reduce the anxieties of (perhaps other) military personnel.

A best-case scenario might show a future, totally civilian, regime unofficially constrained by the threat of intervention or coup to maintain its legitimacy by controlling corruption, following constitutional principles, and enacting and implementing policy in response to citizens' priorities. In this widest view of diarchy, the military would play the role of "loyal opposition."

END NOTES

1. Young, The African Colonial State in Comparative Perspective, pp. 285-286.

2. Joseph, Democracy and Prebendal Politics in Nigeria, p. 3.

3. Olowu, "Centralization, Self-Governance and Development in Nigeria," p. 203.

4. Federal Republic of Nigeria, Report of the Constitutional Conference Containing the Resolutions and Recommendations, Vol. 2, pp. 60-62.

5. Nordlinger, Soldiers in Politics, p. 161.

6. Luckham, The Nigerian Military, pp. 310-315.

7. Luckham, The Nigerian Military, pp. 315, 320, 322, 323.

8. Forrest, Politics and Economic Development in Nigeria, p. 111.

9. Olowu, Lagos State: Governance, Society and Economy, p. 11.

10. Donald L. Horowitz, Ethnic Groups in Conflict (Berkeley: University of California Press, 1985), pp. 613-619.

11. Horowitz, Ethnic Groups in Conflict, pp. 614-615.

12. Olowu, "Centralization, Self-Governance and Development in Nigeria," pp. 204-5. Olowu quotes Egite Oyovbaire, Federalism in Nigeria: A Study in the Development of the Nigerian State (London, Macmillan, 1985), pp. 19-20.

13. Timothy Mead, "Barriers to Local-Government Capacity in Nigeria," American Review of Public Administration 26 (2, June), p. 160, quoting Richard Vengroff, "The

Transition to Democracy in Senegal," In Depth: A Journal for Values and Public Policy 3, pp. 23-52.

14. See, e.g., Edward J. Schumacher, Politics, Bureaucracy and Rural Development in Senegal (Berkeley: University of California Press, 1975).

15. J. A. A. Ayoade, "The Development of Democratic Local Government in Nigeria," in O. Aborisade and R. Mundt, eds. Local Government in Nigeria and the United States (Ife: University of Ife Press, 1995), pp. 19-22.

16. Mead, "Barriers to Local Government Autonomy in a Federal System: The Case of Nigeria," p. 164; Richard H. Leach, Studies in Comparative Federalism: Australia, Canada, the United States and West Germany (Washington: Advisory Commission on Intergovernmental Relations, 1981), pp. 6, 11, 23; and Russell J. Dalton, "Politics in Germany," in Almond and Powell, eds. Comparative Politics Today, p. 276.

17. Mead, "Barriers to Local Government Autonomy in a Federal System," pp. 164-65; O. O. Oyelakin, ed. Handbook on Local Government Administration (Abuja: Office of the Vice President, 1992), p. 28.

18. Alex Gboyega, "Protecting Local Governments from Arbitrary State and Federal Interference: What Prospects for the 1990s?" Publius: The Journal of Federalism 21 (4, Fall) p. 57.

19. Jane I. Guyer, "Representation without Taxation: An Essay on Democracy in Rural Nigeria, 1952-1990," African Studies Review 35 (1, April, 1992), pp. 48-49.

20. C. E. Emezi, "The 1976 National Local Government Reform and the Three Phases After," in O. Aborisade, ed. Nigerian Local Government Reformed (Ile-Ife: Obafemi Awolowo University, Local Government Publication Series, 1989), pp. 75-76.

21. Alex Gboyega, "Protecting Local Governments from Arbitrary State and Federal Interference: What Prospects for the 1990s?" pp. 47, 53-54.

22. Mead, "Barriers to Local-Government Capacity in Nigeria," p. 169.

23. Forrest, Politics and Economic Development in Nigeria, p. 51; Ahmad Khan, Nigeria: The Political Economy of Oil, pp. 192-93.

24. Koehn, Public Policy and Administration in Africa, pp. 17-18, cites various sources for these totals.

25. See Ladipo Adamolekun, "Introduction: Federalism in Nigeria," Publius 21 (4, Fall) pp. 1-11 and the references therein.

26. Juan J. Linz, "The Perils of Presidentialism," in Larry Diamond and Marc F. Plattner, eds. The Global Resurgence of Democracy, 2nd edition (Baltimore: Johns Hopkins University Press, 1996), pp. 124-142.

27. Arend Lijphart, "Constitutional Choices for New Democracies," in Larry Diamond and Marc F. Plattner, eds. The Global Resurgence of Democracy, 2nd edition (Baltimore: Johns Hopkins University Press, 1996), p. 171.

28. Donald L. Horowitz, "Comparing Democratic Systems," in Diamond and Plattner, eds. The Global Resurgence of Democracy, pp. 143-149.

29. Horowitz, "Comparing Democratic Systems," p. 144.

30. J. H. Price, Political Institutions of West Africa (London: Hutchinson, 1977), analyzes the constitutions in effect until that date of publication.

31. Veronica Nmoma presents the arguments for this plan, and cites the literature on it, in "Ethnic Conflict, Constitutional Engineering and Democracy in Nigeria," pp. 343-345.

32. Federal Republic of Nigeria, Report of the Constitutional Conference Containing the Resolutions and Recommendations, Volume II (Lagos: The Federal Government Press, 1995), p. 68.

33. Anthony A. Akinola, "Nigeria: The Quest for a Stable Polity - Another Comment," African Affairs 87 (1988), p. 443; Akinola, "The Concept of a Rotational Presidency in Nigeria," The Round Table 337 (1996), pp. 21, 23-24.

34. James D. Cockcroft, Neighbors in Turmoil: Latin America (New York: Harper and Row, 1989), pp. 358-370.

35. Julius O. Ihonvbere, "Are Things Falling Apart? The Military and the Crisis of Democratisation in Nigeria," Journal of Modern African Studies 34 (2, 1996), p. 221.

36. Jadesola Akande, "The Legal Order and the Administration of Federal and State Courts," Publius (4, Fall), pp. 61-73.

37. The ambiguity in these relationships is well described in Lloyd Fallers's "The Predicament of the Modern African Chiefs," American Anthopologist 57.

38. Reuters News Service, June 17, 1996.

39. Cohen, The Kanuri of Bornu, pp. 14-18.

40. Cohen, The Kanuri of Bornu, p. 8.

41. "The Roles of Traditional Rulers in Local Government in Borno State," in O. Aborisade, ed. Local Government and the Traditional Rulers in Nigeria (Ife: University of Ife Press, 1985), pp. 351-356.

42. Olufemi Vaughan, "Assessing Grassroots Politics and Community Development in Nigeria," African Affairs 94 (October), p. 511.

43. I. B. Bello-Imam, "The Paralysis of Traditional Rulers in Nigerian Politics," in O. Aborisade, ed. Local Government and the Traditional Rulers in Nigeria, p. 182. William F. S. Miles notes that it also happens that traditional chiefs are awarded honorary doctorates by universities. See Miles, "Traditional Rulers and Development Administration: Chieftaincy in Niger, Nigeria, and Vanuatu," in Studies in Comparative Inte3rnational Development 21 (Fall, 1993), no. 3, p. 43.

44. Olu Omopariola, "Financing the Traditional Rulers," p. 201.

45. William F. S. Miles, "Traditional Rulers and Development Administration, pp. 38-39.

46. Victor Ayeni, "Traditional Rulers as Ombudsmen: In Search of a Role for Natural Rulers in Contemporary Nigeria," in Aborisade, ed. Local Government and the Traditional Rulers in Nigeria, pp. 305-319.

47. Dudley, An Introduction to Nigerian Government and Politics, pp. 87, 90, 101-102.

48. Larry Diamond, "Nigeria's Search for a New Political Order," pp. 33-34.

49. Diamond, "Nigeria's Search for a New Political Order," p. 35.

50. Adams, "Reign of the Generals," p. 28.

51. Nigeria, Federal Republic of, Report of the Constitutional Conference (vol. 2), p. 4.

52. AfreeNet, Lagos, July 15, 1996.

53. See Larry Diamond, Anthony Kirk-Greene, and Oyeleye Oyediran, eds. Transition Without End: Nigerian Politics and Civil Society Under Babangida (Boulder: Lynne Rienner, 1997), and O. Oyediran, "Transition Without End: From Hope to Despair—Reflections of a Participant-Observer," in Paul A. Beckett and Crawford Young, eds. Dilemmas of Democracy in Nigeria (Rochester, NY: University of Rochester Press, 1997), pp. 175-192.

54. Human Rights Watch, "'Permanent Transition': Current Violations of Human Rights in Nigeria," Human Rights Watch Publications 8 (No. 3, A, September, 1996), http://www.hrw.org/hrw/summaries/s.nigeria969. html.

55. Richard Joseph, Democracy and Prebendal Politics in Nigeria, pp. 79-80.

56. Quoted in Olagunju, Jinadu and Oyovbaire, Transition to Democracy in Nigeria (1985-1993) (Ibadan: Safari Books, 1993), p 53.

57. Olagunju, Jinadu and Oyovbaire, Transition to Democracy in Nigeria (1985-1993), pp. 52-54, 103-104.

58. J. Isawa Elaigwu, "Ballot   Box or Barracks for Nigeria?" Peace Review (Winter), p. 31.

Chapter 6

THE POLITICAL PROCESS

♦ What kind of associational life is there in Nigeria, and how lively has it been?
♦ In what other forms are interests expressed?
♦ In what ways, as individuals and as groups, have Nigerians participated in politics?
♦ What has been the role of political parties in Nigeria's electoral and governing processes?

The process by which political decisions are made is at the center of any study of a political system. By analyzing the process carefully, one can identify the individuals and institutions possessing power and influence, and see the ways in which individuals and institutions exercise that power and influence.

The Organization of Political Interests

There are at least two aspects of influence in Nigeria: First is the effect of organized interest groups such as unions and trade associations, and religious bodies; the second describes the more informal channels of involvement through individual relationships that are often described by the term *clientelism* (see the definition in Box 3.7).

THE FORMATION OF ASSOCIATIONS IN THE COLONIAL PERIOD

Nigerian author Wole Soyinka describes how some of the first formal interest groups formed during the colonial period, out of previously nonpolitical associations:

> . . .much later, we heard of the formation of the Nigerian
> Women's Union. The movement of the *onikaba*, begun over cups
> of tea and sandwiches to resolve the problem of newly-weds who
> lacked the necessary social graces, was becoming popular and
> nation-wide. And it became all tangled up in the move to put an
> end to the rule of white men in the country.
>
> Soyinka, *Aké*, pp. 199-200

The activities of formal associations and institutions often offer the most
vigorous expression of societal independence from a government, and the
development of an array of movements and associations of this sort has been
identified by many writers on politics as essential to democratic rule. In Chapter
Three, we introduced the concept of *civil society* to the discussion of political
culture. Because this term describes the extra-governmental aspect of the political
system, it is also relevant to the role interest groups play in a democracy. Its
importance to democratic governance was asserted 160 years ago by Alexis de
Tocqueville, who in his analysis of *Democracy in America*, credited the vitality of
that democracy largely to the lively associational activity he observed.

> . . .there is widespread agreement across a range of theoretical
> perspectives that political accountability is an essential condition
> of democracy, and that the degree of accountability depends upon
> the capacity of a robust, autonomous civil society to curb the
> hegemony of the state.[1]

While the term "civil society" encompasses all government-society
interactions, the activities of formal associations and institutions often offer the most
"robust" expression of societal independence from government.   Colonial
administrations in Africa were generally suspicious of such activity, and tried to
restrain the development of associational life to those activities that were clearly
nonpolitical. Before World War II, the only associations allowed were sponsored
by churches or employers, although ethnic-based groups were also frequently
tolerated. Thomas Hodgkin described how, after the war, associational life in
Nigeria (and elsewhere in British West Africa) flowered.[2] After independence, the
many authoritarian regimes that took root in Africa either brought voluntary
associations under control or abolished them. The Nigerian case was exceptional in
Africa, for even during military regimes organizations such as the Nigerian Women's
Union have maintained an independent existence, even as their political influence
was reduced. However, there is an important distinction between the evolution of
civil society in a country like the United States and that in Nigeria. In the latter case,
the state is in a relatively much stronger position because it was the creation of a
colonial power and therefore had no corresponding set of non-governmental
institutions. It furthermore prevented the evolution of voluntary associations, and

bequeathed to the independent state a central position that was both difficult to challenge and tempting to join with. Nevertheless, a survey of the continent as of 1989 found Nigeria to have the largest number of legally-registered non-state organizations in Africa, with 66 trade unions, 53 business associations, and 730 church-based development institutions.[3]

Many of the first formal associations in Nigeria had an ethnic base. There was the Igbo Federal Union (later the Igbo State Union) "inaugurated by politically conscious representatives of the Igbo intelligentsia."[4] The Egbe Omo Oduduwa was organized among young, urban, Yoruba professionals. Minority groups especially found comfort in formal associations such as the Ibibio State Union, the Edo National Union, the Urhobo Renascent Convention, and others. These associations often formed the organizational base for parties when they emerged, and contributed to the latter associations' ethnic orientations. In the North, where individual clientelist ties are relatively stronger, associations even of the ethnic type have played less of a role, although the precursor of the Northern People's Congress, the first political party formed in the North, was the *Jam'iyyar Mutanen Arewa* (the Association of Peoples of the North), a "cultural association" formed by educated northerners in 1951.[5]

CONTEMPORARY ETHNIC-BASED ASSOCIATIONS

An ethnic association of contemporary significance is the Movement for the Survival of the Ogoni People (MOSOP), an organization representing the 500,000 (by their own count) Ogoni people, whose traditional homeland, in the Niger River delta (in Rivers State), is now occupied by Shell Oil drilling rigs. The Ogoni, who live in 111 villages in three Local Government Areas, complain that they have borne the brunt of the inconvenience of Nigeria's oil industry—pollution of fishing streams and water supplies, of the land through oil spills and blowouts, and of the air through the flaring of natural gas at the wells. On the other side, they argue that they have received little in return. All Nigerians outside the government and the Nigerian National Petroleum Corporation (NNPC) wonder what has happened to the mammoth oil revenues that were the basis for grand promises in the 1970s, but the Ogonis and others in the Niger delta are particularly curious. They claim to have received very few multiplier effects in the way of jobs or other economic opportunities from the capital-intensive oil industry. MOSOP, which was founded at the end of the Biafran War, drafted an "Ogoni Bill of Rights" in 1990 based on the principal of *derivation*, which states that the greatest benefit should go to those making the greatest contribution, although the larger issue in the Ogoni case is determining the ownership of the petroleum under their traditional homeland. MOSOP got worldwide visibility through the activities of a well-known Ogoni author, Ken Saro-Wiwa. First named MOSOP's publicity secretary, Saro-Wiwa's elegant pleas on the movement's behalf led to his selection as president of MOSOP and the movement's symbol in the world at large. He led a very sophisticated political action, targeting both Shell and the Nigerian government. A MOSOP briefing paper charged that:

> In the 35 years, Shell have [sic] operated with such total disregard of the environment that the Ogoni people have come to the conclusion that the company is waging an ecological war on them. . . . The response of Shell has been to appeal to the rulers of Nigeria for whom oil means a lot of money in private pockets and in the public purse. Together, the two have mounted a campaign of intimidation and terrorism against the Ogoni people and its leaders.[6]

Shell was not passive, and responded that at least half the oil spills in 1992-93 were the result of sabotage; MOSOP in reply accused Shell of using old equipment that succumbed to metal fatigue.

By the early 1990s MOSOP (and perhaps Ogoni not under the direction of MOSOP) had grown more militant. They organized a large protest demonstration in January 1993, and the government and Shell grew increasingly anxious. Three months later, Nigerian soldiers guarding workers on a pipeline project that cut through farms fired on demonstrating villagers, killing one and wounding eleven. One result was that Saro-Wiwa was arrested and his passport impounded. Amnesty International intervened, his passport was returned, and he went to Europe to engage in a propaganda war with Shell Oil and the Nigerian regime.

The violent confrontation in January brought a crisis to MOSOP. Some of the Ogoni chiefs, including founders of MOSOP, charged that Ken Saro-Wiwa was too confrontational in his approach, and resigned from the organization, leaving him in control. His mostly younger followers charged the chiefs with selling out. The conflict grew: In July 1993, Saro-Wiwa was charged on six counts, including sedition and unlawful assembly. He and other MOSOP leaders were arrested, prompting more demonstrations, with the situation complicated by interethnic conflict between the Ogoni and their neighbors.

This fight on economic issues turned ethnic, with incitement by political leaders, as members of the Andoni group attacked and destroyed several Ogoni villages (MOSOP claimed one thousand deaths). In October, the government convened a peace conference, which concluded that there were no outstanding issues, and that all parties had accepted an immediate resolution to the conflict. However, Saro-Wiwa did not sign the agreement and political scientist Claude Ake called the agreement a "shotgun solution." In reality, Shell's expansion plans were on hold (the company suspended its drilling operations in Ogoni territory in 1993), government figures were angry at MOSOP, and the Ogoni continued to feel aggrieved. In May 1994 the conflict between MOSOP and the more conservative Ogoni elders took a fateful turn: Four chiefs, two of them related to Saro-Wiwa, were gruesomely murdered by young Ogoni militants. Saro-Wiwa was arrested with fourteen other Ogoni leaders for inciting the violence with his rhetoric. It was several months before they were charged with murder, although it was clear that Saro-Wiwa was not directly involved in the killing. He remained in prison for over a year, during which time he received the Right Livelihood Award and the Goldman Environmental Prize for his environmental campaign against Shell. In October 1995, he and eight codefendants were convicted of murder by a military court, and in November 1995, they were executed by hanging despite pleas of clemency from around the world.[7]

MOSOP has continued its activities, with predictable responses by the government. In advance of a pending visit by a British Commonwealth Ministerial Action Group (CMAG), MOSOP charged that sixteen of its members had been arrested in July–August 1996, including a radio station producer accused of broadcasting an Ogoni song. The government denied that the arrests had in fact occurred.[8]

The MOSOP leaders have gained the support of Amnesty International, other human rights nongovernmental organizations (NGOs), and the World Council of Churches. The British Commonwealth has suspended Nigeria's membership, and many governments have condemned the persecution of the Ogoni activists, ensuring worldwide publicity for their cause and effective representation in the international community. Other Nigerian communities have problems with the government that are perhaps more serious than those of the Ogoni, but have not succeeded in acquiring such powerful allies.[9]

Although there is now a wide variety of associational life in Nigeria, the ethnic-based origins of this life in the colonial period continue to be seen throughout the country, such as the contemporary *Oha Eze Ndi Igbo* (Igbo Peoples' Assembly) in the East, and a Northern Elements Coalition in the North. The trend is especially pronounced among the Yoruba, where the sense that a major group is being locked out of national power is most pronounced. There the *Afenifere*, the *Egbe Omo Yoruba*, and the Oodu'a Youth Movement (OYM) reflect a hardened ethnic base. In December 1994, the OYM issued the Yoruba People's Charter for Self-Determination, which declared a lack of "faith in Nigeria as presently constituted."[10]

Religious Institutions And Associations - As in many other countries, religious groups have played an important part in Nigerian politics. These groups are especially durable and resilient, because when political activity is repressed they remain organized around denominational objectives, and whereas ethnic associations might in some instances have to play a less obvious role, neither Christian nor Muslim religious groups and leaders find it necessary to camouflage their identities. As in other countries, religious-based interest groups take several forms: formal institutions (churches, koranic schools), leadership roles such as bishops, pastors, and *mallams* (Muslim teachers and learned men), and voluntary denominational associations. For instance, in 1984 many church leaders, including the country's Catholic bishops, condemned the Buhari regime's detentions and secret trials, and in 1997 the Catholic Bishops Conference of Nigeria called for release of all political detainees and spoke out against the campaign to make Abacha a civilian head of state. However, the effectiveness of religious institutions in articulating concerns to government has been reduced by intergroup conflicts, most frequently between Christians and Muslims, that put the government in the role of mediator. Two "peak associations" should be mentioned: The Christian Association of Nigeria (CAN) was formed in 1976 in response to the government's announcement that all schools would be taken over by the government. It broadly represents Christian denominations, and this ecumenical spirit was strengthened as a result of the government's announcement in 1986 that Nigeria would join the Organization of the Islamic Conference (OIC). The chairman of the CAN was the Roman Catholic archbishop of Lagos, Anthony Okogie, but Anglicans, Baptists, evangelical churches (e.g., the Evangelical Community of West Africa) and others have been represented, and the chairman as of 1997 is Dr. Sunday Mbang, bishop of the Methodist Church. The CAN has criticized northern predominance in government, and has pushed for a categorical renunciation of Nigerian membership in the Organization of the Islamic Conference and for the release of political detainees.

On the Muslim side, the Supreme Council of Islamic Affairs (SCIA) is headed by the sultan of Sokoto as president, with the Shehu of Borno as vice president, and a Yoruba Muslim as general secretary.[11]

An Advisory Council on Religious Affairs was created by the government in 1987 with equal numbers from the CAN and the SCIA, in order to advise on the outbreak of strife between Christians and Muslims in Kaduna State, but the council proved to be ineffective.[12]

Not surprisingly, associational life is most active in the South; however, the North is home to an Islamic "mystic brotherhood," the *Tijaniyya*, which is particularly influential among lower-class Hausa Muslims, and is looked on with suspicion by the representatives of orthodox Islam (another brotherhood, the *Khadiriyya*, is identified with the Sokoto emirate). These groups, which blur the distinction between "modern" associations and "traditional" institutions, have been challenged since the 1970s by the Muslim Students Society (MSS), which was formed in reaction to socialists and other student radical movements of a Western type. In the process, the MSS also came to question the particular regional traditions of the brotherhoods, and to advocate a return toward a more "pure" Islam.[13]

Modern Economic Interest Groups - In the more urban and industrialized areas of the country there is a range of associational interest groups common to the politics of any modern nation. In the late colonial and early independence periods, Nigerian businesspeople did not tend to form associations, but rather depended on their personal connections to take advantage of political and administrative decisions. A major exception to this rule was the Market Women's Association (MWA), which was formed in the 1920s. As noted earlier, the market women were one of the more politically active social groups under colonialism, and the MWA represented them not just economically, but also in support of political movements. A formal association emerged in other sectors of the economy only in the late 1960s when the Small Businessmen's Committee of the Lagos Chamber of Commerce was formed.[14] The Manufacturers Association of Nigeria (MAN) was formed in 1971, and in the 1970s principally represented expatriate businesses. Partly as a result of indigenization policy, the MAN gradually came to include a significant number of Nigerian-owned firms: 40 percent of the membership in 1984.[15] In the mid 1980s, the MAN played a central role in the conflict over the Structural Adjustment Program, calling for protection of "fledgling industries," and warning of a widespread deindustrialization if World Bank restructuring plans were carried out. As part of their lobbying activities, manufacturers took out full-page newspaper ads that "urged Nigerians to buy Nigerian and lobbied the government for lower interest rates and other relevant policies."[16] Under the Abacha regime, arguments in favor of restoring and extending market-based reforms have been most clearly articulated by the Economic Summit Group, representing a wide base of sectors in the economy, which has replaced the MAN and Chamber of Commerce as chief spokesperson for business.

In a country as vast as Nigeria, transportation plays an important part in the economy. Although the British left Nigeria with a rail system that is still in operation, it does not handle a large share of the country's passengers and freight. Air transportation was once a monopoly of state-owned Nigerian Airways, but the opening of that market to competition in the early 1990s led to the creation of a number of competing privately owned air services. The vast majority of passengers and freight, however, are carried by private bus, taxi, and trucking companies, organized as the National Transport Owners Association. This group has been particularly vocal, of course, on the price of fuel, especially when the government has considered reducing its subsidy, and on government regulations of fares.[17]

Trade unions have played a role in Nigerian politics since the colonial period, although before independence unions were small, weak, and concentrated in Lagos. In 1964, the independent unions formed a joint action committee and called Nigeria's first general strike, which won substantial concessions from the government. Interest in unions grew as part of a general resentment of the newly emerging privileged classes. After the civil war, a ban on strikes remained in effect, but was largely ignored. Nigerian workers competed for their share of the new petroleum wealth, and in 1974-1975 there were over two hundred trade disputes.[18] Late in 1975 the four existing trade union federations merged into the Nigerian Labour Congress. Fearing a strong and radical union movement, the Muhammed administration arrested the movement's leaders and appointed a panel to investigate them. In 1976-1977, strikes in essential services (especially banking and oil) were prohibited, and all existing unions were dissolved. In 1978, a government-controlled Nigeria Labour Congress (NLC) was created by decree and all legal unions were forced to affiliate. There were then forty-two affiliated unions, where there had been over one thousand previously. Although unions were forbidden to participate in party politics in the elections that reinstituted civilian government in 1979,[19] the vote-based Second Republic was fertile ground for union activities. These reached a high point in 1981, when the government agreed to establish a national minimum wage. Yet, in spite of its origin and efforts to limit its activities, the NLC quickly developed its own agenda (especially in opposition to agreement with the IMF on dealing with the economic crisis of the mid-1980s) and sponsored several strikes.

The government responded with wage freezes and bans on further strikes. In an unusually bellicose move on May Day 1987, the NLC demonstrated vigorously against Structural Adjustment Program policies during a celebration at the national stadium in Lagos. Shortly thereafter the government rescinded its decision to abolish the minimum wage in firms employing less than five hundred workers.[20] In December of that year, the NLC led the national protest against government efforts to cut the petroleum consumer price subsidy. The government was eventually successful in partially cutting the subsidy, but only after waves of strikes and protests had caused several postponements.[21] Still, the economic downturn in the 1980s caused the NLC to lose influence, given the large number of layoffs and sharp decline in real wages.[22]

In retaliation for anti-SAP activities, the NLC was again dissolved in December 1987 by Babangida and recreated by him in 1988. It rebounded once more after the annulment of the 1993 presidential election, declaring a general strike in the summer of 1994; as a result, its leaders were replaced by Abacha appointees.

Labor action has been organized more frequently by sector: Groups representing the petroleum workers can have an immediate impact on the national economy, and consequently have the potential for great political influence, as was demonstrated in 1994 strike actions by the National Union of Petroleum and Natural Gas Workers (NUPENG) and the Petroleum and Natural Gas Senior Staff Association (PENGASSAN). NUPENG, the blue-collar petroleum workers' union, claims 150,000 members. The strike by NUPENG and PENGASSAN in support of the installation of Moshood Abiola as president lasted several months, and caused at least a 20 percent drop in oil production for the domestic market. The Abacha regime responded by dismissing the leaders and appointing its own administrators of the striking unions. Most members of these unions eventually returned to work; the government announced that the strike among petroleum workers had been ended, and the secretary of NUPENG, Frank Kokori, was arrested for leading the strike (Kokori and another NUPENG leader were among the first political prisoners released by Abubakar following the death of Abacha.)

Groups such as NULGE (the Nigerian Union of Local Government Employees) are also influential because of their immediate impact on government. Professional organizations such as the Nigerian Bar Association, the Nigerian Medical Association, and especially the Nigerian Union of Journalists, have been politicized as issues have concerned them directly. The Nigerian Bar Association has seen its interests directly affected by the arbitrary nature of recent government actions; in the absence of the rule of law, lawyers' usefulness is considerably diluted. Thus, the Nigerian Bar Association boycotted the military tribunals that were in operation after the 1983 coup. Military governments periodically force the dissolution of such groups by arresting their leaders, as they have done with the NLC and petroleum workers' unions. The Nigerian Association of Resident Doctors, which gave Dr. Beko Ransome-Kuti his start as a human rights and democracy advocate, was banned in 1985 after a doctors' strike protesting low funding for health and higher fees in government hospitals.[23]

Women's Organizations - The Market Women's Association (MWA) is both an economic interest group and a women's movement. As we have seen, the MWA was already active in the colonial period and remained politically involved after independence:

> . . .in the mid 1980s free education was stopped and tuition fees were introduced. . .In January 1987, secondary school fees were dramatically increased after the introduction of primary school fees. At the time that school fees were being increased, MWA members were asked to pay N.50 per stall daily in the markets. The MWA mobilized against these taxes on the premise that they were already paying too many levies and taxes. A procession of women singing war songs went to the government secretariat where the leadership of the Association discussed their grievances with government officials. When the issue was not resolved, the women continued with their demonstration up to the fourth day when they threatened to go naked. This led to the intervention of the Oba (Paramount leader) of Benin because naked women's demonstration in public is considered as the highest expression of anger. . .The government reaction to the demonstrations by women was that the women were "unpatriotic."[24]

Other women's organizations have been less independent of regimes, and less effective. Women's organizations are supposed to affiliate with the National Council of Women's Societies (NCWS); although founded in 1959 and non-governmental, the NCWS offers the only channel of state recognition for women's organizations. The tendency in military regimes to want to incorporate associational life into their hierarchy was seen especially in the creation, at the national level, by the Babangida regime of the Better Life Program(BLP) and the National Commission for Women (NCW). The BLP emerged from a conference sponsored by the Directorate of Food, Roads and Rural Infrastructure (DFRRI) in 1987 on "Better Life for the Rural Woman." With fairly substantial government funding (amounts were never published), the BLP furnished start-up capital for various income-generating cottage industry and agricultural projects for women. The

National Coordinator of the BLP was Maryam Babangida, wife of the president, with governors' wives serving as state-level coordinators.   Mrs. Babangida was assisted by a committee composed of the wives of the Vice-President and other senior military officers, known as the "M Team."   This arrangement led one observer to suggest that the organization appears "to have been created to provide a useful and appropriate occupation for the wives of important state officials."[25]

The NCW was created by government decree in 1989, ostensibly as a part of the National Development Plan.   In preparation for the state-level primary elections of 1991, the NCW did carry out a political awareness campaign, and made a public case for women's greater participation in politics.

The National Association of University Women (NAUW), founded in 1964, is affiliated with the International Federation of University Women. Membership is open to women who have completed at least two years of university. Although such organizations are primarily welfare-oriented and not especially political, the NAUW cites as a main goal the promotion of women's education, and in this respect sometimes functions as an interest group.[26]

Membership in these organizations is concentrated in urban areas in the South. In the North, the Muslim Sisters' Organization and the Federation of Muslim Women's Associations of Nigeria "encourage women to explain their situation within a religious context."[27]

Women's rights have been championed to a degree by Women in Nigeria (WIN), an association of upper-class women engaged in "research, advocacy and action," and the closest thing in Nigeria to a feminist movement. It claims to have branches in most states, and while it does not claim a "grassroots" membership, it does assert that it represents a "cross section of Nigerians," at least in some states. WIN was commissioned under the Babangida regime to provide input to the Political Bureau charged with moving the country back to civilian rule. Although the association conducted an elaborate series of regional workshops and conferences, and labored over its final report, it is not clear that the report had any impact on decisions, especially as the structure which they hoped to influence was never put into place. WIN's influence on the military regime may have been reduced by its decision not to affiliate with the National Council of Women's Societies, which the military regime had developed as an "official" umbrella organization for women's groups.   Involvement in the country's political and human rights umbrella movements, especially the close relationship to the Campaign for Democray (in 1991, WIN was among the organizations that launched the CD) has been internally controversial, with opponents arguing that the association's ability to serve in an advocacy role for women is reduced by involvement in "national politics."

With the exception of the MWA, and of WIN (which has had a marginal role in Nigerian politics), no women's organization has espoused positions that might be characterized in the West as "feminist." According to its director general,

The NCW does not endorse for Nigeria the western stand of
women's liberation. What we are after is emancipation, which
means release from constraints wherein people (both males and
females) can participate fully in the development of this country,
irrespective of their sex.[28]

University Staff and Students - The universities are another modern
sector that has a tradition of political activism. University staff (In Nigerian usage,
the term "staff" includes the teaching faculty) and students were some of the earliest
critics of military rule, and military governments have tried to marginalize their role
in the country. In the political history of Africa since independence, student groups
have been one of the most active interests in politics. They are the children of the
elite (to a much greater degree than in industrial countries), and the probable
successors to power. Moreover, they have been exposed to radical ideologies and
to organizing efforts more than most other constituencies. In Nigeria, students
organized one of the first public protests against military rule in reaction to cuts in
the educational budget in 1978. An army response to unrest on the campus of
Ahmadu Bello University in Zaria resulted in several deaths, which event was
followed by nationwide protests and demonstrations by university and secondary
students. The government then banned the National Union of Nigerian Students.
An organized student voice soon reemerged as the National Association of Nigerian
Students (NANS), which organized a boycott of classes in 1984 to protest the
introduction of tuition payments and the cutting of subsidies. In response, campuses
were closed and some student leaders were arrested.[29] Students were also in the
forefront in organizing protests against the Babangida administration's Structural
Adjustment Program (SAP) in 1988 and 1989. As part of their strategy, they always
enlisted the Market Women's Association to join them. Shettima gives three reasons
for this: (1) "the involvement of women in demonstrations has the symbolic value
of motherhood; even security agents feel restrained from reacting brutally"; (2) the
involvement of the MWA results in closing the markets, which adds to the drama of
the protest; and (3) widening the scope of the demonstrations draws more attention,
including that of the media.[30]
    The NANS has continued to be active up to the present, but has been the
object of efforts on the part of the government to coopt its leadership and divide its
ranks.
    The pay and perquisites of university staff have suffered relative to those
elsewhere in government service. Lecturers declared their first political strike in
1973, and the Gowon administration responded with a threat to evict university staff
from university-provided housing. The academic community eventually went back
to work, but relations with government have continuously been strained under
military rule, and strikes by staff (organized through the Academic Staff Union of
Universities—ASUU) and students (through NANS) have been increasingly
common.[31] Babangida banned both organizations for their criticisms of the

Structural Adjustment Program (see Chapter Seven), and also used the threat of eviction (unsuccessfully) against university staff in 1992. The campuses have remained the most vocal opponents of the Abacha continuation of military rule, and also have tried to use strikes to improve their economic situations. In April 1996, the faculties of the thirty-six state and federal universities acted on an overwhelming vote to strike, and ASUU demanded a tripling of the average annual salary (which then would still be just $1800).[32] However, because recent military regimes have been content to let the universities deteriorate as the price of their political marginalization, campus political activities have not had the impact on policy as have parallel actions of, say, petroleum workers. The Abacha government did respond by outlawing ASUU and giving university staff a seven-day ultimatum to leave their campus housing. As of September 1996, the situation was in stalemate; the strike continued on most campuses, lecturers were defying the threat to move them from their homes, but beginning to make plans for an ultimate eviction. On the other hand some faculty at a few campuses had returned to the classroom, and at the University of Ilorin 291 lecturers had resigned. In October, the government reiterated that ASUU was outlawed, and banned all meetings of the organization, threatening arrest and trial for "saboteurs." ASUU then called off its six-month-old strike, and professors returned to their classrooms. The government continues to neglect the university system's needs.

Teachers - Teacher associations have faced the same frustrations as their professorial counterparts. According to a survey of a national sample of elementary teachers, most teachers belong to a union, and support union objectives. They have not, however, found the union effective at maintaining their standard of living or improving their working conditions. Still, they claim to attend union meetings, and to be willing to strike if asked.[33]

The Oil Companies - Interests of another kind are the international oil companies that control the production and export of Nigeria's principal product. These are powerful, if discreet, players in Nigerian politics. The Shell Petroleum Development Company (SPDC) is the Nigerian subsidiary of the Royal Dutch Shell Group, which has a stake in over three thousand companies and activities in one hundred countries. Through its joint venture with the Nigerian National Petroleum Corporation (NNPC), Shell controls 60 percent of the land known to have commercially viable oil reserves in the country. With the Nigerian operation accounting for 14 percent of Shell petroleum production worldwide, their stake in Nigerian government policy is enormous, but quite narrow, and given differences of opinion in the country (particularly in the oil-producing states themselves) as to the distribution of benefits from oil production, the companies have tried to minimize their involvement in domestic affairs. They were seriously discomfited by the Biafran War, when each side was demanding royalty payments, and that experience reinforced their resolve to limit their contacts to those in the government responsible for oil policy. This involvement is normally low-key. However, open confrontations have occurred: British Petroleum suffered a nationalization in 1979, and only returned to activity in Nigeria in 1993.[34] More recently, competing consortia, one European, the other American and Japanese, have been lobbying the government over contracts for the production of liquified natural gas (see Chapter Two), and the process to be used in its production.[35] The Nigerian government has found its membership in OPEC of great use in negotiating tax and royalty rates with the companies, and thus in blunting each company's individual influence.

The Biafran nightmare has returned to the oil companies in the struggle of MOSOP for more attention to the costs of oil drilling and production to people living in the oil-producing region, and Shell, as we have seen, has had to defend its operation in Nigeria against charges by human rights organizations of its complicity in human rights violations, and to prepare for the as-yet-remote possibility that industrial nations might boycott Nigerian oil. The conflict has already been costly to the oil companies: Three companies estimated losses of $200 million in 1993, because of "unfavorable conditions in their areas of operation."[36]

Human and Civil Rights Organizations - The National Democratic Coalition (NADECO) and the Campaign for Democracy (CD) are groupings of civil rights and democracy activists that are particularly influential in intellectual circles and among students, and in 1994 were at the front of much anti-Abacha activity. NADECO was formed in 1994, calling for a boycott of Abacha's constitutional conference and the return to power of previously elected officials, including Abiola. Although NADECO is seen as a predominantly Yoruba organization, and consequently is not strong outside the Southwest, it received support from prominent northerners, including retired general T. Y. Danjuma. It has been severely harassed by the government. Because it had vowed disruptions over the continued detention of Moshood Abiola, NADECO was under investigation for arson in a major fire that destroyed a telephone exchange in Lagos and shut down fifty thousand lines on July 3, 1996.[37]

CD is a coalition of forty-two organizations, including the Committee for the Defense of Human Rights, the National Association of Democratic Lawyers, the National Association of Nigerian Students (NANS), Women in Nigeria (Lagos branch), and the Nigerian Union of Journalists. This grouping was originally formed in 1991 in opposition to military rule, with Beko Ransome-Kuti elected as chair at its first convention. The regime responded by immediately detaining a number of the leaders, including Ransome-Kuti. This worked to the association's advantage in the long run, because Ransome-Kuti had become well known, and his arrest was widely discussed. CD advocated a national conference to draft a new constitution, as had happened in a number of other, principally French-speaking, African countries. It was CD that published the results of the 1993 election, in the face of regime efforts to suppress them, and CD organized massive demonstrations, said to be the largest in Nigerian history, when the June 1993 presidential elections were annulled. As with NADECO, however, CD had trouble extending its activities outside the Southwest and Lagos, although this was more because of the greater political consciousness in Lagos, and greater anger against Babangida than because a Yoruba had been denied election. Also, as protest grew, there was chaos in Lagos, during which young hoodlums began looting. The breakdown of law and order frightened many opponents of the regime into inaction. CD became one of the few credible opponents of the Abacha regime, but it also started to splinter apart: Ransome-Kuti was accused by other activists of not consulting them before making contact with the interim government formed by Babangida when he resigned.[38] It was also reported that the CD had consultations with Abacha during the Shonekan interim government, and, knowing that Babangida and Shonekan did not intend ever to approve the June 12 election outcome, actually *encouraged* Abacha to seize control. Their expectation that Abacha would intervene on the side of those demanding implementation of the election outcome proved to be a "very poor reading of the character of the Nigerian armed forces," and by later in the year they had realized their error and called for international sanctions against the Abacha regime.[39]

In May, 1997, a new coalition of twenty-two opposition groups was announced in Lagos, the United Action for Democracy (UAD). The constant reformulation of structures for opposition activity testify to the difficulty of maintaining coordinated opposition in the context of both repression and of efforts to coopt respected opponents. Shortly after the UAD was announced, a group appeared under the label United Action for Nigeria (apparently in reaction to the UAD) that called for an extension of military rule, to be followed by the installation of Sani Abacha as civilian president.

Civilian Politicians - During the long periods of military rule, politicians at all levels who were turned out by the military have constituted an interest group united around their desire to be allowed back into the circles of power. They have been a force pushing for the return to civilian rule, even as many of them have been content to be "co-opted" into administrative service under the military. They can scarcely be considered a single interest when they are competing for power under a civilian constitution, and ethnic and regional considerations make them highly suspicious of one another; yet they constitute a significant force working against the intentions of those military leaders who would like to remain in power indefinitely.

The Kaduna Mafia - A clear Nigerian example of the nonassociational interest group, but shadowy in its definition, is the famous "Kaduna Mafia." At least before the establishment of the Abacha regime, hardly any informal conversation on Nigerian politics failed to mention this network of powerful northern leaders (not a mafia in the criminal sense, but as an informal network of power and influence) who were said to maintain strong influence over the military and to have orchestrated the evolution of Nigerian politics in recent years. According to Richard Joseph:

> In a general sense [Kaduna Mafia] refers to members of the northern intelligentsia who assumed positions of political and social influence during the decade of military rule after the civil war. These individuals are, on the whole, better educated than their predecessors in the emirate North who held similar positions in the first decade after independence. [They also] were less dependent on the patronage of the traditional rulers to advance in their careers.[40]

The city of Kaduna, the old regional capital of the North, is symbolic in that it represents the North as a whole. The leaders of the Mafia have controlled various state agencies, including the *New Nigerian* newspaper, the northern radio and television facilities, and financial institutions. They lost a contest for control of the National Party of Nigeria in the 1983 election campaign, and thus lost status vis-á-vis businesspeople who were profiting from party and state patronage. They had close links with the military, and supported the 1983 coup that restored the northern-dominated military rule that has continued to the present.[41] However, Sani Abacha distanced himself from this group, and the arrest and death in prison of General Yar'Adua, a leading figure in the Kaduna Mafia, suggested that the organization had at least temporarily lost its influence.

Peasant Farmers - Given that most of Nigeria's labor force is involved in agriculture, one would expect to find strong associational activity among them. However, the ethnic divisions in the country have prevented the formation of any national-level farm organizations, except among modern entrepreneurial farmers operating on a large scale. Such groups as do exist among peasant farmers are usually engaged in cooperative activities at the local level, and have never been active beyond the regional level. A well-documented farm movement emerged in the Western region in 1968 and 1969, that is, during that later years of the Biafran War. The *Agbekoya* (literally, "farmers reject suffering" in Yoruba) movement was an example of agrarian populism building on peasant unrest that became a tax revolt. This movement had its roots in Akaran, near Ibadan, where farming of cocoa, palm kernels, and cola nuts was the main occupation. Tax collection was suspended for most of two years in rural southwest Nigeria; traditional leaders were attacked, and an *oba* was murdered. Farmers attacked the prison in Ibadan and freed its occupants, and pitched battles were fought with the army and police. Eventually the government was unable to quell the revolts, and negotiated a settlement. The *Agbekoya* movement was one of the most successful mass movements of peasant farmers in Nigeria.

More recently, large-scale development projects in northern Nigeria that have displaced large numbers of farmers, or real or threatened appropriates of land by corporations or wealthy individuals have resulted in peasant mobilization, and have contributed support to political parties challenging the dominant political forces in the region. Here again, however, mobilization has been sporadic and focused on a single event.[42]

The failure of agricultural producers to mobilize politically is attributed by Forrest to the general absence of policies having an impact on their livelihood (counting as exceptions situations such as that spawning the *Agbekoya* movement), the weakness of agricultural class alignments, and "the great dispersion of farming communities and the variation in social organization and culture."[43] More commonly, the interest articulation activities of farmers have been of the anomic variety, or have taken the form of clientelism (see below). This is to be expected among poor and widely illiterate rural populations.

The Military - Finally, one institution has become far more than an interest group: the military itself. Because of Nigeria's extensive experience with direct military rule, their political role is addressed in a separate section of this chapter. Here we can observe that military forces play a role in the politics of all countries that have them, ranging from that of a simple institutional interest group to the situation epitomized by Nigeria, where the military forces themselves control the political regime. Still, the Nigerian military is not a cohesive interest. The enlisted personnel and lower-ranking officers have not seen any direct benefit from military rule, and many have supported efforts to return to civilian rule. Also, the country's ethnic divisions are reflected in the military as well, although they compete there with a well-ingrained military professionalism. The military rank and file were originally drawn mostly from northern non-Hausa minorities. Later recruitment drew from all over the country, but the minorities, especially from the Middle Belt, remain disproportionately numerous. The early preponderance of Igbo officers ended with the second coup and the Biafran War, which resulted in the Northern dominance in the officer corps that is present today. However, there is wide ethnic diversity among the officers, and ethnicity is only one factor in the complex disputes within the military. There is a constant possibility that new factions will emerge to challenge the current leadership, either to supplant them or to redirect the country to civilian control.

The role of a vital **civil society** as a balance to political authority has been played by a range of interest groups in the wake of General Sani Abacha's seizure of power in November 1993. As we have seen, trade unions and unions of the academic staff at secondary schools and the universities have engaged in a series of strikes against the Abacha regime. These activities were designed to force Abacha to release Moshood Abiola from prison, to agree to political activity on Abiola's part, and to turn over power to a civilian regime. Their strike stimulated an increase in world prices of raw crude oil, and in pressing shortages in refined petroleum products in Nigeria. Abacha responded by arresting the union leaders and replacing them with his hand-picked successors. Although the strike may have been broken, it is not yet clear that Abacha has eliminated the petroleum workers' potential for political disruption. Yet, although their effect on the nation's economy was crippling, Abacha stubbornly clung to power until his death. The situation changed under Abubakar, who released union leaders Frank Kokori and Milton Dabibi. They and others could constitute a force in the country strong enough to drive the military from power; however, it is not clear whether the necessary coalition can be formed under a leadership sufficiently influential and determined to accomplish the task.

Abacha's regime was not without substantial support. An organization called the Association for a Better Nigeria (ABN) was formed under Babangida. Headed by Chief Francis Nzeribe, a former aspirant to the SDP presidential nomination and an Igbo, the ABN went to court to seek an injunction against certification of the 1993 election. Although their claim of twenty-five million members must be treated with great skepticism (that would have been about half the adult population, and many more than the fourteen million who voted that year),[44] and although the association may be nothing more than a front for the military regime, there are many in the country who profit from the existing arrangement, and are not eager for a new constitutional regime. Similarly, a number of prominent delegates to the constitutional conference called by Abacha signed a two-page letter in the *New York Times* of October 25, 1994, including Odumegwu Ojukwu, Igbo leader of the Biafran secession, and Shehu Yar'Adua, a candidate for president before Babangida disallowed the 1992 primaries who was then considered one of the most serious contenders for the presidency. The letter called upon the U.S. government to end its support for the presumed Abiola electoral victory. (Yar'Adua was later arrested by Abacha, and presumably lost his enthusiasm for the regime. As noted previously, he died in prison on December 9, 1997).

An alternative, and perhaps more consistently operative structure for interest representation is found in **clientelism**, a concept first introduced in Chapter Three. Powerful Nigerian political figures are able to mobilize support through personal "connections" with subordinates, who may themselves serve in a corresponding role of "patron" for a yet-lower set of "clients." Clientelism was an integral aspect of political life in the larger-scale precolonial systems of the Hausa, the Yoruba, and others. Those who are not represented by formal associations may be able to take advantage of their connections to achieve political ends, particularly at the local level, and where traditional rulers and their political systems maintain some influence. Furthermore, the pattern of personal contacts is ingrained in the culture, and thus remains important as an approach to powerful modern figures independent of any local traditional context. Indeed, clientelism may be a rather universal "first growth" form of political organization where a patrimonial culture is not in place, where the direct power of a state on its subjects is weak, and where modern forms of association based on class or economic interest have not yet been formed. Resting on the intricate and far-reaching patron-client networks in Nigeria is a political system that Richard Joseph has characterized as "prebendal." A "prebend" (a term originally from the Anglican Church, referring to that part of a cathedral's income used to pay the pastor, and given more general meaning by the

---

**Box 6.1 An Example of Clientelist Relations
Between Military Officers and the Public**

"On evenings and at the weekends, there is a
constant stream of 'brothers,' kinsmen,
acquaintances from the same village or town-
ward or the same ethnic group who come to pay
their respects at an officer's house and to drink
his beer and Fanta orange. They may be there
for advice on recruitment into the army, to raise
a contribution for a funeral or some other
common function, to bring messages from
family and friends, to pay homage, to listen to
the radiogram or watch television, or merely to
seek company. . .Ease of access does not,
however, free the more humble visitors of the
obligation to make the suitable gestures of
deference toward their host. Similarly, an
officer, because of his high social position, will
feel strongly obliged to demonstrate the
appropriate hospitality, to keep an ever-open
fridge, or to send his servant scurrying over to
the mess for drinks, and in appropriate instances
to expect his wife or manservant to produce a
large supply of food for visitors

(Luckham, 1971, pp. 112-113)

nineteenth-century sociologist Max Weber) is a public office given by a ruler to an individual client in return for his loyalty in delivering political support at some lower level, and in privatizing public resources. Prebendalism, then, is not a concept clearly separated from clientelism (see Box 3.7), but is rather a form or aspect of clientelism in which the "patron" supports his or her clients through the rent-producing use of public office, and where a principal focus of political activity by clients for their patrons is to help them obtain the prebendal offices that will be the source of income. Joseph sees the rise of prebendalism in Nigeria as independent of the nature of particular regimes, civilian or military,[45] and Luckham identified an openness of recruitment into the military as a factor in the "high accessibility of army officers (like other elites) to persons of nonelite background" (see Box 6.1). The durability of clientelist, or prebendal, politics has made difficult the "restructuring" of Nigerian administration when budgetary concerns have been raised.

Clientelism in the modern Nigerian state is a product of the interaction of precolonial political systems with colonial rule. Lagos, for example, was a "small city state" in 1850, just before British colonial rule in Nigeria first established itself there. The surrounding villages were already tied to Lagos through patron-client ties in which a Lagos chief was the patron of a village which submitted to his authority, or more commonly where the Lagos chief simply *represented* a village's interest at the Lagos *oba*'s court and in the marketplace. In the latter case, there was even competition among Lagos chiefs for the right to represent a village, which had the right to change from one patron to another.[46] When, in 1861, the British imposed a treaty, they intended to govern the whole area directly. However, the climate was not attractive to Europeans, and the resources were never sufficient for intensive staffing by colonial administrators. The district outside Lagos City proper was especially neglected: "the territory was of little interest to foreign rulers so long as the inhabitants supplied foodstuffs to city markets and refrained from interfering with their lucrative North-South trade."[47] The villagers thus arranged their own governance, drawing on their precolonial tradition, with a chief (*baale*) assisted by a council of elders. These officials created patron-client links with the colonial system through Lagos chiefs as they had done previously with the *oba*. These links were broken when, in the 1930s, the British created a separate district for the northern environs of Lagos, but they did not disappear completely.

After World War II, urban development began to engulf the area, and new intermediaries emerged from the multiethnic settler population. Because administrative officials were still remote, and because there were few lateral ties among villages, the need for intermediaries remained, and those individuals occupying such positions became politically influential.[48] Through the accumulation of wealth, and especially, their development of real estate, such patrons acquired high status and authority. In the period leading to independence and during the First Republic, the patronage networks became allied with political parties, especially the Action Group and the faction which split from it and emerged as the Nigerian National Democratic Party. The chieftaincies which had been claimed by those at higher positions in the networks were challenged under the first military regimes, which looked into the authenticity of such titles. Those who were eventually officially recognized as chiefs were landowners and entrepreneurs, who combined political and economic power. In her study of clientelism in a suburban area of Lagos, Barnes concludes:

> Clientelism helps account for much of the stability in leadership which exists despite the many changes that take place in regimes. It helps account for the paucity of overt class conflict despite extraordinary disparities between rich and poor. And it helps account for the fact that integration occurs despite the formidable barriers of ethnicity.[49]

When the petroleum-based economic boom began in the late 1970s, clientelist structures already in place saw massive increases of scale: The oil economy was entirely under state control, and state agencies issued contracts for the infrastructure projects that oil made possible. Foreign oil companies and construction companies competed for state contracts and contacts with the appropriate public officials. Middlemen offered to provide the necessary links:

> For the foreign firms competing, it is more rational to increase the price by a one percent commission for the key government official(s) than to try to make a more attractive offer by lowering

the price of the goods. And, to secure this kind of deal, it is necessary to use a local middleman whose services can only be obtained by the payment of a high retaining fee, bonuses and commissions.[50]

Thus, clientelist structures provided the means by which petroleum-produced funds could pass from the public sector—that is, from government treasuries—into private hands.

Participation

The forms of action that Nigerians have taken in pursuit of political goals since independence covers the whole spectrum of possibilities, from the casting of a ballot to participation in the terribly violent civil war of 1967–1970.

VOTING

Given the lack of either good census data or reliable voter registration figures, it is difficult to be precise about voter turnout figures, but estimates are in the range of 40–60 percent in some earlier elections; 66 percent of Nigerian respondents in a national survey claim to have voted for president in 1964, and 59 percent said they voted in local elections.[51] These are impressive levels of activity for a populace that includes a large proportion of poor and illiterate voters. There are many indications that some of the explanation is found in clientelism, in its "machine politics" that ties even uneducated, rural voters into the electoral process through personalistic ties with political activists. Clientelist ties are combined with various appeals based on "moral sentiment" toward any of the range of possible identities to which a given individual or group might respond. Often, voter motivation must be manipulated differently in different elections, to support electoral alliances across regions and ethnic groups.[52] It is never a simple matter to decode the motives behind a given voting decision.

In contrast to such complex calculations, we can be sure of one group that did not vote: Women were not given the right to vote in northern Nigeria until the local elections of 1976 and the federal election of 1979. Even after that, women in the North voted in small numbers, because many northern states had no voter registration list, but relied on income tax receipts as proof of eligibility. Since over 90 percent of women did not pay income tax in the North, there were very few eligible women voters.[53]

Interest in elections, even in the mobilization of clientelist networks, declined during the long process imposed by military regimes for the return to civilian rule. In the presidential election of June 12, 1993—the last national election in the country—out of 39 million registered voters, only 14 million cast ballots, a turnout of 36 percent. This cannot be taken as a sign of voter apathy, however, since it was an election between parties created and imposed by the government, between two relatively unknown presidential contenders. Voter turnout plunged in the election of delegates to the Abacha-sponsored Constitutional Conference on May 23, 1994. This was not surprising, given that there was no campaigning and little voter awareness of the purpose of the election, except that generated by NADECO's call to boycott it! There was no official count, but even government media outlets described a low turnout.[54] Such exercises have undoubtedly lowered Nigerians' expectations of the efficacy of voting. The National Electoral Commission announced in March 1997 that over 55 million had registered to vote in partisan local elections, but it is not known how many actually voted. The registration figure, which would represent nearly the entire voting-age population of the country, must be inflated.

On the other hand, an active local community life, at least in previous periods, was reflected in survey data. In a cross-national survey conducted in the 1970s, Nigerians showed a level of communal activities—organizational membership and group work on community problems—on a par with respondents in the United States, and much higher than respondents from the European and Asian countries involved in the study.[55] As noted above, Nigeria has the highest number of legally registered organizations in Africa. These findings coincide with the vigorous community life often depicted by Nigerian novelists.

"UNCONVENTIONAL" PARTICIPATION

This is a term used to indicate political behavior that is not a routine part of the political process, usually including protest demonstrations and political violence. It is epitomized by the kinds of activity in which people might be engaged when "pushed to the edge."

The tumultuous nature of Nigerian politics has provided many stimulations for demonstrations and protests, often at considerable risk of injury or arrest. The Campaign for Democracy staged what must have been the largest nationwide political protest in the country's history when, in early July 1993, it organized strikes and demonstrations against Babangida's annulment of the June 12 election of Moshood Abiola:

> The CD had done its homework by having meetings with special interest groups—meat sellers, market women, shop keepers, students, trade unions and road transport workers—and by enlisting their co-operation and support. The country became paralysed as banks, markets, schools, and government offices were closed, while many streets in the major cities were deserted. . .The action. . .received unprecedented encouragement from abroad, notably from Nigerians in Europe and the Americas.[56]

Observers were hopeful that this unprecedented action from Nigeria's civil society would force the regime to retreat, but the reaction was harsh: The leaders of the various groups were arrested (and many of them later coopted to support the government), and unprecedented security measures were implemented.

In spite of the risks, the Nigerian tradition of political protest persists. There have been many reports of direct actions of sabotage against oil refineries and pipelines, seen by some as the most effective way to hurt the national regime, to highlight demands for greater return of oil profits to the producing region, or to settle other local disputes. Protest actions are not limited to the petroleum-producing areas. Late in 1997, government workers struck in Kaduna state, in the North, over arrears in pay and denial of benefits; the State Administrator threatened to fire 22,000 workers. A few months later, thousands of secondary school students also demonstrated in Kaduna over non-payment of their teachers' salaries, and called for the removal of the Kaduna State Administrator. Opposition to the regime is most intense in the southwest, where a number of bombings directed against military personnel have taken place, including the attempted assassination of the military administrator of Ekiti state.

Demonstrations were a central part of the struggle over whether Sani Abacha would be transformed into a civilian president. The regime invited, or at least encouraged, "solidarity visits" to Abuja by traditional rulers, religious leaders, and association officers, and supported an organization called Youth Earnestly Ask for Abacha (YEAA) to "demand" his candidacy. YEAA sponsored a massive demonstration in support of Abacha's candidacy in Abuja on March 3, 1998; an anti-Abacha demonstration planned for the same day in Lagos was broken up by police. These projects were the most visible of demonstrations increasingly used to show or to test the legitimacy of government and opposition across the country.

The pattern of political *violence* by region can be seen in Box 6.2, which attempts to log the major outbursts of political violence—coups, the civil war, communal violence, and violence by police and military personnel against civilians. The greatest example of political violence was, of course the Biafran civil war in 1966-1969: Nigeria has experienced over two million deaths in wars from 1960 to 1992, the vast majority of them during the civil war. Still, there have been almost regular reports of violence throughout the independence period, from the use of "thugs" by political parties in both republics through rioting such as broke out in western and northern Nigeria in 1966, in Kano state between the rival northern movements in 1981, and the increasing level of violent political conflict across the country from 1981 to the military coup of 1983, to the confrontations with police in Lagos and the Southwest during the last days of the Babangida regime and in the challenges to Abacha's seizure of power. Conflicts involving associational economic and antiregime groups against the state have been concentrated in the Southwest, especially in Lagos. Eastern Nigeria has seen less reported political violence since the Biafran War, as it has sat somewhat on the sidelines of political competition since then (with the exception of Ogoni-police and interethnic conflict in the Delta, which has claimed thousands of lives in the 1990s).

Ethnic-based violence is unfortunately common in much of the world, and Nigeria has had its share, from the killings that immediately preceded the Biafran conflict through many more localized interethnic conflicts that turn to violence over inequities real or perceived.   While disputes among ethnic groups can have many causes, the role of political authority plays a major role, as we have seen in the siting of local governments in the Ife-Modakeke conflict (Box 3.3). Deciding the location of local governments, with the resources that are perceived to flow therefrom, has been the source of violent conflicts in various parts of Nigeria, including, besides Ife, a bloody dispute between the Ijaws and Itsekiris (and also involving a third group, the Urhobo) in and around the city of Warri in Delta State. As one of a long list of federal government redrawings of local government boundaries, a new local government designated Warri South was created in December 1996. Officials in Abuja were responding to a request by Itsekiri spokesmen for the new unit, which involved moving the local government headquarters from Ogbe-Ijoh (dominated by the Ijaws) to Ogidigben, in Itsekiri territory. Ijaw spokesmen, caught unawares, alleged that this was another instance in a long history of Itsekiri oppression, and violence designed to prevent the move turned into general interethnic attacks that seriously disrupted Shell Oil operations around Warri. In March 1997, Ijaw villagers in the Delta oil region took 126 employees of Shell Oil hostage. The villagers had decided that this was the most effective way to draw the government's attention to their displeasure over the local government issue. The hostages were

BOX 6.2. NIGERIA - POLITICAL VIOLENCE LOG

Year	West and Midwest	East	North and Middle Belt
1953			Kano riots, 36 deaths
1958			NPC/NEPU riots, Maiduguri
1960			Tiv riots, 16–50 deaths
1964			Tiv riots, 300–several thousand deaths
1965	election thuggery		
1966	January "Majors" coup	Outbreak of Biafran War; October violence against northerners	January "Majors" coup; May, Anti-Igbo riots: 92–600 deaths. October violence against easterners (5,000-10,000 deaths)
1967	Peasant tax riots	BIAFRAN WAR	
1968		BIAFRAN WAR	

1969–1971	Student/police clash Ibadan Univ. "loss of life"	BIAFRAN WAR	Student/police clash, ABU
1978	Student/police clash, Lagos Univ.		
1980			'Yan Tatsine uprising, Kano: 4,177 civilians killed. Peasant uprising, violent police suppression, Bakolori irrigation project. 100s killed/wounded
1981			'Yan Tatsine uprisings, Kaduna, Maiduguri.
1982	Election rigging response: 100+ killed, $100M property loss		Maitatsine riots, Gongola State (130 deaths) and Maiduguri ; church burnings, Kano.
1983			Maitatsine riots, Gombe
1984			Police repression of ABU student riots (20 killed)
1985	Anti-SAP riots		Anti-SAP riots, Jos
1986	Anti-SAP riots - over 70 deaths		
1987			religious-based rioting, Kaduna, Kano, Sokoto, Jos
1988			Riots over appointment of sultan of Sokoto
		SAP riots in cities.	Taraba - Tiv/Jukun land disputes. Up to 5,000 deaths by 3/92
1989	Transport fare riots— widespread. "Several" deaths. SAP riots in cities.	Protest at Shell facilities, Umuechem (Delta); 80 killed.	religious-based rioting and looting religious rioting, Bauchi; estimates of thousands of deaths.
1990	Lagos—riots over Ransom-Kuti arrests		anti-Christian violence, Katsina , Kaduna, Kano

1991			
			Religious rioting, Zagon Kataf
		Mobile police attack Ogoni villages 80 deaths	
1992	Demonstrations against annulment of presidential elections. 30—100 deaths		
1993			
	July—20 to 168 deaths in Lagos riots against regime; Fighting between Igbo traders & Yoruba youths in Lagos over whether to strike.		
		Attacks on Ogoni villages; 100s of deaths	Kaduna - Hausa-Kataf (Christian) clashes - 30 deaths in Jan.,300 in May
1994		Ethnic and police conflict with Ogoni; 100s of deaths	Katsina - Muslim/ security forces clashes
		Ogoni-Okrika clashes; at least 90 deaths	Muslim students, police clash in Kaduna; 8 deaths.
1995	Bombings directed against military personnel, Lagos; government blames NADECO.		
1996	Murder of Kudirat Abiola in Lagos.		
		Conflict at Idmili (Anambra)	
	Modakeke/Ife conflict in ife; 100s killed		Kaduna State civil servants strike, student demonstrations
1997	Warri – Ijaw/Itsekiri conflict village burned, 5 deaths		
			Shiite Muslim demonstrations, Kaduna
	At least 3 deaths in clash of police and pro-and anti- Abacha demonstrators, Ibadan		
1998			
	Bomb explosions in Lagos, Ife May 1 demonstration, Ibadan		

Sources: Africa South of the Sahara 1994; Anifowose 1982:124,132; Beckman 1987; Diamond 1988b:59; Forrest 1995: 49, 81, 110, 113, 118,, 238,249; Gboyega 1997: 176 ; Ibrahim 1997; Kirk-Greene 1971: 48, 63; Lubeck 1987: 268; Luckham 1971: 309; Okeke 1992: 109; Oyewole 1987:181, 198; Suberu 1997; Theobald 1990: 159; Welch 1996: 11,12,115; Zartman 1983: 56.

later released, but the conflict continued, with further attacks on Shell installations and a total of ninety deaths reported by April 1997.[57]

The major religion-based violence has been in the North and the Middle Belt. Polarization based on religion dates only to the 1970s, when the question of the role of Shari'a law came up in discussions of a new constitution. The early 1990s were marked by riots against non-Muslim communities in the North with many deaths, large-scale destruction of property, and concerns about the seeming inability of government at all levels to provide security.[58]

Nigeria has been a highly politicized country ever since independence, although alienation and frustration with the failure to develop stable, honest, and responsive institutions is increasingly evident.

Parties and Elections

When the national election of 1993 was voided by the Babangida government, party activities were banned. As is normally the case under military regimes everywhere, Nigeria's military governments have always abolished and banned all political parties and movements, except as they have reconstituted party systems to return to civilian rule before the Second Republic (1979-1983), in the early 1990s under Babangida's aborted movement toward a Third Republic, and most recently (September 30, 1996), when the National Electoral Commission (NECON) created by the Abacha regime registered five new parties to contest local, state, and national elections on the way to a stated goal of turning over power to civilian governments in 1998. The military has seen parties as the source of political disorder, but also as potential bases for challenges to military rule. This, of course, means that the military regime operates without any institutions for *interest aggregation*, "the activity in which the demands of individuals and groups are combined into significant policy proposals."[59] The word "significant" is especially relevant here: In political systems where parties have significant resources, in the form of support manifested through votes, campaign contributions, and the like, they allow contenders for office to cobble together coalitions of interests that provide a sufficient base for the winners to claim legitimate rule, and they transmit a broad range of demands to those officials. Where power is seized by force, parties may no longer have "significant" resources and can be ignored; yet the military rulers also lose an important source of information on policy issues and problems, and on their legitimacy with the public. Demands are then, as in the Nigerian case, aggregated through patron-client networks, which accumulate individual and community desires to share government revenues, rather than the wishes of national-level interests. General policies are then formed through consultation with the bureaucracy, which occupies the vacuum between the military leadership and the population.

Because parties have played an important role in Nigerian politics in the past, their bases of support continue to exist. The five parties that the Abacha regime allowed to form may not evolve into enduring organizations, but it is certain that some constellation of parties will re-emerge in future constitutional arrangements. Thus the evolution of political parties and their effect on Nigerian politics to date is worthy of attention.[60]

The first modern party was formed by Herbert Macaulay to contest Nigerian Legislative Council elections in Lagos in 1923. Several such movements contended for power at the local level under the colonial regime, and a diverse nationalist movement emerged in 1944, under the leadership of Macaulay and Nnamdi Azikiwe, the National Council of Nigeria and the Cameroons, or NCNC.
("Cameroons" here refers to the English-speaking portion of the contemporary country of Cameroon on Nigeria's eastern border. The NCNC was meant to include members from the British trust territory as well as from Nigeria, but in a pre-independence plebiscite, the English-speaking Cameroonians opted for incorporation into Cameroon. The NCNC then was re-named the National Convention of Nigerian Citizens.) This organization advocated greater representation in the Nigerian colonial government. Chapters were established across Nigeria. However, when the British introduced a more democratic but more decentralized constitution in 1951, the NCNC broke up along ethnic lines. The 1951 constitution mandated indirect elections in Houses of Assembly in the three regions; Lagos was in the Western region, where the Yoruba were in the majority. An opposition party, the Action Group (AG), emerged under the leadership of a young Yoruba lawyer, Obafemi Awolowo, with an initial organizational base in the Egbe Omo Oduduwa, a Yoruba cultural society. Although Azikiwe's NCNC won in multiethnic Lagos, the AG won the majority of seats in the Western region. The NCNC won overall in the Eastern region, where Azikiwe's own Igbo ethnic group was in the majority.

From the beginning there were forces within both the NCNC and the AG arguing for movement in a multicultural, issue-based, cross-regional direction. The Action Group was especially split along liberal (cross-regional, pushing for quick movement toward independence) and conservative (ethnic-based, evolutionary) lines. The fact that elected offices were established first at the regional level, and only later (1957) at the national level, favored the forces of regionalism. Azikiwe particularly was committed to action at the national level, but it became clear that a regional power base would be essential to the subsequent contestation for control at the national level, and Azikiwe also was constrained to center his party on its strength in the East. Thus the NCNC came to be identified with that region and the Igbo people.

In the North, Britain's successful application of indirect rule had resulted in an alliance between the colonial administration and the traditional emirs that impeded the formation of modern political movements. Whereas in the South such movements had arisen among a Western-educated elite outside the control of any traditional authority, in the North the only youth to receive a modern education came from the families of the traditional elites. Although reformist political organizations were formed, notably the Northern Elements' Progressive Union (NEPU) under Mallam Aminu Kano, they were able to operate only at the margins and tension points of the emirates. A more conservative movement, the Northern Peoples' Congress (NPC) was taken over by the Sardauna (a traditional title) of Sokoto, a direct descendent of the Fulani empire's founder, and a Hausa commoner, Abubakar

Tafawa Balewa. The NPC, the traditional emirates, and the pre-independence administrative structure were intertwined such that young administrators could run successfully for public office, but only if they had the support of their administrative superiors and of the local traditional elite. This political structure grew up among a population that was not as affected by education (less than 15 percent were literate) and mass communication as in the South, and much more loyal to their traditional authorities. In the 1959 northern House of Assembly, 24 percent of NPC delegates were sons of incumbent or former emirs, and over a third were blood relatives of emirs.[61] The elite origins of the party's officers and candidates were de-emphasized through both communal (ethnic) and religious (Muslim) appeals to the electorate. At NPC meetings, the political choice was seen as between tradition and social breakdown, and good against evil. At NPC meetings in the Kanuri region of the Northeast,

> listeners. . .[were] constantly presented with moral choices; "are you against our own chiefs, the district heads. . .our Shehu [emir]?—Well *they*, the opposition parties, are; are you against wives being obedient to their husbands?—well *they* are; are you against children being obedient to their parents?—well *they* are," and so on. Stories are told of people whose parents were fine and upstanding citizens who supported and were supported by their leaders. Then their children ran away and supported opposition parties having first rejected the authority, love, affection and support of their own parents. Such people are now vagrants with no families, no proper connections to a respectable Kanuri household, no place in society, and no proper place in the social and moral life of the community. It is prophesied that morality and family life as it is now known could be destroyed if opposition parties ever come to power. Finally, it is always pointed out that opposition parties represent the southern Nigerians and that a vote for such a group is a vote against Islam, the true religion, and a vote for paganism covered by a thin cloak of Christianity.[62]

Not surprisingly, the NPC did not give high priority in its program to achieving national independence.

Regional elections in the North were contested by the NEPU, but the NEPU was only occasionally successful, only in the towns, and only through support obtained by an alliance with the NCNC. Officials and elders were rather tolerant of political movements organized by southern Nigerians, probably because they felt they had little to fear from them, but indigenous competition was another matter: In the Kanuri emirate, a Bornu Youth League formed, and battled with NPC supporters in riots in Maiduguri in 1958; it was ruthlessly suppressed and its leaders driven out of the region.[63] In the southern, predominately Christian part of the

Northern region (the Middle Belt), other opposition parties arose. One, the United Middle Belt Congress, formed an alliance in 1958 with the Action Group, but in 1963, broke off from the AG to combine with the NEPU. Unlike the NCNC and AG, neither the NPC nor the NEPU even tried to obtain political support outside their own region. The southern parties, however, found limits placed on their freedom to campaign in the 1964 federal elections, and urged a boycott of the elections there.

The federal election of 1964 and the Western regional election of 1965 proved to be pivotal in the country's history. They were conducted in a climate of violence and corruption that increasingly alienated the voting public. Chief S. L. Akintola had become premier of the Western region when Awolowo resigned to campaign at the federal level in 1959. In 1962, he broke from Awolowo and the Action Group over what he saw as Awolowo's radical socio-economic positions and opposition to working with the northern-dominated government. Akintola formed the Nigerian National Democratic Party (NNDP), which formed a victorious coalition with the NPC in 1964; in return, the federal government supported the NNDP in the Western regional elections the next year. When an NNDP victory was declared in the West amid charges of fraud, federal troops were sent in to support Akintola (Awolowo had been tried and imprisoned for treason in 1963). Chinua Achebe wrote a fictional account of this situation in *A Man of the People*, in which he predicted the coup that ended the disorder.

When General Ironsi assumed power following the breakdown of political order in the Western region and the first coup, one of his first moves was to abolish all parties and a large number of political associations. The country remained without formal parties from 1966 until the preparations for a return to civilian rule in 1979. General Yakubu Gowon (head of state from 1966 to 1975), had considered the creation of a one-party state in Nigeria, with himself as leader of a "national movement."[64] Nigeria's diversity, and the plurality of its power bases, made that concept impossible to achieve: To northern leaders, it suggested southern domination, while to the politicians waiting for the return of civilian rule, it meant the end of their ambitions. Gowon was unable to decide on a course of action, and was deposed before any plan had been adopted.

After taking power, Murtala Muhammed set in motion a process to return to civilian rule. The military regime established a Constitution Drafting Committee, and in his address to its opening session, Murtala Muhammed laid down several principles relating to parties. He encouraged them to "discover some means by which government can be formed without the involvement of political parties," but otherwise that they should draft a plan to guarantee "genuine and truly national political parties," while striving to work out "specific criteria by which their number would be limited."[65] The drafters responded with a constitution that was carefully crafted to promote national parties. It specified that to be elected president, a candidate would have to poll at least 25 percent of the votes cast in each of at least two-thirds of the states. Elections were to be controlled by a Federal Election

Party	Igbo	Yoruba	Hausa-Fulani
NCNC (1958)	49.3	26.7	2.8
Action Group(1958)	4.5	68.2	3.0
NPC	-	6.8	51.3

Table 6.1. Ethnic Distribution of Party Leaders, 1958. *Source:* Richard Sklar and C. S. Whitaker Jr., "Nigeria," in James s. Coleman and Carol Rosberg, *Political Parties and National Integration in Tropical africa* (Berkeley: Univ. of California Press, 1964), p. 612.

Commission (FEDECO), with which all parties must register. Parties were to be open to membership of any Nigerian, and party governing boards were to reflect the country's "federal character," specifically, coming from at least two-thirds of the states. The Electoral Decree was published in 1978; in that same year political parties were again made legal, and they came in a flood—some 150 were formed.

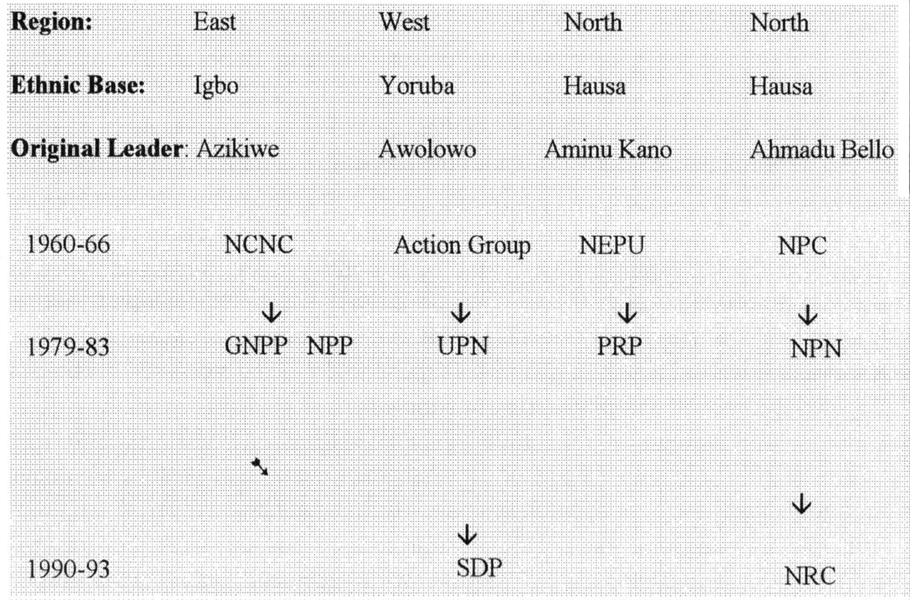

Region:	East	West	North	North
Ethnic Base:	Igbo	Yoruba	Hausa	Hausa
Original Leader:	Azikiwe	Awolowo	Aminu Kano	Ahmadu Bello
1960-66	NCNC	Action Group	NEPU	NPC
	↓	↓	↓	↓
1979-83	GNPP NPP	UPN	PRP	NPN
				↓
		↓		
1990-93		SDP		NRC

(The parties formed under Abacha, 1996-1998, were artificial constructs that were not part of this evolution.)

Figure 6.1. The Evolution of Political Parties in Nigeria.

Most of these could not expect to receive FEDECO certification, but could then negotiate among themselves for positions in larger blocs. FEDECO finally qualified just five parties:

The **National Party of Nigeria (NPN)**, led by upper-income northerners, was seen as the successor to the former Northern People's Congress. However, given the constraints of the new constitution, the NPN was much more interethnic and interregional than its predecessor. For example, its chairman was chief A.M.A. Akinloye, an Ibadan-based lawyer. It particularly enjoyed the support of wealthy businessmen from all regions, who looked to it for contracts and franchises, and for protection against predatory competitors who might have greater political influence.[66] It was openly supported by General Obasanjo himself, and included in its membership Moshood Abiola, the Yoruba businessman who was later to win the last free presidential election, in 1993. The **Unity Party of Nigeria (UPN)** was led by Obafemi Awolowo and thought to be a reincarnation of the Action Group. The **Nigerian Peoples' Party (NPP)** was formed by a young entrepreneur from Maiduguri in the northeast, Alhaji Waziri Ibrahim. Waziri appealed to the minorities in each region against domination by the three large ethnic groups. However, Igbo politicians gained control of the NPP, which then splintered into two parties; one of them asked Nnamdi Azikiwe to take the lead. That segment retained the NPP title but became a new manifestation of the NCNC. The other became The **Great Nigeria Peoples' Party (GNPP)**, under the leadership of Waziri.[67]

Finally, there was the **Peoples' Redemption Party (PRP)** under the northern radical Aminu Kano. Each of the parties had the potential to be national in scope, and they had somewhat differing ideological positions (see Figure 6.1).

The elections of 1979 and 1983 are difficult to analyze, because five parties competed for president, Senate and House seats, and state assemblies with varying degrees of success by state and by office.[68] Looking at the control of the Senate, House and state assemblies overall, however, it is clear that most states were controlled by a single party. Awolowo's Unity Party dominated five of the nineteen states in 1979, all in the Yoruba west and the midwest (a "minority" area). Azikiwe's NPP carried three states, two of which were in the Igbo-dominated east. Aminu Kano, who led the NEPU in challenging the NPC in the North in the First Republic, now headed the PRP, strongly committed to national unification. However, the PRP carried only his own state, Kano, in the North. The GNPP won two states in the Northeast, home region of its presidential candidate. However, the ethnic factor was complicated by the success of the NPN in building cross-regional alliances. The NPN controlled eight states; five of these were in the North, but three were in the Southeast. The GNPP showed some ability to generate votes outside the Northwest, but only in other "minority-dominant" states in the other regions.

LOCAL ELECTIONS

The first elections held under the colonial administration in 1952 were for local councils; local council elections have been held in conjunction with each phase of elections in independent Nigerian history, and in a few cases (under the military) when there were no elections at higher levels. On the other hand, civilian rule does not automatically mean elections at all levels: There were no local elections after the first election of the Second Republic, as elected officials were replaced by those appointed by state governments.

Councils with a majority of elected representatives (some could be appointed by governors) were chosen in nonpartisan elections in 1976 as a prelude to the return to civilian rule. However, under the Second Republic, civilian governors appointed and reappointed "Caretaker Committees" composed of their own political clients. These councilors were replaced following the 1983 coup by military-appointed "sole administrators," and then by appointed five-member councils. In 1987, nonpartisan councils and local government chairmen were chosen, in elections generally perceived to be "free and fair." The Constitution of 1989 provided for elected councils and *secretaries* (executives) of Local Government Areas. Local elections were scheduled for 1989, but were postponed to 1990 to accommodate the two-party system imposed by the Babangida regime. The councils elected in 1990 remained in office until all civilian institutions were terminated by Babangida's suspension of the 1989 constitution in 1993.

The Abacha regime scheduled nonpartisan elections for local chairmen (executives) in 1996, then sponsored the registration of the five new parties to contest local council elections in March 1997. NADECO called for a boycott of these elections, charging that all certified parties were under the control of the government. According to election results from the 774 local council races, the most pro-Abacha of the parties, the United Nigeria Congress Party (UNCP) won 369 chairmanships, followed by the Democratic Party of Nigeria (DPN) with 192 wins. NADECO has charged that the UNCP was seen by the regime as the possible vehicle for its return to power (and in April, 1998 the UNCP was the first party to endorse Abacha as its candidate for the presidency), but the DPS and the other three parties also pledged to support Abacha in an eventual run for the presidency. The three other parties won a total of 203 chairmanships. This "top-down" creation of parties was even more controlled than Babangida's creation of a two-party system.

ETHNIC SOLIDARITY AND PARTY LOYALTY

Nigeria did not share in one experience common to many African states after independence: It never was under the control of a single political party. In many countries, although their real purpose may have been to rationalize a grab for power, leaders argued that multiparty systems exacerbated ethnic tension in the African context, because parties inevitably formed along ethnic lines. Indeed, ethnic-based parties have been a common feature of multipartyism in Africa, and Nigeria was no exception in this regard. Single-party systems (or at least one-party-dominant systems) indeed existed *de facto* in each of the three major regions of Nigeria from shortly after independence until the first coup, and again at the level of the nineteen states during the Second Republic, but it would never have been feasible to impose single-party control over the whole country, as was common elsewhere.

Figure 6.1 shows the history of Nigerian political parties, notably their re-emergence with the same ethnic bases after suppression by military regimes. Governments, especially the military ones, have tried to force Nigerians to express their will through cross-ethnic parties. However, because ethnicity drives much of the political organizing in the country, political leaders have succeeded in subverting the goal of truly national parties through their calls to ethnic identity. A political career is started in a local community on an ethnic basis, and a cross-ethnic party is in that situation nothing more than a coalition of ethnic interests. The Hausas have been most successful in this situation, having captured the presidency each time this national office was filled by election. With envy and bitterness, many political activists in the south are convinced that the Hausas know they can assemble an electoral majority dominated by them, and that they base all their political activity on that belief.

The NPN won the ultimate prize in 1979, the presidency, essentially on the basis of a combination of northern voters and minority voters in the southern regions. The most significant difference for parties between the First and Second Republics turned out to be the carving up of the original three regions into nineteen states. Ethnic groups other than the "big three" were dominant in a number of these states, and had thus broken free of regional ethnic dominance. Party strategists would henceforth need to combine a strong base in one of the main ethnic group areas with a successful appeal for support among minorities and potentially among dissident groups in the home bases of the other two major groups. The potential for success of this strategy if pursued by southern politicians was seen in Aminu Kano's 1979 victory against the NPN in Kano State, demonstrating the rift between Hausa-Fulani notables in Kano and Sokoto. Capturing the support of one of these groups would be difficult for a southerner; but encouraging a separate northern candidacy to split the northern vote was an obvious possibility.

The constitutional requirement that a successful presidential candidate receive at least 25 percent of the vote in at least two-thirds of the states was, as we have seen, an ingenious Nigerian device to ensure that the winner of the most powerful office have wide-based support, which could only be obtained through conciliation and compromise among a variety of important constituencies. However, this complex formula was fraught with danger: At the time of the 1979 elections, there were nineteen states. What, for constitutional purposes, is two-thirds of nineteen? The question had been raised in the Constitution Drafting Committee in 1976. As the election approached, projections suggested that this outcome was quite possible, and the issue continued to be discussed. It particularly occupied the attention of the NPN, which was the party most likely to need an answer. The results confirmed the importance of the question: Shehu Shagari, the NPN candidate, had received 5.7 million votes, compared with 4.9 million for Awolowo, 2.8 million for Azikiwe, and 1.7 million each for Aminu Kano and Waziri. He thus received the highest number of votes, a plurality of just over one-third, but he won over 25 percent of the vote in just twelve of the nineteen states. However, the NPN put forth the suggestion that, since two-thirds of nineteen is actually twelve and two-thirds, the successful candidate needed to win just 25 percent of *two-thirds* of the vote in a thirteenth state; Shagari had won 20 percent of the vote in Kano state, but that was more than one-fourth of two-thirds of the vote! (Richard Osuolale Akinjide, the Ibadan lawyer who pleaded the case for the NPN, was given the nickname "Two Thirds." He later was named Attorney General and Minister of Justice.)

The Obasanjo government could have called a new election, or convened an electoral college to negotiate a conclusion, and Shagari still would likely have been the ultimate victor. However, the military leadership wanted the transition to proceed as smoothly as possible, and found it expedient to accept the NPN logic. FEDECO declared Shagari the winner; Awolowo challenged the outcome in the courts, but was unsuccessful.[69]

The NPN was less successful in the legislative elections, winning 165 of 443 (37 percent) seats in the House of Representatives and 36 of 95 (38 percent) Senate seats. An attempt was made to form a legislative coalition with the NPP, which would in effect have reconstituted the North/East alliance of the First Republic. One observer contends that the old NCNC leadership was split on this issue, with most assuming that the NPN would win, that an Igbo-led party could not do well nationally in the post-Biafra period, and that therefore the best alternative was a renewal of that alliance to at least take part in majority-coalition patronage. Others thought the long-term advantage for Igbo politicians lay in a southern alliance which, after the departure of Chief Awolowo, they would have a chance to dominate.[70] Those urging alliance with the North won the day; however, agreement on the distribution of appointments proved elusive, and the coalition was ended in 1981.

The same five parties remained in existence through the four years of the Second Republic, and contested again in 1983 for the presidency, seats in the Senate and House, and state-level positions. However, the smallest parties, the PRP and the GNPP, had been weakened by their lack of access to resources. And, as is normal in a presidential system where the ultimate prize, the presidency, is a "winner take all" election, there were pressures on the two major opposition parties to combine against the incumbent. Such cooperation proved impossible, however, when neither Azikiwe nor Awolowo would defer to the other as presidential candidate. In a campaign marked with violence and vote-rigging, the NPN won a solid victory, recording gains against the opposing parties in their home areas. The NPN increased its number of governorships from seven to twelve, and Shagari won the minimum

25 percent of the presidential vote in sixteen states, compared to twelve in 1979. The NPN won an absolute majority of seats in both the federal House (61 of 95 seats, or 64 percent) and Senate (307 of 450, 68 percent).

The NPN victory was short-lived. Three months into its second term it met an early demise at the hands of Nigeria's fourth military coup. Party financing in the 1983 elections was based on a system of unprecedented political corruption, even as the country's financial situation had greatly deteriorated,[71] and was among the reasons offered by the military for once again abolishing the country's political parties.

Tom Forrest has postulated that the nature of the NPN itself was at fault for its failure to govern effectively. Although it incorporated persons from other areas much better than the old NPC of the First Republic, it was still perceived as being dominated by northerners, if only somewhat more subtly. Furthermore, although it appeared to be a classic political machine, building on clientelist relationships within more major groups, in fact it did not have strong centralized control at the top.

The power of "big men" in the party to wield personal patronage rather than operate a system of party machine patronage weakened the capacity of the party to discriminate against non-NPN states. It also meant that there was the potential for serious friction between Lagos-based members of the party and state-based members including governors.[72]

The public's *acceptance* of the reimplementation of military rule was rooted in the civilian government's failure to address in policy the issues they had raised during the campaign. For example, both the UPN and the NPP promised full employment and free education at all levels. These promises were beyond the regime's fiscal capacity and showed a serious lack of responsibility; it is not surprising that they contributed to greater voter cynicism.

The two-year reign of Muhammedu Buhari (1983-1985) presented no timetable for a return to electoral politics. However, Buhari's successor, Ibrahim Babangida, began outlining conditions for a return to civilian rule in 1986 that revealed his view of the country's problems. Babangida announced that forty-nine politicians convicted of corruption would be banned from politics for life. Between 1987 and 1989, a series of decrees:

1) specified the categories of former holders of political office who would be disqualified from participation in political activities;
2) created a National Election Commission (NEC) to replace the defunct FEDECO in managing the electoral process;
3) provided for the non-partisan election of local councils in 1987;
4) set a timetable for the creation of political parties and the sequential election of legislators and executives at the local, state, and national levels;
5) promulgated a constitution to come into effect in 1992.

The Political Bureau created by Babangida to draw up recommendations for the return to civilian rule had also suggested that the system be structured to foster a *de-facto* two-party system. The Babangida government accepted the recommendation, and entrusted the NEC with the task of establishing guidelines for party formation that would have this result. In 1989 the ban on party activities was lifted, and associations were invited to form with specifications providing that they have a national following and an internally democratic structure. Some fifty parties sprang up overnight.

The likely effect of forcing a two-party system on this political chaos was not clear. Some feared it would lead to a polarization along north-south Christian-Muslim lines. However, such a polarization would imply the papering over of serious splits *among* northerners and between powerful interests in the Southeast and Southwest; in this context, the emergence of two monolithic political movements would not automatically occur. Thirteen groups eventually petitioned the NEC for recognition. After careful scrutiny the NEC certified five parties to the Armed Forces Ruling Council (AFRC) as having met their specifications. At the same time, the NEC report was quite disparaging of all the applications they had received. The AFRC response was extremely innovative: All thirteen associations, including those certified by the NEC were dissolved, and two parties were established by the military government. . .perhaps the only time in history that an authoritarian leadership had imposed a two-party system!

The NEC now was charged with examining the various documents of the dissolved parties and synthesizing them into two discrete philosophies. President Babangida specified that one party should be "a little to the left," the other "a little to the right" on the political spectrum. However, they were to have identical constitutions, providing for the choice of candidates by primary election. Even the parties' names were assigned by the government: The party on the left would be the Social Democratic Party, that on the right the National Republican Convention. The impact of the American model on Nigerian constitution-making had never been more obvious.

The government built headquarters buildings for both parties at each local government, and provided generous "take off grants" to sustain their organizing efforts. In a first round of elections, party officials at all levels were elected. However, powerful politicians had naturally formed parallel organizations and set about using their clientelist networks to capture one or the other party at various levels. The government tried to discourage these "old breed" politicians by infiltrating their organizations in turn, and threatening dire consequences if banned activists from earlier regimes regained control. The politicians were not easily dissuaded, however; many had borrowed extensively or depleted their personal assets in building up loyal followings, and they hoped to recoup their investments through influential positions in the new government.

Nigerians reacted to these developments with a mixture of cynicism and hope. It was difficult for intellectuals to accept a "democracy" based on parties and elections mandated by an authoritarian government; yet, it was the "only game in town," and promised to bring the country back to civilian rule, however constraining

---

Box 6.3. Moshood Abiola

Bashorun M. K. O. Abiola was the twenty-third child of his father's three wives. His mother was a kola nut trader who paid for his early education. Abiola was an entrepreneur at an early age, selling firewood when he was nine and saving money to buy a truck within a year. Although a Muslim, he attended Baptist Boys High School in his home city of Abeokuta (one year ahead of former head of state Olusegun Obasanjo), but did not convert to Christianity. His good academic work kept him in school even when his fees were not paid. He also established an orchestra to perform at social functions. He studied accounting at the University of Glasgow on a scholarship (1961-1963), then returned home to a job with Guinness breweries, but left after sensing a "glass ceiling" for Nigerian staff. He combined personal business initiatives with paid positions for large companies, finally joining the International Telephone and Telegraph Corporation (ITT) in 1969. He was successful in collecting a large debt owed by the Nigerian government to ITT, and came to own 49 percent of ITT (Nigeria).

Entering politics, he chaired the northern-based National Party of Nigeria in Ogun State during the Second Republic, and launched two newspapers which supported the NPN in power; he later left the NPN and continued to develop his media empire. Abiola became known among African American leaders, winning the Black Heritage Award of the NAACP in 1987 and 1988. His investment portfolio and list of wholly owned firms continued to expand. He has been a major philanthropist, especially in funding Islamic education and secondary schools and libraries. His calls for the West to compensate Africa for the costs of slavery received great attention in Nigeria. In 1993 he was nominated the presidential candidate of the Social Democratic Party, and won the election, but was prevented from taking office by Ibrahim Babangida. When a year later he proclaimed himself president, he was arrested and has been detained ever since. Reportedly he could be released upon renouncing his claim to the presidency (and his son has urged him to renounce to save his ailing businesses), but he has refused. Abiola's wife Kudirat, who has supported his claim to office, was murdered in June, 1996. Officials suggested she died in a family feud; opponents of the government suspect a political assassination. Following Abacha's death, Abubakar entered into negotiations with Abiola to find acceptable conditions for his release, and an agreement was said to be imminent when he died of a reported heart attack on July 7, 1998.

Source: Forrest, The Advance of African Capital, pp. 98-102; AfreeNET, July 1, 1996.

the new rules might be. Many participated in the 1990 elections of local government secretaries and councils under the two party labels. The next year saw the election of state governors and legislators, and a National Assembly. And the process was inevitably building to the election of a president, in 1992, at which time the military would hand over power. The process was set back late in 1992 when the regime nullified the results of the parties' efforts to produce presidential candidates. The process had indeed been so poorly handled as to give justification to a postponement of the process. Yet Nigerians were ever more skeptical as to whether the military really intended to leave, or were just playing an elaborate game to buy time.

Babangida scheduled a new election for June 1993, ordered the parties to produce new candidates, and set August 27, 1993 as the date for turning over power to the civilian government. Under more careful control, the parties reconvened their national conventions and nominated new candidates. The National Republican Convention selected a relatively unknown figure from the North, Bashir Tofa (a Kanuri from the northeast), while the Social Democrats nominated a rich businessman from the southwest, Moshood Abiola. Like Tofa, Abiola had close ties to the military hierarchy. He seemed to have an ideal combination of identities for Nigeria's plural culture: Although a Yoruba, he, like his opponent, is also a Muslim. Significantly, both had been active supporters of the NPN in the Second Republic. Based on NPN pledges of rotation of candidacies to regions other than the North, Abiola had even dreamed of being an eventual NPN presidential candidate, but tried in vain to succeed Shagari.[73]

The election finally took place on June 12, 1993. Nigerian and international observers reported that it was a generally fair election, certainly the cleanest Nigeria had ever seen; the NRC never contested the outcome. Perhaps equally as important as its relative fairness, the election produced a unifying outcome that was everything advocates of a two-party system could have desired: Abiola, from the South, appears to have won in nineteen of the thirty states, and won a majority of the votes in nine northern states, including his opponent's home state of Kano. The results seemed to suggest that, under a two-party system, factionalism in each region and state could be exploited to prevent a strictly regional outcome.

Besides his adept use of the country's clientelist structures, however, Abiola was a personally popular candidate. He was known for his philanthropy, and claimed to have given out 3,750 scholarships across the country, to have built mosques and churches, and to have paid for the digging of wells (Box 6.3). In his campaign, he visited every local government. He also claimed immense popularity within the military; by his own analysis, he had won 97 percent of their vote.[74]

As we have seen, however, the results were never officially announced (although the NEC chairman had "unofficially" announced eleven states), and two weeks later Babangida annulled the election. Party politics, even the contrived variety invented by the Babangida regime, had once again proved to be an exercise unacceptable to the military leadership and their allies. The question is, how was it possible for the leadership of a military force that itself appears to have supported the winner in the election to thwart the widely held support of the election process?

We must point to Nigeria's weak civil society, which allowed Babangida to balance off the various interests in the country: He talked about fresh elections, which obviously had some interest for the NRC, but which was totally unacceptable to SDP loyalists in the Yoruba areas of the Southwest; he managed to break up the SDP alliances that Abiola had carefully constructed, so that support for Abiola among party leaders outside the Southwest began to weaken; and according to Chinua Achebe, he fanned North-South divisions "more flagrantly than any other leaders we have had."[75] A number of activists with solid prodemocracy credentials abandoned their opposition to accept positions in the Abacha government, including Abiola's running mate and the president of the erstwhile Senate, which as a body had denounced the cancellation of the elections. Those who were not co-opted were in hiding, their organizations in disarray. Nigerians still hoping for a responsive, democratic political system had no obvious leaders or associations around which to rally. Abiola himself stubbornly refused to renounce his claim to the presidency even after several years in detention, but few outside of prison were willing to publicly support him. He made a strategic miscalculation by traveling to Europe and North America to seek support, rather than to lead opposition to the annulment of the election within the country. This action reduced his legitimacy in the eyes of many Nigerians (some of whom remembered that Abiola had himself supported the military coup against Shehu Shagari in 1983), and did not result in strong international support. In addition, conservative northerners found his conduct unseemly; to them he should have accepted his treatment at the hands of Babangida as Allah's will.

The Abacha regime's declaration that party activity would be resumed was ostensibly made policy when, in June 1996, it announced rules and guidelines for the formation and recognition of political parties. According to these rules, each party must have an office and at least 40,000 members in each state (a total of 1,240,000), and must file an application fee of 500,000 naira ($6000). Although NADECO condemned the exercise, and continued to stand behind Abiola, political entrepreneurs immediately began planning their organizations. Five parties were certified for the partisan elections of local chairmen in March 1997, but none of them gave any opposition to the regime, and all of them eventually supported a run by Abacha for the presidency. State and federal elections, including the election of a federal president, were scheduled for August 1998. However, on July 20, 1998, Abubakar announced the dissolution of the five parties, the nullification of the local and state elections, and a new start toward democracy with a promise to hand over power to an elected president on May 29, 1999.

Conclusion

There are two aspects of support for the return to party competition in Nigeria that should be kept in mind. On the one hand, democratic ideologues, including many academics, cannot conceive of any kind of real democracy that does not allow for party activity. Party competition has, in Nigeria's experience, been the only alternative to military rule. On the other hand, party activity has been powerfully stimulated by "prebendal" desires among political activists. Richard Joseph has, as we have seen, found a prebendal base in both civilian and military regimes, yet apparently sees a difference in the scale of prebendal office creation, for "a competitive electoral system, with its vast array of ministerial and sub-ministerial appointments, with legislative offices and their private staff positions to be filled, is a veritable boon to prebendal politics." The need to aggregate votes in order to obtain such offices gives political activists at the lower levels of the hierarchy access to a resource that is only available under conditions of electoral competition.[76] It is this double set of motives that constantly pressures the military regime to name the date of the next election.

END NOTES

1. Pearl T. Robinson, "Democratization: Understanding the Relationship between Regime Change and the Culture of Politics, *African Studies Review* 37 (1, April), p. 44.

2. Thomas Hodgkin, *Nationalism in Colonial Africa* (New York: New York University Press, 1957).

3. Michael Bratton and Nicolas van de Walle, *Democratic Experiments in Africa*, p. 147.

4.Richard Sklar and C. S. Whitaker, "Nigeria, in James S. Coleman and Carl G. Rosberg Jr., *Political Parties and National Integration in Tropical Africa* (Berkeley: University of California Press, 1964), p. 636.

5. Billy Dudley, *An Introduction to Nigerian Government and Politics*, p. 49.

6. Quoted in Welch, *Protecting Human Rights in Africa*, p. 114.

7. Welch and Sills, "The Martyrdom of Ken Saro-Wiwa and the Future of Ogoni Self-Determination," pp. 12-13.

8. Reuters News Service, Lagos, August 20, 1996.

9. Welch, *Protecting Human Rights in Africa*, pp. 111-116.

10. Ihonvbere, "Are Things Falling Apart?" pp. 215, 218.

11. Paden, "Nigerian Muslim Perspectives on Religion, Society, and Communication with the Western World," p. 9.

12. Forrest, *Politics and Economic Development in Nigeria*, pp. 114, 117.

13. Paden, "Nigerian Muslim Perspectives on Religion, Society, and Communication with the Western World," pp. 8-9.

14. Forrest, *Politics and Economic Development in Nigeria*, p. 27.

15. Jane Guyer, "The Spatial Dimensions of Civil Society in Africa," in John W. Harbeson, Donald Rothchild and Naomi Chazan, eds. *Civil Society and the State in Africa* (Boulder: Lynne Rienner, 1994), pp. 220-222.

16. Thomas M. Callaghy, "Lost Between State and Market: The Politics of Economic Adjustment in Ghana, Zambia, and Nigeria," in Joan M. Nelson, ed. *Economic Crisis and Policy Choice: The Politics of Adjustment in the Third World* (Princeton, NJ: Princeton University Press, 1990), p. 310.

17. Forrest, *Politics and Economic Development in Nigeria*, p. 218.

18. Oyelele Oyediran, ed., *Survey of Nigerian Affairs, 1975* (Ibadan: Oxford University Press, 1978), p. 130.

19. Forrest, *Politics and Economic Development in Nigeria*, pp. 61, 65.

20. Callaghy, "Lost Between State and Market," p. 311; Forrest, *Politics and Economic Development in Nigeria*, pp. 221-22.

21. Callaghy, "Lost Between State and Market," p. 311.

22. Forrest, *Politics and Economic Development in Nigeria*, pp. 221-22.

23. Forrest, *Politics and Economic Development in Nigeria*, pp. 96-97.

24. Shettima, "Engendering Nigeria's Third Republic," p. 85.

25. Hussaina Abdullah, "'Transition Politics' and the Challenge of Gender in Nigeria," *Review of African Political Economy* 56, 1993, p. 33.

26. Hussaina Abdullah, "'Transition Politics'," pp. 30-31.

27. Hussaina Abdullah, "'Transition Politics'," pp. 36-37.

28. Hussaina Abdullah, "'Transition Politics'," p. 33.

29. Forrest, *Politics and Economic Development in Nigeria*, pp. 62, 96.

30. Shettima, "Engendering Nigeria's Third Republic," p. 86.

31. Sklar and Whitaker, "Nigeria," p. 636.

32. *Chronicle of Higher Education*, March 22, 1996, p. A41.

33. Sunal, Sunal, and Ose, "Nigerian Primary School Teachers' Perceptions of Schooling," p. 65.

34. Ahmad Khan, *Nigeria: The Political Economy of Oil*, p. 33.

35. Ahmad Khan, *Nigeria: The Political Economy of Oil*, pp. 14, 175.

36. Welch and Sills, "The Martyrdom of Ken Saro-Wiwa and the Future of Ogoni Self-Determination," p. 12.

37. AfreeNet, Lagos, July 5, 1996.

38. Welch, *Protecting Human Rights in Africa*, pp. 251-55.

39. Julius O. Ihonvbere, "Are Things Falling Apart?" pp. 194-95.

40. Joseph, *Democracy and Prebendal Politics in Nigeria*, pp. 133-134.

41. Forrest, *Politics and Economic Development in Nigeria*, pp. 57, 88-89.

42. Forrest, *Politics and Economic Development in Nigeria*, p. 202.

43. Forrest, *Politics and Economic Development in Nigeria*, p. 201.

44. Soyinka, *The Open Sore of a Continent*, p. 42.

45. Joseph, *Democracy and Prebendal Politics in Nigeria*.

46. Sandra T. Barnes, *Patrons and Power* (Bloomington: Indiana University Press, 1986), pp. 19-23.

47. Barnes, *Patrons and Power*, pp. 29-31.

48. Barnes, *Patrons and Power*, pp. 31-46.

49. Barnes, *Patrons and Power*, p. 201.

50. Barber, "Popular Reactions to the Petro-Naira," p. 436.

51. Verba, Nie and Kim, *Participation and Political Equality*, pp. 58-59.

52. Joseph, *Democracy and Prebendal Politics in Nigeria*, p. 58.

53. Shettima, "Engendering Nigeria's Third Republic," p. 62.

54. "Election of constitutional conference delegates," *West Africa*, May 30- June 5, 1994, pp. 954, 966.

55. Verba, Nie and Kim, *Participation and Political Equality*, pp. 58-59.

56. Ihonvbere, "Are Things Falling Apart?" pp. 202-03.

57. T.C. McCaskie, "Recent History," in *Africa South of the Sahara 1998* (London: Europa Publications, 1997), p. 791; *The Guardian* (Lagos), April 30, 1997.

58. Rotimi T. Suberu, "Religion and Politics: A View from the South," and Omar Farouk ibrahim, "Religion and Politics: A View from the North, in Diamond, Kirk-Greene, and Oyediran, eds. *Transition Without End*, pp. 401-425, 427-447.

59. Almond and Powell, *Comparative Politics: A Theoretical Framework*, p. 104.

60.This account of party development through the first years of independence is taken from Sklar and Whitaker, "Nigeria."

61.Sklar and Whitaker, "Nigeria," p. 617.

62.Ronald Cohen, The Kanuri of Bornu, pp. 109-110.

63.Ronald Cohen, The Kanuri of Bornu, p. 110.

55. Dudley, An Introduction to Nigerian Government and Politics, pp. 94-100.

65.Address of Brigadier Murtala Muhammed, reprinted as the preface to the Report of the Constitution Drafting Committee (Lagos, Ministry of Information, 1976), quoted in Dudley, An Introduction to Nigerian Government and Politics, p. 127.

66. Tom Forrest, Politics and Economic Development in Nigeria, pp. 77-78.

67. A lively account of the breakup of the NPP is provided by Kole Omotoso, in his essay

Just Before Dawn, pp. 35-36.

68.A detailed analysis of the 1979 election by office and by state is found in Dudley, An Introduction to Nigerian Government and Politics, pp. 198-225.

69. Dudley, An Introduction to Nigerian Government and Politics, pp. 168-178; Omotoso, Just Before Dawn, pp. 39-49.

70. Kole Omotoso, Just Before Dawn (Ibadan, Spectrum Books, 1988), pp. 35-36.

71.Beckett, "Elections and Democracy in Nigeria,", pp. 103-109.

72.Tom Forrest, Politics and Economic Development in Nigeria, pp. 75-76.

73. Wole Soyinka, The Open Sore of a Continent, pp. 103-104.

74. O. Oguibe, ed. Democracy in Nigeria: The June 12 Mandate (London: African Research and Information Bureau, 1993), cited in Forrest, Politics and Economic Development in Nigeria, p. 257, fn 5.

75. quoted in Forrest, Politics and Economic Development in Nigeria, p. 237.

76.Richard Joseph, Democracy and Prebendal Politics in Nigeria, p. 57.

Chapter 7

POLICY FORMATION AND IMPLEMENTATION: EXTRACTION AND DISTRIBUTION

♦ Given the environment of Nigerian politics, how effective has the political system been in improving the quality of life?

♦ How has central state planning affected Nigerian economic conditions? What has been the effect of subsequent privatization?

♦ How pervasive is political corruption, and how has it affected government and private-sector performance?

♦ How does the Nigerian government finance its expenditures?

♦ What are the patterns of distribution of government expenditures?

♦ How does the Nigerian government's distributive performance (on education, health, and defense) compare with earlier times, and with other countries at similar levels of development?

♦ What has been the effect of efforts to Nigerianize the economy?

♦ How have inflation and international debt, and steps to deal with these problems, affected quality of life?

Many people have stopped bothering themselves with classifying African regimes as democratic or otherwise. They instead keep asking: How much do the regimes address themselves to the needs and aspirations of the people? I am one, I tell you, all these noises about democracy and democratic are mere luxuries to the sufferers.

- Letter to the editor, Lagos, 1983 (quote in Richard Joseph, *Democracy and Prebendal Politics in Nigeria)*

In comparing the various civilian and military regimes Nigeria has experienced, the ultimate question must always be their *performance*. This is certainly the "bottom line," for Nigerians, whose support of these various regimes has been based on the quality of life they have experienced under them. This chapter, then, focuses on the *decisions* governments have made, particularly in raising revenues, dispersing funds, and implementing programs. Secondly, it discusses some background issues such as the level of corruption, the results of which underlie all policy. Finally and very importantly it presents the constraints imposed on Nigerian decision- making by the outside world, particularly in the World-Bank-supported Structural Adjustment Program. Dealing with "SAP," as the structural adjustment program is commonly called, leads us back to the discussion of environment which we began in Chapter Two. Policy relating to Nigeria's international economic situation has had to respond to initiatives from other African countries, world powers, international organizations, and such powerful economic entities as international corporations. Here we consider the critical constraints that the world economy puts on the choices available to a Third World country, even one as large and resource-rich as Nigeria.

In order to follow the overall outline of this book's description of the Nigerian political process it is helpful to remember that policy decisions must always be viewed in the environmental context in which they are taken; however, those decisions have effects, intended and unintended, that, at least over time, alter that environment. In a systems analysis, it is only theoretically possible to disengage treatments of environment and policy, because in the real world they are constantly feeding back to one another. The central empirical question that comes from this relationship is: Does a government have real options in dealing with a problem or opportunity, or is the only option already determined by environmental limitations, whether historical, physical, socio-cultural, or international? Policy frustrations come from the limited range of options available, even though regime opponents and perhaps the general public insist that more could be done.

Thus, an examination of policy must attempt to measure how policy initiatives have *changed* the environment. To approach that issue, in Chapter Two we first compared Nigeria with other countries in terms of the gravity of the problems facing them in health, education, etc. Here, in order to focus on the impact of Nigerian policy, we revisit those same problem areas, but here we focus on changes in the indicators in these policy areas since independence, in comparison with other African countries and with countries elsewhere that were in roughly the same situation as Nigeria in 1960. In comparing similar environmental contexts we hope to separate out the effect of policy; where accomplishments seem to diverge, we can then identify differences in policy approaches, and with some confidence report which regimes have been most successful. First, however, we must consider those aspects of the decision-making situation that cannot be manipulated by policy.

Situational Barriers to Effective Performance

It will come as no surprise to learn that Nigerians by and large have been disappointed with the performance of their political system, and (as exemplified in the quote opening this chapter) disillusioned with the limited channels open to them to affect the political decisions that concern them. Because the attainments of thirty-five years of independence have been so meager in Nigeria and elsewhere in Africa, we should expect that the causes of poor performance transcend mere ill will or incompetence of political leaders.

A first cause of disappointment in Africa generally grew from the heightened expectations from government at independence. Late colonial administrations had promoted a development ideology, and independent regimes were compelled to do at least as well. In the multiparty competitive politics of newly independent Nigeria, candidates had made extravagant promises of educational opportunities, health care, technical support for agriculture, roads and communications, and other fields of activity that did not at the time seem far-fetched. But resources did not generally multiply to meet demands, except during the heady years of the oil boom in the late 1970s, when government expenditure grew at an even greater rate than private consumption, both in absolute terms and as a proportion of GDP[1] Taxes are difficult to impose on the attentive political public in any country, except in time of war or other national emergency, and have not grown to offset the spending habits of Nigerian governments. Furthermore, except for petroleum, the economy did not grow to provide the necessary resource base.

CENTRAL PLANNING: BARRIER TO DEVELOPMENT?

Dele Olowu, noting the failure of either mineral extraction, agricultural production or international aid to stimulate economic growth in Africa, suggests that such growth requires "institutions which encourage and facilitate a diversity of human organizations." Just as an active democracy seems to require a vibrant civil society, so, Olowu suggests, economic development cannot be produced from above by a control-oriented centralized state. The infusion of new capital and new technology is wasted, in this view, if there are not already in place "effective systems of contract, credit, and money markets; municipal services including public education, health, and transportation; effective systems of weights and measures; institutions for transmitting and exchanging information cheaply; an effective public bureaucracy; and institutions for the discovery and adaptation of new ideas."[2]

Olowu's concerns for breaking the state's hold on the development process (and giving it instead a major role in infrastructure development) is in line with the dominant ideology in the world economy since the breakup of the Soviet Union and the disappearance of the socialist bloc of economies. In the

Cold War period, Western governments and development agencies followed the Soviet lead in promoting and funding massive showcase projects, not only for their propaganda and foreign policy impact (although those helped to sell them with legislators at home), but also because of a widely shared belief in such projects as stimuli for economic growth. In Nigeria, this approach was first seen in the Niger Agricultural Project, launched in 1948 by the colonial administration to increase the production of peanuts. Political considerations plagued the project from the beginning. It was located in a sparsely settled, poor, and disease-plagued area in the North, and was to be highly mechanized. However, the project could not attract sufficient volunteer labor from other areas (and the administration excluded the possibility of bringing laborers from the Eastern region, which might pose political problems). Profitability was limited by the colonial marketing board's conflicting need to maximize revenues from the difference in market price and the price paid to producers. Finally, the project ran into ever-increasing labor costs, attributed to the rise in food prices.[3]

After independence, large-scale planning for agricultural development found fruition in the River Basin Development Authorities (RBDAs), which were multipurpose agencies built around dam and reservoir projects on major river systems. The prototype for these was the Tennessee Valley Authority created in the United States in the 1930s to help lift a poor rural region out of the Depression. Such projects became very popular in the developing world in the 1960s, for they fit well with the emphasis in that period on centralized planning for development. The movement of populations out of reservoir areas and the introduction of new economic activities provided the rationale for direct state involvement in the economy. These projects also appealed to officials bent on self-enrichment, since they provided opportunities for corruption and offered financial windfalls to those with political access. The largest such project in Nigeria was the Kainji Dam and Reservoir in the Northwest, planning for which was begun before independence in 1959. In 1960 the World Bank agreed to finance the project, which was completed between 1964 and 1968. A long-term review of that project points out that, although its original purpose was to make the Niger navigable, its most important product has been electric power.[4] The Nigerian dam projects were originally the product of cooperation with international development agencies; however, the projects received large-scale domestic funding once petroleum production provided the necessary revenues. Although the Kainji Dam seems to have served Nigeria well, subsequent projects became so heavily political that in 1979 nine of them were defined in terms of political boundaries rather than natural river basin areas, and in 1984 it was proposed that there be one RBDA for each state.[5] By that time, of course, funds were no longer available for large-scale centrally planned development projects.

Another large-scale irrigation project, at Bakolori, with 80,000-100,000 people living in the project area, ended disastrously about ten years after it was begun. Farmers were to be brought into the project under the condition that they take direction from project administrators. After a standoff emanating from the demand of better lands or cash compensation by farmers whose fields had been taken over for the project, the federal government sent in paramilitary forces to suppress the rebellion. Hundreds were killed and wounded, but the rebellion could not be controlled; this project too ended in complete failure.[6]

The heavy hand of state direct capital investment was seen in industrial development as well. In addition to the difficulties inherent in making economic choices based on complicated central plans, Nigeria's state-directed industrial development was also plagued by political (federal character) investment criteria (a problem common in other centrally planned economies, notably the former Soviet Union). For example, when the government decided to encourage the introduction of automobile assembly plants, it reached agreements with Peugeot and Volkswagen to build facilities in Nigeria. Because the Volkswagen plant was to be built in Lagos State, politics dictated that the Peugeot plant be located in the North, and it was built in Kaduna. However, because of higher costs at the latter location, the government agreed to pay Peugeot a premium for each car produced—and later followed with a similar premium to Volkswagen! Another massive investment involved the decision that Nigeria should have its own steel industry. A steel-producing plant was built at Aladja, in the center of the country, but politics dictated a wide distribution of the steel rolling mills that would receive the Aladja output. They were put in Oshogbo, Jos, and Katsina, between 300 and 1,000 km. from Aladja, and with no direct rail or water connection between them. Although the Aladja plant has operated at less than 20 percent of capacity, a much larger steel operation has been under construction at Ajaokuta, in Kwara State, since 1979, at a cost of over $6 billion. When Western capital sources proved to be hesitant about the viability of this project, the Soviet Union stepped in as "technical partner." Eventually some five thousand Soviet technicians came to Ajaokuta, and the training of Nigerian personnel both in Nigeria and in the U.S.S.R. began in 1981. In spite of numerous difficulties, successive Nigerian regimes have pushed ahead with the project as the keystone of Nigerian industrial development. After the downturn of the early 1980s, only the Ajaokuta project and the fourth petroleum refinery in Port Harcourt were continued by the Nigerian government.[7] The Soviet connection at Ajaokuta was brought up to date in January 1997, when a Russian delegation came to Lagos to discuss completion of the project. Two months later the Nigerian government announced that it would spend an additional $600 million to bring Ajaokuta to completion.[8]

Since the debt crisis, the thrust of World Bank efforts and the condition of most foreign aid in the developing world has been to disengage government from the control of resource and factor allocation, and to let these be determined by market factors (inevitably including a large role for international financial and industrial entities). In the case of Nigeria, however, Tom Forrest argues that the state's role in economic decision may have been exaggerated all along because of earlier dominant development ideologies that presumed a central state role in economic development.[9] As noted in Chapter Two, Forrest does not see Nigeria as having a policy-induced food production crisis. He argues that Nigerian regimes have intervened very little in domestic food production and marketing, and he argues against such intervention in the future. He finds that some government expenditures on agricultural projects have been wasteful, and concludes that "in some cases it would have been better if the state had literally 'neglected' agriculture." In line with presently fashionable economic thought, he argues against direct state involvement in agricultural production, but supported efforts in the late 1980s and early 1990s to build roads and other rural infrastructure through the Directorate of Foods, Roads and Rural Infrastructure (DFRRI).[10] However, because of resentment from local governments at DFRRI competition for local development funds, the agency was abolished by the Babangida government.

In the particular case of desertification in the Sahel region, including northern Nigeria, the record of "top-down" technology and management-based solutions has been "unimpressive." One author calls instead for reliance on the resilience and adaptive capabilities of indigenous peoples: Their diversification and mobility should not be discouraged by government policies. Noting that Nigerian regimes have consistently attempted to discourage urban-rural and rural-rural mobility, Mortimore feels they have confused "migration" with "circulation." (See our discussion of urbanization in Chapter Two.) As an example, he cites the 1984 military government's action in driving unauthorized traders off the streets, which action "paid scant regard to the impact of such action on rural areas scarred by another drought." Circulation, as opposed to permanent migration to the city, should be encouraged as less socially disruptive, redistributing income from urban to rural areas, and disseminating useful knowledge. Similarly, pastoral nomadism should not be treated with permanent resettlement projects without safeguards of the economic advantages in herding. All in all, the situation calls for less regulation (which government is usually unable to accomplish in any case) and for more structuring of incentives based on inhabitants' adaptive abilities.[11]

Privatization was consciously pursued by the Babangida government, not so much from ideological commitment to the concept, but rather as a means to reduce the government budget. However, according to Forrest *de facto* privatization had long taken place through corruption. "[P]rivate gain surrounded all state companies and corporations. Private accumulation was often dependent on state contracts and various forms of state intervention in the economy." Thus, the question was one of efficient, less costly government. In 1985, government agencies withdrew from large-scale agricultural operations, and the government announced the commercialization of fertilizer procurement and distribution. In 1988, 135 enterprises were offered for privatization, 67 of them completely, and the rest in part. By late 1990 fifty companies had been sold. Those to be partially privatized included Nigeria Airways, the National Shipping Line, the Nigerian National Petroleum Corporation (NNPC), Nigerian Telecommunications, the National Insurance Company, the Nigerian Railway Corporation, the National Electric Power Authority (NEPA), and toll collections along the country's turnpikes. However, in 1995, the Abacha regime officially abandoned further privatization, and announced its intention to regain control of the four largest commercial banks. NEPA and Nigerian Railways had been largely unaffected by the privatization policy, and extensive government involvement in enterprises continued.[12]

For Nigeria, the most important case over which the privatization (and Nigerianization) issue has been fought is in the exploitation of its oil fields. The colonial government had given British companies sole rights to tap this resource, and British companies maintained a monopoly until the Petroleum Decree of 1969 made the petroleum the property of the Nigerian state and created the Nigerian National Oil Corporation (NNOC) to exploit it. In 1977 the NNOC was merged with the Ministry of Petroleum Resources to create the Nigerian National Petroleum Corporation (NNPC), which has represented the Nigerian interest in oil production since that time.[13] This concentration of power over the most important Nigerian asset caused serious problems of accountability, and in 1986 the military regime re-created the Ministry of Petroleum as the Department of Petroleum Resources. However, the association between the two units remains so close that it is not clear that the separation has produced any noticeable degree of control. The NNPC was declared "commercial and autonomous" as of January 1992; it was expected to be self-financing and to provide revenues to the state, rather than to request subsidies from the state. However, it is a company in need of downsizing:

> With excessive red tape and bureaucratic delays in the organization, mechanical and management problems, it is unlikely that the company and the Nigerian oil industry can do without the investment and participation of foreign oil companies. The latter, therefore, have little to fear from the particular clause in the join operating agreements which allows NNPC to take over exclusive operation of a concession when desired.

It also appears that, after it has paid its due to the government, there is not adequate revenue remaining for the NNPC to meet its investment commitments to its joint operations with private companies.[14] This has led the government to shift, in the 1990s, from joint-venture arrangements to production-sharing contracts, which allow the government to have equity participation in production without having to share up-front costs. Even so, joint-venture contracts already negotiated are costing the NNPC about $2 billion per year in development costs. The NNPC is behind in its contributions to the joint ventures, which were asked to cut expenditures in 1993 and 1994, even as its divestments from joint ventures with Shell, Agip, Texaco, and Pan Ocean have reduced its participation from 60 to 50 percent.[15] Nigeria's ability to control its own petroleum industry and to prolong production as far in the future as possible have increasingly been compromised by the country's general financial difficulties.

If the Nigerian government has generally abandoned direct investment of capital in industrial projects, there is at least one exception in the petrochemicals industry. Since early in the 1980s, Nigerian planners have seen petrochemical production as a way to diversify exports and substitute domestic for imported products, in a type of production based on raw materials derived from petroleum refinery byproducts. Because this is a highly technical field, however, the capital needs are considerable, and development must be gradual. Two plants built by the NNPC opened in 1988, and now produce detergents, lubricants, insecticides, woven sacks, plastic crates, tubes and tires, and other goods for the domestic market, but are not sufficient to meet demand. New plants would provide a wider range of chemical products. Planners have hoped that a petrochemical industry would provide the missing link between the petroleum industry and local small-scale manufacturing, and the Nigerian government has listed incentives to encourage private investment in petrochemicals.[16]

Unfortunately, potential private investors in the petrochemical subsector are wary of investing in permanent plant in light of the unsettled political and economic conditions in the country. Still, government promotion of this industry based on its likely multiplier effects in stimulating industrial growth seems rational, in spite of the country's poor record of development through planning.

In addition to situations of direct state ownership of enterprises, Nigeria has had its experience with efforts at central control of prices, money, and markets of which the unintended effects had greater impact on the country than did progress toward the policy goal. For example, in attempting to deal with foreign indebtedness, the military government wanted to increase the proportion of foreign exchange funds applied to debt relief. In an effort to limit the payment of foreign currencies for imported goods, the government attempted to encourage domestic production and discourage imports. The decision was made to require prospective importers to obtain a government-issued import license. The program, which also provided import protection for domestic food production, was effective in reducing the level of imports, but, because the demand for imported goods exceeded the supply allowed in the total value of import licenses, the cost of imported goods increased, and the issuance of the licenses became a focal point of corruption. Individuals having political connections but nothing to import obtained licenses, which they could then sell at a considerable profit.

CORRUPTION

Indeed, a major further constraint on Nigeria's development has been the problem of massive corruption that we first addressed in Chapter Three. In trying to explain how Nigeria has achieved so little in the past twenty years, it is not enough to cite the usual constraints on Third World development. Those are real enough, and sufficient explanation for poor countries without natural resources, but they cannot explain the situation of oil-rich Nigeria. For that explanation, we must ask, as many Nigerians have, what has happened to the billions of dollars in oil receipts since the 1970s?

Political corruption exists at some level in every polity, and was present in Nigeria from the beginning. However, the arrival of massive oil revenues is highly correlated with rising levels of corruption that put Nigeria in a foremost position among contemporary nations on this dimension: As evidence, a survey of international business people by management and risk-analysis organizations ranked Nigeria at the top of a list of countries considered "most corrupt," among fifty-four countries included in the rankings.[17]

One observer has listed, as necessary conditions for corruption, (1) the existence of surplus national wealth, in (2) a rapidly growing economy, with (3) economic and political authority highly concentrated in the hands of public officials. Added to these as the "sufficient conditions" are (4) a moral code such as the "amoral familism" introduced in Chapter Three, and (5) an authority structure of deference to those with power, also presented in the discussion of political culture in Chapter Three. These conditions have been found in Nigeria at optimal levels for corruption, and the evidence is persuasive that the level of corruption grew with the nation's oil wealth. One study correlates annual percentage changes in Nigerian GDP with the incidents of corruption reported by the media (Figure 7.1). However, the peaks on both trends themselves correlate with, first, the end of the Biafran War and, second, the coup of 1975 and its revelations of corruption in the previous few years, with the coup coming shortly after record prices were recorded for petroleum in world markets. Thus, the correlation, although thought-provoking, may reflect the impact on both variables of historical events.[18]

The first major scandal came during the Gowon administration in 1975, and was particularly devastating because many had put great hope in the military's pledge to eliminate corruption. The Nigerian government placed orders for 20 million tons of cement that year, with 80 percent of that total designated for defense purposes. This was about two-thirds the amount of cement normally ordered in all of Africa in one year, and was to be paid for at

Box 7.1 Major Corruption Scandals in Nigeria
First Period of Military Rule

1975 Cement Scandal - over 16 million tons ordered and delivered in single year to ports with a capacity for 6.5 million tons, cost $2 billion

1977 FESTAC - corruption in contracts

Universal Primary Education

Second Republic (1979-1983)

Abuja, Federal Capital Territorial Administration, $20 million construct contract fraud.

1979-1980: Nigerian National Supply Company - London manager stole 1.9 million British pounds.

NNPC lost N17 billion in oil smuggling (1979-1983)

1982: Nigerian External Telecommunications N53 million unaccounted for.

1983: Federal Housing Scheme N43 million missing

> Federal Mortgage Bank

> Delta Steel Company

> National Youth Service Corps (N16 million)

> Central Bank foreign exchange manager exported N24 million

British Aerospace, N30 million in kickbacks.

Current Period of Military Rule (1983 to present)

1990-1992: Gulf War oil profits skimming, $12.6 billion. In 1992, World Bank reports gap between reported and estimated earnings from petroleum at $2.7 billion, or 10 percent of GDP.

Babangida/Abacha: More than $1 billion per year flow to smuggling networks and confidence teams, many operated with the collusion of top elites. Over $2 billion diverted from state oil refineries, contributing to major fuel shortage.

Sources: Forrest 1995: 86; Khan 1994: 32; Lewis 1996: 97; Washington Post, June 9, 1998.

a price that was $15 a ton higher than the market rate. Cement producers the world over began shipping cement to Lagos, and soon the port was filled with up to 455 ships waiting to be unloaded. The military government was paying demurrage charges (penalty for failure to unload on schedule) of $500,000 per day, and "a nice return was to be had simply by chartering a rusting hulk, loading it with cement and pointing it in the direction of Nigeria. The whole exercise is thought to have cost at least two billion dollars or one quarter of Nigeria's oil revenue for 1975."[19] It had to have been carefully planned for personal enrichment in its various aspects by top government officials.

In the intervening years, a fairly large proportion of reported political corruption has had to do with the accounts of the Nigerian National Petroleum

Figure 7.1 Annual Percentage Changes in GDP and Reported Corruption

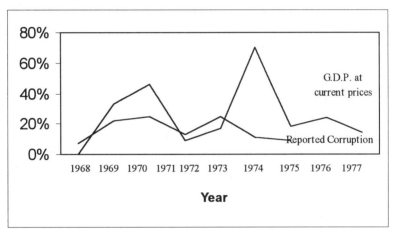

From Varda Eker, "On the Origins of Corruption: Irregular Incentives in Nigeria."
Sources: International Financial Statistics Yearbook (IMF, Washington, 1980) and
Fed. Republic of Nigeria, Crime and the Quality of Life in Nigeria (Lagos, 1980), p.
14.

Corporation itself. Nigeria should have reaped a windfall during the Gulf War, as petroleum prices temporarily shot up, but increased revenues never showed up in national accounts. In 1994, Pius Okigbo examined the books of the Central Bank of Nigeria; a report he submitted as he left the country found that $12.6 billion were not accounted for. For the single year of 1992, the World Bank found a discrepancy between the official earnings reported by government and estimated earnings based on production and price data of $2.7 billion, or about 10 percent of the country's Gross Domestic Product.[20] Skimming of the oil profits had indeed reached astronomical proportions.

Government officials often have echoed public outcries at excessive, market-based corruption, and at times, especially after the 1983 coup, serious measures have been applied. In 1983 and 1984, many former officials of the Second Republic were brought to trial on corruption charges. A Nigerian observer wrote that the Buhari regime was "the only government in Nigeria's history that attempted not only to probe, but also to prosecute and punish fraud in high places."[21] A potentially more effective move was the sudden currency change of 1984. People were given a short amount of time to exchange their holdings of naira for new bills, up to a maximum of N5000 or $6250 per person. Those wishing to exchange more than that amount had to swear an affidavit on how they had acquired the money. The intent was to make hoards of illegal cash suddenly useless. Effects were noticeable, but some of them were unintended: There was a sudden boom in consumer spending and in the paying-off of bills, and some in rural areas lost savings because of the difficulty of getting to a bank in time. Also, the Central Bank underestimated the size of the money supply, although it perhaps intentionally wanted to reduce that amount. As a result, there was a shortage of cash, which caused a deflation after the first spending burst.[22] These measures were taken by a regime that is remembered for heavy-handedness in its reaction to the Second Republic. Unfortunately, no more democratic regime has dealt any effective blows against the corruption problem.

Extractive Performance

> The tax people brought this paper, they say that, because I have a large farm, I am to get a special assessment. They say that I am *Gbajumo* (well-to-do) because I have a large farm, but they say nothing about the thirteen children and four women who depend on the farm for *gari* [food], no. They say I am *gbajumo* with a large farm.
>
> Wole Soyinka, *Aké.* p. 201

Most African societies provided for some form of tribute to political leaders before the arrival of colonialism. Indeed, the highly centralized states often had sophisticated systems of taxation. In the Kanuri kingdom of Bornu,

> There were two main taxes and innumerable smaller ones. indeed in the Kanuri language it is possible to denote the meaning of taxation, a tax on something, by simply adding the suffix "ram" to the activity or the object.[23]

Colonial administrations in Africa used taxation to force populations into the money economy: If tax payments in cash were required, the inhabitants could not remain totally in a subsistence, cashless, or non-European-currency form of economy. In their terms, taxation was seen to provide "the recognition of allegiance and. . .inculcation of habits of work."[24]

However, individual-level taxation did not seem to play a big role in colonial Nigeria as a source of revenue; where "produce and labor markets did not have to be provoked by forceful measures. . ."colonial attention to taxation seems to have been a little absent minded."[25] Guyer tells us further that in Ibadan (western Nigeria), there was a capitation tax of seven shillings per year on adult males, which would have been 2-1/2 percent of mean annual estimated income. In fact, however, because these taxes were collected through chiefs under indirect rule, rates were in fact quite arbitrary, and contributed greatly to the resentment of the chiefs' role in the colonial system.[26] Peoples like the Igbo, with their decentralized political systems, had not experienced any kind of formal taxation in the precolonial period, and took to it very reluctantly under British rule. As we have seen, indirect rule was a failure in the Southeast in any case, but particularly when illegitimate chiefs attempted to collect taxes. The Igbo Women's War of 1929 (see Chapter Three), a very serious challenge to the colonial administration, grew from a rumor that the head tax already imposed on men was to be extended to women, children, and animals.

The fiscal system that Nigeria inherited in 1960 depended mainly on taxes on international trade. Indirect taxes provided 64 percent of total revenues, direct taxes only 16.5 percent, and other revenues 19 percent.

In the 1980s, export duties and the sales tax on agricultural products were eliminated, the poll tax was reduced to a standard level throughout the country, personal income tax rates were made uniform, and the ability to charge a sales tax on petroleum was taken from the states.[27] As part of the austerity program introduced after the 1983 coup, some states reintroduced school fees and cattle taxes, and special levies were established for various development and education projects. It is unclear, however, what effort was made to collect these taxes, or whether they resulted in significant increases in revenue.[28] Particularly at the local level, "the taxation systems set up by colonial governments have been all but dismantled."[29] Nationalist rhetoric was not appropriate for maintaining or raising taxes, and as new local tax units were created to replace the Native Authorities, that most unpopular of colonial functions was abandoned. Although local taxes have been accepted when tied directly to opening schools, an example of when they were not legitimated in the eyes of citizens was in support of the war against Biafra. In fact, because of a decline in commodity prices at that time and the burgeoning cost of local government, resistance to taxation eventually resulted in violence in western Nigeria. The annual capitation tax was reduced to £2, then raised to 8 naira in 1980, and at present is N7.5 (7.5 naira) on the adult male population, and the personal tax of anyone earning over 600 naira per year was taken away from local governments by the states in the 1970s. (The Nigerian monetary unit at independence was the Nigerian pound. In January, 1973 the pound was replaced by the naira at a rate of two naira per pound. At that time the naira exchanged with the dollar at roughly N1 = $1.50.) Thus, in those periods when Nigeria has experienced elected local governments, their agendas have not been focused on the classic issue of local politics—the creation of a budget. Nigerian local government has been based on a principle that Jane Guyer has labeled "representation without taxation!"[30] As noted earlier, petroleum has become the main source of revenue for government at all levels, which makes the national development of Nigeria rather unique. Peasants in premodern Europe were estimated to have had up to one-third of their incomes extracted from them, whereas Nigerian peasants have never paid direct taxes that were anywhere near that amount.[31] As local governments struggle to find revenues, their efforts serve mostly to keep the edge on tax resistance. On entering Enugu, in eastern Nigeria, the authors once came upon local tax collectors attempting to assess the owners of car radios. Drivers drove heedlessly over and around the barriers that the hapless tax collectors had put up. Since the car radio tax was collected on the spot, it was not obvious that the funds gathered by these entrepreneurial collectors would make it to the local treasury in any case.

Extractive performance at the local level is tied to the issue of government accountability. Not only does the absence of an effective tax structure deprive citizens of their usual handle on the state, but it also prevents them from formulating a theory of equality based on the progressivity of taxation, and in fact gives them no basis on which to hold wealthy citizens accountable for providing their share of support. In Guyer's words, "the material basis for a familiar form of democratic struggle for accountability and control is more or less defunct."[32] This is a central aspect of the difficulty of achieving responsible government in Nigeria.

For the central government the colonial system had developed an alternative source of revenue, the Agricultural Marketing Boards. Ostensibly created to provide price stability to farmers, marketing boards were created for each of six principal products. The boards were to accumulate surplus funds in good years that would be available to support the prices paid to farmers when market prices were low. However, the accumulated funds were tempting to government officials with development projects in mind. Thus, in essence, Nigeria's rural commodity producers funded the construction of an urban infrastructure and in addition paid for the import of foreign consumer goods into the cities. The Marketing Boards were regionalized in 1954, inheriting at that time a surplus of 87 million pounds. The regions then began their practice of using the surpluses for development projects, through a gap created between the prices they obtained on the world market and the prices they paid to farmers. When the price paid to farmers was constant, it was not widely perceived as a tax. However, in 1965, faced with widespread refusal to pay taxes, the Western region government decided to reduce the price paid to cocoa farmers from £110 to £60. Farmers could not meet their costs at this price level, and were unable to pay their laborers, who rioted and set cocoa farms on fire. The violence spread to the cities and contributed to the unrest that led to the first coup of 1966.[33] The Marketing Boards were later re-nationalized, and finally, in 1986, were disbanded as the privatization program was implemented.[34]

Peasant farmers also paid direct taxes, of which they were much more aware: Widespread tax riots broke out in the Western region in 1968-1969, during which tax collection was halted, eventually to be replaced by a lower, much simpler flat tax.

In the First Republic and under the Gowon administration, the personal income, sales, and poll taxes were collected by states. The implementation of the Land Use Decree in 1978 (see the discussion under Regulative Performance in Chapter Eight), also gave governors the ability to charge fees for land occupancy applications, and to demand rent for property thus allocated[35]—the functional equivalent of a property tax under Nigeria's concept that all land ultimately belongs to the state. However, tax collections generally declined as new states were created, without fiscal institutions in place and with smaller tax bases than the old regions. At the same time, rising oil revenues strengthened the fiscal position of the federal government (and those states with oil fields).

Oil exploration began in 1938; after being interrupted by World War II, it was resumed in 1947, and production began in 1958. At independence, the federal government was collecting modest royalties from private Western oil companies. In 1971, within a few years of the Biafran War, Nigeria joined the Organization of Petroleum Exporting Countries (OPEC), and also formed the Nigerian National Oil Company (NNOC) to participate directly in oil production. NNOC acquired a one-third interest in the Agip Company and Elf, both French-controlled. At the time, this was seen as retribution for French support of the Biafran separatist effort, but within a few years the government had acquired a majority interest in all oil production activities. The NNOC was merged with the Ministry of Petroleum Resources to form the Nigerian National Petroleum Corporation (NNPC).[36] Over this same period (the mid 1970s), petroleum prices had risen dramatically, from $3.30 per barrel in 1972 to $21.60 in 1979. Thus, the taxation and royalties collected by the Nigerian federal government from multinational oil companies came to provide the greater part of federal government revenues and, through the federal system, of state and local revenues as well (Table 7.1).

In a pattern typical of Third World oil exporting countries, Nigeria has come to depend almost entirely on the revenues from this single industry. Since there is no indication that the world's appetite for oil will diminish in the near future, it is basically a reliable revenue source that substitutes for the various forms of imposition of taxes on private income. Thus, Nigerians are fortunate that they have not been burdened with the cost of supporting government programs; they are perhaps *unfortunate* that governments, especially authoritarian military regimes, can tap this vast wealth without

Table 7.1: Oil Taxes and Royalties as % of Federal Government Revenue

1970	26.8
1975	77.5
1980	81.1
1985	77.8
1988	78.2
1995	83.6

Source: John Ohiorhenuan, *Capital and the State in Nigeria* (New York: Greenwood Press, 1989); *Europa World Yearbook 1997,* Vol. II(London: Europa Publications, 1997, p. 2486.

risking the wrath of taxpayers. The exceptions to this general rule appear to be enterprises and property owners in Lagos State, which has a large share of the country's modern enterprises and generates over half its revenues, and the Ogonis and other peoples who inhabit the oil producing region, who do not feel they benefit from the natural resources of their home area, and who, as described in Chapter Two, have paid the environmental price for oil exploration and extraction.

How well have Nigerian governments done in collecting their "fair share" from oil company profits? An assessment of the conditions of the 1959 Petroleum Profits Tax Ordinance implemented in the last year of colonial rule determined that Nigeria was not getting as great a share of oil operation profits as were other oil producing and exporting countries at that time.[37] In 1964, the Nigerian government attended an OPEC conference for the first time, as an official observer. The 1967 Petroleum Profits Tax (Amendment) Decree adopted OPEC terms for tax assessment. (Nigeria became a member of OPEC in 1971.) An issue that changes over time is the magnitude of fiscal incentives needed to encourage additional exploration and development by the companies. A Memorandum of Understanding on this topic was concluded in 1986 and amended annually in the early 1990s, providing various changes in profit margins and tax incentives for development and exploration. Finally, Nigeria moved toward a gradual and partial nationalization of the industry by providing that the NNPC have an equity stake in the foreign companies of 35 percent (1971), increased to 55 percent (1974), and 60 percent in 1979. The trend toward privatization in the 1990s produced some divestments of oil company equity where the Nigerian side could not meet its investment obligations.[38]

Given their control of vast petroleum reserves, Nigerian regimes have not actively sought large amounts of direct foreign aid. Whereas low-income countries received an average of $10.2 per capita ($24.50 excluding China and India) in 1991, Nigeria's per capita aid totaled only $2.60 that year—a mere .8 percent of GNP. On the other hand, Nigeria used its oil reserves as the collateral for massive borrowing from foreign and international banks in the 1970s and 1980s. While the funds thus obtained supported massive capital expenditures, they also gave Nigeria a share in the common scourge of Third World governments over the past twenty years, external debt. Total external debt went from 10 percent to *140.5* percent of GNP between 1980 and 1995, and annual debt service rose from 4.1 percent of the value of exports to 12.3 percent in the same period.[39] Thus, oil wealth has not brought the country financial independence; quite the contrary, the debt has given international lenders a predominant voice in Nigeria's allocation of public funding.

There are other difficulties on the horizon: The Abacha regime may have been killing the golden goose. In 1993, the Nigerian National Petroleum Corporation (NNPC) was behind $800 million in paying its share of costs in its joint ventures with foreign companies, which led to slowdowns in new drilling and development. The federal government and the oil corporations were also facing increased hostility, as noted above, from groups representing the peoples who live in the oil fields. The government responded in 1992 by creating the Oil Mineral Producing Areas Development Commission (OMPADEC), which was to have 3 percent of federation revenues to spend in those areas. Critics were scornful of the funding made available, and it is unclear whether any improved relationships have resulted (see Chapter Six). It is difficult to imagine how difficult the situation would be if oil revenues begin to decline, which could be the result of increasingly short-range perspectives on the part of military rulers.

Distributive Performance

We have seen that government revenues at all levels have come to be predominantly derived from export sales of oil. Naturally, both the division of those revenues among federal, state, and local governments, and the reliability with which they have in fact been distributed, have been central issues of public policy. As a policy issue, distribution in a large country such as Nigeria is also seen as a geographic question, not just one of policy priorities. Nigerians have a fondness for referring to the federation budget as the "national cake," and they see state and local governments as the major recipients of slices. Under the First Republic, when Nigeria was truly a federation, the regions were largely responsible for their own finances, and revenues in the country were largely distributed on the basis of *derivation*. That is, funds stayed in the region where they were collected. In the 1960s, the regions raised about half of total revenues in the country, and took primary responsibility for expenditures on education, health, and agriculture. Given a very modest level of capital in the private market, the funds available through the Marketing Boards to the regions were the major resources for investment. However, consistent with the model for oil-producing states with high absorptive capacity (Chapter Two), the increase in oil revenues in the 1970s helped the military regime then in control to consolidate power into an effectively unitary system. In order to fund local governments, the RAS (Revenue Allocation Systm) was extended to cover them directly by the 1979 constitution, and, beginning in 1982, federal revenues were shared according to set percentages among the three levels of government, with 10 percent originally allocated to local governments.[40]

Given the set formulas in the RAS, it is not surprising that regions and localities strive for statehood and for independent local government areas over which they will have greater control, and that population counts loom large as a political issue. Generally, LGAs derive less than 10 percent of their revenues from local sources, and at the state level, only 10 to 30 percent of recurrent expenditures (all expenditures other than capital development) were covered by internally generated revenues (see Figure 5.1). Lagos State has been the major exception, generating over half its own revenues from the industrial and commercial enterprises concentrated there. As of 1992, LGAs collectively received 20 percent of almost all federal revenues, and were to receive 10 percent of internally generated state revenues. However, the states were notorious for not making the required payments to the LGAs, and indeed for laying additional costly burdens on them. Also, until late in the Babangida era the federal funding also was passed through the states for distribution to LGAs, and local chairmen often complained that the transmissions were late and never entirely paid. One must also assume that corruption at the highest level keeps a significant portion of federal revenues from ever reaching the Federation Account, from which they are to be allocated to the three levels of government.

The question of *vertical* distribution of revenues, i.e., among the different levels of government, is relatively simple to answer, in terms of some overall distribution by percentage. More complex is the question of *horizontal* distribution: On what basis should monies be distributed among states and among local governments? In any federal system, a myriad of equity and political factors come into play on this issue, and Nigeria is certainly no exception.

In the colonial period and under the First Republic, *ad hoc* revenue commissions met periodically to determine the bases of revenue distribution. Revenue allocation from the federal government to the states became a major issue under the Second Republic: States with large population and few resources argued for distribution among states on the basis of population; the oil-producing states supported the derivation principal. The federal government now spends between two-thirds and three-fourths of public monies, and also has great control over how the money distributed to state and local governments will be spent. On the contentious question of how to distribute resources as the number of states and local governments expanded, governments settled on relatively straightforward formulas, a combination of equality (across-the-board distributions to all states) and population. States other than Lagos depend on the federal RAS for 70 to 90 percent of their recurrent revenues. The Shagari government's compromise solution to the derivation vs. need controversy was to give 40 percent of the total state-level allocation of federal funds in identical amounts to each state, with another 40 percent based on population. Fifteen percent was given based on primary school enrollment, to encourage states to focus on education, and 5 percent was to match states' internally generated revenues to encourage them toward greater fiscal independence.

With marginal adjustments the Shagari formula has remained the basis for allocation through the present regime. The large education allotment has not been administered to the satisfaction of state and local governments, since a Federal Primary School Education Board has been created to provide a direct allocation of education funds to schools. In 1988 the Babangida regime created a permanent National Revenue Mobilization, Allocation, and Fiscal Commission to advise on "fiscal federalism." Although a wide variety of new criteria have been advanced, none have replaced population and simple equality among units at a given level—states or LGAs.[41] In addition, the principle of derivation is still much discussed, especially as concerns the oil-producing Niger River delta, but used quite sparingly by northern-dominated regimes. The RAS in use in recent years is not much different from that of the last civilian government. It provides that 40 percent of revenues available at both the state and the local level is to be allocated equally among units, with 30 percent to be allocated on the basis of population. As we will see in Chapter Eight, census figures have been controversial throughout the history of independent Nigeria, and the controversy erupts precisely around this issue. Another 10 percent of revenues is to be allocated according to a "social development factor," which in fact is closely correlated with population. Ten percent is distributed according to "land mass and terrain," and the final 10 percent as a matching fund in proportion to the success units have at generating internal revenues. Of a separate allocation of 5 percent of federation revenues, half goes to mineral-producing states—in other words, 2.5 percent of total federal revenues is distributed based on derivation.[42] However, in a 1995 radio broadcast the last category was stated differently: "13 percent of all revenue accruing to the Federal Account *directly from natural resources* [emphasis added] shall be set aside as derivation. . .[in order] to compensate communities which suffer severe ecological deprivation as a result of the exploitation in their areas."[43] This figure would seem to compare favorably with 2.5 percent of total federal revenues, which, as we have seen, are over 90 percent from petroleum sales. Will the promise be implemented?

It may be argued that the states' reliance on federal revenues has encouraged financial irresponsibility at that level. This was particularly noticeable under the Second Republic, when states were more influential than in other regimes: States budgeted large deficits and simply let them accumulate; they funded expensive projects, free medical services and education, and covered massive debts of state-owned banks. Federal auditing, presumably obliged by the constitution, had not been applied. When the military took over in 1983, the states were found to have a total debt of N13.3 billion.[44]

To summarize this discussion of the "horizontal" distribution of revenues, political decision-makers at all levels have agreed with and responded to a public perception that the application of government resources is not for the attainment of national-level development objectives, but should rather be seen as wealth to be distributed according to one's influence and access to those in control of distribution. Given the locational and communitarian nature of their clientelist structures, Nigerians have a great interest in the equality of the distribution of federal funds to the states. Because over time the principle of "need" (generally defined, as above, as based on population) has taken precedence over the principle of derivation in the distribution of revenues by the federal government among the states, there has been steady growth of the proportion of funds allocated to the northern states, so that, in Forrest's estimation, their share was brought "roughly into line with their share of the total population." Since the 1970s, casual observation would suggest that the North has done well in the allocation of federal funds in specific areas such as agriculture, industrial development, and road construction.[45] Major highway mileage has been significantly expanded and roadways improved in the North, whereas even the major highways in the South are in a deplorable state.

DISTRIBUTIVE OUTCOMES: THE ROLE OF THE PRIVATE AND PUBLIC SECTORS

The sentiment of despair with which this chapter opens reflected the belief of at least one Nigerian that the level of prosperity in the country derives from state activity or lack thereof. Forrest would remind us, however, that much of the economic activity in the country has been found in the private sector, where Nigerian and foreign entrepreneurs respond to market incentives. Governments have had a major effect on the course of Nigerian economic development, but they are not the whole picture. It is for this reason that in

Chapter Two we have set this work on Nigerian politics in the context of a larger economic environment. Nor should one assume that political and administrative decisions are *exclusively* prebendal in motivation. In all regimes, resources have been applied to general policies, and policy initiatives have had real, broad, and general consequences.[46] Here we examine the specifically governmental performance of its economic development and welfare roles.

As a producer of high-grade petroleum, Nigeria has had an unusually great potential to move out of the ranks of the less-developed into the middle-income nations. The Nigerian share of petroleum profits has almost exclusively flowed into the hands of government institutions and, informally, into the hands of government officials as the revenues considered in our discussion of extractive performance. Between 1973 and 1978, the proportion of Nigeria's GDP expenditure controlled by government increased from 12 percent to 36 percent. Between 1970 and 1980, impressive government projects such as road development, irrigation projects, and the launching of Abuja as the nation's capital were signs that government was playing a role in making the country's petroleum-based potential a reality.

Unfortunately, political corruption grew apace, and probably began consuming a higher proportion of national wealth than in the pre-oil period. When oil revenues suddenly began their decline in 1980, "corruption and mismanagement prevented any kind of disciplined adjustment," and "the economy was plunged into depression and mounting international indebtedness. . .Sucked dry of revenue by the corruption, mismanagement, and recession, state governments became unable to pay teachers and civil servants or to purchase drugs for hospitals, and many services (including schools) were shut down by strikes."[47] This does not mean that the petroleum revenue did not flow into the economy, but that it flowed in large part through the clientelist networks described in previous chapters.

Thus, in spite of the country's raw material advantage, Nigerians have not seen their lives improve in recent years. The United Nations Development Program has produced a Human Development Index (HDI) based on three factors: life expectancy at birth, adult literacy, and GDP per capita. Table 7.2 shows some development rankings for Nigeria, her immediate neighbors (Benin, Niger, and Cameroon), and a sample of other countries. Nigeria ranks 141st among 174 countries on the HDI, but it ranks 135th in GDP per capita. It is not surprising to find the less-developed countries low on these listings. However, GDP per capita is a good measure of distributive potential; thus the comparison of GDPPC and the HDI ratings can be an indicator of how well a country has done for its people compared with other countries with similar capacity. Although the Nigerian data are comparable to those of its neighbors, and to Africa as a whole, this suggests that the Nigerian advantage in oil revenue has had no noticeable impact on the overall quality of life. (Cameroon is also an oil exporter, but its exports are not nearly as important as

Table 7.2 Nigeria's ranking on GNP Per Capita and Human Development Index

Country	Life Expectancy at Birth, 1992	Adult Literacy Rate (%) 1992	Real GDP p.c. $, 1992 (PPP$)	Human Devel. Index , 1992	Rank in GDPPC, 1992	Rank by HDI	GDPPC-HDI
USA	76	99	23760	0.937	1	2	-1
Japan	79.5	99	20520	0.937	2	2	0
Britain	76	99	17160	0.916	23	18	5
Mexico	71	89	7300	0.842	47	53	-6
Botswana	65	67	5120	0.763	67	74	-7
Indonesia	63	82.5	2950	0.637	99	104	-5
P.R.China	68.5	79	1950	0.594	123	111	12
Cameroon	56	60	2390	0.503	115	127	-12
NIGERIA	50	52.5	1560	0.406	135	141	-6
Benin	48	33	1630	0.332	133	155	-22
Niger	46.5	12	820	0.207	157	174	-17

UN Development Program, *Human Development Report 1995, pp. 155-157.*

Nigeria's, yet it shows a much higher GNP per capita, and is marginally ahead on the other indicators as well.) A recent survey found that the health and educational situation of Nigerians is "poor relative to other developing countries. Moreover, these indicators have shown very little improvement over the last fifteen years."[48]

In analyzing distributive performance, it is important to examine budgetary priorities as well: Given a level of revenue, to what uses is it put? What proportion of national income does each purpose represent? How heavy is it in per capita terms?

In the case of a military-dominated country, one might expect that military expenditures would loom especially large. This is not the case in Nigeria, where published sources put the 1992 military budget at $255 million. This is a per capita expenditure on the military of only $2 per annum, for a rank of 125 out of 140 countries, and less than 1 percent of GNP. However, there are believed to be significant additional military expenditures that are not publicly reported. Extremely modest in size at independence, Nigeria's armed forces grew to a strength of 250,000 at the height of the Biafran War. Then the Gowon regime began a program of gradual attrition that reduced the force to about 100,000 in the mid-1980s. Further shrinkage since then has resulted in a total force of 94 thousand. Over 80 percent of the personnel are in the army, with less than 10,000 in the air force and 5000 in the navy.[49] This still leaves Nigeria a major military force, with army manpower equal to that of the other fourteen West African countries combined. Although per capital military expenditures are relatively modest, their net effect given Nigeria's overwhelming size is a military predominance in the region.

As we saw in Chapter Three, Nigerians have shown great enthusiasm for education, and parties and regimes have promised universal access to it. It was noted there that the Nigerian 6-3-3 system of primary, junior secondary, and senior secondary schools parallels that found in most U.S. school systems. In the federal structure, primary education is now a function of the the Federal Primary School Commission, which is active in regulating programs. Children are admitted to elementary school at the age of six, and follow a six-year curriculum, finishing with a Primary School Leaving Certificate. (Very few families have access to kindergartens and nursery schools, which are mostly private.)

Secondary education is primarily the responsibility of the states. It also consists of six years, divided into three years of junior and three years of senior secondary school. At the end of junior secondary school, some children leave formal education for apprenticeship or go directly into the job market. Those who proceed to senior secondary school follow either an academic curriculum that can lead on to university, or a technical or commercial program. Beginning in 1970, the states one-by-one took control of private (mostly church-related) schools, and thus are the sole providers of education at the primary and secondary levels. Free public education has been a popular political goal for many years. It is, however, the case that primary and secondary education is in all states partially funded through school fees.

Although university education is in theory a federal responsibility, there has been such a demand for access to higher education that a number of states have created their own institutions. As of 1991, all but two states in southern Nigeria had at least two universities (Oyo State had three). No northern state had two campuses, although Kano State is establishing a multicampus state university.[50] The proliferation of campuses has stretched already-strained funding for higher education. Because Nigerian university students and educators have always been vocal interest groups, university-level policy has been an area of controversy and occasional violence. As in other countries, the location and funding of university campuses is a central, and expensive educational issue. A new issue that has recently been raised by religious groups is whether to allow the organization of private universities. The academic staff union (ASUU) has been opposed to the proposal, arguing that private institutions, which would charge tuition of at least 50,000 or 60,000 naira (about $700) per year would draw away the children of the wealthy, and thus further weaken the numerous public institutions. Nevertheless, if the public universities continue to deteriorate, parents who cannot afford an overseas education for their children will continue to press for the private option. An idea floated by the Abacha regime in 1997, to alleviate the universities' fiscal crisis by instituting a tuition payment system, has not met with a warm response.

Some educational progress can be noted: In 1964 Nigeria ranked twenty-ninth in Africa in per capita enrollments, with 5 percent of the school-age population in primary school; it was nineteenth in secondary enrollments, with .5 percent of the appropriate age group in school. Ten years later, 24 percent of the school-age population was in school, and Nigeria was fifteenth in Africa on this measure. In 1990, 60 percent of the school-age population was in primary school, an impressive accomplishment given population growth in that period; but it had fallen back to nineteenth in rank on the continent. Moreover, none of the inequalities in the provision of education that had been identified since before independence had been erased: A report by the International Labor Office in 1981 found that the North still lagged in schooling, as did girls behind boys and rural children behind those in the cities. Federal statistics for the same time showed that, while 48 percent of primary students in the Southeast and 53 percent in the Southwest were female, only 34 percent were female in the northern states.[51]

Measures of school attendance do not, of course, address the issue of quality of education. Nigeria's educators have made progress on some measures of quality, in spite of resource constraints. To be employed as a primary teacher in Nigeria has until recent reforms normally required a Grade II Teacher's Certificate, which attests to the completion of a teacher's college curriculum. For some enrollees, the teachers' college was actually a secondary school, roughly equivalent to grades 7-11 (if entered immediately after primary school) in the United States; for secondary graduates, the teacher's college provides one to three years of further training depending on students' grades in secondary school. Federal governments have attempted to upgrade teacher preparation with the creation of Advanced Teachers' Colleges providing a three-year post-secondary curriculum leading to the National Certificate of Education (NCE), as described above. However, federal education statistics showed that only 5 percent of primary teachers had the NCE (or equivalent university training) in 1988, and a recent survey of primary teachers found that only 9 percent had the NCE, while 86 percent had the Grade II certificate, and 7 percent (all in the North) were not even at the Grade II level.[52]

There is great controversy in the education world on the effectiveness of various teaching methods. In Nigeria, as in many Third World settings, the normal classroom practice is memorization and recitation. A survey of primary school teachers showed that 61 percent most often used these methods, compared with findings in the United States that 60 percent of primary teachers favor a discussion approach.[53] Whatever the educational effects of these different methods, the lack of discussion does not bode well for the creation of a participatory political culture.[54] In the words of teacher education specialists,

> Memorization and recitation strategies do not develop students' critical thinking, reflective thinking, problem-solving and decision-making skills. These overall thinking skills are important to prepare individuals to be effective citizens in a democratic society that is competitive in regional and international markets.[55]

Nigerian governments' most mediocre performance has been in the area of *health*. This may be in part a result of a health-delivery system that has been oriented to curative, high-cost service, although this does not distinguish Nigeria from most other African countries, which inherited colonial and missionary health facilities that themselves focused on cure rather than prevention. In the Nigerian case, a particular cost factor growing from the imitation of Western health facilities was the opening of expensive teaching hospitals in the 1970s.

Nigeria's health system has been primarily market-based, such that medical personnel are much more available to the wealthy than to the poor. Government hospitals are divided into general wards and amenity wards. The former are very inexpensive, but the care is very poor; the amenity wards provide better care, but are affordable only to the better-off. The Buhari regime attempted to coerce doctors out of private practice and into public health care. "Under the Private Practice Decree of 1984, public officers were forbidden to engage in the management or running of any private business, profession, or trade. Unable to go private, many doctors left the government service."[56]

Nigeria's health-care system is highly concentrated in urban areas. The doctor/population ratio was estimated at 1:2600 in Lagos State, compared to 1:38,000 in more rural Ondo State (it was 1:630 nationally in the United States in 1970). In Ogun State in 1979, the doctor/population ratio in Abeokuta, the state capital, was 1:11,245, while in two rural local government areas, Egbado North and Ijebu North, it was 1:192,615 and 1:200,861.[57] An effort was made to distribute health care more evenly through the National Youth Service Corps, established in 1973, which sent young doctors into rural areas. However, very few of them remained in those areas beyond their required terms.[58] Health care is also imbalanced regionally, with, in 1980, 3,800 people per hospital bed in the north, 2,200 in the Middle Belt, 1,300 in the Southeast, and 800 in the Southwest.

Lower expenditures on health followed from the general economic decline of the 1980s. As government hospitals deteriorated, private facilities grew. In 1987 the Babangida regime announced a Primary Health Care Plan (PHC), which promised more and better training of personnel, better health data, greater availability of drugs, improved nutrition, promotion of health awareness among the population, development of a family health program, promotion of oral rehydration therapy (to combat the effects of diarrhea in children), partial responsibility for the government's population control program, and an Expanded Programme of Immunization (EPI). The Ministry of Health had responsibility for implementation of these programs, in cooperation with Local Government Councils, which would be provided direct financial support for the programs from the federal government.

There has been some progress in outcomes in absolute terms: Nigeria's infant mortality rate (IMR) has dropped from 185 in 1960 to 139 in 1970, 114 in 1980, and 80 in 1995 (See Figure 7.2). However, the under-five mortality rate (U5MR, meaning the number per 1,000 children born who die before their fifth birthday) was 191 in 1993; almost one-fifth of Nigerian children do not reach the age of five.[59] These rates are means for the entire country, however, and conceal significant internal variations. The Western State's rate overall was lower than that for Nigeria as a whole in 1971, but was 109 in rural areas and 77 in urban centers.[60] The immunization program (EPI) should have the greatest effect on the U5MR, because it is focused on the major childhood diseases: whooping cough, diphtheria, measles, and polio, as well as on tetanus and tuberculosis. The program was established in over three hundred LGAs, with the goal of achieving 90 percent immunization by the end of 1990; three days were set aside in 1988 for the mass immunization of pregnant women and children under two years of age, so as to achieve a stage goal of 60 percent coverage. Although EPI probably fell short of these numbers, it did expand coverage significantly—probably exceeding that in some areas of the United States. In the then Kwara State, over 4.5 million doses of vaccine were distributed under EPI in January, 1985, with coverage as high as 70 percent in some LGAs.[61]

The federal government's 1990 expenditure for health care of $906 million was only $9 per capita, compared to a continent-wide average of $24. This represented 2.7 percent of GDP, only one-third of that from public funds. Part of this poor performance must be seen in the low foreign assistance component in Nigeria's effort: Only six percent of its health expenditure came from that source, the third lowest proportion in Africa.

Where international and domestic agencies have cooperated, there have been some dramatic attacks on health problems. For example, as we saw in Chapter Two, guinea worm infestation has been a chronic disease in Nigeria. However, a coalition of international organizations launched a worldwide eradication project in 1986, hoping to make guinea worm the second major disease (after smallpox) to be thus eliminated from the entire world. In 1995, one participating agency, the Carter Center, announced a 97 percent reduction in the disease. In 1995, only about 130,000 cases were reported worldwide, and half these were in war-torn Sudan.[62] It is difficult to accept the implication of these statistics for Nigeria, given the high estimate of guinea worm infestation less than ten years earlier, but it is clear that progress has been made.

In order to determine the relationship between governmental public health efforts and changes in the health indicators of the population, it is not enough to examine health expenditures exclusively, as a large proportion of the resources needed to combat Nigeria's health problems are for expenditures other than on medical personnel and facilities. It has been estimated that 95 percent of disease cases in Nigeria are preventable, and that the most effective preventive measures include providing a safe water supply, sanitary waste disposal, adequate housing, and proper drainage.[63] Slow progress in these areas as the country's population rapidly increases prevents meaningful improvements in health statistics.

Comparative health *outcomes* in a number of countries comparable to Nigeria in assets and in health environment are an additional manner of assessing the Nigerian regime's performance in this area.   Figure 7.2, comparing infant mortality rates over time since independence in Nigeria and its immediate neighbors, shows that the declining IMR in Nigeria is in fact correlated with parallel declines in those neighboring countries, although between 1975 and 1985, Nigeria's position improved from being at the top of the range to being near the bottom.

    Even this comparison does not allow for different capacities in these countries. However, the United Nations Children's Fund (UNICEF) has calculated "national performance gaps" on several general measures of children's health that place countries above or below the health level that would be predicted based on GNP alone. The under-five mortality rates (U5MR), for example, generally fall as GNP levels rise. If the data on these two variables are plotted, we can see this linear relationship, and observe that

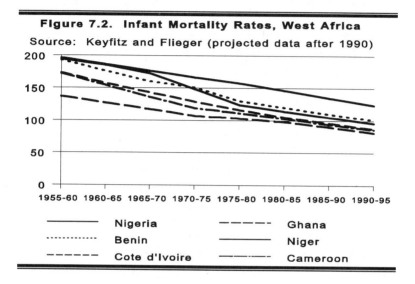

Figure 7.2. Infant Mortality Rates, West Africa

Source: Keyfitz and Flieger (projected data after 1990)

——————— Nigeria	– – – – – Ghana	
·············· Benin	——————— Niger	
– – – – – Cote d'Ivoire	—–—–— Cameroon	

some data points are below and some above that line. We assume that countries with relatively low GNPs *and* low U5MRs have applied their resources more effectively than those with relatively high GNPs and high U5MRs. Using 1993 data, Nigeria's GNP predicts an expected U5MR of 139; the actual rate was 191, a difference of -52. The relationship between GNP and the percent of under-five children underweight shows that Nigeria would be predicted to have 31 percent of under-five children underweight, whereas the actual proportion in 1993 was 36 percent. The difference, minus 5 percent, shows Nigeria tied for twentieth among twenty-seven African countries for which the necessary are available. These negative values show national performance gaps that do not speak well of the regime's efforts on those factors affecting children's health.

    Capital Expenditure: The Construction of Abuja - Although Lagos pre-dates colonialism, it was developed by the British as the colonial capital of Nigeria, and served as the capital of the independent country. However, in the historical tradition of Washington, D.C., Canberra, and more recently Brasilia, the military government charged a committee in 1975 to study the feasibility of keeping the seat of the federal government at Lagos. That body recommended the creation of a new, centrally located city. Although such a program entails tremendous expenditures even in the best of conditions, planners felt justified in promoting a political capital that would be free of the congestion, pollution, and chaos of Lagos. Accordingly, the Murtala Muhammed regime cut an 800 km^2 area from three of the then-existing states for a federal district. In 1976, the Federal Capital Territory (FCT) was created in the south-central part of the former Northern region (see map, Figure 1.1), to be administered by a Federal Capital Territory Authority. Construction was authorized for a new capital city within the FCT, to be named Abuja (the name of a village at the site), and to be completed in fifteen to twenty years at a cost of N10 billion (at an exchange rate at that time of one naira = $1.50).[64]

On December 12, 1991 the Office of the Presidency was officially transferred to Abuja, and has since come to be called, because of the topographical feature that dominates the site, "Aso Rock." According to the (disputed) 1991 census, the FCT had a total population of 378,700.

The Abuja project is an impressive accomplishment. In fact, it has been criticized because of the high standards for housing, sewage system, roads, etc. designed to equal those in the capitals of industrial countries but with costs of living effectively excluding all but upper income officials from living comfortably there.[65] The cost, now impossible to calculate, is far beyond original estimates, and has been well padded with corrupt overcharges. The project was also plagued with inefficiencies due to politically inspired pushes for rapid progress. Construction was given highest priority by the Shagari, Buhari, and Babangida administrations so that each of them could claim credit for this showpiece. Less visible programs suffered by comparison. Finally, as seems to have been the case in Washington, Canberra, and Brasilia, the move to Abuja has been made with great reluctance by those comfortably established in Lagos. For example, the absence of international air connections means that Nigeria's capital can only be reached from abroad through a stop in Lagos or Kano. Foreign embassies are only gradually relocating.

There have been fears in the South that the shift to Abuja was meant to bring the government more under the influence of the Islamic north (Abuja is about two hours by highway from the traditional "capital" of the north, Kaduna), and the move was generally welcomed in the north. Nonetheless, great store was put in creating a neutral capital as a symbol of the country's unity, and in making Abuja a modern, planned city.

NIGERIANIZATION AND THE DISTRIBUTION OF WEALTH

There is little doubt that the colonial political economy in Africa was developed to serve the interests of Europe. At least until the end of World War II, private investment decisions and policies concerning the development of infrastructure were joined in the goal of extracting maximum profits from the colonies. Not surprisingly, then, a major policy goal of independent African states was to transform the political economy into one that primarily benefited their own citizens. "Africanization" became a key part of that policy in virtually all states, embodied in directives that Europeans be replaced as quickly as possible by nationals, not only in the public service, but in the private sector as well.

In Nigeria the military government of Yakubu Gowon first addressed the problem of "Nigerianization" in its Second National Development Plan (1970-74). By that time, the public sector was completely staffed by Nigerians (and the completion of that process in the military made possible the first coup in 1966). The regime's approach took aim at both the hiring of personnel and the ownership of enterprises. In its rationale on the personnel dimension, the government argued that Nigerianization of private-sector personnel would reduce the "earnings leakage" that drained away the benefits of the country's industrialization, and would end the situation where "high-level Nigerian personnel educated and trained at great cost to the nation, are denied employment in their own country by foreign business establishments."[66]

As concerns the ownership of property, the 1970-1974 plan argued that "a truly independent nation cannot allow its objectives and priorities to be distorted or frustrated by the manipulations of powerful foreign investors." The government promised to acquire "equity participation in a number of strategic industries that will be specified from time to time." The Nigerian Enterprises Promotion Decree of 1972 established the Nigerian Enterprises Promotion Board, empowered to "advance and develop the promotion of enterprises in which citizens of Nigeria shall participate fully and play a dominant role." The decree included a list of industries in which only Nigerians could invest, including bakeries, casinos, cinemas, road transport, newspaper publishing, and radio and television broadcasting. A second list of industries could have foreign equity participation of up to 60 percent, with minimum investment and income standards that ensured these would be large-scale companies. The decree was supplemented by various measures designed to encourage Nigerian investment, including training programs for Nigerian businessmen on both acquisition and management. The next year, the government acquired 40 percent ownership (later increased to 60 percent) of the three major foreign-owned banks, which at that time controlled 70 percent of bank activity. The banks were required to offer 40 percent of their loans to Nigerian nationals. A 1977 decree replaced the two schedules in the 1972 decree with three: One requiring 100 percent Nigerian ownership, the second requiring 60 percent, and the third 40 percent. The overall effect was to further restrict foreign ownership, but also to limit the concentration of Nigerian ownership by providing that no individual could control more than one enterprise regulated by the decree. Early implementation coincided with the period of Nigeria's greatest economic growth, including the money supply, and was therefore almost painless, because the pie was constantly expanding.

As of 1985, some 930 out of 1,200 existing companies had been certified as in compliance. However, very few companies met the requirements through public stock offers. Most met the Nigerian ownership requirement through privately arranged transactions, which allowed them to choose their Nigerian partners, and presumably to use those partners as "front men" to get around the intent of the regulations. Those Nigerians benefiting most directly were members of the country's commercial elite.[67]

> The personnel provisions of the 1972 decree resulted in a gradual decline in the promotion of expatriate employees. A 1973 study found that expatriates already constituted less than 3 percent of the total number of employees in the modern sector, although because this was a time of rapid economic growth, the absolute number of expatriates was still increasing. There was a strange coalition of interests colluding to limit indigenization at the top:
> Generally, positions have been indigenized only in so far as they are of limited importance. . .In the top echelons of enterprises especially at board level, Nigerians have largely been given honorific, administrative and public-relations roles while the really substantive power roles such as the management of production and the control of the technology of production have been retained by foreigners. . .The problem here is that the foreigners do not want to give up the control any more than most Nigerians want them to give it up. For the foreigners, the control is critical for the protection of their technology and hence their leverage for ensuring protection of their technological dominance, a greater share of profits and the repatriation of surplus. *For the Nigerians the feeling is [that] the presence of the expertise of foreigners is [a] critical condition for their profit making..Not surprisingly, it is members of the Nigerian bourgeoisie who have taken up the cause of the foreigners, pressing for higher expatriate quotas and the relaxation of the restrictions...it is they who have put the Nigerian Enterprises Promotion Board in a no-win position.* (emphasis added) [68]

The Nigerianization policy also extended the degree of government participation in the economy. "By 1980 there were 70 noncommercial and 110 commercial federal enterprises and parastatals, many of which depended on government support to cover their operational losses."[69] Soon thereafter, economic decline and international pressure forced the beginning of a reverse movement toward privatization.

With petroleum the major source of foreign exchange, and with that under government control, the distribution of wealth in the country is greatly influenced by public policy decisions. Private consumption surged as oil revenues multiplied in the 1970s, about 8 percent per year. However, this average figure conceals tremendous increases in wealth at the top; the lower 40 percent of the population benefited very little. In the economic depression of the 1980s, those at the top of the income scales remained well-off, while incomes generally declined sharply. According to one estimate, the real income of urban households fell 57 percent between 1980 and 1987; although rural incomes also fell, they were estimated to be higher than urban incomes by 1985-1986.

> **Box 7.2 The Effects of Inflation: A Case Study**
>
> A young man with a new doctoral degree won a position as instructor at a Nigerian university in 1977. His salary and benefits totaled 6,000 Naira per year. At that time, one Naira equaled $1.50, so his salary was the equivalent of $9000—modest by industrial-world standards, but very comfortable in Nigeria. Twenty years later (1997), this same young man achieved the rank of full professor, at a salary of 51,000 naira per year, with fringe benefits raising his total annual compensation to 90,000 naira. However, at the parallel market exchange rate of 80 naira to the dollar, he now makes $1125 per year, and this does not take into account the effect of inflation on the purchasing power of the dollar since 1977.

Income distribution has also been affected by inflation, which followed from the rapid increase in the money supply during the 1970s oil boom, and continued apace later on, as governments followed a time-honored approach to balancing budgets when revenues declined: They printed money. Inflation has been a continuous problem, but has become especially serious in the 1990s, as shown in Figure 7.3. The case study (see Box 7.2) shows the effect of this inflation on individual income. Governments have attempted to deal with inflation by enforcing an official exchange rate. However, once the official and the market or parallel rates diverge, there is chaos in the financial system. Investments dry up, and corruption is stimulated, since anyone with access to foreign exchange at the official rate can then sell the foreign currency "on the street" for a large profit.

DEALING WITH DEBT AND STRUCTURAL ADJUSTMENT

During the 1970s oil boom, insufficient attention was paid to the productivity of the uses to which public funds were put. Much of the money was applied to an increase in welfare expenditures, to developing an unprofitable steel industry, and to building the new capital at Abuja. We described in Chapter Two how, late in the 1970s, commodity prices fell while oil prices remained high; African governments borrowed at an even faster pace, and the continent's total indebtedness increased. Foreign lending agencies turned to international financial institutions, principally the International Monetary Fund and the World Bank, to work with African and Latin American governments in "restructuring" the debts and the conditions of repayment.[70]

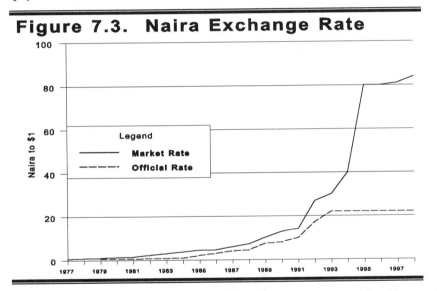

Figure 7.3. Naira Exchange Rate

The debt problem had begun during the first period of military rule, but became much more acute during the Second Republic (1979-1983). In its turn, the Buhari regime approached the International Monetary Fund for relief in the form of new loans and more favorable repayment terms, but rejected the severe conditions the IMF attached to its help: The national currency, the naira, would have to be devalued, trade restrictions would have to be dropped, and subsidies for domestic gasoline consumption ended. Buhari's government implemented some of the austerity measures favored by the international lenders: Wages of public officials were frozen, 250,000 government workers were laid off, and foreign-exchange-consuming imports were cut back. Unfortunately, these measures were not sufficient to slow the crisis. It was clear to the military leadership that measures severe enough to win lender approval would be extremely unpopular with the Nigerian public, and would lead to outbursts of political violence. Even to hold talks with the IMF would cause unrest in the country. However, just the servicing costs on the foreign debt of $25 billion equaled over 70 percent of Nigeria's annual export earnings; no new funds were coming into the country, and creditors would not talk about the situation until the Nigerian government had reached an agreement with the IMF. When Ibrahim Babangida seized power in 1985, he showed considerable political skill in opening a "national debate" on the issue. A broad range of voices from economic interests and the media spoke against an agreement; only the Lagos Chamber of Commerce, some corporate managers and chairmen and some senior civil servants supported it. Some critics believed the conditions should be accepted, but that no loan should be negotiated, because it would allow officials to continue their mismanagement and waste. (The immediate need was to have existing debt payment restructured.) Babangida then suspended negotiations with the IMF—a very popular move—but proceeded to claim to fashion a Nigerian version of structural adjustment, and instead opened negotiations with the World Bank, which convinced the Nigerian government to let it develop a Structural Adjustment Program that would be acceptable to the IMF and allow for debt rescheduling.[71]

Babangida's supposedly home-grown Structural Adjustment Program (SAP) resulted in an adjustment in the value of the naira from 1.6=$1 in 1986 to 4.62=$1 in 1988. Still, there was no immediate outcry, as the effects of the new policies were not immediately clear, and also because many Nigerians assumed that the drop in oil revenues was only temporary and that the government had simply gone through the motions of an IMF-style solution to meet short-term needs.[72] However, as the SAP's austerity measures began to be felt, the policies became extremely unpopular. In his parallel program of moving back toward civilian rule, Babangida forbade candidates to criticize the program, but at the same time eased off on the necessary austerity measures. The net result was that, although Nigerians were suffering from the country's poor position in international finance, the SAP had not been effective in reducing the debt, reforming the financial system, or reducing the economy's dependence on oil. GDP in current dollars was about the same in 1992 as in 1986, although, if measured in constant naira, there was growth in the GDP of about 5.6 percent per annum over that four-year period. The federal budget deficit increased from 2.8 percent of GDP in 1990 to 9 percent in 1992. This deficit was financed by external borrowing and growing domestic debt. The total external debt continued to rise, passing $30 billion by the end 1988, then stabilizing at just over that amount (it was $32.5 billion in 1993), then rising again to $35 billion by 1995. However, the structure of the debt was improved, with the proportion of short-term debt dropping from 40 percent in 1980 to 12 percent in 1993; the proportion of total debt owed to private banks also declined. This led to a drop in the debt service from a peak of 38.7 percent in 1985 to about 30 percent in 1988.[73] Interestingly enough, in its own evaluation of the SAPs of twenty-nine African countries, the World Bank identified Nigeria and five other countries as having made "large improvements" in economic policy in the 1980s, with modest growth in gross domestic product between 1987 and 1991. According to the Bank, countries that implemented the recommended reforms reduced their deficits, and increased exports, production, savings and investment.[74] In 1994, rather than allow the naira to float as urged by the IMF, the Abacha regime maintained an official exchange rate of 22 naira to the dollar, certainly with the support of those who are able to take corrupt advantage of it. In 1995, the exchange rate was partially opened to market forces, but the N22 to $1 exchange rate was maintained for government transactions. This was not effective at stabilizing the economy, nor did it improve relations with the international sector. The total external debt reached almost $8 billion, and the National Petroleum Corporation owed over $1 billion to its foreign partners.[75]

On the other hand, in responding to gasoline shortages the government has lowered the subsidy on petroleum products. Nigeria once had the lowest fuel prices in the world: In 1993, gasoline cost eight U.S. cents per gallon in Nigeria, compared to 11 cents in Iran, 24 cents in Venezuela and Libya, 35 cents in Saudi Arabia, $1.12 in the United States and $3 to $4 per gallon in Europe. In 1994, the Nigerian gasoline price was raised 400 percent, but was still in the low end of the price range. Holding the price down deprives the country of gasoline, as stocks are spirited over the borders to fetch higher prices—at least fifteen times higher in Benin, Cameroon and Niger—or sold along the roadside in Nigeria at "unofficial" prices. Estimates of the amount of petroleum smuggled out of the country range from 20,000 to 100,000 barrels per day; the amount sent to Cameroon was such that Cameroon reportedly closed down its main refinery in 1992 because internal demand was met by smuggled fuel from Nigeria. Nigeria has almost never been able to fill domestic demand from its own refineries, and in 1991 25 percent of that demand was met by imports.[76] However, the sharp price rise of 1994 seemed one more hardship to endure for those on low and fixed incomes, already suffering from rapid inflation. The country's transportation system has developed around the availability of cheap petroleum products, and raising the price to the level of cost would force painful dislocations. The government's best option on this issue is not obvious, but one writer has suggested that if the NNPC were run "transparently," and it was clear that the problem was not primarily one of inefficiency and corruption, cost-based prices for fuel might be more palatable to the Nigerian public.[77] Concern over availability joined concern over cost in 1997, as periodic shortages crippled industries and brought transportation to a crawl. Long queues at official stations prompted a black market that charged up to 80 naira per liter, or about seven times the normal price. The immediate cause for the shortage was not the pricing system, but rather the deteriorating conditions in Nigeria's four refineries, with responsibility for the crisis attributed to mismanagement and diversion of maintenance funds.

A major reason why the severe conditions of the SAP were not more effective at addressing the country's economic problems was in their implementation. To be effective, the policies required coordinated and even application. But although Nigeria's supply of trained and experienced administrators is higher than in most of Africa, it was also demoralized by the SAP's attacks on the public sector, and thus not in a mood to put its heart into the implementation of these extremely unpopular programs.[78] And, as we have noted elsewhere, the effectiveness of the SAP and other policies was also undermined by corruption. In 1992, the IMF ended its endorsement of Nigerian economic policy, leaving Nigeria with interest payments on its external debt of $5 billion per year, or over one-third of total revenue from exports.[79]

Conclusion

Given the stagnant or declining economic conditions prevalent in Nigeria since the early 1980s, many people there have survived only because of the continued vitality of extended family structures. The large family units that result from polygamous marriages and the common residence of multiple generations have proven to be the social security available to rural people in their old age or when they become disabled, a valuable function since the Nigerian government would never have the resources to provide such a safety net.

In much of the world, the attraction of democracy has been its association with prosperity. Nigerians are like other people in that they are more interested in the outcome of the political process than in the process itself. Calls for better leadership and the welcome initially extended to some military regimes suggest that Nigerians' highest priorities are economic security and the rule of law. If these could be provided by generals, the country would probably accept an authoritarian system. However, at least since Plato we have known that benevolent authoritarianism is an elusive concept. Western democracies have developed on the premise that democracy is a necessary, if not sufficient, condition for accountable leadership. And Nigerians have had sufficient opportunity to compare the results of military rule with their expectations that a majority of them are ready for another try at elective civilian rule. Perhaps another constitutional correction will be enough to usher in the long-term political stability for which they have hoped.

We have focused the above discussion on those aspects of the Nigerian situation most amenable to correction. There remain several rather intractable problems that will only be overcome with truly revolutionary change. Larry Diamond has identified as a central problem for Nigeria *the relationship between the economy and the state.* In his words, "stable democracy is associated with an autonomous, indigenous bourgeoisie, and inversely associated with extensive state control over the economy. . .In Nigeria, and throughout much of Africa, the swollen state has turned politics into a zero-sum game in which everything of value is at stake in an election, and hence candidates, communities, and parties feel compelled to win at any cost."[80] The answer appears to be the emergence of a vigorous private sector less dependent on government subsidies and freed from the kind of bureaucratic rent seeking that have drained the initiative and resources of the private sector. Nigerians have a reputation for entrepreneurship in West Africa and the world. A major challenge for Nigeria and other countries is to reduce the role of government to the provider of necessary infrastructure so that Nigerian entrepreneurial initiative can thrive. The nongovernmental civil society must grow for there to be a demand for government accountability and for a policy orientation to decision-making rather than a clientelist vision of a "national cake."

A parallel challenge, however, is to define infrastructure broadly enough to include the health, education, and income safety net provisions that will reduce the tremendous inequalities between haves and have-nots, or at least slow the continually growing disparity between these two groups, if only to provide the social and political stability in which economic development can proceed. Such measures inevitably involve a governmental role in redistribution, through taxation of income and profits and the allocation of the revenues to health, education, and income maintenance programs.

END NOTES

[1]1. I. William Zartman with Sayre Schatz, "Introduction," in Zartman, *The Political Economy of Nigeria* (New York: Praeger, 1983).

2. Dele Olowu, "Centralization, Self-Governance, and Development in Nigeria," pp. 196-97.

3. Shenton, "Nigerian Agriculture in Historical Perspective," pp. 54-55.

4. Wolfe Roder, *Human Adjustment to Kainji Reservoir in Nigeria* (Lanham, MD: University Press of America, 1994).

5. Forrest, *Politics and Economic Development in Nigeria*, pp. 191-192.

6. Bjorn Beckman, "Public Investment and Agrarian Transformation in Northern Nigeria," in Watts, ed. *State, Oil, and Agriculture in Nigeria*, pp. 127-130.

7. I. Osayimwese and S. Iyare, "The Economics of Nigerian Federalism," *Publius* 21 (Fall, 4), pp. 96-97; Shehu Othman, "Les relations internationales globales du Nigeria," in Bach, Egg and Philippe, eds. *Le Nigéria: Un pouvoir en puissance*, p. 68; Jean Philippe, "L'enjeu industriel: nationalisme et indépendance économique, p. 167.

8. AfreeNet (www.Afreenet.com), January 30 and March 28, 1997.

9. Forrest, *Politics and Economic Development in Nigeria*, p. 4.

10. Forrest, *Politics and Economic Development in Nigeria*, pp. 183, 188.

11. Mortimore, *Adapting to Drought*, pp. 223, 230.

12. Forrest, *Politics and Economic Development in Nigeria*, pp. 223-224, 245, 248.

13. Augustine A. Ikein, *The Impact of Oil on a Developing Country: The Case of Nigeria* (New York: Praeger, 1990), pp. 2-3.

14. Ahmad Khan, *Nigeria: The Political Economy of Oil*, pp. 26-28.

15. Ahmad Khan, *Nigeria: The Political Economy of Oil*, pp. 91-92.

16. Ahmad Khan, *Nigeria: The Political Economy of Oil*, pp. 147-49.

17. *New York Times*, November 29, 1996. See also L. W. J. C. Huberts, "Expert Views on Public Corruption Around the Globe," p. 11, who reports that a panel of experts drawn from four international conferences judged Nigeria to have the reputation for most corruption among twenty-one selected countries included in his survey.

18. Eker, "On the Origins of Corruption: Irregular Incentives in Nigeria," pp. 173, 180.

19. Robin Theobald, *Corruption, Development and Underdevelopment* (Durham, NC: Duke University Press, 1990), p. 96.

20. Ahmad Khan, *Nigeria: The Political Economy of Oil*, p. 32, citing the *Economist Survey* of 21 August, 1993.

21. Forrest, *Politics and Economic Development in Nigeria*, p. 102, quoting Onwuchekwu Jemie in the *Guardian* (Lagos), May 10, 1987.

22. Forrest, *Politics and Economic Development in Nigeria*, p. 99.

23. Cohen, *The Kanuri of Bornu*, p. 28.

24. Guyer, "Representation Without Taxation: An Essay on Democracy in Rural Nigeria, 1952-1990," p. 43, quoting from Sir Alan Pim, "Public Finance," in Margery Perham, ed. *Mining, Commerce and Finance in Nigeria* (London: Faber and Faber), pp. 225-280.

25. Guyer, "Representation Without Taxation," p. 54.

26. Guyer, "Representation Without Taxation," pp. 54-55.

27. Forrest, *Politics and Economic Development in Nigeria*, p. 53.

28. Forrest, *Politics and Economic Development in Nigeria*, pp. 98-99.

29. Guyer, "Representation Without Taxation," p. 43.

30. Guyer, "Representation Without Taxation," pp. 56-57.

31. Guyer, "Representation Without Taxation," p. 57

32. Guyer, "Representation Without Taxation," p. 57.

33. Dudley, *An Introduction to Nigerian Government and Politics*, pp. 72-73.

34. Egg, "La nouvelle insertion de l'agriculture nigériane dans le marché mondial," p. 190.

35. A. O. O. Ekpu, "Making the Land Use Act Work," *Edo State University Law Journal* 2 (no. 1), 1993, p. 29.

36. John F.E. Ohiorhenuan, *Capital and the State in Nigeria* (New York: Greenwood Press, 1989), p. 66.

37. L. H. Schatzl, *Petroleum in Nigeria* (Ibadan: Oxford University Press, 1969), pp. 84, 94.

38. Ahmad Khan, *Nigeria: The Political Economy of Oil*, pp. 18-19.

39. The World Bank, *World Development Report 1997* (New York: Oxford University Press, 1997), p. 246.

40. Osayimwese and Iyare, "The Economics of Nigerian Federalism"; Phillips, "Managing Fiscal Federalism."

41. Adedotun O. Phillips, "Four Decades of Fiscal Federalism in Nigeria," *Publius* 21 (Fall, 4), pp. 104-105.

42. A.O. Phillips, "Four Decades of Fiscal Federalism in Nigeria," p. 107.

43. Ihonvbere, "Are Things Falling Apart?" pp. 222-23.

44. Forrest, *Politics and Economic Development in Nigeria*, pp. 83-84.

45. Forrest, *Politics and Economic Development in Nigeria*, pp. 53-54.

46. Forrest, *Politics and Economic Development in Nigeria*, p 6.

47. Diamond, *Nigeria: Pluralism, Statism, and the Struggle for Democracy*, p. 53.

48. Paul Francis et al, *State, Community and Local Development in Nigeria* (World Bank Technical Paper No. 336, Africa Regional Series)(Washington, D.C.: World Bank, 1996), p. 6.

49. Ruth Leger Sivard, *Military and Social Expenditures 1993* (Washington, D.C.: World Priorities, 1994); testimony of James L. Woods, Deputy Assistant Secretary of Defense for African Affairs before the Subcommittee on Africa, U.S. House Committee on Foreign Affairs, August 4, 1993; Metz, ed. *Nigeria: A Country Study*, pp. xix-xx; Nadir A. L. Mohammed, *Military Expenditures in Africa* (Abidjan, Côte d'Ivoire: African Development Bank, 1996), p. 20-22.

50. Osayimwese and Iyare, "The Economics of Nigeria Federalism: Selected Issues in Economic Management," p. 92.

51. International Labor Office, *First Things First: Meeting the Basic Needs of the People of Nigeria* (Addis Ababa, 1981), p. 10, cited in Olowu, *Lagos State* (Lagos: Malthouse Press, 1990), p. 32; Nigeria, Federal Ministry of Education, *Statistics of Education in Nigeria 1985-1989* (Lagos: Statistics Branch, 1990), p. 7.

52. Sunal, Sunal, and Ose, "Nigerian Primary School Teachers' Perceptions of Schooling," p. 61; Nigeria, Federal Ministry of Education, *Statistics of Education in Nigeria 1985-1989*, p. 16.

53. Sunal, Sunal and Ose, p. 63; see the research citations therein.

54. See Almond and Verba, *The Civic Culture* (Prineton: princeton University Press, 1963).

55. Sunal, Sunal and Ose, p. 72.

56. Forrest, *Politics and Economic Development in Nigeria*, p. 97.

57. Tola Olu Pearce, "Health Inequalities in Africa," in Toyin Falola and Dennis Ityavyar, eds. *The Political Economy of Health in Africa* (Athens, OH: University Center for International Studies, 1992) p. 201; Metz, ed. *Nigeria: A Country Study*, p.

147; World Bank, *World Development Report 1995* (New York: Oxford University Press, 1995), p. 215.

58. Metz, ed. *Nigeria: A Country Study*, p. 149.

59. World Bank, *World Development Report 1995.*

60. Pearce, "Health Inequalities in Africa," p. 203.

61. D. Olubaniyi, "Primary Health Care at Local Government Level in Kwara State," in O. Aborisade, ed. *On Being in Charge at the Grassroots Level in Nigeria* (Department of Local Government Studies, Obafemi Awolowo University, Ife, 1989), p. 198.

62. Metz, ed. *Nigeria: A Country Study*, p. 151; "Guinea Worm Eradication: The Future," *Africa Demos* 3 (No. 5, May, 1996), p. 14.

63. Lasun Ajao, "Environmental Sanitation: The Concern of the Local Government," in O. Aborisade, ed. *Nigerian Local Government Reformed* (Department of Local Government Studies, Obafemi Awolowo University, Ife, 1989), p. 273.

64. Anthony Oyewole, *Historical Dictionary of Nigeria*, pp. 127-28.

65. Erasmus U. Morah, "Why Nigeria Obtained the New Capital That it Did."

66. Claude Ake, "Indigenization: Problems of Transformation in a Neo-colonial Economy," in Ake, ed. *Political Economy of Nigeria* (New York: Longman, 1985), pp. 174-175.

67. Ake, "Indigenization," pp. 177-182.

68. Ake, "Indigenization," p. 188.

69. Ebenezer C. Ugorji, "Privatization/Commercialization of State-Owned Enterprises in Nigeria," *Comparative Political Studies*, 27 (4, January), p. 540.

70. Gordon, "Debt, Conditionality, and Reform: The International Relations of Economic Restructuring in Sub-Saharan Africa," pp. 92-96.

71. Forrest, *Politics and Economic Development in Nigeria*, pp. 210-12.

72. Callaghy, "Lost Between State and Market: The Politics of Economic Adjustment in Ghana, Zambia, and Nigeria," p. 309.

73. Forrest, *Politics and Economic Development in Nigeria*, pp. 218-219; *World Development Report 1995*, Table 20; Ahmad Khan, *Nigeria: The Political Economy of Oil*, pp. 190-192, 199 (fns 8 and 9).

74. Peter Lewis, "The Politics of Economics" *Afria Report* 39 (3, May-June); World Bank, *Adjustment in Africa: Reforms, Results, and the Road Ahead* (New York: Oxford University Press, 1994).

75. Peter Lewis, "From Prebendalism to Predation: the Political Economy of Decline in Nigeria," *Journal of Modern African Studies* 34 (1), p. 97.

76. Ahmad Khan, *Nigeria: The Political Economy of Oil*, pp. 127-130, 151 (fn 1).

77. Ahmad Khan, *Nigeria: The Political Economy of Oil*, p. 150.

78. Callaghy, "Lost Between State and Market," p. 312.

79. Forrest, *Politics and Economic Development in Nigeria*, p. 247.

80. Diamond, "Nigeria: Pluralism, Statism, and the Struggle for Democracy," p. 69.

Chapter 8

REGULATIVE PERFORMANCE, HUMAN RIGHTS, AND NIGERIA'S WORLD ROLE

- ◆ How are the laws enforced?
- ◆ What is the extent of crime?
- ◆ What is the government's record in protecting or violating civil rights?
- ◆ What measures have been taken to control corruption?
- ◆ How is Shari'a (Islamic law) integrated into the legal system?
- ◆ How are property rights defined and enforced?
- ◆ Why is the taking of censuses controversial?
- ◆ How big a player is Nigeria in international affairs? What are its principal foreign policy objectives? How do other governments see Nigeria?

Regulative Performance

By regulative performance, we mean "the exercise of control by a political system over the behavior of individuals and groups in the society."[1] The means of regulation most centrally include legal coercion or its threat, but authorities also employ exhortation or material and financial inducements as well.

CRIME AND LAW ENFORCEMENT

At independence, although the constitution provided for a federal Nigerian police force, its organization was essentially regionalized: The regional commissioner reported to the premier of each region. In addition, local authorities in the North had already maintained their own police units, and the Western region developed a separate regional police force after independence. Because this latter force was inserted into the rough-and-tumble political campaigning of the early

1960s, the military regime decided to consolidate the police function at the national level. The inspector-general of police heads this organization, under the supervision of the head of state through a minister charged with police affairs; there is a commissioner in control of the police contingent in each state.[2]

This federal police organization was itself politicized under the Second Republic, when President Shagari built up the police presumably as a balance to the military. The ruling National Party of Nigeria developed close links to the police organization, and they were again reported to be intervening in election activities. There were also charges of harassment, extortion, and protection of criminals. The independent influence of the police was reduced dramatically when the military resumed control in 1983, but it is this national police organization that now enforces traffic laws and other government legislation. In Chapter Three we presented observations on police corruption; there are also popular perceptions that police officers are excessively arbitrary and brutal, which has led to a number of riots and violent attacks on the police in recent years. In 1989, a police raid ostensibly against stolen goods in the Katsina market led merchants to fear robbery by the police; a mob gathered, which itself was dispersed by riot police.[3]

The Nigerian secret police, the National Security Organization (NSO) was created in 1976. Its activities were greatly expanded with the return of the military to power in 1983, but it was split up under Babangida into a Defense Intelligence Agency, the Nigerian Intelligence Agency, and the State Security Services (SSS). Only the last of these would have had a formal mission of domestic surveillance; although SSS activities were at first greatly reduced under Babangida, it has been reactivated as Babangida and then Abacha relied on it to develop a more personalized, centralized, and less tolerant system of rule. It is widely believed that the SSS monitors public meetings, educational activities, and the like, and employs informers from various walks of life to keep the government apprised of activities that might generate opposition to its policies.

There are no reliable statistics on crime rates, but there is great fear of theft and robbery. Urban residences are surrounded by high walls, and the wealthy retain their own security guards. Travel is held to be unsafe even on major intercity highways after dark because of the presence of armed robbers. One of the consequences of the civil war was the demobilization of thousands of trained fighters, many of whom took their weapons with them; firearms are plentiful in the country.

It is often still the case that "law and order" is maintained in individual communities—especially in rural areas—through traditional institutions and norms. Traditional leaders not only prevent deviant behavior, but also take responsibility for the welfare of the "strangers" who, in accord with accepted procedures, have taken up residence in their communities. Even without access to reliable data, observers would consistently report lower crime rates in rural than urban areas:

In the rural areas, cultural values, especially of honesty, good neighborliness, respect for elders and authorities, etc. play a major role in minimizing rate of crimes. Religious injunctions inhibit criminal tendencies, while social interaction between communities and villages makes everybody his brother's keeper. In spite of the fact that law enforcement agents are far away from the rural community, these values have played a major role in the security of life and property.[4]

Lack of confidence in police protection has inevitably led to citizens taking the law into their own hands. Vigilante groups have not only closed off whole neighborhoods to nighttime traffic, they have sometimes meted out justice on the spot. In Onitsha (eastern Nigeria), in 1989, an armed gang was terrorizing a neighborhood without police intervention; residents angrily attacked known and suspected criminals and lynched four of them. Government officials are naturally concerned about the impact of such a trend on the rule of law, and on their ability to control their communities. However, in Oyo State in 1987, the governor issued an edict authorizing "the establishment of ward or village level vigilance groups or committees," and authorized them to register inhabitants, monitor movements into and out of the area, respond to calls of distress, to hire private security guards, and even "to collect information in respect of persons with criminal tendencies and pass such to the police for investigation." Obviously missing is the power to arrest and prosecute.[5] The program is similar (although broader reaching) to "neighborhood watch" organizations in the United States. However, because the action of the vigilante groups depends on the police for arrest and prosecution, the lack of confidence in police effectiveness is still a problem, and, at the other extreme, overzealous compensation by the vigilantes for the absence of police protection leads to the breakdown of the rule of law. Military rulers have responded in an *ad hoc* manner to crime: General Buhari established Armed Robbery and Firearms Tribunals (ARFT), continued by President Babangida, which tried most capital offenses without appeal. By 1988, nearly four hundred executions had been carried out after ARFT convictions.[6] Public executions for those convicted of violent crime by these tribunals (whose decisions cannot be appealed) continued through the Abacha years,[7] but with little perceptible effect on crime.

In spite of the perceptions of inadequacy of police protection in Nigeria, some 350,000 crimes were reported in Nigeria in 1984-1985, and Nigerian prisons held 54,000 individuals in 1986, up from 26,000 in 1976. This represents roughly 40 to 66 prisoners per 100,000—compared to a range over the same decade of 123 to 216 prisoners per 100,000 in the United States.[8] Thus, the use of prisons has been growing in both countries, but at a more rapid rate in the United States than in Nigeria.

This reflects, first of all, the increasing reliance on imprisonment as a control of crime in the United States, even compared with other industrial countries, but also shows the limitations on policy options under the fiscal constraints typical of Third World countries. In that context, communities are often forced to rely on informal controls on behavior.

Fear of crime is, along with the decline of purchasing power, the central problem in the lives of most Nigerians, especially in urban areas. A regime, whether civilian or military, that could provide security against criminals would be popular with most Nigerians.

Participation by Nigerians in international crime has received a fair amount of attention in world media. A principal focus abroad has been on the employment of young men as "mules," transporting illegal narcotics on international flights. Given the poverty and unemployment in Third World cities like Lagos, it would not be surprising that a young man would accept a single task offering payment greater than he might otherwise make in a lifetime, even though some 2000 Nigerians are in prison around the world for drug trafficking.[9] The Babangida government launched several well-publicized measures to combat participation in the drug trade: As noted earlier, it established special drug tribunals that imposed long prison terms and heavy fines, and in 1986-1987 produced 120 convictions. In 1988, the defense minister established a special "drug squad" to track drug traffickers "at home and abroad," and Nigeria signed the 1988 United Nations Drug Convention. The regime created the National Drug Law Enforcement Agency (NDLEA) in 1990 "to eliminate the growing, processing, manufacturing, selling, exporting, and trafficking of hard drugs." Extradition treaties covering drug crimes were signed with Benin, Ghana, and Togo. These efforts received international encouragement: The United States and Nigeria signed a mutual law enforcement agreement in 1987, and a special antidrug Memorandum of Understanding in 1990. The latter set up a joint task force on narcotics, and the United States began to provide financial and technical aid to the NDLEA (and a United States-Nigeria Joint Narcotics Task Force is still in existence in spite of difficult relations between the two countries). Similar agreements were concluded with Britain and Saudi Arabia.

Besides its effect on health and criminality rates, drug abuse takes a toll around the world in official corruption. Just as a Latin American peasant or a "mule" can make more in this industry than they could dream of making in the legal options available to them, a law enforcement agent with discretion as to whether or not a wealthy criminal should be arrested is tempted by short-run gains that may easily exceed the salaries of a career. With corruption already a major problem in Nigeria, keeping a "clean" enforcement operation in drug trafficking has to be a challenge. Within a few years after U.S.-Nigerian cooperation began on controlling the drug trade, the U.S. government decided that Nigeria was lax in its enforcement of drug laws and, in accord with U.S. law, withdrew all foreign aid support from the country (a move also prompted by the Babangida/Abacha annulment of the 1993 election and continuation of military rule). The Abacha regime showed some signs that it had continued its anti-drug effort. In August 1996, it was announced that almost 600 employees of the NDLEA had been relieved of their positions "for various offences... completely prejudicial to the corporate interest of the agency. The announcement continued that thirty other employees were already facing various tribunals for "offences regarded as outright betrayal to the nation."[10]

Nevertheless, the U.S. State Department opened the section on Nigeria in its International Narcotics Control Strategy Report for 1997 by declaring that "Nigeria is the hub of African narcotics trafficking, and Nigerian poly-crime organizations continue to expand their role in narcotics trafficking worldwide."[11] There are suspicions in the international law enforcement community that drug-related corruption reaches very high levels in the country.

THE REGULATION AND PROTECTION OF CIVIL RIGHTS

Nigeria has been under continuous military rule since 1983, and those used to political activity and free discussion in the media felt the effect in that year of the more authoritarian-minded Buhari regime. However, the political climate seemed to relax under Babangida, and the average citizen has not felt oppressed by an authoritarian state. That citizen is aware of the police presence at checkpoints along the country's highways, but fear of authority does not restrict the citizen's actions to any degree. The Nigerian government, like those of most Third World countries, simply does not have the resources available to keep close tabs on its large population. The matter is different, however, if one becomes politically active, and publicly critical of the government.

Judicial Process - As we have seen, the country's judicial system remains active, and has been surprisingly diligent at following a rule of law through the various informally constituted regimes. Still, military regimes have seriously compromised that rule of law. The regime imposed the State Security (Detention of Persons) Decree in 1984, which allows detention without trial of those "suspected of posing a threat to national security." State officials have intervened with increasing frequency into the judicial system where political questions are involved. Finally, drug trafficking, armed robbery, embezzlement, and other crimes have been put under the jurisdiction of military tribunals, which have a somewhat lesser concern for the niceties of procedural rights than do their civilian counterparts. The precedent of creating special tribunals to combat crime has led to the use of such tribunals to circumvent the judicial process in political trials: Most recently, Ken Saro-Wiwa and his colleagues were convicted by such a special tribunal, and the military officers accused of an attempted coup in 1997 were judged by a secret tribunal.

Press freedom and the right to a speedy trial were seriously abridged when General Buhari took control and vigorously "cleaned house" in the civil service. His Decree no. 2 of 1984 permitted the government to hold without trial anyone considered a "threat to the state"; Decree no. 3 established military tribunals to try former public officials for corruption and misconduct; finally, Decree no. 4

prohibited publishing or broadcasting anything false in any detail "that might bring government officials into ridicule or disrepute." Under the combined effect of these decrees the National Security Organization (NSO) could act against regime opponents at will. Furthermore, when brought to trial, defendants had the burden of proving their innocence, and harsh punishments were meted out. Although the public had generally welcomed punishment of corrupt politicians, their attitude changed when prominent journalists and editors were arrested.[12] This was a level of repression theretofore unknown in Nigeria.

However, when General Babangida came to power he proclaimed a government based on the respect for civil rights. Buhari's Decree no. 4 (criminalizing media stories embarrassing to the government) was repealed, and thousands of people under detention were released. The Babangida regime thus gained instant legitimacy, but its respect for human rights was short-lived. Soon this regime also closed newspapers, fired critical civil servants, and banned organizations that challenged government policies. Agbese places the blame for this turnaround on the conditions necessary to implement the Structural Adjustment Program. He argues that Nigerians would not have given their consent to the stringent budgetary cutbacks and fiscal controls imposed under SAP, and that, once Babangida had determined that SAP was necessary, he had no choice but to muzzle public opinion, even as he asked for a "national debate" on the issue. Agbese concludes that the external forces imposing the SAP as a condition of Nigeria's reinstatement were responsible for the abridgement of Nigerian democracy.[13] Freedom of expression seems to have been reduced even further—in that repression touches members of the political and military elite who hitherto appeared safe, and famous figures presumably protected by international opinion—as Sani Abacha strove to hold onto power. In 1994, writer Wole Soyinka was prevented from leaving the country by air, and his passport was seized. He later slipped across the border, and is now criticizing the regime from America. The Nigerian government, charging his involvement in bombings directed against the regime, asked in August 1997 that he be extradited to face charges of conspiracy and treason. Prominent political prisoners included (until Abacha's death) former head of state Olusegun Obasanjo, and of course Moshood Abiola (former presidential candidate Shehu Yar'Adua died in prison in December 1997). Unprovoked attacks on Ogoni villages in the oil-producing region cannot be blamed with certainty on the government, but the government had a vested interest in chilling the protest climate. It did so publicly with Babangida's Treason and Treasonable Offenses Decree of May 1993, which allowed the death penalty for *advocacy* of "ethnic autonomy."[14]

Because Abacha seemed concerned about international opinion, and generally followed the example of his predecessors in striving for a level of control that would not result in some form of international sanctions, there was much optimism that Ken Saro-Wiwa, head of the Nigerian Writers' Union and champion of the rights of the Ogoni people, would not be convicted by a military tribunal of complicity in murder; when he was convicted and sentenced to death on October 31,

1995, many assumed he would be pardoned, or serve a prison term, because of international attention to his case. There was great shock, then, when the execution was carried out ten days later (see Chapter Six).

Nigerians have traditionally been lively political debaters, generally unreserved at voicing their opinions. However, a climate of fear concerning political expression was evident for the first time in the country's history as the Abacha regime consolidated control. The death of Sani Abacha and the assumption of office by General Abjulsalam Abubakar raised hopes that Nigeria would move toward a more legitimate regime, with greater respect for the rule of law. One of Abubakar's first acts was the release of nine prominent political prisoners, including former military ruler General Obasanjo, and human rights advocate Beko Ransome-kuti. On the other hand, there are still powerful voices in government arguing against a change from the repressive regime developed by Abacha, and Abubakar will only gradually be able to move toward reconciliation.

CONTROLLING CORRUPTION

The topic of corruption has already been addressed in earlier discussions of political culture and distributive performance (Chapters Three and Seven). Here it is appropriate to describe official efforts to combat corruption. Successive Nigerian regimes have come to power vowing to root out the corruption of the previous administration. When Yakubu Gowon was overthrown amid the first major corruption scandal in Nigeria, the successor regime of Murtala and Obasanjo instituted "Operation Purge the Nation." Over 10,000 civil servants were removed from office, mostly on charges relating to corruption or abuse of office, but it is not clear that public service was less corrupt thereafter. Obasanjo later instituted a Corrupt Practices Investigation Bureau (CPIB). The CPIB commissioner was empowered to investigate corruption, and to gather evidence in appropriate cases, but could not initiate proceedings. The CPIB was poorly funded, and seen as relatively toothless. It was replaced under the Second Republic by a Code of Conduct, to be enforced by a Code of Conduct Bureau and Code of Conduct Tribunal. Unfortunately, its provisions that public officials declare their assets were never enforced, and only President Shagari and his vice president ever complied. Concerning these failed efforts, one must conclude that "where the political will is absent no amount of laws, bureaux, commissions or draconian punishments will ever begin to make an impact on let alone deal with corruption."[15]

THE ROLE OF SHARI'A

The Shari'a is the Muslim legal code. Its sources are the Koran, the Sunna (the tradition coming from the Prophet Muhammed himself), the Kiyas (analogical deductions from other sources) and Ijma, or consensus among Islamic jurists. In the constitutional debates leading up to the Second Republic (1979-1983), northern

Muslims raised the issue of extending the availability of Shari'a courts from the state level in the northern region to federal courts all over the country. The 1979 constitution recognized the validity of Shari'a in the North, and provided for a line of appeal through a Shari'a Court of Appeal to the Federal Court of Appeal. Provision for also made for a Shari'a court of appeals in the constitution of 1989 and the report of the 1994/95 Constitutional Conference.[16] For southerners, a secular state does not permit such a separate legal track, and certainly not outside the northern states. Muslims counter that there are Muslims throughout the country, and that they should have access to the Shari'a, especially in the realm of marriage and family law.

PROPERTY RIGHTS

Throughout history and in all societies the allocation of use of property, especially land, has been a major aspect of law and politics. It receives little attention in most descriptive works on politics in industrial nations, because policies are usually long in place. (Except in such cases as the demands of prerevolutionary owners for title to lands confiscated by Communist governments, or suits brought

---

Box 8.1 The Umbilical Cord in Igbo Culture

"The burial of the umbilical cord. . .has given rise to a social institution which may be called 'the navel complex.' The Igbo who cannot point to the burial place of his navel cord is not a *diala*—freeborn. A child whose navel cord was not buried is denied citizenship. For the burial, the mother selects the most fruitful oil palm tree out of the many that the husband may indicate. At the foot of this tree the umbilical cord is buried. ... This palm belongs to the child. It cannot be alienated. Not only is it a symbol of *diala* status; it is the foundation for the socially ambitious."

Victor C. Uchendu, *The Igbo of Southeast Nigeria* (New York, Holt, Rinehart and Winston, 1965), p. 59.

---

by North American Indian peoples for lands alienated in violation of treaties.) In Africa, slowly evolving traditions on land ownership and use were jolted by colonial administrations, and have grown more complex and insecure under conditions of urbanization and capital-intensive farming.

Most African traditions did not include the concepts of absolute private ownership or land as a commodity that could be bought and sold by private persons. Rather, allocation of land use was a communal right; an individual or family would be granted the use of a field, but for a fixed or indeterminate period of time, never permanently. The community that controlled this allocation included the deceased of the family unit or community, such that even community or family leaders could not decide on a different form of allocation. In those societies with traditional rulers, such as the Yoruba, one of the principal royal duties and privileges was the allocation of land use. A stranger could "rent" a piece of land, but was limited in how he could use it; generally, annual crops were permitted, but permanent crops like kola, rubber, and cocoa would be prohibited as a use that suggested long-term alienation. The difficulty of land alienation in the Igbo culture is illustrated in the practice of burying the umbilical cord (see Box 7.2); this custom is common to many other Nigerian cultures as well (although it is dying out among those who give birth in hospitals).

The situation was somewhat different in northern Nigeria, where the Fulani overlords who established control over Hausa communities early in the nineteenth century claimed from those communities the right to allocate land ownership and use.[17] They apparently did not succeed in applying this authority universally, however, as in the densely populated area around Kano, "individuals who are recognized as owners are afforded a remarkable degree of security regarding the retention and disposition of their land," and this with little recourse to either Islamic or state courts.[18]

As colonial administrations pushed the development of market agriculture, land tenure became a policy issue of great importance in Africa. European settlers and companies wanted clear private title to land, and where they came in considerable numbers, conflicts over land tenure were inevitable. In Nigeria, the colonial administration generally supported the traditional authorities' right to allocate land, but also introduced the concept of private ownership where it had not been known previously, and established the right of government to appropriate land in return for compensation. Expatriates in Nigeria were not allowed to acquire title to any land from a native Nigerian. This policy helps to explain why neither large numbers of Europeans nor any significant European capital investment were to be found in Nigeria. Furthermore, the system discouraged northern Nigerians from purchasing land in the South, or southerners from doing so in the North. In 1916 Lord Lugard declared all land in northern Nigeria to be under "native" authority, although in some northern areas, "native" authority in the form of Fulani lords was, as we have seen above, not universally applied. However, in 1962 the government of the Northern region claimed for itself the right of land-use allocation, and in 1978 the Obasanjo military regime promulgated a Land Use Decree stating that all land is publicly owned in Nigeria, "vested in the Governor of [each] State and such land shall be held in trust and administered for the use and common benefits of all Nigerians in accordance with the provisions of this Act."[19] In a later section, local governments were given the authority to approve transactions transferring the right of land occupancy.[20] Theoretically, the law supports traditional beliefs that land cannot be privately owned; but it departs from tradition in taking the right of allocation for use away from traditional authorities, and land tenure becomes a matter of agreement between private persons and the government. In practice, land continues to be "bought" and "sold" (for some time after the decree, this was done with backdated receipts), and in rural areas to be allocated by traditional rulers (who receive fees for such transactions), but without the support of law. In the region around Kano, the population has "successfully deluded itself that individuals own land. The external realities that have redefined what constitutes 'customary land tenure' over the last seventy-five years have been avoided for the most part." To rural populations in northern Nigeria, the Land Use Decree is not much different from the precolonial claims of Fulani overlords or the edicts of Lord Lugard, but they share with people in other regions the

> anxiety, not over the public ownership and control of land per se but (given the extraordinary power of the state in affecting the distribution of land) how it is administered, by whom, and for whose benefit.[21]

The understanding that land rights are communal in Nigeria clearly distinguishes the impact of petroleum production there from that in a "private property" state like the United States. In Nigeria there was never a question that certain individuals, or even certain villages, had a legal claim to the extraction of petroleum from land that they "owned." There have been disputes over the allocation of profits among different regions of the country, but these disagreements are not phrased in terms of who "owns" the land.

In terms of agricultural development, a central government role in land tenure is part of the state-centered development strategy of many African countries, but seems to be an anomaly in Nigeria with its dynamic private sector. This policy seemed to afford some protection to the peasant farmer, in that his land could not be alienated; however, both before and after the Land Tenure Act, wealthy and influential people have been able to acquire occupancy of land, before, through traditional authorities, and since, through state officials. Forrest reports that "the expropriation of land by the state accelerated in the 1970s, especially in the vicinity of state capitals [and] increased the number of landless and land poor." Also, "there is some evidence that the acquisition of land by companies and wealthy individuals and investment in large-scale farming speeded up after 1983," as "federal agencies and state governments used their powers to lease land to companies and individuals."[22]

Another disadvantage of the act for the smallholder is that the farmer does not have the possibility of using "his" land as collateral for loans, and therefore has little access to credit.[23] In urban areas, the act ostensibly prevents speculation in land values, and allows governments to acquire land for public works projects at little cost. In the words of the Supreme Military Council statement on the decree,

> the previous system. . .created unnecessary delay in acquisition, hampered a lot of development both agricultural and industrial. A lot of projects were abandoned in the past because as soon as such

projects were conceived certain people have the means or interest of knowing the intentions of Government, and before we know what was happening they would have gone to acquire these lands. And by the time the government decides to go ahead with its projects, we would find that millions of Naira had been paid into compensation. So with this decree all these problems have been eliminated.[24]

Even in advanced industrial countries, one should not assume that a change in statutory law automatically transforms reality—we only have to look at laws forbidding the sale and use of narcotics in industrialized countries to see the gap between prescription and practice. This is even more the case in less-developed countries, where the resources available for law enforcement are meager. Yet reality can be *affected* by legislation, even if the effects are not those intended by the legislator. In the case of the Land Use Decree, many Nigerians have continued to sell or lease land, either ignorant of the law or ignoring it. The outcome of these transactions is in doubt, however, whenever the parties become involved in a civil action. In Nigeria, the Land Use Decree was the subject of litigation in the 1989 case of *Savannah Bank Ltd. v. Ajilo.* The plaintiff, Savannah Bank, claimed that a deed of mortgage with the defendant was void because it was not approved by the governor of Lagos State. This claim was upheld by the Ikeja High Court and an appeal was dismissed by the Court of Appeal. On further appeal, the Nigerian Supreme Court also sided with the plaintiff. The decision was widely criticized in Nigeria as unfair, yet the courts' legal opinion was clearly in accord with the decree. Those who persist in ignoring the law have no recourse if a contractual partner reneges on an urban real estate agreement not approved by the governor. Secondly, governments at all levels were removed from the obligation to negotiate a fair price through eminent domain procedures when land is acquired for a public purpose.

The overall effect of this decree was to reduce the control of traditional rulers in southern Nigeria over the allocation of land, although they remain influential wherever traditions continue to respect their powers. The gatekeeping function is, however, shifted to local administrators (rural) or state governors (urban), where the potential for "rent-seeking" is increased enormously.[25] Although bankers treat a "certificate of occupancy" issued by the state as commensurate with a title, it has happened that multiple certificates of occupancy have been issued for a single property. Cases have been reported of three-year waits for a certificate of occupancy. Finally, "allocations of land have been made mostly to relatives, friends, party faithfuls and other associates of those in power at any particular time. . .the various Land Use and Allocation Committees set up under the act to advise the governors on these matters have been of little use. It could hardly be otherwise when all the members of the committee are single-handedly appointed by the governor."[26]

The Land Tenure Act has caused far-reaching changes in access to land in Nigeria. Traditional land tenure was in most cases communal, so that individuals' access to land was treated as entitlement to use or occupancy, not absolute ownership. That principle is continued in the modern legislation, but in a context of more concentrated power over occupancy and use decisions, with fewer checks on arbitrary decisions than existed in either the precolonial, the colonial, or the early independence periods. Most scholarly treatments of the issue see the harmonization of the land tenure system and easier access of government to land needed for development projects as positive achievements; they urge a more efficient and rule-bounded method of administering the decree.

THE CENSUS ISSUE

One policy issue has overshadowed all the others since independence, because the outcome often determines how political goods will be distributed. A minor policy issue in some countries, population counts in Nigeria have been fraught with conflict. In a country where federal subsidies make up the lion's share of budgetary allocations at all levels, the distribution of population directly affects the distribution of resources. (Americans will recognize that a similar issue arose concerning undercounting of some ethnic groups, the homeless, etc., after the 1990 census in the United States, and that a Census Bureau proposal to expand the use of sampling in place of full counts in the 2000 census emerged as an important point of conflict between Congress and the Clinton administration.)

The colonial administration carried out the first national census of Nigeria in 1952-1953. There was considerable doubt as to its accuracy, because inhabitants feared its relationship to tax collection, and because of logistical problems, political tensions, and inadequate training of census takers. Nonetheless, in retrospect it may have been more accurate than any attempt since then.[27]

A census conducted in 1962 reported a Nigerian population of 45 million, with just 47 percent of the total in the North; it was highly controversial, and was finally rejected. A new census conducted in 1963 reported a total population of 55.6 million, making Nigeria the tenth largest country in the world. However, contrary to the count of the previous year, it found a majority of that population (30 million) to be in the North, a finding that was then and is always questioned by southern Nigerians, who maintain that a fly over or drive through the North and South will easily demonstrate that population densities are higher in the latter. Aboyade believes that the 1963 count may have overestimated the total by 30 percent.[28] Nevertheless, that census, or straight-line projections from it, remained the official source of population statistics for almost twenty years. At the same time, voices were continually raised in the regions that perceive themselves undercounted for a new, "fair" count.

In 1973, General Gowon's Supreme Military Council attempted a census update, and ordered that enumerators be accompanied by unarmed soldiers. With the prestige and integrity of the armed forces behind the count, the resulting figures presumably could be trusted, and used for economic planning, electoral preparation, and military disengagement. Gowon's optimism was misplaced. The 1973 census figures, when finally released, appeared as politically manipulated and inflated as the discredited results of a decade earlier.   Apparent overcounting in certain areas, especially in the North, revived the latent fears of regional domination that periodically roil Nigerian politics.[29]

After almost two additional decades of continued reliance on the 1963 figures, the Babangida government commissioned a new census to be conducted by a National Population Commission. Following methodical pre-testing and sampling, a census was conducted in November 1991 that put the country's total population at 88.5 million, a figure that caused substantial downward revision from estimates that exceeded 100 million, and seemed to substantiate the findings of Aboyade and others that the 1963 count had been inflated. According to this census, the highest population concentrations were in the states of Bauchi, Kaduna, Kano, Katsina and Sokoto in the North, and Lagos, Oyo and Rivers States in the South. These figures caused new consternation in the South, where feelings ran high that the figures had again been "cooked" to give a disproportionate population share to the North.

Conclusions on Performance

While our judgments on performance should be nuanced given the complexity of Nigeria's political environment and the problems it faces, an overall conclusion emerges unfailingly: In comparison to other countries with equivalent natural resources, pool of skilled human resources, and size, Nigeria has not done well.

That obvious conclusion caused writer Chinua Achebe to write *The Problem with Nigeria*, in which he concluded that the "problem" was leadership. Until Nigerians can settle on a constitutional arrangement that provides responsive leadership from the national to the local level, the country will continue to fall far short of its potential. Although the Second Republic failed, it was a significant improvement over the First in reining in the politicization of ethnicity. There was reason to be optimistic that the constitution developed in the late Babangida years would have introduced another increment of correction. It is clear that the present military regime is not interested in moving toward a new legitimate system; there will be no further progress in democratization until a coalition can be formed with the strength to force it in that direction.

There may also be a fatal flaw in the political culture that has developed in Nigeria since independence, and that is part of the "curse of oil": As noted earlier, public policy is often seen in Nigeria as the "national cake," and the unfortunate analogy suggest that "they"—the government—bake a cake which is distributed in slices sized to match the political influence of various constituencies. At least at the mass level, but with the encouragement of political office seekers, constituencies are defined in ethnic terms, and politics becomes a competition among ethnic groups for larger slices of cake. The analogy could of course be used to describe the politics of many countries, but not to the extreme degree that it applies in Nigeria. There, communities look to the government to provide for them. A successful Nigerian constitution will not only provide responsive leaders; it must also shift responsibility so that extractive and distributive performance come from the same budget, and so that there is some relationship between the amounts one pays into and receives from the public sector. Public goals based on community effort were the norm in most Nigerian traditions; that norm must be rediscovered.

Political scientist Julius Ihonvbere reasons that new elections would do no good in contemporary Nigeria: "Until accountability, social justice, equality, and human rights become part of the political agenda of transition from authoritarianism. democracy stands practically no chance of success or consolidation."[30]

Nigeria in Africa and in the World

Nigeria (now along with South Africa) has the population and resource base to be a regional power, and it has stimulated hopes and fears among its neighbors concerning that potential. Under the First Republic (1960-1966), Nigeria generally focused inward, and played a rather minor role in the continent's turbulent politics. But then came the civil war over Biafra: Nigeria's army grew from 10,000 to 250,000; the country's oil potential became known; and, as we have seen earlier, world powers took an interest in the war's outcome.

Some West African governments offered clear support to Biafra, a support Nigerians suspected grew from a desire to see their country divided up and thus reduced in influence. This was thought especially to be the case with Côte d'Ivoire (the Ivory Coast) under President Houphouet-Boigny, who favored Biafra with French support. When the war ended, relations among these countries were appropriately strained.

Nigeria took a leading role in drafting successive versions of the Lome Convention between the ACP (Africa, Caribbean and Pacific) countries and the European Union (EU). Under a series of agreements going back to 1975, sixty-six less-developed countries are given customs exemptions on their exports to Europe, with Europe giving up previous reciprocal provisions that give European goods preferential access into the less-developed countries. Lome also gives access to technical and financial aid of about $2 billion per year, as well as loans from the European Investment Bank. Finally, the EU compensates these countries for some losses on commodity exports.[31] The first Lome agreement followed Britain's entry into the the European Economic Community (EEC) which subsequently became the EU. The accord was the result of Commonwealth countries' insistence that they enter into the special preferences that the European Community had provided the colonies of the original members (especially France). Because of Nigeria's heavy dependence on oil exports, rather than on agricultural commodities, the impact of

Lome has been less there than in other African countries (and has not had the overall impact on Africa in general that was originally anticipated, as the importance of African trade has continued to decline in an expanded Europe).[32]

Success in the Lome accords in bridging the gap between French-speaking and English-speaking African countries gave hope that further region-wide economic cooperation was possible. Nigeria under General Gowon took a leading role in establishing the Economic Community of West African States (ECOWAS), hoping both to bring Nigeria closer to other West African countries, while at the same time countering French influence in the region. The Ivoirian government had already taken the lead in forming the Economic Community of West Africa (CEAO in French), an exclusively French-speaking organization, and were naturally wary of the predominant position that Nigeria might play in a wider regional organization. But Nigeria was successful in first approaching Togo, Benin, and Niger, the francophone (French-speaking) countries with which it already had close ties, offering attractive economic inducements that included special petroleum prices. With this group in hand, Nigerian diplomats cast their net wider, and in 1975 the Treaty of Lagos was signed by representatives of sixteen West African governments. The ECOWAS treaty specified a two-year phase during which intra-community tariffs would be frozen, followed by an eight-year period that would end with the removal of duties on trade among members. Finally, a common external tariff wall would be created.

Thus, West Africa under Nigerian leadership has been partaking in the worldwide movement toward free-trade zones. As elsewhere, however, progress has been difficult. Ten years after its creation, ECOWAS reported that it had not made "tangible progress in practical terms," and by 1989 the member governments were $80 million in arrears in their contributions to the organization. The proportion of intra-community trade in the member countries' total international trade has not changed since 1980. On the other hand, ECOWAS has had better success as a regional political organization, especially in mediating disputes among member states, and in 1990 a Nigerian proposal was approved that created a standing mediation committee.[33]

Nigeria has played a prominent role in the region through commitment of its substantial military capacity, notably in supplying the leadership and the majority of troops for ECOMOG, the ECOWAS-sponsored peacekeeping force in Liberia. That operation has largely been seen as a success, with armed conflict halted and a truce negotiated among the Liberian contenders that allowed for a national election to take place. As a part of that operation, Nigeria also stationed troops in Sierra Leone, to protect that country's borders from incursions of Liberian rebels, and finished by confronting a military junta in Sierra Leone that overthrew an elected civilian government there in May 1997. . .an action more than a bit ironic, given the origins of the Abacha regime. The operation in Sierra Leone was ultimately successful in restoring the democratically elected president, Ahmad Kabbah, in February 1998. Although other West African governments are wary of the new

Nigerian propensity to use force in the region, even under ECOMOG sponsorship, the Sierra Leonean intervention on the side of democratic civilian rule stands out as the most effective public relations initiative Abacha used in influencing world opinion.

Nigeria has also participated in wider-ranging United Nations operations including in Lebanon, Rwanda, the former Yugoslavia, and Somalia. However, as in other countries, these overseas deployments are seriously questioned, given the country's serious financial difficulties.

During the oil-boom years, Nigeria's wealth attracted immigrants from across the region(causing Nigeria to obtain a delay in the adoption of an ECOWAS provision for the free flow of labor among member states), but in especially large numbers from English-speaking Ghana. When oil production fell and the Nigerian economy weakened in 1983, one aspect of the government's response was a sudden mass expulsion of Ghanaians, who were forced to return to their homeland. (Ghana had itself expelled Nigerians and other West Africans in 1970 and 1972 in order to deflect anger from the government over economic problems.) Relations with Ghana were strained for several years thereafter.

Nigeria and Cameroon have a long-standing border dispute (see the background in Chapter One) over the Bakassi peninsula and adjacent islands. This area is potentially oil- and gas-rich, and is also a productive fishing area. According to Wole Soyinka, it was ceded to Cameroon by Yakubu Gowon in return for Cameroon's support of the Federal side in the Biafran War. Nigeria now claims that the transfer was never legally approved in Nigeria.[34] The conflict has resulted in military skirmishes over the years. In 1981, five Nigerian soldiers were killed in such a clash. More recently (1994-1996), a renewal of such incidents resulted in Nigeria's deployment of 1,000 troops there, and threatened to involve France, which has a defense agreement with Cameroon (but substantial interest in improving its relations with Nigeria as well). In July 1996, the Organization of African Unity met in the Cameroonian capital of Yaoundé. Nigeria's foreign minister accused Cameroon of simultaneously massing troops on their common border. Cameroon filed suit over the issue in 1994 in the International Court of Justice in the Hague, and in March 1996, the International Court asked the two countries to refrain from military action while the case was under consideration by them, but vituperations continued: In August 1996, Cameroon barred imports of Nigerian flour, stating the flour was suspected of causing cancer. In response, Nigeria's minister of agriculture called the ban "part of Cameroon's campaign of calumny against Nigeria over the border conflict." The Cameroonian claim before the International Court was extended to include territory around Lake Chad in the North.[35] The two governments finally agreed to allow a United Nations fact-finding mission to visit the Bakassi peninsula and attempt to broker a peace. The International Court agreed to a request by Cameroon to broaden the case to consider the entire frontier between the two countries, and was not expected to reach a decision in the case until late in 1998. The potential for serious conflict is always present, however, not just because of the potential value of the territories involved: Rather, regimes in each country may be motivated to use the need for "defense against an enemy" to shore up weak legitimacy.

Because of the country's prominence on the continent, Nigeria's international financial problems have been especially embarrassing to it. Forced along with other African nations to accept stringent structural adjustment planning from the World Bank and International Monetary Fund, Nigeria has reacted with frustration and anger, and has led the region's governments in their critique of international lenders' policies, and sometimes in more general calls for African self-reliance: It hosted the meeting that led to the OAU's adoption, in 1980, of the Lagos Plan of Action as a response to western calls for greater integration into the world market system.

Through the Organization of Petroleum Exporting Countries (OPEC), Nigeria has a separate international identity not preponderantly African, but one which acts within a limited frame of reference.

With some ambivalence, northern-dominated governments have been encouraged by Muslim interests to develop closer relationships with the Islamic world, which led among other things to the abortive effort under Babangida to join the Organization of the Islamic Conference (see Chapter Three). As in other Muslim regions of the world, there is an ongoing competition in Nigeria between a conservative establishment and a younger generation of Islamic reformists who are influenced by media and personal contacts with the Middle East, especially Iran. The English-language *Teheran Times* is circulated in the North.[36] A prime motivation for the pressure to associate with Islam internationally is said to have been the need for conservative Islamic leaders to affirm their position against reformers through identification with orthodox (especially Middle Eastern) Islam, while challengers such as the Mai Tatsine movement are linked to "foreigners" from Cameroon, Chad, and Niger.[37] The construction of mosques, printing and distribution of literature, etc., have been supported by the Gulf states, especially Saudi Arabia, to the discomfiture of some Christian groups. This is evidenced in an edifice competition in Abuja, where a magnificent mosque dominates the skyline, with a yet-to-be completed ecumenical church not far away.

From the Biafran War through the end of the Cold War, Nigeria's relations with the West were often on edge, as Nigeria emerged from that war a major military power on the continent and attempted to assert a foreign policy position that did not always coincide with the West's Cold War stances. Nigeria's role as a regional power pitted it particularly against France, which of all the Western powers has continued to play the most prominent role in West Africa. Bolaji Akinyemi, director general of the Nigerian Institute of international Affairs, once called France "Africa's Enemy Number One" for its trade relationship with South Africa and its involvement, both clandestine and overtly military, in its former colonies and as a surrogate for Belgium in its former colony, Zaire. Although French interest has indeed been focused on its former colonies, France began to take a clearer stand against South Africa after the election of François Mitterand as president in 1981, and relations with Nigeria began to improve.[38] As described below, the two countries cooperated in thwarting the insertion of Libya's Qaddafi in Chad, and in recent years the French have decided that Nigeria's size and potential wealth should not be overlooked: France has actively promoted closer economic ties with Nigeria, a move that in turn has upset Nigeria's French-speaking neighbors. The territorial conflict between Nigeria and Cameroon (see above) has put France in a very difficult position, as it may have to choose between maintaining its economic and defense commitments to its former colony with its substantial economic interests in Nigeria and its desire to cultivate this potential regional power.

Southern Africa was the chief source of conflict between Nigeria and the United States. In 1976 Nigeria attempted to intervene in the Angolan conflict, and attempted to get the three contending groups to form some type of unity government. The United States, on the other hand, was alarmed at the close Soviet and Cuban ties of the MPLA administration, and actively supported its opponents, seeing this strategy as balancing the designs of the socialist camp on southern Africa. At the height of this disagreement the Nigerian government even took over the U.S. Information Service buildings and radio-monitoring stations in Lagos and Kaduna.

Relations became much warmer during the Carter administration, when Andrew Young, as U.S. Ambassador to the United Nations, took a special interest in relations with Africa, and entered into a particularly warm relationship with General Obasanjo, then the Nigerian head of state.[39] Relations cooled again during the Reagan administration, starting with a comment by the Nigerian foreign minister that Nigeria preferred a Carter victory in the 1980 American presidential election. More importantly, Nigeria strongly disapproved of Reagan's "constructive engagement" with South Africa and Britain's support of the constructive engagement approach and its "soft approach" to sanctions against white-dominated Rhodesia (now Zimbabwe). Nigeria even nationalized British holdings in BP in an effort to influence British Rhodesian policy.[40] U.S.-Nigerian cooperation in African affairs disappeared as the administration also asked for and won a senatorial repeal of the Clark amendment, which had required congressional approval for any clandestine aid to the UNITA movement in Angola. In spite of these differences of opinion over southern Africa, Nigeria shared with the West a fear that Chad might come under the influence of Qaddafi's Libya, and cooperated with Britain, France, and the United States in late 1981 by committing ground troops to a military action in that neighboring country to the north. The Reagan administration also came to show strong symbolic support for Nigeria's Second Republic as an example of "African democracy." Finally, Reagan continued the Carter initiatives in commercial exchange and technical aid in agriculture and banking.

The first Reagan administration coincided with the end of Nigeria's petroleum-based boom. American imports of Nigerian oil dropped over 15 percent from 1980 to 1981. Nigeria had been the second most important source of U.S. oil imports, but dropped to third place in 1982, and to seventh place in 1983, far behind

Mexico, Canada, Venezuela, Britain, Indonesia, and Saudi Arabia.[41] As explained in Chapter Two, the end of the oil boom came about because of decreased demand in the industrial countries and the entry into the market of North Sea oil from Britain and Norway, and put Nigeria in direct competition with Britain for the North American and European markets.

With the renewal of military rule in 1983, relations between the United States and Nigeria remained correct, but the Western powers, especially Britain and the United States, were openly critical of Nigeria's military rulers, and showed support for the country's return to civilian rule, especially during the Babangida regime. Relations with Britain were dramatically worsened over the Umaru Dikko affair (see Box 8.2). The U.S. Agency for International Development and the U.S. Information Service both began aid programs in support of democratization in Nigeria. Babangida's 1993 election annulment brought condemnation from the

---

Box 8.2 The Umaru Dikko Affair

For many Nigerians, Alhaji Umaru Dikko, former minister of transportation in the Shagari government (1979-1983), "represented what the J. R. Ewing character meant for millions of viewers of the television series 'Dallas': A man that many loved to hate." Son-in-law of President Shagari, he was often considered the unofficial prime minister. Access to him meant access to wealth, a privilege from which a small number of individuals had benefited. In 1983, he had managed the Shagari re-election campaign, which put him in touch with the world of important business deals. He presided over the Presidential Task Force on Rice, and reportedly became very wealthy as a result.

After the coup of December 1983, Dikko fled to Britain, where he appeared on television with a threat to wage a *jihad* (holy war) against the Buhari regime. When the British refused a Nigerian demand for Dikko's extradition, Buhari's administration took matters into their own hands: Customs officials at Gatwick Airport opened a suspicious-looking crate marked "diplomatic materials" and addressed to the Foreign Ministry in Lagos. Inside they found an unconscious Dikko in the presence of an Israeli physician. Britain recalled its high commissioner (Ambassador) from Lagos in protest.

(More recently, Dikko returned voluntarily to Nigeria, and is again active in politics.)

From Shehu Othman, "Les relations internationales globales du Nigeria," pp. 73-74.

United States and Britain, and a suspension of aid. However, this relationship has not been important enough to the military rules to modify their behavior. Presumably an embargo on purchases of Nigerian oil would have that effect, but it does not appear that the industrial nations' governments have the will to take such a drastic step.

Most observers saw the Abacha regime's treatment of dissenters as a calculation of how far they could silence opposition without provoking more severe international sanctions. They pushed suppression to the limit with the Ogoni hangings of November 1995, provoking the withdrawal of ambassadors by all the major Western powers. Perhaps the most official condemnation at the international level came from the United Nations Human Rights Commission (UNHRC), composed of eighteen experts on human rights from around the world. The UNHRC expressed its displeasure over "the high number of extra-judicial and summary executions, disappearances and cases of torture" in which army and security forces were involved.[42]

The European parliament voted a condemnation of Nigeria. The British Commonwealth suspended Nigeria's membership for two years, although Prime Minister John Major rejected a call by President Nelson Mandela of South Africa for a boycott of Nigerian oil. In April 1996, a Commonwealth Ministerial Action Group (CMAG) recommended a set of actions against the Abacha regime, including a ban on arms exports to Nigeria, and a prohibition of athletic exchanges with Nigerian teams. In response, Nigeria released eight political prisoners, promised a return to civilian rule in 1998, invited the United Nations Human Rights Commission team that investigated human rights abuses, then invited the CMAG to Abuja for talks. Those talks later broke down over the question of whether the CMAG could meet with private (i.e., opposition) groups. The CMAG states have kept their sanctions on hold, presumably to have continued leverage on the Nigerian government. Only Canada has taken strong measures against the regime, unilaterally implementing the recommended sanctions. Canadian foreign minister Lloyd Axworthy has denounced the "appeasers" in the Commonwealth, and the Abacha administration has accused Canada of supporting terrorist activities in Nigeria. Canada and Nigeria have closed their embassies in Lagos and Ottawa, respectively.

President Clinton halted direct U.S.-Nigeria air travel and all U.S. foreign aid to Nigeria, withdrew U.S. support for assistance to Nigeria by the World Bank and IMF, and extended a ban on travel in the United States by Nigerian officials. However, within three months, all countries but the United States and Canada had resumed normal relations, and the United States said it was "carrying out a comprehensive review of its policy on Nigeria." Nigeria responded with a twelve-member lobbying delegation in Washington that included an Igbo army colonel, Roy Innis of the Congress on Racial Equality, and Askia Muhammed of the *Washington Observer*. The son of one of the Ogoni chiefs murdered in 1994 took out a two-page ad in the *New York Times* (December 6, 1995) holding Saro-Wiwa responsible for all the misfortune of the Ogoni people.[43] Indeed, Nigeria has gotten some mixed messages from the United States, as when Louis Farrakhan, on a trip through western and southern Africa, Libya, Iraq, and Iran in January 1966, praised Abacha's plan for the return to civilian rule, and Senator Carol Mosely-Brown of Illinois, maintaining good personal relations with the Abacha family, visited them in Nigeria. The Nigerian regime has also invested heavily in public relations in the United States, having bought the services of well-connected lobbying and public relations firms in Washington. In April 1997 Nigeria paid almost $600,000 for a

16-page advertising supplement in the *Wall Street Journal*, featuring a "soft" interview with Abacha that praised the "political, economic, and social stability" of his government.[44]   By August 1996, the Clinton administration concluded that it did not have sufficient international support for tough sanctions, and sent Bill Richardson to Nigeria to use "gentle diplomacy" on the issues of human rights and democracy.[45]   As President Clinton prepared for a trip to six African nations in March 1998, Washington sent a stronger message: The itinerary pointedly left out Nigeria, and Assistant Secretary of State Susan Rice stated that "an electoral victory by any military candidate in the forthcoming presidential election in Nigeria would be unacceptable." Nonetheless, unless the Abacha regime had committed a major human rights violation, and again captured world attention, it appeared unlikely that western governments would play an active role in forcing a change in Nigeria's form of government. Even a plea from Pope John Paul, in connection with a pastoral visit to Nigeria that came just before Clinton's Africa trip, for the release of sixty political prisoners did not appear to have any effect.[46]   Things looked more promising with the assumption of power by Abubakar. On July 20, 1998 he announced to a wary Nigerian public that he would release all political prisoners and would hand over power to a civilian president on May 29, 1999.

Through much of the independence period, Nigeria has played the role of a major regional power, a role its governments have emphasized in their bids for Nigeria to become a permanent member of the United Nations Security Council. However, Nigeria's place in the world has been compromised in recent years by her economic weakness, by the low legitimacy of her rulers both internally and abroad, and by the deepening fault lines along her regional and religious boundaries. It has further been called into question by the defeat of apartheid in South Africa, which, with the emergence of Nelson Mandela as the most highly respected leader on the continent, makes that country a more congenial model for African development and a more respected voice for Africa.[47]   Given Nigeria's great potential (and the daunting problems which South Africa still faces), an economic revival and a new and legitimate political regime might yet return Nigeria to the purposeful involvement in world affairs that characterized the Murtala/Obasanjo period.

END NOTES

1. Almond and Powell, Comparative Politics: A Theoretical Framework, p. 161.

2. Olu Adediran, "Security of Life and Property and Law Enforcement Agents at the Local level in Nigeria," in Aborisade, ed. Nigerian Local Government Reformed (Ife: Local Government Publication Series, Obafemi Awolowo University, 1989), p. 303.

3. Forrest, Politics and Economic Development in Nigeria, pp. 80-81, 111-12; Metz, ed. Nigeria: A Country Study, p. 318.

4. Adediran, "Security of Life and Property and Law Enforcement Agents at the Local Level in Nigeria," p. 305.

5. O. Adediran, "Security of Life and Property," pp. 307-309; Helen Chapin Metz, ed. Nigeria: A Country Study, p.318.

6. Metz, Nigeria: A Country Study, p. 320.

7. Amnesty International, "Nigeria: Resumption of Public Executions."

8. Metz, ed. Nigeria: A Country Study, p. 318; U.S. Bureau of Justice Statistics, Sourcebook 1994 Justice, p. 541.

9. "L'Afrique des Trafics," Le Monde Hebdomadaire, April 25 - May 2, 1991.

10. Reuters Press Agency, Lagos, August 6, 1996.

11. Metz, Nigeria: A Country Study, pp. 320-321; U.S. Department of State, Bureau for International Narcotics and Law Enforcement Affairs, "Africa and the Middle East," International Narcotics Control Strategy Report, 1997 (Washington: http://www.state.gov/www/global/na...997_narc-report/afrme97_part2.html).

12. Larry Diamond, "Nigeria: Pluralism, Statism, and the Struggle for Democracy," pp. 56-57.

13. Pita Ogaba Agbese, "The State versus Human Rights Advocates in Africa: The Case of Nigeria."

14.Claude E. Welch, Jr., Protecting Human Rights in Africa: Roles and Strategies of Non-Governmental Organizations, p. 112.

15. Billy Dudley, An Introduction to Nigerian Government and Politics, pp. 136-137; Robin Theobald, Corruption, Development and Underdevelopment, pp. 138, 141-143.

16. Anthony Oyewole, Historical Dictionary of Nigeria, p. 305; Report of the 1994/95 Constitutional Conference, pp. 88-89.

17.E. Wayne Nafziger, "The Economy," p. 177.

18.Paul J. Ross, "Land as a Right to Membership: Land Tenure dynamics in a Peripheral Area of the Kano Close-Settled Zone," p. 225.

19.Quoted in M.B. Adegboye, "The Impact of the Land Use Act on Traditional Rulers in Local Administration in Nigeria," p. 211.

20. M.B. Adegboye, p. 214.

21. Paul J. Ross, "Land as a Right to Membership: Land Tenure Dynamics in a Peripheral Area of the Kano Close-Settled Zone, pp. 245-247.

22. Tom Forrest, Politics and Economic Development in Nigeria, pp. 197-98.

23. The situation is similar to the ejido policy in Mexico, a similar shared land ownership scheme enacted after the Revolution to protect peasants' access to land, but which has had the same effect on the credit worthiness of peasants as in Nigeria.

24. L.O. Dare, "Administration of the Decree," in Omolade Adjuyigbe and Leo O. Dare, eds., Land Tenure Reform in Nigeria: Implications and Implementation of the Land-Use Decree 1978, pp. 106-107. The described practices are reminiscent of William Plunkitt's "honest graft" in Nineteenth-Century New York City, where Plunkitt "seen his opportunities and he took 'em" (William Riordan, Plunkitt of Tammany Hall).

25. M.B. Adegboye, "The Impact of the Land Use Act on Traditional Rulers in Local Administration in Nigeria," p. 218; L.O. Dare, "Administration of the Decree," pp. 109-114..

26. A. O. O. Ekpu, "Making the Land Use Act Work," p. 28.

27. Ronald Cohen and Abe Goldman, "The Society and Its Environment," p. 93.

28. Ojetunji Aboyade, "The Economy of Nigeria," p. 131.

29. Claude E. Welch, Jr. No Farewell to Arms?, p. 10.

30. Julius O. Ihonvbere, "Elections and Conflicts in Nigeria's Nontransition to Democracy," p. 1

31. A. Leroy Bennett, International Organizations: Principles and Issues, p. 257.

32. Naomi Chazan et al, Politics and Society in Contemporary Africa. pp. 303-305.

33. The preceding treatment of ECOWAS' formation is drawn from Carol Lancaster, The Lagos Three, pp. 253-257.

34. Wole Soyinka, The Open Sore of a Continent, p. 22.

35. Reuters News Agency, Lagos, July 7 and August 6, 1996; "Nigeria/Cameroon: Blundering into battle," Africa Confidential 35 (No. 8, April 15, 1994) pp. 4-5.

36. John N. Paden, "Nigerian Muslim Perspectives on Religion, Society and Communication with the Western World, " pp. 11, 14.

37. Last, Murray. 1988. "Tradition musulmane et diplomatie," p. 271.

38. Shehu Othman, "Les relations internationales globales du Nigeria," pp. 75, 78.

39. H.E. Newsum and Olayiwola Abegunrin, <u>United States Foreign Policy Towards Southern Africa: Andrew Young and Beyond</u> (New York, St. Martin's, 1987), pp. 72-84; Shehu Othman, "Les relations internationales globales du Nigeria, pp. 56-57.

40. Sarah Ahmad Khan, <u>Nigeria: The Political Economy of Oil</u>, p. 70; Shehu Othman, "Les relations internatinales globales du Nigeria," p. 69.

41. Shehu Othman, "Les relations internationales globales du Nigeria," pp. 57-64.

42. Reuters Press Agency, Geneva, July 26, 1996.

43. Reuters News Agency, February 26, 1996; Claude E. Welch, Jr. and Marc Sills, "The Martyrdom of Ken Saro-Wiwa and the Future of Ogoni Self-Determination," pp. 13-14.

44. Mother Jones, January-February 1998 (http://www.motherjones.com/mother_jones/JF98/cook.html).

45. <u>New York Times</u>, August 22, 25, 1996.

46. New York Times, March 22, 1998, p. 1.

47. See Shehu Othman, "Les relations internationales globales du Nigeria," pp. 80-81.

Chapter 9

NIGERIA: PROSPECTS FOR DEVELOPMENT AND DEMOCRACY

The Nigerian political setbacks we have documented do not equal the tragedies of a Bosnia, Rwanda, or Liberia, but the frustrations are nonetheless deep and enduring, and the threat of political cataclysm hangs over the country: Wole Soyinka sees a "spiral of murder, torture, and leadership dementia that is surely leading to the disintegration of a once-proud nation."[1] Any close observer must admit that, since independence, billions of desperately needed naira have been wasted, a few have grown rich at the expense of the poor, many of the country's most talented citizens have emigrated, and accountability in government has proven highly elusive. In the words of poet Tanure Ojaide:

> *We have lost it,*
> *the country we were born into.*
> *We can now sing dirges*
> *of that commonwealth of yesterday --*
> *we live in a country*
> *that is no longer our own.*[2]
> (from "No Longer Our Own Country," written in 1986)

In this concluding chapter, we would like to revisit the questions raised in the introductory chapter concerning democratization and economic development and the model presented by Weingast for achieving democracy, to determine what the preceding description of Nigerian politics can tell us about these issues.

The Preconditions for Democracy

The Nigerian case is consistent with the general hypothesis that countries with low levels of economic development, with low educational levels, and with a middle class that is a relatively small proportion of the population will have difficulty implementing a democratic decision-making process. Yet, although these factors are indeed powerful predictors, they are not determinant. India's experience with political pluralism in roughly similar conditions (including severe ethnic and religious strife) shows that the maintenance of a stable liberal democracy is possible, even though India itself stands out as unique in its region, where Pakistan, Bangladesh, Sri Lanka, and Burma have political histories rather like Nigeria's. Weingast states that India is "characterized by institutions that provide incentives for political leaders to encourage mutual tolerance and by a citizen consensus that wants these institutions preserved."[3] What differences in the two experiences explain why India was able to achieve this democratic equilibrium, and what appears to be a consolidated democracy, while Nigeria (and other countries) have not?

Crawford Young's comparative study of the colonial experience provides the central arguments here.[4] A first difference is in the length of that experience, several hundred years for India, less than one hundred for Nigeria. The first Indian was admitted to the civil service in 1871; the first Indian was commissioned in the army in 1763.[5] This helps explain why Nigeria's inherited institutions have remained foreign to many of its citizens, while in India, "the legitimacy [of colonial transplants] is not questioned even by. . .those that draw their inspiration from cultural nationalism or class conflict."[6] A second difference is less clear, but perhaps critical: In India, after the split with Pakistan, a one-party-dominant system built around the great personal legitimacy of the movement's leaders in a long struggle for independence, evolved into a multiparty system. One cannot but observe that, had India and Pakistan remained a single political unit, its chances of developing a sense of legitimacy of opposition would have been much less; Nigeria has held together equally disparate parts. The success of this process was by no means assured, but the contrast in time is again important, when one considers that the competing independence movements in Nigeria had only sixteen years from the founding of the NCNC in 1944 to independence in 1960, while the Indian Congress was formed in the nineteenth century. In terms of Weingast's model, Indian elites, having experienced the tearing apart of their political system, and having come close to crisis confrontations several times, have determined that their optimal choice is to respect the democratic rules.

One might conclude that India, and not Nigeria, is the unique and limiting case. This is not, however, to despair of democracy in Nigeria, but merely to point out that its consolidation has all the impediments of a large, poor, multicultural state, but did not have some of the advantages experienced by the largest democracy in the World in the evolution of its political system.

The Co-Requisites for Democracy

Weingast's model describes the maladies of the Nigerian political system: Because citizens hold different views about limits on the state, and are (mostly) unwilling to defend those limits—"the sovereign can violate these limits and retain sufficient support to survive."[7] Nigeria has the mistrust among communal groups that renders cooperation impossible: When the Eastern region was considering secession in 1966-1967, Igbo leaders thought they had heard assurances from the Western region that it to would also secede. In classic "prisoner's dilemma" terms, the West sided with the federal government in the subjugation of Biafra. In later years, when western activists called for unified resistance against a northern-dominated regime, many easterners seem to have found grim satisfaction in leaving the West isolated in its resistance.

In his discussion of the special problems of achieving democratic stability in divided societies, Weingast describes the success of constitution-writing in Belgium and Switzerland, and attributes their success to their having "devised a set of constitutional provisions to limit the effect of ethnic and religious divisions. The important characteristics of these constitutions is that, where practical, decision-making is decentralized, while majority rule is limited at the center: Special majorities are required to change basic laws."[8]

> **Box 9.1 What is the Prisoner's Dilemma?**
>
> **The 'Prisoner's Dilemma'** refers to the situation of two suspects in custody. Each is told that the other has confessed to the crime with which they are charged, and that confession will bring leniency. Each suspect knows that, if the other has confessed, he should also, but that both are better off if neither confesses. The repetition of such dilemmas builds long-term trust if the suspects are true to each other, but one betrayal means that both are likely to continue suffering at the hands of the arresting officers. Thus, in general the prisoner's dilemma model refers to situations where players must decide whether or not to trust one another in situations where betrayal pays off in the short run but is costly in the long run.

Nigerian constitution writers have already been aware of these rules. There is already a wide consensus there that stable democracy will not be achieved under a unitary system. Indeed a principal source of Nigerian instability is that the systems imposed by military regimes have been intrinsically unitary, both because of the hierarchical nature of military rule, and because they provide almost all public goods through a single, centrally controlled funding source—petroleum. Nigerian democracy will require the decentralized decision-making of a genuine federation, with vetoes in the hands of all sizeable minorities and the continuation of a public policy of geographic allocation of public funds. The constitution should provide for immediate participation from all regions of the country, because "zoning," with its promise of future control for those who wait their turn, will not be a credible promise to those who are last in line for a turn. Zoning has its own dilemma: If rotation participants are few (say, North and South), many minorities will feel forever left out by the prescription. If many groups are included in the rotation, the wait between terms for any group will seem interminable. However, the automatic rotation of a zoning arrangement might be one of the first guarantees of long-term limitation on power that Nigerian elites would accept, and might be even more acceptable if there were genuine power sharing from the beginning between the top executive position (president) and the other positions (vice-president, prime minister, speaker of the house, etc.). Nigerians will be skeptical, of course, about whether a president might really agree to a genuine sharing of executive power.

Nigerians have done well at writing constitutions for their set of circumstances, but they have not succeeded in convincing the military that their optimal choice is to accept civilian rule. Access to oil revenues increases the payoff from political control, and leads to what Weingast calls an asymmetric equilibrium, based on the formation of a pact between the rulers and one group (or several) to exploit another (or others), with groups easily identified by ethnicity and religion.

The good news for Nigeria in the Weingast model is that democracy does not depend on the prior achievement of democratic values in the population. It requires that, perhaps as the result of a crisis in which all have suffered, groups and their leaders accept a pact, a feature of which is that short-term gains that might result from a single betrayal of democratic limitations will be outweighed by the long-term destruction the betrayal engenders. When junior military officers and ethnic "mafias" are put in such a position, a fundamental prerequisite for Nigerian democracy will have been established.

THE RELATIONSHIP BETWEEN DEMOCRACY AND THE MARKET

One of the first questions we posed in this study was whether there is a relationship between liberal democracy and a free market. In the present context, economic liberalization has usually been accompanied by an increased income differential between rich and poor, with economic stress for much of the middle class. This would not seem to be auspicious for democracy. Achieving a democratic equilibrium can be rendered as difficult by class and wealth distinctions as by ethnic and religious divisions. Forrest postulates that the demand for civilian, democratic rule is not related in Nigeria to support for a more market-based economic system. The former is supported by "politicians and some businesspeople who see military rule as narrowing the channels of access to state power and wealth," by "professional and intellectuals who uphold the universal ideal of bourgeois democracy," and by trade unions. Economic liberalization, he suggests, is supported only by international financial institutions, who have persuaded military regimes to move toward a market-based economy out of the necessities imposed by debt and trade problems.[9] However, international financial institutions have pushed democracy and economic reform as a joint package.

A stable polity in Nigeria will require intervention in the market to protect disadvantaged regions and to give the lower classes some evidence that they will benefit under conditions of economic liberalization. Nigeria with its oil wealth is better positioned than most Third World countries to provide such a cushion, but needs political leaders with the will and incentives to serve the wider public in the longer term, and with the credibility to restore citizens' faith in the fairness of the revenue system and the allocation of costs and benefits. Could an elected government impose austerity measures, as painful as they are for many constituents in the short term, in order to achieve long-term development? Some might argue that Nigeria needs the strength of an authoritarian leader (with clean hands) if it is to get its economic house in order. A model is found in the tough, disciplined rule of Jerry Rawlings in nearby Ghana (which seems to be evolving toward a more democratic polity). Babangida seemed at times to be following the Rawlings model, but ultimately set Nigeria back again, not only by annulling the presidential election he had so carefully nurtured, but perhaps even more importantly by his abolition of state and local civilian rule already in place. His government had increased the share of national revenues designated for local governments from 10 to 20 percent, and had directed it to the LGAs directly from the center (i.e., without going through the states). Functioning local governments were in place, and even if rather cumbersome in the complex separation of powers among their institutions, they had the advantage of being accessible. Nigerian citizens had begun to compare their locality with those adjoining them, and to demand better services. Again, a federal distribution of power among hundreds of local governments may be the most attainable approach to limiting the power and its payoffs that are so tempting to authoritarian military leaders. The federal government would still control the oil wealth, but local governments could develop other sources of revenue and exercise new if limited autonomy, and the federal government could vigorously prosecute local corruption and support the development of professional administration at the local and state level. Huntington's admonition to consolidate institutions before participation is widened could have been heeded. It remains to be seen whether local elections held under the Abacha regime in 1996 and, with political parties, in 1997 have restored any of the limited capacity local governments had begun to acquire before the Babangida intervention.

The Difficulties of Ending Autocratic Rule in a Petroleum Economy

Although we have introduced many factors into our explanation, oil revenues remain at the base. As the sense of public duty among some of the military elite declined from Gowon and Murtala to Babangida and Abacha, a subculture developed among officer ranks that can be identified as "When do I get my turn?" Such corruption of values is common in the world, but the availability of oil revenues means that authoritarian leaders need not seek their rents directly from the populace. Rather, they have learned that all they must do is control the spigot and the narrow slice of the population that operate and protect it, and opponents will be helpless. The oil workers' unions and the people of the Ogoni homeland where the drilling is done must be neutralized; the rest can be safely ignored. Oil wealth is even more secure if a larger proportion of the petroleum is extracted off-shore.

The alliance between the military and the "Kaduna Mafia" strengthened the military hand and the dominant political position of the North, and, even though Abacha ultimately ruled almost entirely through control of the military, as long as the petroleum was marketed and human rights violations did not become too severe or too publicized, there was little likelihood of substantial intervention from the international community.

Mancur Olson observed that "resolute autocrats can survive even when they impose heinous amounts of suffering upon their peoples. When they are replaced, it is for other reasons (e.g., succession crises) and often by another stationary bandit." He then built on the literature postulating that democracy appears under "historical conditions and dispersions of resources that make it impossible for any one leader or group to assume all power,"[10] or, in Weingast's terms, when elites must pay too high a price for violating democratic limitations. The conditions necessary for democracy are not close at hand for Nigeria in the short term, that is, as long as the economy depends overwhelmingly on oil, and the state's resources are increasingly controlled by the regime.

Likely Short-Term Scenarios

Peter Lewis has drawn on patterns in other African countries to show what might happen in the shorter run—i.e., before the achievement of a stable democratic equilibrium of any sort. He described Abacha's personalistic rule as moving Nigeria along one of three roads:[11]

The Road to Kinshasa - This refers to the Kinshasa of the now deposed Mobutu Sese Seko, in which there was (before Laurent Kabila) "no large-scale eruption of civic violence or significant political instability. Rather, a stable predatory regime would preside as the country experienced domestic decay and international isolation." This would appear to be the road Nigeria has traveled thus far.

The Road to Monrovia - The most frightening possible outcome of Nigeria's internal political struggles, in which the Nigerian state would crumble under ethnic and factional conflict. This is an outcome for which there is precedent on the continent (and in other areas of the world such as Serbia), especially in countries with deep-seated ethnic, regional and religious divisions. The regime's heavy oppression in the Niger delta and frustration with perceived northern domination in the Southwest are causing resentment and anger among the youth in those areas that is overwhelming any sense of identity with the Nigerian state and could lead to a breakdown of public order in those areas. The threat thus posed to petroleum production would result in a violent regime response, with a tragic outcome much larger in scale than that experienced by tiny Liberia.

The Road to Accra - This might be the road followed if Abubakar chooses to be more faithful than his predecessors Babangida and Abacha to the model of Ghana's Rawlings, not only in identifying a popular leader who can win an orchestrated electoral victory, but also in pushing for important economic and political reforms. This is a road that many Nigerians would see as the country's best short-run hope if Abacha were followed by a more idealistic military officer. Even though many people underestimated his resilience and survival instincts, few people credited Abacha with Rawlings's vision and strength of character. With the near-total breakdown of national political institutions and the availability of petrodollars, Nigerians' most common short-run hope is that good and conscientious military leaders will take control, and will put the country on a new road. In the longer run, Nigerians must nurture the leaders' incentives to restrain themselves, so that their incentives become congruent with the exercise of conscientious leadership.

END NOTES

1. Soyinka, The Open Sore of a Continent, p. 153.

2. Tanure Ojaide, The Blood of Peace and Other Poems (London: Heinemann, 1991), p. 9.

3. Weingast, "The Political Foundations of Democracy and the Rule of Law," p. 258.

4. Young, The African Colonial State in Comparative Perspective.

5. Young, The African Colonial State in Comparative Perspective, p. 273.

6. Subrata K. Mitra, "Politics in India," in Almond and Powell, Comparative Politics Today, p. 670.

7. Weingast, "The Political Foundations of Democracy and the Rule of Law," p. 246.

8. Weingast, "The Political Foundations of Democracy and the Rule of Law," p. 257.

9. Forrest, Politics and Economic Development in Nigeria, pp. 125-26.

10. Mancur Olson, "Dictatorship, Democracy, and Development," American Political Science Review 87 (3, September), p. 573.

11. Peter Lewis, "The Politics of Nigeria's Economic Decline," 1996.

References

Abernethy, David B. *The Political Dilemma of Popular Education: An African Case.* Stanford, California: Stanford University Press, 1969.

Aborisade, Oladimeji. "An Appraisal of Local Government in Nigeria from 1976 to 1986," in O. Aborisade, ed. *Readings in Nigerian Local Government.* Ife: Obafemi Awolowo University Press, 1988.

Aboyade, Ojetunji. "The Economy of Nigeria," in P. Robson and D. A. Lury, eds. *The Economies of Africa.* London: Allen and Unwin, 1969, pp. 127-193.

Abdullah, Hussaina. 'Transition Politics' and the Challenge of Gender in Nigeria. *Review of African Political Economy* 56, 1993, pp. 27-41.

Achebe, Chinua. *Arrow of God.* New York: Doubleday-Anchor, 1969.

_____. *A Man of the People.* New York: Doubleday-Anchor, 1967.

_____. *The Trouble with Nigeria.* Enugu: Fourth Dimension Press, 1983.

Adamolekun, Ladipo. Introduction: Federalism in Nigeria. *Publius* 21 (Fall, no. 4), 1991, pp. 1-11.

Adams, Paul. Reign of the Generals. *Africa Report* (Nov.-Dec.), 1994, pp. 26-29.

Adediran, Olu. 1989. "Security of Life and Property and Law Enforcement Agents at the Local Level in Nigeria," in O. Aborisade, ed. *Nigerian Local Government Reformed.* Ife: Local Government Publication Series, Obafemi Awolowo University, 1989, pp. 301-313.

Adegboye, M. B. "The Impact of the Land Use Act on Traditional Rulers in Local Administration in Nigeria," in O. Aborisade, ed. *Local Government and the Traditional Rulers in Nigeria.* Ife: Nigeria, University of Ife Press, 1985, pp. 207-220.

Adejuyigbe, Omolade and Leo O. Dare, eds. *Land Tenure Reform in Nigeria: Implications and Implementation of the Land-Use Decree 1978.* Ile Ife: University of Ife Press, 1978.

Ademoyega, A. *Why We Struck: The Story of the First Nigerian Coup.* Ibadan: Exams Publishers. 1981.

Agbese, Pita Ogaba. "The State versus Human Rights Advocates in Africa: The Case of Nigeria," in Eileen McCarthy-Arnolds, David R. Penna, and Debra Joy Cruz Sobrepeña, eds. *Africa, Human Rights and the Global System: The Political Economy of Human Rights in a Changing World.* Westport, CT: Greenwood Press, 1994, pp. 147-172.

Ahmad Khan, Sarah. *Nigeria: The Political Economy of Oil.* Oxford: Oxford Univerity Press, 1994.

Ajao, Lasun. "Environmental Sanitation: The Concern of the Local Government," in O. Aborisade, ed. *Nigerian Local Government Reformed.* Ife: Local Government Publication Series, Obafemi Awolowo University, 1989, pp. 272-280.

Akande, Jadesola. The Legal Order and the Administration of Federal and State Courts. *Publius* (4, Fall), 1991, pp. 61-73.

Ake, Claude. "Indigenization: Problems of Transformation in a Neo-colonial Economy," in Claude Ake, ed. *Political Economy of Nigeria.* New York: Longman, 1985, pp. 173-200.

_____. Rethinking African Democracy. *Journal of Democracy* 2 (1, Winter), 1991.

Akinnaso, F. Niyi. "The National Language Question and Minority Language Rights in Africa: A Nigerian Case Study," in Ronald Cohen, Goran Hyden and Winston P. Nagan, eds. *Human Rights and Governance in Africa.* Gainesville: University Press of Florida, 1993, pp. 191-214.

Akinola, Anthony A. The Concept of a Rotational Presidency in Nigeria. *The Round Table* 337, 1996, pp. 13-24.

_____. Nigeria: The Quest for a Stable Polity - Another Comment. *African Affairs* 87, 1988, pp. 441-447.

Almond, Gabriel A. and G. Bingham Powell. *Comparative Politics: A Theoretical Framework.* New York: HarperCollins, 1996.

_____. *Comparative Politics Today: A World View.* New York: HarperCollins, 1996.

Almond, Gabriel A. and Sidney Verba. *The Civic Culture*. Princeton: Princeton University Press, 1963.

Amnesty International. Nigeria: Resumption of Public Executions. *Amnesty International Press Release*. London: Amnesty International, AI Index: AFR 44/12/94, October 12, 1994.

Andreski, Stanislav "Kleptocracy as a System of Government in Africa," in Arnold J. Heidenheimer, ed. *Political Corruption: Readings in Comparative Analysis.* New York: Holt, Rinehart and Winston, 1970, pp. 346-357.

Arnold, Guy. *Modern Nigeria.* London: Longman, 1977.

Awa, Eme O. *Federal Government in Nigeria.* Berkeley: University of California Press, 1964.

Awe, Bolanle. Women's Political Activism in Nigeria; A Stepping Stone to Government Participation. *The Urban Age* 2 (2, Winter), 1994, p. 17.

Awolowo, Obafemi. *The People's Republic.* London: Oxford University Press, 1968.

Ayeni, Victor. "Traditional Rulers as Ombudsmen: In Search of a Role for Natural Rulers in Contemporary Nigeria," in O. Aborisade, ed. *Local Government and the Traditional Rulers in Nigeria.* Ife: University of Ife Press, 1985, pp. 305-319.

Ayoade, John A. A. "The Development of Democratic Local Government in Nigeria," in O. Aborisade and R. Mundt, eds. *Local Government in Nigeria and the United States: Learning from Comparison.* Ife: Local Government Publication Series, Obafemi Awobwo University, 1995, pp. 19-28.

Barber, Karin. Popular Reactions to the Petro-Naira. *Journal of Modern African Studies* 20 (3), 1982, pp. 431-450.

Barnes, Sandra T. *Patrons and Power: Creating a Political Community in Metropolitan Lagos.* Bloomington: Indiana University Press, 1986.

_____. *Markets and States in Tropical Africa.* Berkeley: University of California Press, 1981.

Bates, Robert H. *Essays on the Political Economy of Rural Africa.* Cambridge: Cambridge University Press, 1983.

Bayart, Jean-François. *The State in Africa.* London: Longman, 1993.

Beckett, Paul, "Elections and Democracy in Nigeria," in Fred M. Hayward, ed. *Elections in Independent Africa.* Boulder: Westview Press, 1987, pp. 87-119.

_____ and James O'Connell. *Education and Power in Nigeria: A Study of University Students.* London: Hodder and Stoughton, 1977.

Beckman, Bjorn. "Public Investment and Agrarian Transformation in Northern Nigeria," in Michael Watts, ed. *State, Oil, and Agriculture in Nigeria.* Berkeley: Institute of International Studies, University of California at Berkeley, 1987, pp. 110-137.

Bello-Imam, I. B. "The Paralysis of Traditional Rulers in Nigerian Politics," in O. Aborisade, ed. *Local Government and the Traditional Rulers in Nigeria,* 1985, pp. 181-194.

Bennett, A. Leroy. *International Organizations: Principles and Issues,* 2nd ed. Englewood Cliffs, NJ: Prentice-Hall, 1995.

Berry, Sara C. *Custom and Socio-economic Change in Rural Western Nigeria.* Oxford: Clarendon Press, 1975.

_____. *No Condition is Permanent.* Madison: University of Wisconsin Press, 1993.

_____. "Oil and the Disappearing Peasantry: Accumulation, Differentiation, and Underdevelopment in Western Nigeria," in Michael Watts, ed. *State, Oil, and Agriculture in Nigeria.* Berkeley: Institute of International Studies, University of California at Berkeley, 1987, pp. 202-222.

Bienen, Henry with Martin Fitton, "Soldiers, Politicians and Civil Servants," in Keith Panter-Brick, ed. *Soldiers and Oil: The Political Transformation of Nigeria.* Totowa, NJ: Frank Cass, 1978, pp. 27-57.

Bohannon, Paul. "The Tiv of Nigeria" in James L. Gibbs, Jr., ed. *Peoples of Africa.* New York: Holt, Rinehart and Winston, 1965.

BP Statistical Review of World Energy. London: The British Petroleum Company, 1994.

Bratton, Michael. "Civil Societies and Political Transitions in Africa," in John W. Harbeson, Donald Rothchild, and Naomi Chazan, eds. *Civil Society and the State in Africa.* Boulder: Lynne Rienner, 1994.

_____ and Nicolas van de Walle. 1997. *Democratic Experiments in Africa: Regime Transitions in Comparative Perspective.* New York: Cambridge University Press.

Callaghy, Thomas M. "Lost Between State and Market: The Politics of Economic Adjustment in Ghana, Zambia, and Nigeria," in Joan M. Nelson, ed. *Economic Crisis and Policy Choice: The Politics of Adjustment in the Third World.* Princeton, NJ: Princeton University Press, 1990. pp. 257-319.

Callaway, Barbara. "The Political Economy of Nigeria," in Richard Harris, ed. *The Political Economy of Africa.* Cambridge, MA: Schenkman Publishing, 1975.

_____. *Muslim Hausa Women in Nigeria.* Syracuse: Syracuse University Press, 1987.

Castañeda, Jorge G. "Democracy and Inequality in Latin America: A Tension of the Times, in Jorge I. Domínguez and Abraham F. Lowenthal, eds. *Constructing Democratic Governance: Latin America and the Caribbean in the 1990s.* Baltimore: Johns Hopkins University Press, 1996, pp. 42-63.

Chazan, Naomi and Victor T. LeVine. "Africa and the Middle East: Patterns of Convergence and Divergence," in John W. Harbeson and Donald Rothchild, eds. *Africa in World Politics.* Boulder, CO: Westview Press, 1991.

Chazan, Naomi, Robert Mortimer, John Ravenhill, and Donald Rothchild. *Politics and Society in Contemporary Africa.* Boulder, CO: Lynne Rienner, 1992.

Claeson, Matthew and Elaine El Assal, eds. *Global Information Sources: Where Audiences Around the World Turn for News and Information.* Washington: Office of Research and Media Reaction, U.S. Information Agency, 1996.

Cockcroft, James D. *Neighbors in Turmoil: Latin America.* New York: Harper and Row, 1989, pp. 358-370.

Cohen, Abner. *Custom and Politics in Urban Africa: A Study of Hausa Migrants in Yoruba Towns.* Berkeley: University of California Press, 1969.

Cohen, Ronald. *The Kanuri of Bornu*. New York: Holt, Rinehart and Winston, 1967.

Cohen, Ronald and Abe Goldman. "The Society and Its Environment," in Helen Chapin Metz, ed. *Nigeria: A Country Study* . Washington: U.S. Government Printing Office, 1992, pp. 85-153.

Coleman, James S. *Nigeria: Background to Nationalism*. Berkeley: University of California Press, 1958.

The Constitution of the Federal Republic of Nigeria. Lagos: Federal Ministry of Information, 1979.

Crawford, Gordon. Whither Lomé? the Mid-Term Review and the Decline of Partnership. *Journal of Modern African Studies* 34 (3, 1996), pp. 503-518.

Crowder, Michael. *The Story of Nigeria* (4th ed.). London: Faber and Faber, 1978.

Dahl, Robert A. *After the Revolution*. New Haven: Yale University Press, 1971.

Dalton, Russell J. *Citizen Politics* (Second Edition). Chatham, NJ: Chatham House, 1996.

_____. "Politics in Germany," in Gabriel A. Almond and G. Bingham Powell Jr., eds. *Comparative Politics Today: A World View*. New York: HarperCollins, 1996, pp. 264-325.

Dare, L. O. "Administration of the Decree," in Omolade Adjuyigbe and Leo O. Dare, eds., *Land Tenure Reform in Nigeria: Implications and Implementation of the Land-Use Decree 1978*. Ife: University of Ife Press, 1978.

Dennis, C. "Women and the State in Nigeria: the Case of the Federal Military Government, 1984-5, in H. Afshar, ed. *Women, State and Ideology*. London: Macmillan, 1987.

Diamond, Larry. *Class, Ethnicity, and Democracy in Nigeria: The Failure of the First Republic*. Syracuse: Syracuse University Press, 1988.

_____. "Nigeria: Pluralism, Statism and the Struggle for Democracy," in Diamond *et al.*, eds., *Democracy: Africa*. Boulder: Lynne Rienner, 1988, pp. 33-91.

_____. "Economic Development and Democracy Reconsidered," in Gary Marks and Larry Diamond, eds. *Reexamining Democracy.* Newbury Park: Sage, 1992, pp. 93-139.

_____, Anthony Kirk-Greene, and Oyeleye Oyediran, eds. *Transition Without End: Nigerian Politics and Civil Society Under Babangida.* Boulder: Lynne Rienner, 1997.

Dudley, Billy. *An Introduction to Nigerian Government and Politics.* Bloomington: Indiana University Press, 1982.

Easton, David. *A Systems Analysis of Political Life.* New York: John Wiley and Sons, 1965.

Egg, Johny. "La nouvelle insertion de l'agriculture nigériane dans le marché mondial," in Daniel C. Bach, Johny Egg and Jean Philippe, eds. *Le Nigeria: Un Pouvoir en Puissance.* Paris: Karthala, 1988, pp. 169-92.

Eker, Varda. On the Origins of Corruption: Irregular Incentives in Nigeria. *Journal of Modern African Studies* 19 (1), 1981. pp. 173-182.

Ekpu, A. O. O. Making the Land Use Act Work. *Edo State University Law Journal 2* (1), 1993.

Elaigwu, J. Esawa. Ballot Box or Barracks for Nigeria? *Peace Review* (Winter), pp. 28-31, 1991-92.

Emecheta, Buchi. *Destination Biafra.* New York: Allison and Busby, 1982.

Emezi, C. E. "The 1976 National Local Government Reform and the Three Phases After," in O. Aborisade, ed. *Nigerian Local Government Reformed.* Ife: Obafemi Awolowo University, Local Government Publication Series, Obafemi Awolowo University, 1989, pp. 73-83.

Enahoro, Peter. *How to be a Nigerian.* Ibadan: Caxton Press, 1966.

_____. *The Complete Nigerian.* Lagos: Malthouse Press, 1992.

Fallers, Lloyd. The Predicament of the Modern African Chief: An Instance from Uganda. *American Anthropologist* 57, 1955, pp. 290-305.

Forrest, Tom. *The Advance of African Capital: The Growth of Nigerian Private Enterprise*. Charlottesville: University Press of Virginia, 1994.

_____. *Politics and Economic Development in Nigeria*. Boulder, Westview, Updated edition, 1995.

Francis, Paul, with J. A. Akinwumi, P. Ngwu, S. A. Nkom, J. Odihi, J. A. Olomajeye, F. Okunmadewa and D. J. Shehu. *State, Community and Local Development in Nigeria* (World Bank Technical Paper No. 336, Africa Region Series). Washington, D.C.: World Bank, 1996.

Gboyega, Alex. "Nigeria: Conflict Unresolved," in I. William Zartman, ed. *Governance as Conflict Management: Politics and Violence in West Africa* (Washington, DC: Brookings Institution), 1997, pp. 149-196.

_____. Protecting Local Governments from Arbitrary State and Federal Interference: What Prospects for the 1990s? *Publius: The Journal of Federalism* 21 (4, Fall), 1991, pp. 45-59.

Geertz, Clifford. *Old Societies and New States: The Quest for Modernity in Asia and Africa*. New York: Free Press of Glencoe, 1963.

Gordon, David F. "Debt, Conditionality, and Reform: The International Relations of Economic Restructuring in Sub-Saharan Africa," in Thomas M. Callaghy and John Ravenhill, eds. *Hemmed In: Responses to Africa's Economic Decline*. New York: Columbia University Press, 1993, pp. 90-129.

Graf, William D. *The Nigerian State: Political* Economy, *State, Class and Political System in the Post-Colonial Era*. Portsmouth, NH: Heinemann Educational Books, 1988.

Grimes, Barbara F., ed. *Ethnologue: Languages of the World*, 11th edition. Dallas, TX: Summer Institute of Linguistics, 1988.

Guyer, Jane I. Representation without Taxation: An Essay on Democracy in Rural Nigeria, 1952-1990. *African Studies Review* 35 (1, April), 1992, pp. 41-79.

_____. "The Spatial Dimensions of Civil Society in Africa: An Anthropologist Looks at Nigeria," in John W. Harbeson, Donald Rothchild and Naomi Chazan, eds. *Civil Society and the State in Africa*. Boulder: Lynne Rienner, 1994, pp. 215-229.

Hodgkin, Thomas. *Nationalism in Colonial Africa.* New York: New York University Press, 1957.

Horowitz, Donald L. "Comparing Democratic Systems," in Larry Diamond and Marc F. Plattner, eds. *The Global Resurgence of Democracy,* 2nd edition (Baltimore: The Johns Hopkins University Press), pp. 143-149.

_____. *Ethnic Groups in Conflict.* Berkeley: University of California Press, 1985.

Huberts, L .W. J. C. "Expert Views on Public Corruption Around the Globe." Amsterdam: PSPA Publications, Department of Political Science and Public Administration, Vrije Universiteit Amsterdam, 1996.

Human Rights Watch. 'Permanent Transition': Current Violations of Human Rights in Nigeria. *Human Rights Watch Publications* 8 (No. 3, A, September), 1996, http://www.hrw.org/hrw/summaries/s.nigeria969. html.

Huntington, Samuel P. 1996. *The Clash of Civilizations and the Remaking of World Order.* New York: Simon and Schuster.

_____. *Political Order in Changing Societies.* New Haven: Yale University Press, 1968.

_____. *The Third Wave: Democratization in the Late Twentieth Century.* Norman, OK: University of Oklahoma Press, 1991.

Husain, Mir Zohair. *Global Islamic Politics.* New York: HarperCollins, 1995.

Ibrahim, Omar Farouk, "Religion and Politics: A View from the North," in Larry Diamond, Anthony Kirk-Greene, and Oyeleye Oyediran, eds. *Transition without End: Nigerian Politics and Civil Society under Babangida.* Boulder, CO: Lynne Rienner, 1997, pp. 427-447.

Ihonvbere, Julius O. Elections and Conflicts in Nigeria's Nontransition to Democracy. *Africa Demos* 3 (No. 5, May), 1996, pp. 8-9, 11.

Ikein, Augustine A. *The Impact of Oil on a Developing Country: The Case of Nigeria.* New York: Praeger, 1990.

Inglehart, Ronald. *Modernization and Postmodernization: Cultural, Economic, and Political Change in 43 Countries.* Princeton: Princeton University Press, 1997.

Dennis A. Ityavyar, "The Colonial Origins of Health Care Services: The Nigerian Example," in Toyin Falola and D. Ityavyar, eds. *The Political Economy of Health in Africa.* Athens, OH: Ohio University Center for International Studies, 1992.

Iwayemi, Akin. "Le Nigéria dans le système pétrolier international," in Daniel C. Bach, Johny Egg and Jean Philippe, eds. *Le Nigeria: Un Pouvoir en Puissance.* Paris: Karthala, 1988, pp. 19-38.

Jackson, Robert H. And Carl G. Rosberg. *Personal Rule in Black Africa: Prince, Autocrat, Prophet, Tyrant.* Berkeley: University of California Press, 1982.

Janowitz, Morris. *The Military in the Political Development of New Nations.* Chicago: University of Chicago Press, 1964.

Jennings, W. Ivor. *The Approach to Self-Government.* Cambridge: Cambridge University Press, 1956.

Joseph, Richard A. *Democracy and Prebendal Politics in Nigeria: The Rise and Fall of the Second Republic.* Cambridge: Cambridge University Press, 1987.

Kane, Ousmane. The Rise of Muslim Reformism in Northern Nigeria: IZALA, in Martin Marty and Scott Appleby, ed. *Accounting for Fundamentalisms.* Chicago: University of Chicago Press, 1994.

Karatnycky, Adrian. *The Comparative Survey of Freedom 1995-1996.* Http://www.freedomhouse. org//Political/summary.htm, 1997.

Keyfitz, Nathan and Flieger. *World Population Growth and Aging: Demographic Trends in the Late Twentieth Century.* Chicago: University of Chicago Press, 1990.

Kirk-Greene, Anthony H. M. *Crisis and Conflict in Nigeria: A Documentary Sourcebook 1966-1969.* London: Oxford University Press, 2 vols, 1971.

Klitgaard, Robert. *Controlling Corruption.* Bloomington: Indiana University Press, 1988.

Koehn, Peter H. *Public Policy and Administration in Africa: Lessons from Nigeria.* Boulder: Westview Press, 1990.

Lancaster, Carol. "The Lagos Three: Economic Regionalism in Sub-Saharan Africa," in John W. Harbeson and Donald Rothschild, eds. *Africa in World Politics.* Boulder: Westview, 1991, pp. 249-267.

Last, Murray. "Tradition musulmane et diplomatie," in Daniel C. Bach, Johny Egg and Jean Philippe, eds. *Le Nigéria: Un Pouvoir en Puissance.* Paris: Karthala, 1988, pp. 257-73.

Leach, Richard H. *Studies in Comparative Federalism: Australia, Canada, the United States and West Germany.* Washington: Advisory Commission on Intergovernmental Relations, 1981.

Lewis, Peter. From Prebendalism to Predation: the Political Economy of Decline in Nigeria. *Journal of Modern African Studies* 34 (1), 1996, pp. 79-103.

_____. The Politics of Economics. *Africa Report* 39 (3, May-June), 1994, pp. 47-49.

_____. "The Politics of Nigeria's Economic Decline." Paper presented at the Annual Meeting of the African Studies Association, San Francisco, CA, November 24, 1996.

Lijphart, Arend. "Constitutional Choices for New Democracies," in Larry Diamond and Marc F. Plattner, eds. *The Global Resurgence of Democracy,* 2nd edition, Baltimore: Johns Hopkins University Press, 1996, pp. 162-174.

Linz, Juan J., "The Perils of Presidentialism," in Larry Diamond and Marc F. Plattner, eds. *The Global Resurgence of Democracy,* 2nd edition, Baltimore: Johns Hopkins University Press, 1996, pp. 124-142.

_____ and Alfred Stepan. *Problems of Democratic Transition and Consolidation: Southern Europe, South America, and Post-Communist Europe.* Baltimore: Johns Hopkins University Press, 1996.

Lipset, Seymour Martin. *Political Man.* Garden City, NY: Doubleday, 1960.

_____. The Social Requisites of Democracy Revisited. *American Sociological Review* 59 (February), pp. 93-139, 1994.

Lloyd, P. C. "The Yoruba of Nigeria," in James L. Gibbs Jr., ed. *Peoples of Africa.* New York: Holt, Rinehart and Winston, 1965, pp 547-582.

_____. *Africa in Social Change.* London: Penguin, 1972.

Lubeck, Paul M. "Islamic Protest and Oil-Based Capitalism: Agriculture, Rural Linkages, and Urban Popular Movements in Northern Nigeria," in Michael Watts, ed. *State, Oil, and Agriculture in Nigeria*. Berkeley: Institute of International Studies, University of California at Berkeley, 1987, pp. 268-290.

Luckham, Robin. *The Nigerian Military: A Sociological Analysis of Authority and Revolt 1960-67*. Cambridge: Cambridge University Press, 1971.

Mackintosh, J.P. *Nigerian Government and Politics*. London: George Allen and Unwin, 1966.

McMullan, M. "Corruption in the Public Services of British Colonies and Ex-Colonies in West Africa," in A. J. Heidenheimer, ed. *Political Corruption: Readings in Comparative Analysis*. New York: Holt, Rinehart and Winston, 1970, pp. 317-330.

Mead, Timothy D. Barriers to Local Government Autonomy in a Federal System: The Case of Nigeria. *Southeastern Political Review* 24 (1, March), 1996, pp. 159-176.

_____. Barriers to Local-Government Capacity in Nigeria. *American Review of Public Administration* 26 (2, June), 1996, pp. 159-172.

Metz, Helen Chapin. *Nigeria: A Country Study*. Washington: Federal Research Division, Library of Congress, 1992.

Miachi, Tom A. "The Role of the Atta of Igala in Nigerian Politics: Analysis of a Political Development in Historical Perspective," in Oladimeji Aborisade, ed. *Local Government and the Traditional Rules in Nigeria*. Ife: University of Ife Press, 1985, pp. 77-92.

Miles, William F. S. *Elections in Nigeria: A Grassroots Perspective*. Boulder, CO: Lynne Rienner, 1988.

_____. *Hausaland Divided: Colonialism and independence in Nigeria and Niger*. Ithaca: Cornell University Press, 1994.

_____. Traditional Rulers and Development Administration: Chieftaincy in Niger, Nigeria, and Vanuatu. *Studies in Comparative International Development* 28 (Fall, 1993), no. 3, 1993, pp. 38-43.

Mitra, Subrata K. "Politics in India," in Gabriel A. Almond and G. Bingham Powell, *Comparative Politics Today*, 6th Edition. New York: HarperCollins, 1996, pp. 669-729.

Mohammed, Nadir A. L. *Military Expenditures in Africa: A Statistical Compendium*. Abidjan, Côte D'Ivoire: African Development Bank (Economic Research Paper No. 21), 1966.

Morah, Erasmus U. Why Nigeria Obtained the New Capital That it Did: An Analysis of Officials' Disposition in Housing Development. *International Review of Administrative Sciences* 59, 1993, pp. 251-275.

Mortimore, Michael. *Adapting to Drought: Farmers, Famines and Desertification in West Africa*. Cambridge: Cambridge University Press, 1989.

Nafziger, E. Wayne. *The Economics of Political Instability: The Nigeria-Biafran War*. Boulder, CO: Westview Press, 1983.

_____. "The Economy," in Helen Chapin Metz, ed. *Nigeria: A Country Study*. Washington, U.S.: Government Printing Office, 1992, pp. 155-202.

Newsum, H. E. and Olayiwola Abegunrin. 1987 *United States Foreign Policy Towards Southern Africa: Andrew Young and Beyond*. New York: St. Martin's Press, 1987.

Nigeria, Federal Republic of. *Report of the Constitutional Conference Containing the Resolutions and Recommendations* (Volume II) (Lagos: The Federal Government Press, 1995).

Nigeria, Federal Ministry of Education. *Statistics of Education in Nigeria 1985-1989*. Lagos: Statistics Branch, Federal Ministry of Education, 1990.

Nmoma, Veronica. "Ethnic Conflict, Constitutional Engineering and Democracy in Nigeria," in Harvey Glickman, ed. *Ethnic Conflict and Democratization in Africa*. Atlanta: African Studies Association Press, 1995, pp. 311-350.

Nnoli, Okwudiba. *Ethnic Politics in Nigeria*. Enugu: Fourth Dimension Publishers, 1980.

Nordlinger, Eric A. *Soldiers in Politics: Military Coups and Governments*. Englewood Cliffs, NJ: Prentice Hall, 1977.

Normandy, Elizabeth. "Nigeria," in Mark W. Delancey, ed. *Handbook of Political Science Research on Sub-Saharan Africa.* Westport, CT: Greenwood, 1992.

Odunfa, Sola. Farewell (Until the Next Time). *BBB Focus on Africa* 4 (Oct.-Dec., 4), 1993, pp. 26-29.

Ohiorhenuan, John F. E. *Capital and the State in Nigeria.* New York: Greenwood Press, 1989.

Ojaide, Tanure. *The Blood of Peace and Other Poems.* London: Heinemann, 1991.

Okeke, Okechukwu. *Hausa-Fulani Hegemony: The Dominance of the Muslim North in Contemporary Nigerian Politics.* Enugu: Acena Publishers, 1992.

Okonjo, Kamene. "The Dual-Sex Political System in Operation: Igbo Women and Community Politics in Midwestern Nigeria", in Nancy J. Hafkin and Edna G. Bay, eds. *Women in Africa: Studies in Social and Economic Change."* Stanford: Stanford University Press, 1976, pp. 44-58.

Olagunju, Tunji, Adele Jinadu, and Sam Oyovbaire. 1993. *Transition to Democracy in Nigeria (1985-1993).* Ibadan: Safari Books.

Olayiwola, Peter O. *Petroleum and Structural Change in a Developing Country: The Case of Nigeria.* New York: Praeger, 1987.

Olowu, Dele. "Centralization, Self-Governance, and Development in Nigeria," in James S. Wunsch and Dele Olowu, eds. *The Failure of the Centralized State.* Boulder, CO: Westview, 1990, pp. 193-227.

_____. *Lagos State: Governance, Society and Economy.* Lagos: Malthouse Press, 1990.

Olson, Mancur. Dictatorship, Democracy, and Development. *American Political Science Review* 87 (3, September), 1993, pp. 567-576.

Olubaniyi, D. "Primary Health Care at Local Government Level in Kwara State," in O. Aborisade, ed., *On Being in Charge at the Grassroots Level in Nigeria.* Department of Governmental Studies, Obafemi Awolowo University, Ife, 1989, pp. 191-205.

Omopariola, Olu. "Financing the Traditional Rulers," in O. Aborisade, ed. *Local Government and the Traditional Rulers in Nigeria.* Ife: Nigeria. University of Ife Press, 1985, pp. 195-203.

Omotoso, Kole. *Just Before Dawn.* Ibadan: Spectrum Books, 1988.

Osayimwese, Izevbuwa and Sunday Iyare. The Economics of Nigerian Federalism: Selected Issues in Economic Management. *Publius: The Journal of Federalism* 21 (Fall, 4), 1991, pp. 89-101.

Ostheimer, J. M. *Nigerian Politics.* New York: Harper and Row, 1973.

Othman, Shehu. "Les relations internationales globales du Nigéria," in Daniel C. Bach, Johny Egg and Jean Philippe, eds. *Le Nigéria: Un Pouvoir en Puissance.* Paris: Karthala, 1988, pp. 53-81.

Ottenberg, Phoebe. "The Afikpo Ibo of Eastern Nigeria," in James L. Gibbs Jr., ed. *Peoples of Africa.* New York: Holt, Rinehart and Winston, 1965, pp. 1-39.

Oyediran, Oyelele. *Survey of Nigerian Affairs, 1975.* Ibadan: Oxford University Press, 1978.

_____, ed. *Nigerian Government and Politics Under Military Rule 1968-79.* London: Macmillan, 1979.

_____. "Transition Without End: From Hope to Despair—Reflections of a Participant-Observer," in Paul A. Beckett and Crawford Young, eds. *Dilemmas of Democracy in Nigeria* (Rochester, NY: University of Rochester Press, 1997), pp. 175-192.

Oyelakin, O. O. *Handbook on Local Government Administration.* Abuja: Office of the Vice-President, 1992.

_____. 1992. "Implementation of the Executive Federal Presidential System of Government at the Local Government Level: Its Logic, Merits and Constraints," Paper presented at the National Workshop for Directors of Local Government at the State Level, Obafemi Awolowo University, Ife, July 21-23, quoted in Timothy D. Mead, "Barriers to Local Government Autonomy in a Federal System: The Case of Nigeria", *Southeastern Political Review* 24 (1, March, 1996), p. 168.

Oyewole, Anthony. *Historical Dictionary of Nigeria.* Metuchen, NJ: Scarecrow Press, 1987.

Paden, John N. "Nigerian Muslim Perspectives on Religion, Society, and Communication with the Western World." Washington, D.C.: Office of Research, U.S. Information Agency, 1990.

Panter-Brick, S. K. *Soldiers and Oil: The Military and the Political Transformation of Nigeria.* London: Frank Cass, 1978.

Pearce, Tola Olu. "Health Inequalities in Africa," in Toyin Falola and Dennis Ityavyar, eds., *The Political Economy of Health in Africa.* Athens, OH: Ohio University Center for International Studies, 1992, pp. 184-216.

Philippe, Jean. "L'enjeu industriel: nationalisme et indépendence économique, in Daniel C. Bach, John Egg and Jean Philippe eds. *Le Nigéria: Un Pouvoir en Puissance.* Paris: Karthala, 1988, pp. 149-167.

Phillips, Adedotun. Four Decades of Fiscal Federalism in Nigeria. *Publius: The Journal of Federalism* 21 (Fall, 4), 1991, pp. 103-111.

Pollock, David and Elaine El Assal, eds. *In the Eye of the Beholder: Muslim and Non-Muslim Views of Islam, Islamic Politics, and Each Other.* Washington, D.C.: Office of Research and Media Reactions, United States Information Service, 1995.

Price, J. H. *Political Institutions of West Africa* (Third Edition). London: Hutchinson, 1977.

Przeworski, Adam and Fernando Limongi. Modernization Theories and Facts. *World Politics* 49 (January), 1997, pp. 155-183.

Riordan, William L. *Plunkett of Tammany Hall.* New York: A. A. Knopf, 1948.

Robinson, Pearl T. Democratization: Understanding the Relationship between Regime Change and the Culture of Politics. *African Studies Review* 37 (1, April), 1994, pp. 39-67.

Roder, Wolfe. *Human Adjustment to Kainji Reservoir in Nigeria: An Assessment of the Economic and Environmental Consequences of a Man-made Lake in Africa.* Lanham, MD: University Press of America, 1994.

"The Roles of Traditional Rulers in Local Government in Borno State," In Oladimeji Aborisade, ed. *Local Government and the Traditional Rulers in Nigeria* . Ife: University of Ife Press, 1985, pp. 351-356.

Ross, Paul J. "Land as a Right to Membership: Land Tenure Dynamics in a Peripheral Area of the Kano Close-Settled Zone," in Michael Watts, ed. *State, Oil, and Agriculture in Nigeria.* Berkeley: Institute of International Studies, University of California at Berkeley, 1987, pp. 223-247.

Schatzl, L. H. *Petroleum in Nigeria.* Ibadan: Oxford University Press, 1969.

Schumacher, Edward J. *Politics, Bureaucracy and Rural Development in Senegal.* Berkeley: University of California Press, 1975.

Shenton, Robert. "Nigerian Agriculture in Historical Perspective: Development and Crisis 1900-1960," in Michael Watts, ed. *State, Oil, and Agriculture in Nigeria.* Berkeley: Institute of International Studies, University of California at Berkeley, 1987, pp. 34-57.

Shettima, Kole Ahmed. Engendering Nigeria's Third Republic. *African Studies Review* 38 (3, December), pp. 61-98.

Sivard, Ruth Leger. *Military and Social Expenditures 1993.* Washington, D.C.: World Priorities, 1994.

Sklar, Richard. *Nigerian Political Parties.* Princeton: Princeton University Press, 1963.

_____. *Nigerian Political Parties: Power in an Emergent African Nation.* New York: NOK Publishers, 1983.

_____ and C. S. Whitaker, Jr. "Nigeria," In James S. Coleman and Carl G. Rosberg, Jr., *Political Parties and National Integration in Tropical Africa.* Berkeley: University of California Press, 1964, pp. 597-654.

Smock, Audrey C. *Ibo Politics: The Role of Ethnic Unions in Eastern Nigeria.* Cambridge, MA: Harvard University Press, 1971.

Soyinka, Wole. *Ake: The Years of Childhood.* Ibadan: Spectrum Books, 1981.

_____ *The Open Sore of a Continent.* New York: Oxford University Press, 1996.

Suberu, Rotimi T. "Religion and Politics: A View from the South," in Larry Diamond, Anthony Kirk-Greene, and Oyeleye Oyediran, eds. *Transition without End: Nigerian Politics and Civil Society under Babangida.* Boulder, CO: Lynne Rienner, 1997, pp. 401-425.

Sunal, Cynthia S., Dennis W. Sunal, and Osayimense Ose. Nigerian Primary School Teachers' Perceptions of Schooling During the Second Decade of Universal Primary Education. *African Studies Review* 37 (3, December), 1994, pp. 51-75. Sussman, Leonard R. "Press Freedom: Media Controls," *Freedom House* (http://www.freedomhouse.org/Political/sussman.htm), 1996.

Theobald, Robin. *Corruption, Development and Underdevelopment.* Durham, NC: Duke University Press, 1990.

Thompson, William R. *The Grievances of Military Coup Makers.* Beverly Hills, CA: Sage Professional Papers in Comparative Politics, 1978.

Ugorji, Ebenezer. Privatization/Commercialization of State-Owned Enterprises in Nigeria: Strategies for Improving the Performance of the Economy. *Comparative Political Studies* 27 (4, January), 1995, pp. 537-560.

United Nations Development Program. *Human Development Report 1995.* New York: Oxford University Press, 1995.

United States. Justice Department. Bureau of Justice Statistics. *Sourcebook 1994.* Washington, D.C.: Department of Justice, 1995.

Van Allen, Judith. "'Aba Riots' or Igbo 'Women's War'? Ideology, Stratification, and the Invisibility of Women," in Nancy J. Hafkin and Edna G. Bay, eds. *Women in Africa: _Studies in Social and Economic Change".* Stanford: Stanford University Press, 1976, pp. 59-85.

Vaughan, Olufemi. Assessing Grassroots Politics and Community Development in Nigeria. *African Affairs* 94 (October), 1995, pp. 501-518.

Verba, Sidney. "The Parochial and the Polity," in Verba and Lucian W. Pye, eds. *The Citizen and Politics: A Comparative Perspective.* Stamford, CT: Greylock Publishers, 1978, pp. 3-28.

_____, Norman H. Nie and Jae-on Kim. *Participation and Political Equality.* Cambridge: Cambridge University Press, 1978.

Watts, Michael, ed. "Agriculture and Oil-Based Accumulation: Stagnation or Transformation?" in Watts, ed. *State, Oil, and Agriculture in Nigeria.* Berkeley: Institute of International Studies, University of California at Berkeley, 1987, pp. 58-84.

Watts, Michael, ed. *State, Oil, and Agriculture in Nigeria.* Berkeley: Institute of International Studies, University of California at Berkeley, 1987.

Weingast, Barry R. The Political Foundations of Democracy and the Rule of Law. *American Political Science Review* 91 (2, June), pp. 245-263, 1997.

Welch, Claude E., Jr. *No Farewell to Arms? Military Disengagement from Politics in Africa and Latin America.* Boulder, CO: Westview Press, 1987.

_____. *Protecting Human Rights in Africa: Roles and Strategies of Non-Governmental Organizations.* Philadelphia: University of Pennsylvania Press, 1995.

_____. and Marc Sills. The Martyrdom of Ken Saro-Wiwa and the Future of Ogoni Self-Determination. *Fourth World Bulletin* 5 (Nos. 1-2, Spring/Summer), pp. 5-16, 1996.

Whitaker, C. S. Jr. *The Politics of Tradition: Continuity and Change in Northern Nigeria,*
1946-66. Princeton: Princeton University Press, 1970.

Wiseman, John A. *Political Leaders in Black Africa.* Brookfield, VT: E. Elgar, 1991.

World Bank. *Adjustment in Africa: Reforms, Results, and the Road Ahead.* New York: Oxford University Press, 1994.

_____. *World Development Report 1995: Workers in an Integrating World.* New York: Oxford University Press, 1995.

_____. *World Development Report 1997: The State in a Changing World.* New York: Oxford University Press, 1997.

Young, Crawford. *The African Colonial State in Comparative Perspective.* New Haven: Yale University Press, 1994.

_____. *The Politics of Cultural Pluralism.* Madison: The University of Wisconsin Press, 1976.

Zartman, I. Willam and Sayre Schatz. "Introduction," in Zartman, ed. *The Political Economy of Nigeria.* New York: Praeger, 1983, pp. 1-24.

Index